CHINA:
A Critical Bibliography

CHINA

A Critical Bibliography

by

Charles O. Hucker

THE UNIVERSITY OF ARIZONA PRESS

TUCSON   ARIZONA

CHARLES O. HUCKER, chairman of the Department of Far Eastern Languages and Literatures at the University of Michigan, is secretary of the Association for Asian Studies. He was chairman of the Committee on Oriental Studies at the University of Arizona when he conceived and set in motion the Critical Bibliographies on China, Japan and Korea, and India, with the support of the Carnegie Corporation. Hucker was historical officer for the Fifth Fighter Command with the U.S. Air Force, during World War II. He received his Ph.D. from the University of Chicago in 1950. The Orientalist is the author of numerous monographs, journal articles and reviews, and of *China: A Critical Bibliography,* and *The Traditional Chinese State in Ming Times* (University of Arizona Press, 1961), and *The Censorial System of Ming Times* (Stanford University Press, 1966).

First Printing, 1962
Second Printing, 1964
Third Printing, 1966

China: A Critical Bibliography is one result of a four-year effort by the Oriental Studies staff of the University of Arizona, largely financed by the Carnegie Corporation of New York, to produce a series of reference guides that might facilitate the study of the major Far Eastern areas in American colleges. When complete, the series will also include Japan-Korea, India-Pakistan, and Southeast Asia guides.

In accord with a general pattern established for the whole series, the present work is a selected, graded, annotated list of books, articles, and individual chapters or sections of books that contribute significantly, in the compiler's opinion, to the academic study of both traditional and modern China. It is designed to be of use equally to introductory and advanced students, to teachers and research workers at all levels, and to librarians.

Entries are arranged in topical groupings, so that the user, by consulting the comprehensive Table of Contents, can readily pin-point those books and articles that pertain to any particular subject in which he might be interested. There are seven major sections: (1) Introduction, (2) Lands and Peoples, (3) History, (4) Intellectual and Aesthetic Patterns, (5) Political Patterns, (6) Social Pátterns, and (7) Economic Patterns. Within each of these sections, entries are divided further among sub-sections — in some cases, several orders of sub-sections — that have been suggested by the subject matter. The sequence of sub-sections reflects a combination of chronological and topical analyses.

With reference to each particular subject, entries appear in the order in which the compiler would recommend them to an introductory college student, proceeding in general from items that are most authoritative to those that are less authoritative, from those of general scope to those of narrow scope, and from those that are readily available to those that are less available. The criterion of availability has suggested giving priority to books published in English since 1940 and articles in standard English-language journals. Works in Oriental languages have not been listed because of their unfortunately limited usability among American college students; but works in

French and German have been listed if they are standard references not substantially duplicated or superseded in English publications.

Within some sub-sections are groupings divided by asterisks. Such groupings denote differences of kind, rather than of quality, among the items listed. Thus asterisks sometimes separate translations from critical studies, biographies from general historical studies, political, cultural, and socio-economic studies of a particular historical era, etc. The whole of each sub-section should therefore be taken note of, not its first listings only. Moreover, although an effort to make each sub-section a complete unit in itself has resulted in much duplication of entries, there nevertheless remains a need for some cross-referencing from sub-section to sub-section. Continual reference to the Table of Contents is essential to the effective use of the bibliography.

For help of various kinds in the preparation of the bibliography I am greatly indebted to all my former colleagues of the Oriental Studies faculty at the University of Arizona; to my students Charles R. Bryfogle, Kathleen Crockett, Bruce Cunningham, Phyllis A. Gibbs, Marianne Gilbert, and Mrs. Lucille B. Williams; and to Mrs. Reta Cruse, N. Patricia Cunningham, and Rosie Morales. I am grateful also for the tolerance and generosity of the whole University of Arizona Library staff.

No one knows better than I how incomplete and inadequate this effort is. I hope it may deserve to be revised and brought up to date in the not too distant future, and to that end I shall welcome the criticisms and suggestions of all my peers who are working in the Chinese studies field. Meantime, I have no choice but to admit that the judgments represented in the order of entries and in their annotations are my own sole responsibility, for which neither the Carnegie Corporation of New York nor the University of Arizona Press can justly be maligned.

Charles O. Hucker

CONTENTS

CONTENTS

CONTENTS

INTRODUCTION

The Chinese, the most numerous of the world's peoples, occupy a land area larger than any other Far Eastern state and proudly look back upon the world's longest history of continuous national existence. Renowned for their urbanity, their practicality and adaptability, their diligence and productivity, and their literary, artistic, architectural, and technological achievements, they were the ancient givers of civilization to neighboring Vietnam, Korea, and Japan and traditionally exerted military, political, and cultural domination over most of Inner Asia, mainland Southeast Asia, and East Asia. Throughout history, on balance, they have been the most prosperous and sophisticated people in Asia and possibly in the world. Confronted by a militant and mechanized outside world in the 19th century, the Chinese in recent decades have been undergoing perhaps the most agonizing renovation experienced by any modern nation. But they have not abandoned their traditional claims to national cohesiveness, international leadership, and cultural greatness. More than ever before, and increasingly, the role of China the Middle Kingdom *(Chung-kuo)* is a decisive one in world affairs.

GENERAL WORKS

1

MacNair, H. F. (ed.) *China.* Berkeley: University of California Press, 1946. A well balanced collection of 34 essays by authorities on major aspects of Chinese history and civilization; still authoritative, though somewhat out of date.

2

Fairbank, John King. *The United States and China.* Rev. ed. Cambridge: Harvard University Press, 1958. On China's traditional civilization and its transformations in modern times, in a general historical framework; analytical, readable, and probably the best general introduction to China for American readers.

3

Hu Chang-tu and others. *China: Its People, Its Society, Its Culture.* New Haven: HRAF Press, 1960. The most up-to-date and comprehensive topical description of China and the Chinese; stronger on contemporary than on historical China, and stronger on socioeconomic than on humanistic aspects.

4

Latourette, Kenneth Scott. *The Chinese: Their History and Culture.* 3d ed. rev. New York: Macmillan, 1946. Part 1: Chinese history in chronological presentation. Part 2: Chinese culture in topical presentation. Standard, with extensive bibliographies following each chapter; but needs revision.

5

Hinton, Harold C. and Marius B. Jansen. *Major Topics on China and Japan: A Handbook for Teachers.* New York: Institute of Pacific Relations, 1957. Pp. 1-226 provide a balanced, descriptive presentation of Chinese culture and history of traditional and contemporary times; addressed primarily to secondary school teachers, but authoritative.

6

Balazs, E. and others. *Aspects de la Chine.* 2 vols. Paris: Presses Universitaires de France, 1959. A collection of succinct, authoritative essays on all facets and periods of Chinese history and civilization through the 19th century; probably the best popular introduction to traditional China in any Western language.

7

Dean, Vera Micheles. *The Nature of the Non-Western World.* New York: Mentor Books, 1957. Chap. 5 provides a succinct analysis of traditional Chinese civilization and its modern transformation under the impact of the West, from a predominantly socio-political point of view.

8

Winfield, Gerald Freeman. *China: The Land and the People.* Rev. ed. New York: William Sloane Associates, 1950. A highly personal, but reliable, description of how the modern Chinese people live and work, emphasizing socioeconomic aspects.

9

Bodde, Derk. *China's Cultural Tradition: What and Whither?* New York: Rinehart, 1957. A brief introduction to some major controversial problems about China's historical civilization.

10

Williams, Samuel Wells. *The Middle Kingdom.* Rev. ed. 2 vols. New York: Scribner, 1883. The best known of many 19th century compendiums about China and Chinese life in general; though of outdated scholarship, still a standard reference.

11

Buck, Pearl, *The Good Earth.* New York: John Day, 1931; repeatedly reissued. A classic novel exemplifying the nature and values of Chinese peasant life.

12

Lin Yutang. *My Country and My People.* Rev. ed. New York: John Day, 1935. A somewhat idealized introduction to the culture of the upper classes in China, by one of its most urbane and articulate spokesmen.

BIBLIOGRAPHIES

13

Goodrich, Luther Carrington and Henry C. Fenn. *A Syllabus of the History of Chinese Civilization and Culture.* 6th ed. New York: The China Society of America, 1958. An unannotated list of books and articles, arranged by topics in a general historical framework; most useful for pre-20th century eras.

14

Hucker, Charles O. *Chinese History: A Bibliographic Review.* Washington: Service Center for Teachers of History, 1958. A descriptive essay about books and articles relevant to the study of Chinese civilization; useful mainly for historical rather than contemporary times.

15

Yuan Tung-li. *China in Western Literature.* New Haven: Yale University Far Eastern Publications, 1958. A comprehensive list of English, French, and German books about China published between 1921 and 1957, arranged by topics.

16

Bibliography of Asian Studies. Published annually as the separate September issue of the *Journal of Asian Studies,* 1956–. The most comprehensive regular lists of books, pamphlets, and articles on China and other areas of South, Southeast, and East Asia; arranged by topics within major areas. Originated as a separate publication, *Bulletin of Far Eastern Bibliography,* under the editorship of E. H. Pritchard (vols. 1-5, 1936–40); then incorporated into the *Far Eastern Quarterly* (predecessor of *Journal of Asian Studies*) from 1941 through 1955, as an annual compilation beginning in 1949.

17

Wright, Arthur F. "The Study of Chinese Civilization," *Journal of the History of Ideas,* XXI (1960), 233-255. A general, interpretive review of the changing character of Western scholarship (and to some extent Chinese and

Japanese scholarship) in reference to China during the 19th and 20th centuries.

18

American Historical Association. *Guide to Historical Literature*. New York: Macmillan, 1961. Pp. 258-295, by C. S. Gardner and E. H. Pritchard, list 1189 books, pamphlets, and articles about China, arranged by historical periods and by subject categories, in no particular order; with some brief annotations. Some Chinese-language works are included.

19

Cordier, Henri. *Bibliotheca Sinica*. Rev. ed. 4 vols. Paris: E. Guilmoto, 1904-08; supplementary volume Paris: P. Guenther, 1924; author index New York: Columbia University East Asiatic Library, 1953. Comprehensive list of Western-language books about China published prior to about 1921, arranged by topics.

20

Revue Bibliographique de Sinologie. Paris: École Pratique des Hautes Études, 1955-. Abstracts of current books and articles in Oriental and Western languages relevant to the study of China's historical civilization, written in English and French; published for each year.

21

Franke, Herbert. *Sinologie*. Bern: A. Francke, 1953. An authoritative bibliographic introduction to the study of traditional Chinese civilization, in German.

22

Quarterly Check-list of Oriental Studies. Darien, Conn.: American Bibliographic Service, 1959-. The most up-to-date lists of current publications (separates only) about China as well as other areas of Asia; cannot be relied on for completeness.

23

Stucki, Curtis W. *American Doctoral Dissertations on Asia, 1933-1958*. Ithaca: Southeast Asia Program, Department of Far Eastern Studies, Cornell University, 1959. A useful bibliography of works many of which are unpublished but are available on microfilm through University Microfilms, Ann Arbor, Michigan.

JOURNALS

24

Journal of Asian Studies. 1941-. Published quarterly as the official journal of the Association for Asian Studies; regularly contains authoritative articles and reviews about both traditional and modern China, of rather general interest. Known until 1956 as the *Far Eastern Quarterly*.

25

The China Quarterly. 1960-. Published in London; devoted exclusively to the study of communist China, with authoritative articles, current chronologies of events, translations of important current documents, etc.

26

Pacific Affairs. 1928-. Published quarterly by the Institute of Pacific Relations; regularly contains articles and reviews relating to modern and contemporary China.

27

Asian Survey. Berkeley: University of California Institute of International Studies, 1961-. Published monthly as a successor to *Far Eastern Survey;* regularly includes brief articles on contemporary China.

28

Harvard Journal of Asiatic Studies. Cambridge, Mass.: 1936-. Published irregularly; contains technical, often philological, articles and reviews about traditional China.

29

T'oung Pao. 1890-. Published irregularly by E. J. Brill in Leiden under a series of distinguished editors; devoted to scholarly articles and reviews about traditional China and other areas of the Far East in German, French, and English. The most prestigeful European journal devoted to Sinological publications; technical.

30

Bulletin of the School of Oriental and African Studies, London University. 1917-. Published annually or oftener; regularly contains articles and reviews about traditional China; somewhat technical.

31

Asia Major. New series, 1949-. Published irregularly by Taylor's Foreign Press in London under scholarly editorship; regularly contains authoritative articles and reviews pertaining to traditional China; somewhat technical.

32

Journal of Oriental Studies. 1954-. Published twice a year by the Hong Kong University Press; regularly contains scholarly articles on traditional China, some in English and some in Chinese.

33

Monumenta Serica. 1935-. Published irregularly by the Catholic University of Peking until 1948, thereafter by the Society of the Divine Word in Tokyo and Nagoya, Japan; a scholarly journal carrying technical articles and reviews about traditional China, principally in English and German.

34

Sinologica. 1948-. Published irregularly in Switzerland; devoted to scholarly articles and reviews about traditional China, in German, French, and English; somewhat technical.

35

Tsing Hua Journal of Chinese Studies. New series, 1956-. Published irregularly in Taiwan; devoted to scholarly articles in English about traditional China.

36

Oriens Extremus: Zeitschrift für Sprache, Kunst und Kultur des Lander des Fernen Ostens. 1954-. Published twice a year by Otto Harrassowitz in Wiesbaden, Germany; regularly contains articles and reviews in German, French, and English about traditional China; somewhat technical.

37

Oriens. 1948-. Published twice a year by E. J. Brill in Leiden, as the journal of the International Society for Oriental Research; occasionally contains articles in German, French, and English pertaining to traditional China; somewhat technical.

38

Journal of the American Oriental Society. 1843-. Published quarterly; regularly contains technical, philological articles on traditional China, especially emphasizing subjects of humanistic rather than social science interest; with authoritative book reviews.

39

Chinese Culture. 1957-. Published irregularly in Taiwan; contains semi-scholarly articles in English about traditional China.

40

Chinese Social and Political Science Review. 1916-37. Published quarterly by the Chinese Social and Political Science Association; devoted to articles in English about both traditional and contemporary China.

41

Journal of the North China Branch, Royal Asiatic Society. 1858-1948. Published quarterly in Shanghai; devoted to scholarly and semi-scholarly articles and reviews about China of both traditional and modern times.

42

Bulletin of the Museum of Far Eastern Antiquities, Stockholm. 1929-. Published irregularly; regularly contains articles about China, almost entirely of a heavily philological and technical nature. Special emphasis given to archeology and art history.

43

Memoirs of the Research Department of the Toyo Bunko. 1926–. Published irregularly by The Toyo Bunko ("The Oriental Library") in Tokyo; devoted to scholarly articles, mostly by Japanese authors but mostly in English, about traditional China; technical.

44

Journal of the Royal Asiatic Society of Great Britain and Ireland. 1834–. Published quarterly in London; occasionally contains scholarly articles about China, mostly referring to traditional times.

45

Far Eastern Survey. 1932–1961. A biweekly publication of the Institute of Pacific Relations, regularly containing very brief articles on contemporary Chinese affairs. Succeeded in 1961 by *Asian Survey.*

LANDS AND PEOPLES

Despite its long heritage of cultural and political cohesiveness, China has no geographic unity. Even the almost square, densely populated heartland called China Proper (18 modern provinces, about 1,350,000 square miles or roughly half the land area of the continental United States) is fragmented into numerous distinctive natural regions. In general, North China, dominated by the Yellow River plain, is a relatively flat, dry, brown terrain, hot in summer and bitter cold in winter, where dry-field cultivation of such crops as wheat and millet predominates. Horses, oxen, and even camels are relatively common. South China, including the Yangtze River valley and the coastal islands Taiwan (Formosa) and Hainan, is contrastingly hilly, moist, and green, with a more even and moderate climate and with wet-field cultivation of rice predominating. Water buffalo are the only common draft animals. Even more distinctive natural regions enclose China Proper on the west and north: mountainous Tibet, the deserts of Sinkiang (Chinese Turkestan), the steppes of Inner Mongolia, and the rich basin of Manchuria, all of which have been incorporated into the Chinese administrative realm in modern times. The whole of this greater China (some 3,900,000 square miles) is alternately warmed and cooled by monsoon air currents moving inland from the oceans in summer and seaward from the Eurasian interior in winter. Both China Proper and Manchuria are rich agricultural regions; Tibet, Sinkiang, and Inner Mongolia are characterized principally by grazing economies. The Chinese have long known and worked substantial deposits of coal and iron, but in general their mineral resources have not been extensively developed and are thought to be relatively poor.

The peoples of China, almost unmixed Mongoloid, are more nearly homogeneous in physical characteristics than the people of any other large Far Eastern nation. Of the total population of about 650 millions (1960 estimate), nearly 95 per cent (the so-called Han people) speak the national language, Chinese. Of these, the majority speak the Mandarin dialect *(Kuo-yü)*. Cantonese and many lesser dialects prevail in the coastal areas of South China. The difficulties of communication that result from dialectal variations are offset by the prevalence of a standard writing system using ideographic characters rather than an alphabet. Important non-Han peoples in China include Tibetans, Mongols, Manchus, Uighurs, and the aboriginal tribesmen of Southwest China, principally related to the Thai.

TOPOGRAPHY, CLIMATE, RESOURCES

46

Cressey, George B. *Land of the 500 Million.* New York: McGraw-Hill, 1955. The most comprehensive, authoritative, and up-to-date geographical survey of China: the people, the topography, the climate, the resources, the economic life in general, and the major regions.

47

Shabad, Theodore. *China's Changing Map.* New York: Praeger, 1956. An authoritative, detailed geographic survey of the various regions of China, with introductory sections on the land, the political organization, and the economic life of China as a whole; emphasizes the situation under Chinese communist control.

48

Cressey, George B. *China's Geographic Foundations.* New York: McGraw-Hill, 1934. A general survey of the land and the Chinese people's use of it, with a detailed breakdown by regions; should be used to supplement Cressey's later *Land of the 500 Million,* which does not wholly supersede it.

49

Ginsburg, Norton (ed.). *The Pattern of Asia.* Englewood Cliffs, N.J.: Prentice-Hall, 1958. Pp. 155-273, apparently by Herold Wiens, authoritatively describe the topography, climate, regions, resources, economic life, and political organization of China Proper, Manchuria, and Sinkiang; other sections deal authoritatively with the surrounding regions.

50

Cressey, George B. *Asia's Lands and Peoples.* New York: McGraw-Hill, 1944. Chaps. 3-9 provide authoritative, brief descriptions of China's physical environment and economic activity, region by region.

51

Stamp, L. Dudley. *Asia: An Economic and Regional Geography.* 10th ed. London: Methuen, 1959. Pp. 480-582 on China, especially emphasizing topography and resources, with descriptions of the major natural regions of China Proper and of Taiwan, Manchuria, and Hong Kong.

52

Lyde, Lionel. *The Continent of Asia.* London: Macmillan, 1933. Pp. 537-641 on China, with especially detailed descriptions of the major natural regions.

53

National Geological Survey of China. *Bulletin.* Peking and Nanking; 1919–48. Published irregularly; technical reports on China's geological resources. Representative of a large number of publications of the National Geological Survey, including a *Memoirs* series and a *Palaeontologia Sinica* series.

54

Lee, J. S. (Li Ssu-kuang) *The Geology of China.* London: Thomas Murby, 1939. The standard geological description, but not reflecting any studies done after the early 1930's.

THE PEOPLE

55

Spencer, Joseph. *Asia East by South: A Cultural Geography.* New York: Wiley, 1954. Pp. 115-123: a concise statement of the racial and linguistic distribution patterns and interrelationships of all the Far Eastern peoples.

56

Latourette, Kenneth Scott. *The Chinese: Their History and Culture.* 3d ed. rev. New York: Macmillan, 1946. Pp. 495-510 survey the racial components of the Chinese people.

57

Li Chi. *The Formation of the Chinese People: An Anthropological Inquiry.* Cambridge: Harvard University Press, 1928. A historical study of the migrations and minglings of racial and ethnic groups to form the present population of China.

58

Wiens, Herold J. *China's March Toward the Tropics.* Hamden, Conn.: Shoe String Press, 1954. Pp. 267-328: a detailed classification of the non-Han peoples of southwestern China.

59

Hudson, G. F. "The Nationalities of China," *St. Antony's Papers,* VII (London: Chatto and Windus, 1960), 51-61. A brief essay on the distribution of minority peoples in China and the policy adopted toward them by the Peking government in the 1950's.

60

Hu Chang-tu and others. *China: Its People, Its Society, Its Culture.* New Haven: HRAF Press, 1960. Pp. 64-94: a general descriptive classification of the various non-Han peoples in China.

61

Shirokogorov, S. M. *Anthropology of Northern China.* Shanghai: 1923. Technical, classical physiometric studies of China's principal physical types. Cf. Shirokogorov's *Anthropology of Eastern China and Kwangtung Province* (Shanghai: 1925).

62

Coon, Carleton S., Stanley M. Garn, and Joseph B. Birdsell. *Races: A Study of the Problems of Race Formation in Man.* Springfield, Ill.: Charles C. Thomas, 1950. A standard reference on the elements that distinguish the races, with brief descriptive remarks about the various Chinese peoples.

THE LANGUAGE

63

Hu Chang-tu and others. *China: Its People, Its Society, Its Culture.* New Haven: HRAF Press, 1960. Pp. 95-109 describe the nature of the language, spoken and written; the distribution of its dialects; and alphabetization and other modern reform movements.

64

Karlgren, Bernard. *The Chinese Language.* New York: Ronald Press, 1949. A general description, with special reference to classical written Chinese and the reconstruction of early Chinese pronunciation.

65

De Francis, John F. *Nationalism and Language Reform in China.* Princeton: Princeton University Press, 1950. A history of efforts to alphabetize Chinese writing, which began with the first appearance of modern Westerners in China and have intensified in the 20th century; with consideration of both linguistic and political difficulties.

66

Forrest, Robert A. D. *The Chinese Language.* London: Faber and Faber, 1948. Evolution of Chinese speech; characteristics of the modern dialects and of related languages of southwestern China; more technical than Karlgren.

67

Winfield, Gerald F. *China: The Land and the People.* Rev. ed. New York: William Sloane Associates, 1950. Pp. 168-186: an anecdotal, non-technical introduction to the Chinese language, spoken and written, and how it is learned and used by the Chinese people.

68

Wright, Arthur F. "The Chinese Language and Foreign Ideas," in *Studies in Chinese Thought* (A. F. Wright, ed.; Chicago: University of Chicago Press, 1953), pp. 286-303. On the Chinese language as a hindrance to the introduction of ideas alien to Chinese culture, with examples drawn from the whole range of history.

69

Chan Shau Wing. *Elementary Chinese.* 2d ed. Stanford: Stanford University Press, 1959. Pp. xi-xxvii: a brief, not overly technical introduction to Chinese linguistics, the writing system, and modern script reforms.

70

Chao Yuen Ren. *Mandarin Primer: An Intensive Course in Spoken Chinese.* Cambridge: Harvard University Press, 1948. Pp. 3-81: a thorough, technical introduction to modern Chinese linguistics.

71

Creel, H. G. and others. *Literary Chinese by the Inductive Method. Vol. 1: Hsiao Ching.* Rev. ed. Chicago: University of Chicago Press, 1948. Pp. 1-33: a thorough explanation of the history and nature of classical written Chinese.

72

Creel, H. G. *Chinese Writing.* Washington: American Council on Education, 1943. A simplified and very brief explanation of what classical Chinese writing is like and of the difficulties in reading it.

73

Quong, Rose. *Chinese Wit, Wisdom, and Written Characters.* New York: Pantheon, 1944. A popular, rather fanciful introduction to Chinese written characters, showing their pictographic-ideographic nature.

74

Karlgren, Bernhard. *Easy Lessons in Chinese Writing.* Stockholm: Naturmetodens Sprakinstitut, 1958. A primer of 1044 basic Chinese characters, arranged according to the principles of their formation, giving pronunciations, definitions, and archaic script forms.

75

Denlinger, Paul B. "Chinese Historical Linguistics: The Road Ahead," *Journal of the American Oriental Society,* LXXXI (1961), 1-7. A general discussion of the scholarly literature on the early development of the Chinese language, with suggestions about fruitful lines of future research.

76

Mills, Harriet C. "Language Reform in China: Some Recent Developments," *Far Eastern Quarterly,* XV (1955-56), 517-540. Description of efforts by the communist People's Republic of China to foster standardization of pronunciation, simplification of written characters, and eventual alphabetization.

77

Hsia Tao-tai. *China's Language Reforms.* New Haven: Institute of Far Eastern Languages, 1956. A manual of simplified written forms promulgated by the People's Republic of China.

78

Chao Yuen Ren. *Cantonese Primer.* Cambridge: Harvard University Press, 1947. Introduction to the South Chinese dialect that is the form of Chinese most commonly spoken by American Chinese.

79

Meillet, A. and Marcel Cohen. *Les langues du monde.* Paris: H. Champion, 1952. Includes an authoritative section on the distribution, statistics, characteristic features, and mutual relationships of the Sino-Tibetan languages by Henri Maspero.

Language textbooks

80

Chan Shau Wing. *Elementary Chinese*. 2d ed. Stanford: Stanford University Press, 1959. Principally useful for reading modern colloquial Chinese.

81

Chao Yuen Ren. *Mandarin Primer: An Intensive Course in Spoken Chinese*. Cambridge: Harvard University Press, 1948. A standard text for modern colloquial Chinese, but dealing only with speech. Six long-play records covering the first 24 lessons are available as Folkways Records album FP 8002 (New York. 1955).

82

Teng Ssu-yü. *Conversational Chinese*. Chicago: University of Chicago Press, 1947. Gives equal emphasis to speaking and reading the modern colloquial style.

83

Creel, H. G. and others. *Literary Chinese by the Inductive Method*. 3 vols. Chicago: University of Chicago Press, 1938–52. Readings in (1) The *Classic of Filial Piety*, (2) the *Analects* of Confucius, (3) the book of Mencius.

Dictionaries

84

Mathews, Robert Henry. *Mathews' Chinese-English Dictionary*. Rev. ed. Cambridge: Harvard University Press, 1944; and *Revised English Index*. Cambridge: Harvard University Press, 1943. The standard student's dictionary; more useful for written than for spoken Chinese.

85

Chan Shau Wing. *A Concise English-Chinese Dictionary*. 2d ed. Stanford: Stanford University Press, 1955. For conversation and writing in the colloquial style.

86

Fenn, Courtenay Hughes. *Chinese-English Pocket-Dictionary*. Rev. ed. Cambridge: Harvard University Press, 1944. The most useful small dictionary for reading Chinese.

87

Giles, Herbert Allen. *Chinese-English Dictionary*. Rev. ed. 2 vols. Shanghai: Kelly and Walsh, 1912. The standard comprehensive dictionary for scholarly use, exemplifying the Wade-Giles system of romanization, used by most English-language writers about China and by most subsequent dictionary-makers.

HISTORY

GENERAL

The long history of China has been, and continues to be, dominated by two major, interrelated themes: (1) the spread of the Chinese people out of their earliest known homes in the Yellow River plain of North China southward, westward, and to a limited extent northward toward an ever more saturated occupance of China Proper; and (2) the struggle of the sedentary, agrarian Chinese to survive against or to overawe and dominate predatory outsiders—first the mostly nomadic frontier peoples of the north and northwest, notably the Huns, Turks, Mongols, and Manchus in succession, and more recently commercial and industrial empire

builders from overseas — always with the eventual result of finding new forms in which to renew national unity and preserve a distinctively Chinese way of life. Since from their known beginnings in the second millenium B.C. down to A.D. 1912 the Chinese were ruled by a succession of royal or imperial families, they traditionally viewed their history as the cyclical rising, flourishing, and decaying of dynasty after dynasty. No other system of periodization has yet been universally accepted, but for present purposes Chinese history is divided into the following large-scale eras:

(1) Prehistory
(2) The Formative Age (1766?–221 B.C.)
(3) The First Imperial Era (221 B.C.–A.D. 220)
(4) The Age of Disruption and Division (220–589)
(5) The Golden Age of Empire (581–1279)
(6) The Age of Renewed Invasions (907–1368)
(7) Indian Summer of the Empire (1368–1840)
(8) The Nineteenth Century
(9) The Nationalist Era (1912–   )
(10) The Communist Era (1921–   )

Reference aids

89

Goodrich, L. C. and Henry C. Fenn. *A Syllabus of the History of Chinese Civilization and Culture*. 6th ed. New York: The China Society of America, 1958. An unannotated list of books and articles, arranged by topics in a general historical framework; most useful for pre-20th century eras.

90

Hucker, Charles O. *Chinese History: A Bibliographic Review*. Washington: Service Center for Teachers of History, 1958. A descriptive essay about books and articles relevant to the study of Chinese history, especially of traditional times.

91

Giles, Herbert A. *A Chinese Biographical Dictionary*. Shanghai: Kelly and Walsh, 1898. The only work of its kind dealing with important Chinese of all periods prior to the 20th century; a standard reference, though outdated and unreliable in detail.

92

Langer, William L. (ed.). *An Encyclopedia of World History*. Rev. ed. Boston: Houghton Mifflin, 1948. The scattered sections on China, by Charles S. Gardner, make an excellent reference for the dates of important events.

93

Moule, Arthur C. *The Rulers of China, 221 B.C.-A.D. 1949*. New York: Praeger, 1957. Chronological tables, full of technical data that make the work an indispensable reference tool for the specialist.

94

Philips, C. H. (ed.). *Handbook of Oriental History*. London: Royal Historical Society, 1951. Pp. 153-214, by O. B. van der Sprenkel: an explanation of systems for romanizing Chinese words and of Chinese usages in naming and dating; a glossary of special terms commonly encountered in writings about China; and chronological tables of Chinese dynasties and rulers up to 1912. Marred by use of the romanization system called Gwoyeu Romatzyh, which is seldom used by Western writers.

95

Herrmann, Albert. *Historical and Commercial Atlas of China.* Cambridge: Harvard University Press, 1935. The standard Western-language atlas dealing with the whole historical development of China.

96

Sellman, R. R. *An Outline Atlas of Eastern History.* London: Edward Arnold, 1954. Includes maps of China from period to period, but too few and too superficial to be very helpful.

97

Yang Lien-sheng. *Topics in Chinese History.* Cambridge: Harvard University Press, 1950. Syllabus for an advanced course on the development of Chinese civilization to about 1800, with lecture outlines, reading assignments, and bibliographic notes on important Chinese, Japanese, and Western-language sources.

General historical surveys

98

Reischauer, Edwin O. and John K. Fairbank. *East Asia: The Great Tradition.* Boston: Houghton Mifflin, 1960. Pp. 32-393 offer the most comprehensive, authoritative, and up to date survey of Chinese history from its beginnings into the 19th century.

99

Goodrich, L. Carrington. *A Short History of the Chinese People.* 3d ed. New York: Harper, 1959. A most useful brief survey; well balanced, but giving special attention to technology and material culture.

100

Latourette, Kenneth Scott. *The Chinese: Their History and Culture.* Rev. ed. New York: Macmillan, 1946. Part I a detailed chronological history; out of date, but still a standard reference.

101

Grousset, René. *The Rise and Splendour of the Chinese Empire.* Berkeley: University of California Press, 1953; paperbound reprint, 1958. Traditional China into the 19th century; episodic in coverage, emphasizing great men and cultural glories.

102

Fitzgerald, Charles Patrick. *China: A Short Cultural History.* 3d ed. New York: Praeger, 1950. Traditional China into the 19th century; highly selective, with special emphasis on thought, art, and literature.

103

Eberhard, Wolfram. *A History of China.* Rev. ed. Berkeley: University of California Press, 1960. Highly interpretive and provocative presentation of Chinese history from a sociological point of view, with special emphasis on early history up to the 7th century.

104

Franke, Otto. *Geschichte des chinesischen Reiches.* 5 vols. Berlin: Walter de Gruyter, 1930–52. Somewhat out of date, but still the most comprehensive scholarly history of China up to A.D. 1280 available in a Western language; particularly strong on the details of political history.

105

Maspero, Henri and Jean Escarra. *Les institutions de la Chine.* Paris: Presses Universitaires de France, 1952. A broad, authoritative survey for the general reader of China's over-all evolution from earliest times to the beginning of the 20th century; defines "institutions" broadly to include the political, social, economic, and intellectual aspects of Chinese life.

Special studies of broad historical sweep

106

Sun, E-tu Zen and John de Francis (trans.). *Chinese Social History.* Washington: American Council of Learned Societies, 1956. Translations of 25 articles by modern Chinese scholars, chiefly dating from the 1930's, relating to socioeconomic aspects of Chinese life from earliest antiquity into the 19th century; an invaluable reference.

107

Yang Lien-sheng. *Studies in Chinese Institutional History.* Cambridge: Harvard University Press, 1961. (Harvard-Yenching Institute Studies, XX). Nine studies of traditional Chinese history, especially emphasizing socioeconomic aspects, all previously published as articles in the *Harvard Journal of Asiatic Studies.* Includes "Toward a Study of Dynastic Configurations in Chinese History" (pp. 1-17; from HJAS XVII [1954], 329-345), suggesting approaches to understanding the successive rise and fall of dynasties in Chinese history.

108

Miyakawa Hisayuki. "An Outline of the Naito Hypothesis and Its Effects on Japanese Studies of China," *Far Eastern Quarterly,* XIV (1954–55), 533-552. Explanation of an influential Japanese theory about the periodization of Chinese history, suggesting that "modern" China began between the T'ang and Sung periods.

109

Wiens, Herold J. *China's March Toward the Tropics.* Hamden, Conn.: Shoe String Press, 1954. A history of Chinese expansion southward out of the Yellow River Valley and of China's historic relations with the aboriginal inhabitants of south and southwest China.

110

Miyakawa Hisayuki. "The Confucianization of South China," in *The Confucian Persuasion* (A. F. Wright, ed.; Stanford: Stanford University Press, 1960), pp. 21-46. On the gradual expansion of dominant North Chinese culture patterns into the south coastal regions and Taiwan, from the 3d century B.C. into the 19th century.

111

Chi Ch'ao-ting. *Key Economic Areas in Chinese History.* London: Allen and Unwin, 1936. An influential economic interpretation of the development of China throughout history, based principally on a study of public works for water control from dynasty to dynasty.

112

Wang Yü-ch'üan. "The Rise of Land Tax and the Fall of Dynasties in Chinese History," *Pacific Affairs,* IX (1936), 201-220. A brief but influential essay suggesting an economic interpretation of China's traditional dynastic cycle.

113

Yao Shan-yu. "The Geographical Distribution of Floods and Droughts in Chinese History, 206 B.C.-A.D. 1911," *Far Eastern Quarterly,* II (1942–43), 357-378. A statistical study, by province and by dynasty; quantitative data only.

114

Lin Yutang. *A History of the Press and Public Opinion in China.* Chicago: University of Chicago Press, 1936. An episodic, untechnical account of public protest in China from earliest times and especially of modern efforts toward establishment of a free periodical press.

115

Muramatsu Yuji. "Some Themes in Chinese Rebel Ideologies," in *The Confucian Persuasion* (A. F. Wright, ed.; Stanford: Stanford University Press, 1960), pp. 241-267. On religious beliefs, "mandate of Heaven" notions, ethnocentrism, and socioeconomic reforms that characterize the programs of rebellions throughout Chinese history.

116

Sun, E-tu Zen and John de Francis. *Bibliography on Chinese Social History.* New Haven: Far Eastern Publications, Yale University, 1952. An annotated list of 176 modern scholarly articles in Chinese about socioeconomic aspects of Chinese history from antiquity; a valuable reference for those who can use the language.

Chinese-foreign relations throughout history

117
Hall, D. G. E. *A History of South-East Asia.* New York: St. Martin's Press, 1955. A standard, general reference for China's relations throughout history with the various peoples of both the mainland and island parts of Southeast Asia.

118
Purcell, Victor. *The Chinese in Southeast Asia.* New York: Oxford University Press, 1951. A voluminous compendium of historical data concerning Chinese migration and settlements to the south, arranged according to the various countries of Southeast Asia.

* * *

119
Bagchi, Prabdoh Chandra. *India and China: A Thousand Years of Cultural Relations.* 2d ed. New York: Philosophical Library, 1951. A survey of Chinese-Indian contacts through history, with special reference to the reciprocal interchange of intellectual and material culture.

* * *

120
Li Tieh-tseng. *The Historical Status of Tibet.* New York: King's Crown Press, 1956. A reliable general survey of Tibetan history from earliest times into the 20th century, with special emphasis on Chinese-Tibetan relations.

* * *

121
Lattimore, Owen. *Inner Asian Frontiers of China.* 2d ed. New York: American Geographical Society, 1951. A highly interpretive analysis of the relations between sedentary Chinese society and the nomadic peoples of the north and west throughout history; a standard reference.

122
Hambis, Louis. *La Haute-Asie.* Paris: Presses Universitaires de France, 1953. A survey of the Inner Asian peoples from earliest times to the present, with chapters on ethnography and intellectual-aesthetic life; brief and in popular style, but reliable.

123
Grousset, René. *L'empire des steppes.* Paris: Payot, 1948. An authoritative general history of the nomadic peoples of Inner Asia from antiquity into the 18th century.

124
Barthold, V. V. *Turkestan down to the Mongol Invasion,* trans. by H. A. R. Gibb. 2d ed. rev. London: Luzac, 1958. A basic, authoritative reference on the Moslem conquest of Central Asia and the subsequent Khitan and Mongol empires.

125
Barthold, V. V. *Four Studies on the History of Central Asia,* trans. by V. and T. Minorsky. 2 vols. of a projected 3. Leiden: E. J. Brill, 1956–58. Basic, authoritative studies of Turkic and Mongol history in Russian Turkestan; vol. 1 includes general surveys of Turkestan and the Kazakistan-Kirchizistan area from antiquity into the 19th century.

* * *

126
Li Chi. "Manchuria in History," *Chinese Social and Political Science Review,* XVI (1932–33), 226-259. A general survey of Manchurian history from earliest times; abstracted from a Chinese essay by Fu Ssu-nien and others.

127
Gibert, Lucien. *Dictionnaire historique et géographique de la Mandchourie.* Hongkong: La Société des Missions-Étrangères, 1934. A monumental sourcebook of data on China's far northeast; unreliable in details, but valuable for general reference.

* * *

128
Nelson, M. Frederick. *Korea and the Old Orders in Eastern Asia.* Baton Rouge: Louisiana State University Press, 1945. An analysis of Chinese-Korean relations from earliest times to the beginning of the 20th century.

129
Osgood, Cornelius. *The Koreans and Their Culture.* New York: Ronald Press, 1951. The second part is a survey of Korean history, emphasizing relations with China.

130
Griffis, William E. *Corea, the Hermit Nation.* 9th ed. rev. New York: Scribner, 1911. A standard reference for China's cultural influence on, and historical relations with, the Korean peninsula.

131
Hulbert, Homer B. *The History of Korea.* 2 vols. Seoul: Methodist Publishing House, 1905. A detailed, standard reference, covering the period from highest antiquity to 1904.

* * *

132
Sansom, George. *Japan: A Short Cultural History.* Rev. ed. New York: Appleton-Century-Crofts, 1943. A standard reference for China's cultural influence on Japan throughout history; cf. Sansom's more detailed works, *A History of Japan to 1334* and *A History of Japan, 1334–1615* (Stanford: Stanford University Press, 1958 and 1961).

133
Tsunoda Ryusaku (trans.). *Japan in the Chinese Dynastic Histories: Later Han Through Ming Dynasties,* ed. by L. C. Goodrich. South Pasadena: P. D. and Ione Perkins, 1951. Annotated translations of successive Chinese notices about Japan, especially valuable for the history of Chinese-Japanese relations.

* * *

134
Hudson, Geoffrey F. *Europe and China: A Survey of Their Relations from the Earliest Times to 1800.* London: Edward Arnold, 1931; paperbound reprint, Boston: Beacon Press, 1961. A well-balanced and readable account of cultural and commercial contacts between Europe and China prior to the industrial revolution; not thoroughly documented, but reliable.

135
Yule, Henry (ed.). *Cathay and the Way Thither, being a Collection of Medieval Notices of China.* New ed. rev. by Henri Cordier. Vol. 1. London: The Hakluyt Society, 1913. Includes a long essay on Western travelers to, and Western writings about, China from antiquity into the 16th century.

136
Needham, Joseph. *Science and Civilisation in China.* Vol. 1. Cambridge: Cambridge University Press, 1954. Pp. 150 ff.: a survey of historic contacts between China and the Indian, Arab, and European worlds, with special reference to the interchange of scientific and technological ideas and techniques.

PREHISTORY

Man's occupance of China has been traced back to perhaps half a million years ago, when hominid Peking Men *(Pithecanthropus pekingensis)* hunted from caves in North China and related protohumans apparently roamed the south. Subsequently cultural influences from Siberia, Southwest Asia, and Southeast Asia seem to have converged in

China. Although the archaeological record is fragmentary and often hard to interpret, it is clear that by 2000 B.C. at the latest the whole of China Proper was dotted by neolithic villages of pottery-making cultivators of the soil. The most advanced of the neolithic peoples inhabited the far northwest (Kansu province), the central Yellow River plain (Honan province), and the eastern part of the Yellow River plain (Shantung province). The Honan "painted pottery" peoples (the Yang-shao culture) and the Shantung "black pottery" people (the Lung-shan culture) were clearly the direct Mongoloid ancestors of the later Chinese people; and from the midst of their villages, soon after 2000 B.C., emerged the first real Chinese civilization, that of the brilliant bronze-age city-state called Shang.

137

Cheng Te-k'un. *Archaeology in China.* Vol. 1: *Prehistoric China.* Cambridge: Heffer, 1959. The most authoritative and comprehensive account of human development in China prior to the Shang era, including the immediately surrounding areas as well as China Proper; not overly technical in style.

138

Fairservis, Walter A., Jr. *The Origins of Oriental Civilization.* New York: Mentor Books, 1959. Within the general context of Asian prehistory, pp. 45-57, 71-114, and 132-141 summarize pre-Shang development in China; reliable, though in popular style.

139

Andersson, Johan Gunnar. "Researches into the Prehistory of the Chinese," *Bulletin of the Museum of Far Eastern Antiquities,* Stockholm, XV (1943). A detailed survey of pre-Shang remains in North China, including a highly personal record of the history of Chinese archaeology in the 1920's and 1930's; now partly superseded by Cheng Te-k'un.

140

Loehr, Max. "The Stratigraphy of Hsiao-t'un (Anyang); with a Chapter on Hsiao-t'un Foundation Burials and Yin Religious Customs," *Ars Orientalis,* II (1957), 439-57. Translated from the Chinese of Shih Ching-ju; includes a concise, untechnical survey of the characteristics of the Yang-shao, Lung-shan, and Shang (Yin) cultures.

141

Academia Sinica Institute of History and Philology. *Ch'eng-tzu-yai: The Black Pottery Culture Site at Lung-shan-chen in Li-ch'eng-hsien, Shantung Province.* New Haven: Yale University Press, 1956. Translation by Kenneth Starr of the official Chinese report on excavation of the principal black pottery site.

142

Andersson, Johan Gunnar. *Children of the Yellow Earth: Studies in Prehistoric China.* New York: Macmillan, 1934. An intensely personal account, in popular style, of the discovery of Peking Man and other prehistoric remains in China; still a standard reference.

143

Movius, Hallam. "Paleolithic Archaeology in Southern and Eastern Asia, Exclusive of India," *Cahiers d'Histoire Mondiale,* II (1954–55), 257-282, 520-553. Pp. 270-282 on North China, pp. 533-534 on South and West China; a very concise, technical survey.

144

Cheng Te-k'un. *Archaeological Studies in Szechwan.* Cambridge: Cambridge University Press, 1957. A comprehensive and readable account of human development in

central West China, extending into the early historic period.

145

Chang Kwang-chih. "A Brief Survey of the Archaeology of Formosa," *Southwestern Journal of Anthropology,* XII (1956), 371-386. Reviews recent discoveries of neolithic sites.

THE FORMATIVE AGE

Shang, 1766?–1122 B.C.?
Chou, 1122?–256 B.C.
　Western Chou, 1122?–770 B.C.
　Eastern Chou, 770–256 B.C.
　　Spring and Autumn *(Ch'un-ch'iu)* Period, 722–481 B.C.
　　Warring States *(Chan-kuo)* Period, 403–221 B.C.

The Chinese traditionally traced their civilization back to a long line of god-like beings (P'an Ku, the Yellow Emperor, and others) who created the universe, begat mankind, and taught the ways of civilization. But genuine history begins in China with the still semi-legendary Shang kingdom, which 20th century archaeology has brilliantly confirmed. The Shang kings, sanctioned by powerful ancestral and other spirits, ruled over most of North China from a large urban capital in Honan. Their subjects practised both agriculture and animal husbandry, produced some of the most exquisite bronze vessels ever created, and fought from chariots and afoot against surrounding "barbarians." Their flourishing state was finally overthrown from the west in the 12th or 11th century B.C. by a related and formerly allied people called Chou, whose kings then established the longest-lived dynasty of Chinese history and came to be revered as the founding geniuses of China's traditional social and moral order. Under Chou rule in general Chinese life settled into the family - oriented, agriculture - based patterns that dominated it thereafter. Literature and the arts developed under aristocratic patronage, and ritualized etiquette characterized social intercourse. The Chou realm spread to include the Yangtze River valley as well as North China. From the beginning it was parceled out feudal-fashion among hereditary regional lords, and the centralized control of the Chou kings steadily waned. During the Eastern Chou period politics became an increasingly intense struggle for ascendancy among powerful regional states, notably Ch'i in Shantung, Ch'in in Shensi, Ch'u in the central Yangtze valley, and Wu in the area of modern Shanghai. Iron was introduced, cavalry and massed infantry came into use, and warfare became more efficient and destructive. China's great philosophical schools arose in reaction to the giving way of the old social and moral values

— the Confucians, the Taoists, and others. When the Chou line was at last extinguished in 256 B.C. China was already long enmeshed in a chaotic multi-state war from which Ch'in emerged victorious in 221 B.C.

Legendary origins

146
Kramer, Samuel N. (ed.). *Mythologies of the Ancient World.* Chicago: Quadrangle Books, 1961; paperbound ed. New York: Doubleday Anchor Books, 1961. Chap. 8 by Derk Bodde is a critical, scholarly study of China's ancient creation myths.

147
Fairservis, Walter A., Jr. *The Origins of Oriental Civilization.* New York: Mentor Books, 1959. Pp. 76-82 summarize legends and myths about Chinese origins.

148
Karlgren, Bernhard. "Legends and Cults in Ancient China," *Bulletin of the Museum of Far Eastern Antiquities,* Stockholm, XVIII (1946), 199-365. Comprehensive, detailed analysis of Chinese myths in their pre-Han forms.

149
White, William Charles. *Bone Culture of Ancient China: An Archaeological Study of Bone Material from Northern Honan, Dating about the Twelfth Century, B.C.* Toronto: University of Toronto Press, 1945. Pp. 11-18 summarize legends of Chinese origins and briefly describe the ancient Chinese literature from which they are derived.

150
MacCulloch, John Arnott. *The Mythology of All Races.* Vol. 8: *Chinese and Japanese.* Boston: Archaeological Institute of America, 1937. Chaps. 2: "The Three Emperors," 3: "Other Prehistoric Emperors," 5: "Cosmogony and Cosmological Theories"; an authoritative statement of traditional Chinese views by John C. Ferguson.

151
Werner, E. T. C. *Myths and Legends of China.* New York: Brentano, 1922. Chap. 3 summarizes traditional Chinese creation myths.

Shang

152
Cheng Te-k'un. *Archaeology in China.* Vol. 2: *Shang China.* Cambridge: Heffer, 1960. Comprehensive, authoritative, and readable account of the Shang civilization in all its aspects.

153
Creel, Herrlee Glessner. *The Birth of China.* Reprint ed. New York: Ungar, 1954. Chaps. 4-14 present the most readable general review of Shang civilization, as reflected in the early excavations of the Shang capital; still reliable, though superseded in detail by Cheng Te-k'un.

154
Fairservis, Walter A., Jr. *The Origins of Oriental Civilization.* New York: Mentor Books, 1959. Pp. 114-132 review Shang civilization; reliable though in popular style.

155
Creel, Herrlee Glessner. *Studies in Early Chinese Culture.* Baltimore: Waverly Press, 1937. Analysis, in technical style, of problems relating to the origins of the Shang people and the probable existence of a still earlier Hsia state in North China, as claimed in Chinese tradition.

156
White, William Charles. *Bone Culture of Ancient China: An Archaeological Study of Bone Material from Northern Honan, Dating about the Twelfth Century, B.C.* Toronto: University of Toronto Press, 1945. Technical study of bone objects, including "oracle bones" or divination records, excavated at the Shang capital; profusely illustrated with drawings.

157
Loehr, Max. *Chinese Bronze Age Weapons.* Ann Arbor: University of Michigan Press, 1956. A detailed, technical study of more than 100 axes, spearheads, dagger axes, knives, daggers, and swords of Shang and early Chou times; with authoritative comment on the difficulties of relating early Chinese culture to outside cultures through stylistic and technological analysis.

158
Eberhard, Wolfram. "The Formation of Chinese Civilization According to Socio-Anthropological Analysis," *Sociologus,* VII (1957), 97-112. Discussion of possible new approaches to an explanation of how, in Shang or pre-Shang times, a high-civilization "Chinese" group emerged among non-Chinese "local cultures."

159
Li Chi. *The Beginnings of Chinese Civilization.* Seattle: University of Washington Press, 1957. Brief and rather technical discussion of the Shang people and culture, with special reference to physical types and bronze technology.

160
Maspero, Henri. "La société chinoise à la fin des Chang et au début des Tcheou," *Bulletin de l'École Francaise d'Extrême-Orient,* XLVI (1954), 335-403. On the socio-economic aspects of the transition from Shang to Chou.

161
Eberhard, Wolfram. *Lokalkulturen im alten China.* 2 vols. Leiden and Peking: 1942. Comprehensive, controversial analysis of the various regional cultures whose interaction, Eberhard believes, created a unique Chinese civilization in ancient times.

Chou

Recommended general histories: Reischauer and Fairbank, pp. 49-84; Fitzgerald, pp. 55-134; Eberhard, chaps. 3-4.

162
Bodde, Derk. "Feudalism in China," in *Feudalism in History* (R. Coulborn, ed.; Princeton: Princeton University Press, 1956), pp. 49-92. An authoritative, brief description of the governmental and social organization of the early Chou period.

163
Creel, Herrlee Glessner. *The Birth of China.* Reprint ed. New York: Ungar, 1954. Chaps. 15-28 present a thorough review of the Chou conquest and of early Chou society and institutions; in a popular style, but authoritative.

164
Walker, Richard Louis. *The Multi-state System of Ancient China.* Hamden, Conn.: Shoe String Press, 1953. Analyzes interstate relations of the Ch'un-ch'iu period.

165
Legge, James (trans.). *The Chinese Classics.* Vols. 3-5 in 6 parts. London: Henry Frowde, 1865-72. (Being reprinted by the Hong Kong University Press, 1961). Include authoritative, annotated translations of the 3 basic Chinese sources of Chou history: *Shu-ching* ("Classic of Documents"), a collection of speeches, etc., attributed to highest antiquity down through the early Chou rulers (vol. 3); *Ch'un-ch'iu* ("Spring and Autumn Annals"), a cryptic chronicle of events from 721 to 481 B.C.; and its principle commentary, *Tso-chuan* (both in vol. 5).

166
Karlgren, Bernhard (trans.). "The Book of Documents," *Bulletin of the Museum of Far Eastern Antiquities,* Stockholm, XXII (1950), 1-81. Translation of the *Shu-ching;* more literal and precise than Legge's.

167
Maspero, Henri. *La Chine antique.* Rev. ed. Paris: Imprimerie Nationale, 1955. Detailed description of the

political history, the institutions, and the culture of the Chou period; a classic reference, though not substantially changed since its first printing in 1927.

168

Sun, E-tu Zen and John de Francis (trans.). *Chinese Social History.* Washington: American Council of Learned Societies, 1956. Includes 5 articles by modern Chinese scholars on the society and economics of Chou China: "The Well-Field System in Shang and Chou" and "Some Agricultural Implements of the Early Chinese," by Hsü Chung-shu; "Feudal Society of the Chou Dynasty," by Chang Yin-lin; "The Investiture Ceremony of Chou," by Ch'i Ssu-ho; and "The Chinese Land System before the Ch'in Dynasty," by Wu Ch'i-ch'ang.

169

Lattimore, Owen. *Inner Asian Frontiers of China.* 2d ed. New York: American Geographical Society, 1951. Part 3 provides a highly interpretive socioeconomic analysis of the rise of the Chinese nation in Chou times and of China's relations with neighboring peoples.

170

Creel, Herrlee Glessner. *Confucius the Man and the Myth.* New York: John Day, 1949; paperbound reprint entitled *Confucius and the Chinese Way,* New York: Harper Torchbooks, 1960. An authoritative and critical study, but in very readable style, of the life, the teachings, the times, and the influence of Confucius.

171

Kaizuka Shigeki. *Confucius,* trans. by G. Bownas. New York: Macmillan, 1956. A brief study of the life and teachings of Confucius, including an analytical description of the political and social institutions of the late Chou period.

172

Swann, Nancy Lee. *Food and Money in Ancient China.* Princeton: Princeton University Press, 1950. An authoritative study of the treatises on economics from Pan Kus *Han-shu* and Ssu-ma Ch'ien's *Shih-chi,* incorporating annotated translations; presents the traditional Chinese view of economic development and planning in Chou times.

173

Chavannes, Édouard (trans.). *Les mémoires historiques de Se-ma Ts'ien.* 5 vols. in 6. Paris: Ernest Leroux, 1895–1905. Authoritative, partial translation of Ssu-ma Ch'ien's *Shih-chi,* the standard Chinese history of China into the 2d century B.C.

174

Debnicki, Aleksy. *The "Chu-shu-chi-nien" as a Source to the Social History of Ancient China.* Warsaw: Panstwowe Wydawnictwo Naukowe, 1956. On a cryptic chronicle of events ("Bamboo Annals") from highest antiquity down into the 4th century B.C., traditionally considered an important source for Chou history but of very questionable authenticity; cf. the translation given in the prolegomena to James Legge's version of the *Shu-ching* in vol. 3 of his *The Chinese Classics.*

175

Creel, Herrlee G. "Bronze Inscriptions of the Western Chou Dynasty as Historical Documents," *Journal of the American Oriental Society,* LVI (1936), 335-349. On how bronze vessels can be used to complement the *Shu-ching* for the study of early Chou history.

176

Harlez, C. de (trans.). "Koue-Yü ou Discours des Royaumes," *Journal Asiatique,* ser. 9, vol. II (1893), 373-419; III (1894), 5-91. Translation of *Kuo-yü,* a collection of documents concerning interstate diplomatic relations of the Warring States era, not available in English rendering.

177

Komai Kazuchika and Takeshi Sekino. *Han-tan: Excavation at the Ruins of the Capital of Chao in the Contending States Period.* Tokyo: Far Eastern Archaeological Society, 1954. Profusely illustrated report on one of the great cities of late Chou times.

178

Biot, Édouard (trans.). *Le Tcheou-li ou Rites des Tcheou.* 3 vols. Paris: Imprimerie Nationale, 1851. An ancient Chinese classic *(Chou-li)* purporting to describe and establish regulations for the government of Chou times, but now generally believed to be a utopian reconstruction attributable to a very late Chou or perhaps even later period; the only complete translation in a Western language.

179

Tschepe, Albert. *Histoire du royaume de Ts'in.* Shanghai: Mission Catholique, 1909. (Variétés Sinologiques, 27.) Uncritical narrative history of the western feudal state of Ch'in and its gradual conquest of all China.

180

Tschepe, Albert. *Histoire du royaume de Han.* Shanghai: Mission Catholique, 1910. (Variétés Sinologiques, 31.) Uncritical narrative history of the central China feudal state of Han from its creation in 453 B.C.

181

Granet, Marcel. *Chinese Civilization.* London: Kegan Paul, 1930; paperbound reprint, New York: Meridian Books, 1958. An original, theoretical analysis of Chinese institutions and society in Chou times, but not generally considered authoritative.

182

Jager, Fritz (trans.) "Die Biographie des Wu Tzu-hsü," *Oriens Extremus,* VII (1960–61), 1-16. On a famous prime minister of the southern state of Wu in the 6th century B.C., whose spirit was thought to have brought ruin upon his unappreciative king; from Ssu-ma Ch'ien's *Shih-chi.*

THE FIRST IMPERIAL ERA

Ch'in, 221–207 B.C.

Former Han, 202 B.C.–A.D. 9

Hsin, 9–21

Later Han, 25–220

The subjugation of all China by the state of Ch'in in 221 B.C. ushered in an important new phase of China's development. The Ch'in king, one of the most determined organizers of Chinese history, adopted the auspicious new title First Emperor *(Shih Huang-ti)* and set about obliterating the regionalism of the old feudal age. Inspired and advised by Legalist thinkers, he introduced a highly centralized, bureaucratic form of government; imposed national standards for weights and measures; established central government control over some fields of industry and commerce; suppressed independent thought and criticism; and subjected all Chinese to a harsh and rigidly enforced system of punishments. He also sponsored the building of highways, irrigation canals, and the famous Great Wall of China. Subsequent historians have condemned him for his totalitarian excesses, and shortly after his death his hated regime was toppled by hordes of rebels. But his vision of national unity persisted: China was soon reunited under an able and humane commoner, Liu Pang, who founded the

Han dynasty. He and his successors stabilized the centralized form of government inherited from Ch'in, adopted a modified form of Confucianism as the official state ideology, defended China vigorously against threatened inroads of nomadic Hsiung-nu (Huns) on the north, extended Chinese occupance to the south coast, and thrust Chinese political authority and cultural influence into Vietnam, Korea, and Chinese Turkestan. The four centuries of their rule were broken into Former and Later (or Western and Eastern) Han periods by the interlude of the Hsin dynasty, founded by a Han minister named Wang Mang who is one of the most controversial figures of early Chinese history. The most renowned intellectual of his time, Wang usurped the throne by popular demand (perhaps cleverly engineered) and plunged into socioeconomic experimentation of the most drastic sorts — nationalization of land, revaluation of coinage, and so on. His attempts to alleviate widespread distress failed, and in the end he was swarmed under by rebels. The Han dynasty was then restored, to be finally terminated two centuries later by the usurpation of a generalissimo. In its final century the glory of the Han dynasty was besmirched by a succession of palace intrigues, by governmental disruptions on the part of court eunuchs, by large-scale popular rebellions which gave rise to warlordism, and by widespread disillusionment and intellectual ferment, perhaps resulting in part from the introduction of Buddhism by missionaries from India. But for four centuries literature, the arts, historiography, classical scholarship, and other forms of cultural expression had flourished to such an extent, and China's all-round domination of East Asia had been so unchallengeable, that the Chinese subsequently ranked the Han period as one of the highest points in the development of their civilization and still proudly call themselves "men of Han." At its height, the Han empire was a worthy counterpart of the contemporary Roman empire in the West.

Recommended general histories: Reischauer and Fairbank, chap. 4; Goodrich, chap. 2; Fitzgerald, chaps. 6-10; Grousset, chaps. 6-12; Eberhard, chaps. 5-6.

Ch'in

183
Bodde, Derk. *China's First Unifier: A Study of the Ch'in Dynasty as Seen in the Life of Li Ssu, 280?-208 B.C.* Leiden: E. J. Brill, 1938. The standard source on the governmental policies of the Ch'in state and their chief architect.

184
Bodde, Derk (trans.). *Statesman, Patriot, and General in Ancient China.* New Haven: American Oriental Society, 1940. Studies of three notable Ch'in personages (Lü Pu-wei, Ching K'o, Meng T'ien), based on biographies in the *Shih-chi* of Ssu-ma Ch'ien.

185
Tschepe, Albert. *Histoire du royaume de Ts'in.* Shanghai: Mission Catholique, 1909. (Variétés Sinologiques, 27.) A detailed but uncritical narrative of Ch'in political history from earliest times until 207 B.C.

186
Haenisch, Erich (trans.). "Der Aufstand von Ch'en She im Jahre 209 v. Chr.," *Asia Major,* II (1951–52), 72-84. A biographical notice from Ssu-ma Ch'ien's *Shih-chi* about the first notable uprising against Ch'in.

Han: General

187
Dubs, Homer H. (trans.). *History of the Former Han Dynasty.* 3 vols. of a projected 5. Baltimore: Waverly Press, 1938–55. Translation of the annals sections of Pan Ku's *Han-shu,* thoroughly annotated, with many addenda and long introductory sections that constitute an authoritative political history of the Former Han period.

188
Watson, Burton (trans.). *Records of the Grand Historian of China.* 2 vols. New York: Columbia University Press, 1961. Extensive and authoritative translations from Ssuma Ch'ien's *Shih-chi* relating to the founding of the Han dynasty and its early history to about 100 B.C.; includes annals, treatises, and biographies.

189
Bielenstein, Hans. "The Restoration of the Han Dynasty," *Bulletin of the Museum of Far Eastern Antiquities,* Stockholm, XXVI (1954), 1-209, and XXXI (1959), 1-287. A meticulous, comprehensive account of the overthrow of Wang Mang and the reestablishment of the Liu family, inaugurating the Later Han dynasty.

190
Watson, Burton. *Ssu-ma Ch'ien, Grand Historian of China.* New York: Columbia University Press, 1958. Biographical and literary study of China's greatest historian, with data on the China in which he lived (2d-1st centuries B.C.).

191
Swann, Nancy Lee. *Food and Money in Ancient China.* Princeton: Princeton University Press, 1950. A monumental, technical study of China's early economic life, incorporating annotated translations from Pan Ku's *Han-shu* and Ssu-ma Ch'ien's *Shih-chi* treatises; an indispensable reference on economic theory, economic planning, coinage, industry, etc., of the Former Han period.

192
Balazs, Étienne. "La crise sociale et la philosophie politique à la fin des Han," *T'oung Pao,* XXXIX (1949–50), 83-131. A survey of social, intellectual, and political ferment in the last Han decades, with a study of three disillusioned and rebellious social critics.

193
Wang Yü-ch'üan. "An Outline of the Central Government of the Former Han Dynasty," *Harvard Journal of Asiatic Studies,* XII (1949), 134-187. An interpretive description, emphasizing governmental functions as well as organization; also deals with the Han emperors as executives, the development of state ideology, etc.

194
Tjan Tjoe Som. *Po Hu T'ung: The Comprehensive Discussions in the White Tiger Hall.* 2 vols. Leiden: E. J. Brill, 1949–52. Translation of a report of a court-sponsored conference on the classics in A.D. 79, with a long technical introduction; a major contribution toward understanding the world-view and intellectual life of Han China.

195
Wilbur, C. Martin. *Slavery in China During the Former Han Dynasty, 206 B.C.-A.D. 25.* Chicago: Field Museum of Natural History, 1943. A standard source on socioeconomic conditions in Former Han China.

196

Chavannes, Édouard (trans.). *Les memoires historiques de Se-ma Ts'ien.* 5 vols in 6. Paris: Ernest Leroux, 1895–1905. Authoritative, partial translation of Ssu - ma Ch'ien's *Shih-chi,* the standard Chinese history of China into the 2d century B.C., with valuable introductory data on early Han life and institutions; should be used to supplement Pan Ku's history.

197

Hulsewé, A. F. P. *Remnants of Han Law.* Vol. 1. Leiden: E. J. Brill, 1955. A valuable source of information on Han administrative techniques and sociopolitical attitudes.

198

Yang Lien-sheng. "Great Families of Eastern Han," in *Chinese Social History* (E-tu Zen Sun and John de Francis, ed.; Washington: American Council of Learned Societies, 1956), pp. 103-134. A sweeping study of the socioeconomic power structure in Han times, with an analysis of the political deterioration of the Later Han dynasty.

199

Wright, Arthur F. *Buddhism in Chinese History.* Stanford: Stanford University Press, 1959. Pp. 7-31 give an interpretive over-view of Han China, with emphasis on intellectual and socioeconomic aspects.

200

Houn, Franklin W. "The Civil Service Recruitment System of the Han Dynasty," *Tsing Hua Journal of Chinese Studies,* I (1956), 138-164. Analysis and evaluation of many types of personnel recruitment, including examinations, used in the Former and Later Han governments.

201

Swann, Nancy Lee. *Pan Chao, Foremost Woman Scholar of China, 1st Century A.D.* New York: Century, 1932. Authoritative study of the scholarly Pan family (including the historian Pan Ku) and of their age in China.

202

Maspero, Henri. *Mélanges posthumes sur les religions et l'histoire de la Chine.* Vol. 3. *Études historiques.* Paris: Civilisations du Sud, 1950. Pp. 63–76, "La vie courante dans la Chine des Han," reconstructs, from archaeological evidence, the material aspects of life in Han China: houses, furnishings, foods, entertainments, the daily routine, etc.; should be used together with the author's earlier, and somewhat different, article on the same subject, "La vie privée en Chine à l'époque des Han," *Révue des Arts Asiatiques,* VII (1931–32), 185-201.

203

Lao Kan. "Population and Geography in the Two Han Dynasties," in *Chinese Social History* (E-tu Zen Sun and John de Francis, ed.; Washington: American Council of Learned Societies, 1956), pp. 83-102. On fluctuations in population and in population distribution, with special reference to Chinese settlement south of the Yangtze River.

204

Gale, Esson M. (trans.). *Discourses on Salt and Iron: A Debate on State Control of Commerce and Industry in Ancient China.* Leiden: E. J. Brill, 1931. Translation of chaps. 1-19 of Huan K'uan's *Yen-t'ieh lun,* reporting a court debate in 81 B.C. about emergent welfare-state ideas; chaps. 20-28 are translated in *Journal of the North China Branch, Royal Asiatic Society,* LXV (1934), 73-110.

205

Levy, Howard S. "Yellow Turban Religion and Rebellion at the End of Han," *Journal of the American Oriental Society,* LXXVI (1956), 214-227. Analysis of a magicoreligious Taoist movement that disrupted the last decades of the Later Han period.

206

Eberhard, Wolfram. "The Political Function of Astronomy and Astronomers in Han China," in *Chinese Thought*

and Institutions (J. K. Fairbank, ed.; Chicago: University of Chicago Press, 1957), pp. 33-70. On how the interpretation of portents was used to check the despotic inclinations of Han emperors.

207

Wilhelm, Hellmut. "The Scholar's Frustration: Notes on a Type of *Fu,*" in *Chinese Thought and Institutions* (J. K. Fairbank, ed.; Chicago: University of Chicago Press, 1957), pp. 310-319. Notes how Han scholars used a form of prose-poem to express their frustration at being dependent upon and unprotected against the rulers.

208

De Francis, John (trans.). "Biography of the Marquis of Huai-yin," *Harvard Journal of Asiatic Studies,* X (1947), 179-215. A rather irreverent biography of a helper in the founding of the Han dynasty, from Ssu-ma Ch'ien's *Shih-chi;* with technical annotations.

209

Jansé, Olov R. T. *Archaeological Research in Indo-China.* 2 vols. of a projected 3. Cambridge: Harvard University Press, 1947–51. A monumental report on Chinese tombs and other remains of the Han period in Indo-China; valuable not only as regards Chinese expansion southward but also as regards the material culture of Han China generally.

210

Lin Yutang. *A History of the Press and Public Opinion in China.* Chicago: University of Chicago Press, 1936. Chap. 4, "Public Criticism and 'Party Inquisitions' in the Han Dynasty," surveys the decay of political morale in the Later Han period.

211

Hughes, E. R. *Two Chinese Poets: Vignettes of Han Life and Thought.* Princeton: Princeton University Press, 1960. Part translations and part summaries of long descriptive poems of life at the Han capitals, by Pan Ku and Chang Heng, with critiques throwing light on Han events and customs.

212

Rudolph, Richard C. and Wen Yu. *Han Tomb Art of West China.* Berkeley: University of California Press, 1951. Reproductions of 100 tomb reliefs of the 1st and 2d centuries, with an introduction and descriptions of the plates; a valuable source on Later Han life and culture.

213

Kato Shigeru. "A Study of the Suan-Fu, the Poll Tax of the Han Dynasty," *Memoirs of the Research Department of The Toyo Bunko,* I (1926), 51-68. Includes useful data on the Han fiscal system in general.

214

Haloun, G. "The Liang-chou Rebellion," *Asia Major,* I (1949–50), 119-132. A technical study of a little-known uprising against the Later Han dynasty among "barbarian" mercenaries on the western frontier, 184-221.

215

Waley, Arthur. "Life under the Han Dynasty: Notes on Chinese Civilization in the First and Second Centuries A.D.," *History Today,* III (1953), 89-98. Comments on everyday life in Han times, prompted by publication of R. C. Rudolph and Wen Yu, *Han Tomb Art of West China* (Berkeley: 1951).

216

Duman, L. I. "On the Social and Economic System of China in the Western Han Period," in *Akten des vierundzwansigsten Internationalen Orientalisten-Kongresses München, 1957* (Herbert Franke, ed.; Wiesbaden: Franz Steiner, 1959). A Marxist reinterpretation.

217

Eberhard, Wolfram. "The Origin of the Commoners in Ancient Tun-huang," *Sinologica,* IV (1954–56), 141-155. Includes sociological data on Han soldiers in the far Northwest, ca. 100 B.C.-A.D. 100.

Wang Mang

218
Dubs, Homer H. (trans.). *History of the Former Han Dynasty.* Vol. 3. Baltimore: Waverly Press, 1955. Devoted almost entirely to the career of Wang Mang, whom Dubs considers a self-seeking opportunist who was finally ruined by those he had alienated.

219
Bielenstein, Hans. "The Restoration of the Han Dynasty," first part, *Bulletin of the Museum of Far Eastern Antiquities,* Stockholm, XXVI (1954), 1-209. Pp. 82-165 suggest that Wang Mang fell, not because of his exploitive misgovernment, but because of the uncontrollable, cumulative social effects of a disastrous change in the lower course of the Yellow River.

220
Sargent, Clyde B. *Wang Mang: A Translation of the Official Account of His Rise to Power as Given in the History of the Former Han Dynasty.* Shanghai: Graphic Art Book Company, 1947. Translation of the biography in Pan Ku's *Han-shu,* now superseded by the more authoritative translation by Dubs; introduction gives an objective, inconclusive interpretation.

China's foreign relations in the Han era

221
McGovern, William Montgomery. *The Early Empires of Central Asia.* Chapel Hill: University of North Carolina Press, 1939. Principally a detailed study of relations between Han China and the nomadic Hsiung-nu on its northern frontier.

222
Lattimore, Owen. *Inner Asian Frontiers of China.* 2d ed. New York: American Geographical Society, 1951. Part 4 provides a highly interpretive socioeconomic analysis of the rise of the imperial Chinese state in Ch'in and Han times and of its rivalry with the Hsiung-nu nomads.

223
Hudson, Geoffrey F. *Europe and China: A Survey of Their Relations from the Earliest Times to 1800.* London: Edward Arnold, 1931; paperbound reprint, Boston: Beacon Press, 1961. Chaps. 2 and 3 summarize East-West relations in Han times, especially noting the 2d century B.C. travels of Chang Ch'ien to Western Asia and the rise of the silk trade.

224
Hirth, Friedrich. "The Story of Chang K'ien, China's Pioneer in Western Asia," *Journal of the American Oriental Society,* XXXVII (1919), 89-152. Detailed study of Chang Ch'ien's mission to Russian Turkestan in the 2d century B.C. in search of an alliance with the Yüeh-chih tribe against the Hsiung-nu.

225
Chavannes, Édouard. "Trois generaux chinois de la dynastie des Han Orientaux," *T'oung Pao,* VII (1906) 210-269. On 3 of Later Han's great proconsuls in Central Asia: Pan Ch'ao, Pan Yung, and Liang Ch'in.

226
Aurousseau, Leonard. "La premiere conquète chinoise des pays Annamites," *Bulletin de l'École Francaise d'Extrème-Orient,* XXIII (1923), 137-264. Detailed account of the expansion of the Chinese empire into northern Indo-China in Ch'in and Han times.

227
Maspero, Henri. "L'expedition de Ma Yüan," *Bulletin de l'École Francaise d'Extrème-Orient,* XVIII (1918), 11-28. On the Later Han reconquest of northern Indo-China.

228
Waley, Arthur. "The Heavenly Horses of Ferghana," *History Today,* V (1955), 95-103. A reappraisal of the motives behind a Chinese expedition in 102 B.C. to acquire "blood-sweating horses" from Western Asia; suggests a magico-religious significance.

229
Maenchen-Helfen, Otto J. "The Ethnic Name Hun," in *Studia Serica Bernhard Karlgren Dedicata* (Copenhagen: Enjar Munksgaard, 1959), pp. 223-238. On the difficulties of establishing linguistic affiliations between the Hsiung-nu and the Huns of Europe; technical.

230
Samolin, William. "Hsiung-nu, Hun, Turk," *Central Asiatic Journal,* III (1956?), 143-150. A brief, inconclusive survey of literature on the problem of identifying the Hsiung-nu with the European Huns and relating them to the later Turks.

231
Enoki, K. "Sogdiana and the Hsiung-nu," *Central Asiatic Journal,* I (1955), 43-62. A technical, authoritative discussion of the problem of identifying the Hsiung-nu with the Huns.

232
Dubs, Homer H. *A Roman City in Ancient China.* London: The China Society, 1957. A brief but complicated suggestion that in 36 B.C. the Chinese captured Roman mercenaries from the Hsiung-nu in Sogdiana, after they had previously been captured by Parthians from Crassus at Carrhae, and settled them in a colony in northwestern China.

233
Cammann, Schuyler. "Archaeological Evidence for Chinese Contacts with India during the Han Dynasty," *Sinologica,* V (1956-58), 1-19. Reports on finding the cocking lever of a 1st century crossbow mechanism at Sirkap in northwestern India, which is tangible evidence of Chinese-Indian contacts in Han times.

234
Ikeuchi Hiroshi. "A Study on Lo-lang and Tai-fang, Ancient Chinese Prefectures in Korean Peninsula," *Memoirs of the Research Department of The Toyo Bunko,* V (1930), 79-95. A brief history of Chinese settlement and government in south Manchuria and north Korea from the 2d century B.C. into the 3d century A.D.

235
Teggart, Frederick J. *Rome and China.* Berkeley: University of California Press, 1939. A study of the correlation between Chinese-Hsiung-nu disturbances and Rome-barbarian troubles between 58 B.C. and A.D. 107, noting that every border conflict in Han China had repercussions on the Roman frontier.

236
Grousset, René. *L'empire des steppes.* Paris: Payot, 1948. Pp. 30-124: on the Hsiung-nu and early Turkic invaders of China in Han and post-Han times.

THE AGE OF DISRUPTION AND DIVISION

The Three Kingdoms, 220–280
  Wei (North China), 220–264
  Shu Han (Szechwan), 221–263
  Wu (Yangtze valley), 222–280
Chin, 265–420
  Western Chin (capital Loyang), 265–317
  Eastern Chin (capital Nanking), 317–420
Southern dynasties (capital Nanking for all), 420–589
  (Liu) Sung, 420–477
  Southern Ch'i, 477–502
  Liang, 502–557
  Ch'en, 557–589

The Sixteen Kingdoms (North China), 304–436
    Han, 304–329
    Chao, 329–352
    Former Yen, 352–370
    Ch'eng Han, 304–347
    Later Yen, 384–409
    Southern Yen, 398–410
    Northern Yen, 409–436
    Hsia, 407–431
    Former Liang, 313–376
    Later Liang, 386–403
    Southern Liang, 397–414
    Northern Liang, 397–439
    Former Ch'in, 351–394
    Later Ch'in, 384–417
    Western Ch'in, 395–431
    Western Liang, 400–421
Northern dynasties (North China), 386–581
    Northern Wei, 386–534
    Eastern Wei, 534–550
    Northern Ch'i, 550–577
    Western Wei, 534–557
    Northern Chou, 557–581

With the collapse of the Han dynasty in A.D. 220 China entered upon a long period of political disunity, social change, and intellectual ferment. But the descent into political chaos was relatively gradual and never reached the extreme of contemporary post-Rome Europe. At first the Han empire was split apart by three contenders for national leadership. Their Three Kingdoms era has been romanticized by China's storytellers ever since as an epoch of courage in battle, comradely sacrifices, and brilliant tactical maneuvers. Then China was reunited under a Chin dynasty and enjoyed a revival of the old Han culture and institutions. But Chin was harassed almost from the first by northern "barbarians" and in 317 was forced to withdraw entirely from North China. Thereafter the Han traditions lived on, but with some neo-feudal aspects, in the Yangtze River valley and the south coast under a succession of so-called Southern dynasties; literature and painting particularly flourished. Concurrently, North China was being overrun by Hunnish, proto-Turkic, and perhaps proto-Mongol peoples from the northern steppes. The most important of their tribal kingdoms and dynasties were the successive Wei dynasties of the Turkic-speaking T'o-pa (or Toba) peoples, who dominated North China for a century and a half and began to forge a new Chinese way of life, an amalgam of Han traditions and foreign influences. As the 6th century neared its end a seemingly permanent stalemate had developed between a unified old-style China in the south and a unified new-style China in the north. But neither China was really old-style, for — just as Christianity was winning Europe —

Buddhism, introduced from India in the Later Han period, had become the most vigorous philosophical force in East Asia and was transforming the cultural and intellectual patterns of both Chinas.

Recommended general histories: Eberhard, chap. 7; Goodrich, chap. 3; Reischauer and Fairbank, pp. 128-153; Fitzgerald, chaps. 11-12; Grousset, chaps. 13-15. Eberhard and Goodrich are especially strong on this period.

237

Fang, Achilles (trans.). *The Chronicle of the Three Kingdoms (220–265)*. Cambridge: Harvard University Press, 1952. Authoritative translation of chaps. 69-78 of Ssu-ma Kuang's comprehensive narrative history of pre-Sung China, *Tzu-chih t'ung-chien;* the most detailed study of 3 Kingdoms history.

238

McGovern, William Montgomery. *The Early Empires of Central Asia*. Chapel Hill: University of North Carolina Press, 1939. Chaps. 14-15 give a detailed political history of the Hunnish states of North China up to 439.

239

Bodde, Derk. "Feudalism in China," in *Feudalism in History* (R. Coulborn, ed.; Princeton: Princeton University Press, 1956), pp. 49-92. Pp. 83 ff. discuss the reemergence of "feudalistic phenomena" in Chinese society during the era of North-South division.

240

Yang Lien-sheng. *Studies in Chinese Institutional History*. Cambridge: Harvard University Press, 1961. (Harvard-Yenching Institute Studies, XX). Pp. 119-197, "Notes on the Economic History of the Chin Dynasty": a translation of the section on economic history in the *Chin-shu*, with a long introductory analysis about post-Han social and economic changes; previously published in *Harvard Journal of Asiatic Studies*, IX (1945–47), 107-185.

241

Zürcher, E. *The Buddhist Conquest of China: The Spread and Adaptation of Buddhism in Early Medieval China*. 2 vols. Leiden: E. J. Brill, 1959. Includes, in passing, much data and authoritative comment on the history and society of the 3rd, 4th, and 5th centuries in China.

242

Sun, E-tu Zen and John de Francis (trans.). *Chinese Social History*. Washington: American Council of Learned Societies, 1956. Includes 3 articles on the neo-feudal and other socioeconomic aspects of the history of the era of North-South division: "Early Development of Manorial Economy in Wei and Tsin," by Ho Tzu-ch'uan; "Evolution of the Status of 'Dependents'," by Yang Chung-i; and "The System of Equal Land Allotments in Medieval Times," by Wan Kuo-ting.

243

Gernet, Jacques. *Les aspects économiques du Bouddhisme dans la société chinoise du Ve au Xe siècle*. Saigon: École Francaise d'Extrème-Orient, 1956. An authoritative study of the economic activities and influence of Buddhist monasteries, with indispensable information about China's economic history generally.

244

Eberhard, Wolfram. *Das Toba-reich nordchinas: eine soziologische Untersuchung*. Leiden: E. J. Brill, 1949. A highly detailed and technical study of T'o-pa society, economy, and bureaucracy, in a sociological approach.

245

Shryock, John K. (trans.). *The Study of Human Abilities: The Jen Wu Chih of Liu Shao*. New Haven: American Oriental Society, 1937. Pp. 7-13 give a very brief but excellent summary of general history from the decline of Han through the Three Kingdoms era.

246

Waley, Arthur. "The Fall of Loyang," *History Today,* IV (1954), 7-10. On the loss of North China to "barbarian" invaders in 317, equated in significance with the Gothic sack of Rome in 410.

247

Frankel, Hans H. *Catalogue of Translations from the Chinese Dynastic Histories for the Period 220-960.* Berkeley: University of California Press, 1957. An indispensable reference aid.

248

Balazs, Étienne. *Le traité juridique du "Souei-Chou."* Leiden: E. J. Brill, 1954. Translation, with introductory data and appendices, of the section on law in the *Sui-shu,* especially emphasizing the development of law and justice between Han and Sui times, with much data of general historical value.

249

Holzman, Donald. "Les Sept Sages de la Foret des Bambous et la société de leur temps," *T'oung Pao,* XLIV (1956), 317-346. On the social and intellectual ferment of 3d century China, reflected by a famous group of free spirits.

250

Holzman, Donald. *La vie et la pensée de Hi K'ang (223-262).* Leiden: E. J. Brill, 1957. A detailed, authoritative analysis of the life and thought of Hsi K'ang, an eccentric philosopher-poet who was one of the "Seven Sages of the Bamboo Grove."

251

Acker, William (trans.). *T'ao the Hermit: Sixty Poems by T'ao Ch'ien.* London: Thames and Hudson, 1952. Includes data on the life and times of a 4th-5th century part official, part recluse who is best known as a nature poet.

252

Link, Arthur E. "Shih Seng-yu and his Writings," *Journal of the American Oriental Society,* LXXX (1960), 17-43. A technical study of the intellectual environment and the writings of an eminent Buddhist monk (d. 518).

253

Wang Yi-t'ung. "Slaves and Other Comparable Social Groups During the Northern Dynasties (386-618)," *Harvard Journal of Asiatic Studies,* XVI (1953), 293-364. A detailed study of the sources, status, treatment, and functions of government and private slaves under the "barbarian" dynasties, as well as of concubines and other "retainer" groups.

254

Grousset, René. *L'empire des steppes.* Paris: Payot, 1948. Pp. 30-124 on the Hsiung-nu and early Turkic invaders of China into the 6th century.

255

Schreiber, Gerhard. "The History of the Former Yen Dynasty," *Monumenta Serica,* XIV (1949-55), 374-480; XV (1956), 1-141. A detailed political history of one of the 16 Kingdoms of North China, ruled by T'o-pa relatives called Hsien-pi; with an introductory survey of the general background, the Hsien-pi peoples, and the basic sources.

256

Liebenthal, Walter. "Chinese Buddhism During the 4th and 5th Centuries," *Monumenta Nipponica,* XI (1955), 44-83. Analyzes how various Chinese social classes reacted to Buddhism and describes the succession of disputes and debates that marked early Buddhist history in China.

257

Ch'en, Kenneth. "On Some Factors Responsible for the Anti-Buddhist Persecution under the Pei-ch'ao," *Harvard Journal of Asiatic Studies,* XVII (1954), 261-273. Reflections on social and political differences between North and South China during the era of division, to explain why Buddhists were sometimes forcefully suppressed by the Northern dynasties (Pei-ch'ao) whereas they were subjected only to debates and intellectual arguments under the Southern dynasties.

258

Balazs, Étienne. *Le traité économique du "Souei-Chou."* Leiden: E. J. Brill, 1953. Translation of the section on economic history of the *Sui-shu,* with detailed introductory data and appendices about the history and institutions of 6th century China; especially relevant to the study of the T'o-pa states.

259

Boodberg, Peter A. "Marginalia to the Histories of the Northern Dynasties," *Harvard Journal of Asiatic Studies,* IV (1939), 230-283. Technical studies of a few limited aspects of Northern dynasties history: prevalence of the word "horn" in titles among the northern nomads, a coronation ritual among the T'o-pa peoples, usurpation of the Chou throne by Yang Chien, etc.

260

Soper, Alexander C. *Literary Evidence for Early Buddhist Art in China.* Ascona, Switzerland: 1959. (Artibus Asiae Supplementum, XIX). Contains abundant data revelant to the general history of the era of North-South division.

261

Ikeuchi Hiroshi. "The Chinese Expeditions to Manchuria under the Wei Dynasty," *Memoirs of the Research Department of The Toyo Bunko,* IV (1929), 71-119. On Chinese conquests in north Korea and Manchuria in the middle of the 3d century.

262

Ikeuchi Hiroshi. "A Study on Lo-lang and Tai-fang, Ancient Chinese Prefectures in Korean Peninsula," *Memoirs of the Research Department of The Toyo Bunko,* V (1930), 79-95. Includes a brief account of Chinese settlement and government in south Manchuria and north Korea in the 3 Kingdoms period.

263

Giles, Lionel. *Descriptive Catalogue of the Chinese Manuscripts from Tunhuang in the British Museum.* London: British Museum, 1957. A complete, technical analysis of about 8,000 texts and text fragments collected by Sir Aurel Stein; an indispensable tool for research on society and literature (especially Buddhist) in the period of North-South division.

264

Chen Shih-hsiang (trans.). *Biography of Ku K'ai-chih.* Berkeley: University of California Press, 1953. On a famous 4th century painter and eccentric; translated from the *Chin-shu,* with detailed annotations.

265

Mather, Richard B. (trans.). *Biography of Lü Kuang.* Berkeley: University of California Press, 1959. Translation of a *Chin-shu* account of the founder of the northwestern frontier state of Later Liang late in the 4th century.

266

Goodrich, Chauncey S. (trans.) *Biography of Su Ch'o.* Berkeley: University of California Press, 1953. On an influential 6th century Confucian scholar-official in the service of the "barbarian" Western Wei state; translated from the *Chou-shu.*

267

Carroll, Thomas D. (trans.). *Account of the T'u-yü-hun in the History of the Chin Dynasty.* Berkeley: University of California Press, 1953. On a "barbarian" state that dominated China's far western frontier, ca. 300-450.

268

Miller, Roy Andrew (trans.). *Accounts of Western Nations in the History of the Northern Chou Dynasty.* Berkeley: University of California Press, 1959. On China's knowledge of, and contacts with, Inner Asian peoples from Turfan to Persia during the 6th century.

269

Maenchen-Helfen, Otto. "The Ting-ling," *Harvard Journal of Asiatic Studies,* IV (1939), 77-86. On a tribe that occupied territory north of the Hsiung-nu in Han and subsequent times.

270

Bazin, Louis. "Recherches sur les parlers T'o-pa," *T'oung Pao*, XXXIX (1949–50), 228-329. A technical study of the linguistic relationships among the T'o-pa peoples and their pre-Turk, pre-Mongol, and pre-Tungus allies.

THE GOLDEN AGE OF EMPIRE

Sui, 581–618

T'ang, 618–907

The Five Dynasties (Yellow River valley), 907–960
    Later Liang, 907–923
    Later T'ang, 923–936
    Later Chin, 936–947
    Later Han, 947–951
    Later Chou, 951–960

The Ten Kingdoms (Central and South China), 891–979
    Former Shu (Szechwan), 891–925
    Later Shu (Szechwan), 925–965
    Nan P'ing or Ching Nan (Hupei), 907–963
    Ch'u (Hunan), 907–951
    Wu (Kiangsi), 892–937
    Southern T'ang or Ch'i (Kiangsi), 937–975
    Wu-Yüeh (Yangtze delta), 907–978
    Southern Han or Yüeh (Kwangtung-Kwangsi), 905–971
    Min (Fukien), 892–946
    Northern Han (Shansi), 951–979

Northern Sung, 960–1126

Southern Sung, 1126–1279

The long post-Han political disunity of China was terminated in 589 by an authoritarian northern state, Sui. Reunification set the stage for a glorious resurgence of Chinese civilization, but the Sui emperors, overextending themselves in costly construction projects and military adventures, failed to realize it. Out of late Sui chaos emerged the most admired man of action in Chinese history, Li Shihmin, who built a stable, vigorous, and long-lived T'ang empire on the Sui beginnings. The T'ang epoch rivals the Han as a notable period of consolidation and growth; all aspects considered, it perhaps marks the high point of China's political and cultural dominance over East Asia. Chinese power was again felt in Central Asia, Southeast Asia, and Korea, and the Japanese began assiduously borrowing T'ang culture and institutions. China's society and government developed new patterns, with an examination-recruited bureaucracy beginning to erode the influence of semi-feudal aristocratic families. Culture flourished as never before, especially in the fields of poetry, painting, and ceramics. The T'ang capital at Ch'ang-an (mod-

ern Sian in Shensi) was probably the most elegant and most cosmopolitan metropolis of the contemporary world. But the early T'ang vigor was eventually sapped by court intrigues and a series of rebellions beginning with that of An Lu-shan in the 750's. Finally in 907 the once-centralized T'ang state broke up, and China suffered another cyclical period of disunity. While nomadic pressures mounted on the north, five shortlived dynasties ineffectively tried to maintain Chinese power in the Yellow River valley ("The Five Dynasties," 907–960) and warlords presided over prosperous regional kingdoms in Central and South China ("The Ten Kingdoms," 891–979). Unity was restored by 979 by Sung emperors of the northern plain, and a new era of cultural development was inaugurated. In Sung times urban sophistication became an outstanding characteristic of Chinese life. Rapid development of printing revitalized intellectual life, and the contemplative arts prospered—scholarship, philosophy, and landscape painting especially. Basic Confucian doctrines, long obscured by the more dramatic appeals of Buddhism, reappeared in a vigorous new metaphysical philosophical system known as Neo-Confucianism and regained their old dominance in Chinese ideology. Bureaucratic civil servants finally destroyed the importance of aristocratic privilege in government. But bureaucratic factionalism, deriving from controversies surrounding an 11th-century reform minister named Wang Anshih, and a notable decline in the military tradition inherited from the T'ang era gradually weakened the Sung state and caused it to lose ground to everpredatory northern nomads. In 1126 the whole Yellow River valley was lost to Jurchen invaders from modern Manchuria, and in 1279, after a generation of dogged resistance, the Sung state finally lost its last stronghold in South China to the all-conquering Mongols under Kubilai Khan.

Recommended general histories: Reischauer and Fairbank, pp. 153-242; Fitzgerald, chaps. 13-22; Goodrich, chaps. 4-5; Grousset, chaps. 16-24; Eberhard, chaps. 8-9.

Sui

271

Bingham, Woodbridge. *The Founding of the T'ang Dynasty: The Fall of Sui and Rise of T'ang, a Preliminary Survey.* Baltimore: Waverly Press, 1941. An analysis of factors contributing to the Sui collapse, including detailed data on public-works construction, foreign relations, and the rise of the Li family, which subsequently founded the T'ang dynasty.

272

Wright, Arthur F. "The Formation of Sui Ideology, 581–604," in *Chinese Thought and Institutions* (J. K. Fairbank, ed.; Chicago: University of Chicago Press, 1957), pp. 71-104. An analysis of how the founder of the Sui dynasty utilized ideological propaganda to sanction his reunification of China by conquest.

273

Boodberg, Peter A. "Marginalia to the Histories of the Northern Dynasties," *Harvard Journal of Asiatic Studies,* IV (1939), 230-283. Pp. 253-270 on the establishment of the Sui dynasty by usurpation and on the personalities of the Sui rulers.

274

Wright, Arthur F. "Sui Yang-ti: Personality and Stereotype," in *The Confucian Persuasion* (A. F. Wright, ed.; Stanford: Stanford University Press, 1960), pp. 47-76. On the second and last Sui emperor, as a historical person and as a stereotyped tyrant denounced in orthodox histories and popular myths.

275

Balazs, Étienne. *Le traité juridique du "Souei-Chou."* Leiden: E. J. Brill, 1954. Pp. 73-93 on law codes and judicial legislation of the Sui dynasty.

276

Balazs, Étienne. *Le traité économique du "Souei-Chou."* Leiden: E. J. Brill, 1953. Pp. 151-173 on economic history and legislation of the Sui dynasty.

277

Frankel, Hans H. *Catalogue of Translations from the Chinese Dynastic Histories for the Period 220–960.* Berkeley: University of California Press, 1957. An indispensable reference aid.

T'ang: General

278

Bingham, Woodbridge. *The Founding of the T'ang Dynasty: The Fall of Sui and Rise of T'ang, a Preliminary Survey.* Baltimore: Waverly Press, 1941. A detailed study, from a political approach, of the background and the establishment of the T'ang dynasty.

279

Pulleyblank, Edwin G. *The Background of the Rebellion of An Lu-shan.* London: Oxford University Press, 1955. An exhaustive, analytical study of the economic, political, and military conditions and events that precipitated the 8th century rebellion that started the T'ang regime on its long decline.

280

Reischauer, Edwin O. *Ennin's Travels in T'ang China.* New York: Ronald Press, 1955. A systematic, topical description of 9th-century Chinese life as seen by a Japanese Buddhist monk, incorporated with an account of his activities in China.

281

Reischauer, Edwin O. (trans.). *Ennin's Diary.* New York: Ronald Press, 1955. The observations of a Japanese Buddhist monk who traveled widely in China between 838 and 847; the earliest large-scale and general account of China by a foreign visitor that is now known.

282

Rotours, Robert des (trans.). *Traité des fonctionnaires et traité de l'armée.* 2 vols. Leiden: E. J. Brill, 1947–48. An authoritative, highly technical, thoroughly annotated translation of treatises from the *Hsin T'ang-shu* on the civil government and military establishment of T'ang times; one of the monuments of modern Sinological scholarship.

283

Balazs, Stefan. "Beitrage zur Wirtschaftsgeschichte der T'angzeit," *Mitteilung des Seminars für Orientalische Sprachen,* XXXIV (1931), 1-92; XXXV (1932), 1-73. A classical and indispensable study of population problems, migrations, land distribution, and tax revenues under the T'ang dynasty.

284

Gernet, Jacques. *Les aspects économiques du Bouddhisme dans la société chinoise du Ve au Xe siècle.* Saigon: École Francaise d'Extrême-Orient, 1956. An authoritative study of the economic activities and influence of Buddhist monasteries, with indispensable information about China's economic history generally. Cf. extensive evaluations of Gernet's provocative hypotheses about the relation of Buddhism to medieval Chinese economic developments by A. F. Wright in *Journal of Asian Studies,* XVI (1956–57), 408-414, and Denis Twitchett in *Bulletin of the School of Oriental and African Studies,* London University, XIX (1957), 526-549.

285

Sun, E-tu Zen and John de Francis (trans.). *Chinese Social History.* Washington: American Council of Learned Societies, 1956. Includes 4 articles on socioeconomic aspects of T'ang life: "The System of Equal Land Allotments in Medieval Times," by Wan Kuo-ting; "Lower Castes in the T'ang Dynasty," by Yang Chung-i; "Official Salaries as Revealed in T'ang Poetry," by Ch'en Yin-k'o; and "The Church-State Conflict in the T'ang Dynasty," by Chia Chung-yao.

286

Chavannes, Édouard. *Documents sur les Tou-kiue (Turcs) Occidentaux.* St. Petersburg: 1903. Classical study of the T'u-chüeh (Turks), who controlled the northern frontier from Sui to mid-T'ang times, with translations of Chinese materials and a detailed historical survey; addenda published in *T'oung Pao,* V (1904), 1-110.

287

Bünger, Karl. *Quellen zur Rechtsgeschichte der T'ang-zeit.* Peking: 1946. (Monumenta Serica Monograph IX). A detailed, technical study of the T'ang law code.

288

Twitchett, Denis. "Lands under State Cultivation under the T'ang," *Journal of the Economic and Social History of the Orient,* II (1959), 162-203. A technical historical study of the role of state-owned lands in T'ang fiscal operations.

289

Twitchett, Denis. "Monastic Estates in T'ang China," *Asia Major,* V (1955–56), 123-146. A detailed, technical study of the extent and economic influence of landownership by Buddhist establishmentts and of government efforts to regulate and control it.

290

Ch'en, Kenneth K. S. "The Economic Background of the Hui-ch'ang Suppression of Buddhism," *Harvard Journal of Asiatic Studies,* XIX (1956), 67-105. An analysis of how tax-exempt church estates disrupted the T'ang revenue system, with a general survey of the T'ang economic structure.

291

Moule, Arthur C. *Christians in China Before the Year 1550.* London: Society for Promoting Christian Knowledge, 1930. Pp. 27-77 on the introduction of the Nestorian heresy and other Christian influences into T'ang China.

292

Waley, Arthur. *The Real Tripitaka and Other Pieces.* London: Allen and Unwin, 1952. Pp. 9-130 on Hsüantsang, a famous 7th-century Buddhist pilgrim from China to India; pp. 131-168 on Ennin, a 9th-century Buddhist pilgrim from Japan to China.

293

Rotours, Robert des. *Le traité des examens.* Paris: Ernest Leroux, 1932. An authoritative study of the T'ang system of recruiting personnel for bureaucratic office through competitive examinations, based on translations from the *Hsin T'ang-shu.*

294

Rideout, John K. "The Rise of the Eunuchs During the T'ang Dynasty," *Asia Major,* I (1949–50), 53-72; III (1952), 42-58. Historical survey, up to about 730, of the recruitment, training, functions, and influence of palace eunuchs.

295

Saeki, P. Yoshiro. *The Nestorian Documents and Relics in China.* 2d ed. Tokyo: The Maruzen Co., 1951. A monumental source book of data on the history of Nestorian Christianity in China, chiefly of the T'ang period; with reproductions and translations of many relevant Chinese texts.

296

Wright, Arthur F. "Fu I and the Rejection of Buddhism," *Journal of the History of Ideas*, XII (1951), 33-47. On an early T'ang warning about the danger of Buddhism to the Confucian state system, with comments on the ideological situation of the 7th century.

297

Pelliot, Paul. "Deux itineraires de Chine en Inde à la fin du VIIIe siècle," *Bulletin de l'École Francaise d'Extrème-Orient*, IV (1904), 131-413. Voluminous data on Chinese references to South and Southeast Asia, especially concerning contacts in T'ang times.

298

Pulleyblank, Edwin G. "Neo-Confucianism and Neo-Legalism in T'ang Intellectual Life, 755-805," in *The Confucian Persuasion* (A. F. Wright, ed.; Stanford: Stanford University Press, 1960), pp. 77-114. On conflicting reform programs of moralists and rationalists in a highly creative period of China's intellectual history, after the An Lu-shan rebellion.

299

Twitchett, Denis C. "The Salt Commissioners after An Lu-shan's Rebellion," *Asia Major*, IV (1954-55), 60-89. A technical study of the history, personnel, and techniques of a government salt monopoly that was relied upon to shore up the T'ang dynasty's sagging economic strength in its final century.

300

Twitchett, Denis C. "The Fragment of the T'ang Ordinances of the Department of Waterways Discovered at Tun-huang," *Asia Major*, VI (1957-58), 23-79. A valuable, technical study of codified administrative law in T'ang times.

301

Drake, F. S. "Mohammedanism in the T'ang Dynasty," *Monumenta Serica*, VIII (1943), 1-40. On the earliest Chinese contacts with Moslems and on Moslem settlement in China.

302

Gernet, Jacques. "La vente en Chine d'après les contrats de Touen-houang (ixe-xe siècles)", *T'oung Pao*, XLV (1957), 295-391. A detailed, technical study of some T'ang and Sung sale contracts discovered at Tun-huang, of great value for general social history of the period.

303

Grousset, René. *L'empire des steppes*. Paris: Payot, 1948. Pp. 124-180 on the various Turkic peoples who dominated China's northern and western frontiers in T'ang times.

304

Barthold, V. V. *Turkestan down to the Mongol Invasion*, trans. H. A. R. Gibb. 2d ed. rev. London: Luzac, 1958. Chap. 2 on the Moslem expansion into Central Asia in T'ang and Sung times.

305

Reischauer, Edwin O. "Notes on T'ang Dynasty Sea Routes," *Harvard Journal of Asiatic Studies*, V (1940-41), 142-164. On the concentration of overseas shipping in ports of the central and southeastern coasts; with some reference to navigational progress among the Chinese, Koreans, and Japanese.

306

Sansom, George. *A History of Japan to 1334*. Stanford: Stanford University Press, 1958. A standard reference for China's cultural influence on Japan, which was most intense during the T'ang era; cf. Sansom's *Japan: A Short Cultural History* (rev. ed.; New York: Appleton-Century-Crofts, 1943).

307

Solomon, Bernard S. (trans.) *The Veritable Record of the T'ang Emperor Shun-tsung (February 28, 805 —*

August 31, 805): Han Yü's Shun-tsung shih-lu. Cambridge: Harvard University Press, 1955. A technical, annotated translation of the only extant T'ang reign-history.

308

Giles, Lionel. *Descriptive Catalogue of the Chinese Manuscripts from Tunhuang in the British Museum*. London: British Museum, 1957. A complete, technical analysis of about 8,000 texts and text fragments collected by Sir Aurel Stein; an indispensable tool for research on T'ang and 5 Dynasties (especially Buddhist) society and literature.

309

Frankel, Hans H. *Catalogue of Translations from the Chinese Dynastic Histories for the Period 220-960*. Berkeley: University of California Press, 1957. An indispensable reference aid.

310

Mahler, Jane Gaston. *The Westerners Among the Figurines of the T'ang Dynasty in China*. Rome: Instituto Italiano per il Medio ed Estremo Oriente, 1959. An illustrated study of non-mongoloids represented in T'ang ceramics; pp. 9-105 chiefly an account of T'ang China's knowledge of, contact with, and material influences from Central and Southwest Asia.

311

Chang T'ien-tse. *Sino-Portuguese Trade from 1514 to 1644*. Leiden: E. J. Brill, 1934. Pp. 1-16 give a general survey of China's overseas trade up through T'ang times, with special reference to Arab relations with T'ang China.

312

Hourani, George Fadlo. *Arab Seafaring in the Indian Ocean in Ancient and Early Medieval Times*. Princeton: Princeton University Press, 1951. Pp. 61-79 on the routes, difficulties, and volume of Persian and Arab sea trade with China in T'ang times.

313

Riasanovsky, V. A. "Mongol Law and Chinese Law in the Yuan Dynasty," *Chinese Social and Political Science Review*, XX (1936-37), 266-289. Includes a rather detailed description of the T'ang dynasty law code.

Some T'ang personalities

314

Fitzgerald, Charles P. *Son of Heaven*. Cambridge: Cambridge University Press, 1933. An admiring biography of Li Shih-min, the real founder and second emperor of the T'ang dynasty, with special emphasis on his military exploits in civil and foreign wars.

315

Bingham, Woodbridge. "Li Shih-min's Coup in A.D. 626," *Journal of the American Oriental Society*, LXX (1950), 89-95, 259-271. An analysis of how Li Shih-min secured his succession to the T'ang throne at the expense of his brothers.

*   *   *

316

Fitzgerald, Charles P. *The Empress Wu*. Melbourne: Australian National University, 1955. A biography of the only woman who ever reigned over China, concentrating on her personal life and the palace intrigues that brought her to the throne in 684 and kept her in power for the next 20 years.

317

Lin Yutang. *Lady Wu: a True Story*. London: Heinemann, 1957. A harshly condemnatory biography of the Empress Wu; somewhat fictionalized, but factually reliable.

318

Toan, Nghiem and Louis Ricaud (trans.). *Wou Tsö-t'ien*. Saigon: Société des Études Indochinoises, 1959. An authoritative translation of the *Hsin T'ang-shu* biography of the Empress Wu, with reproduction of the Chinese text and detailed annotations.

*   *   *

319

Levy, Howard S. (trans.) *Biography of An Lu-shan.* Berkeley: University of California Press, 1961. Technical, annotated translation of the *Hsin T'ang Shu* account, the basic reference for the great 8th century rebellion.

320

Levy, Howard S. *Harem Favorites of an Illustrious Celestial.* Taipei: Chung-t'ai Printing Company, 1958. Translations of biographies of four consorts of the emperor Hsüan-tsung, against whom An Lu-shan rebelled in the 750's; presents detailed introductory material about the reign of Hsüan-tsung and the nature of T'ang palace revolutions; specially emphasizes the most notorious beauty of Chinese history, Yang Kuei-fei; incorporates data from separate articles by the same author in *T'oung Pao,* XLV (1957), 451-89; XLVI (1958), 49-80; and *Sinologica,* V (1957), 101-118.

321

Wu Shu-chiung. *Yang Kuei-fei, the Most Famous Beauty of China.* London: Brentano, 1924. An unscholarly and somewhat fictionalized biography of an 8th century imperial concubine who is traditionally blamed for demoralizing the T'ang court and paving the way for the rebellion of An Lu-shan.

* * *

322

Levy, Howard S. (trans.) *Biography of Huang Ch'ao.* Berkeley: University of California Press, 1955. An annotated translation of an early biography of a 9th century rebel.

323

Hung, William. *Tu Fu, China's Greatest Poet.* 2 vols. Cambridge: Harvard University Press, 1952. A detailed biography of an 8th century poet-bureaucrat whom the Chinese have considered their greatest poetic genius, with much data on political and social conditions in his time.

324

Waley, Arthur. *The Poetry and Career of Li Po.* New York: Macmillan, 1951. A brief biography of an 8th century eccentric who is ranked as one of China's greatest poets.

325

Waley, Arthur. *The Life and Times of Po Chü-i.* New York: Macmillan, 1949. On a 9th century poet and social critic. Cf. Eugene Feifel's annotated translation of the *Chiu T'ang-shu* biography in *Monumenta Serica,* XVII (1958), 255-311.

326

Pulleyblank, Edwin G. "Liu K'o, a Forgotten Rival of Han Yü," *Asia Major,* VII (1959), 145-160. On a minor litterateur and official of the 9th century; chiefly of value for intellectual history.

327

Frankel, Hans H. (trans.) *Biographies of Meng Hao-jan.* Berkeley: University of California Press, 1952. On a famous T'ang poet (691−740); annotated translations of four early accounts.

The Five Dynasties and the Ten Kingdoms

328

Eberhard, Wolfram. *Conquerors and Rulers: Social Forces in Medieval China.* Leiden: E. J. Brill, 1952. Includes analyses of how a bandit leader established the Later Liang dynasty, how a Turkic conquest group (the Sha-t'o) established the Later T'ang dynasty, and how China's ruling classes in general were transformed during the 5 Dynasties era.

329

Schafer, Edward H. *The Empire of Min.* Rutland, Vt.: Charles E. Tuttle Company, 1954. The geography, governmental organization, political history, economy, arts, and religion of one of the more important southern kingdoms.

330

Hamilton, James Russell. *Les Ouighours a l'époque des Cinq Dynasties, d'après les documents chinois.* Paris: Imprimerie Nationale, 1955. (Bibliothèque de l'Institut des Hautes Études Chinoises, X). A study of Uighur Turk dominance of Northwest China during the 5 Dynasties period, including annotated translations of Chinese historical accounts and other documents; technical, but with a useful general recapitulation on pp. 127-138.

331

Chavannes, Édouard. "Le royaume de Wou et de Yue," *T'oung Pao,* XVII (1916), 129-264. Detailed study of the Yangtze delta kingdom, Wu-Yüeh.

332

Schafer, Edward H. (trans.) "The History of the Empire of Southern Han," in *Silver Jubilee Volume of the Zinbun - Kagaku - Kenkyusyo,* Kyoto University (Kyoto: 1954), pp. 339-369. Annotated translation of Ou-yang Hsiu's account in the *Wu-tai shih;* technical.

Sung: General

333

Kracke, Edward A., Jr. *Civil Service in Early Sung China, 960-1067.* Cambridge: Harvard University Press, 1953. An authoritative study of the Sung dynasty's elaborate techniques of personnel administration, with special reference to a system of "controlled sponsorship" or "guaranteed recommendations" for selecting men for high office; includes a general description of Sung governmental organization and policies.

334

Sun, E-tu Zen and John de Francis (trans.). *Chinese Social History.* Washington: American Council of Learned Societies, 1956. Includes 3 articles on socioeconomic aspects of Sung life: "Social Relief during the Sung Dynasty," by Hsü I-t'ang; and "Periodic Fairs in South China in the Sung Dynasty" and "Production and Distribution of Rice in Southern Sung," by Ch'üan Han-sheng.

335

Carter, Thomas F. *The Invention of Printing in China and its Spread Westward.* Rev. by L. C. Goodrich. New York: Columbia University Press, 1955. A standard reference on the development of woodblock printing during T'ang, Five Dynasties, and especially Sung times.

336

Kracke, Edward A., Jr. "Sung Society: Change Within Tradition," *Far Eastern Quarterly,* XIV (1954-55), 479-488. An important refutation of the common belief that traditional Chinese social organization did not permit significant change from within; based on the social changes that accompanied urbanization in Sung times.

337

Lo Jung-pang. "The Emergence of China as a Sea Power during the Late Sung and Early Yüan Periods," *Far Eastern Quarterly,* XIV (1954-55), 489-503. A study of intense sea-oriented interests and activities that developed in 13th-century China in response to social and environmental changes on the mainland.

338

Kato Shigeshi. "On the Hang or the Associations of Merchants in China," *Memoirs of the Research Department of The Toyo Bunko,* VIII (1936), 45-83. A general history of mercantile guilds, with special reference to the development in T'ang and especially Sung times; a valuable source on medieval mercantile practices in general.

339

Gernet, Jacques. *La vie quotidienne en Chine à la veille de l'invasion Mongole (1250−1276).* Paris: Hachette, 1959. A panoramic description of the Chinese, their customs, their institutions, their beliefs, and their material environment in the last Sung decades, with special reference to the magnificent capital city, Hangchow.

340

Goodrich, L. C. and Feng Chia-sheng. "The Early Development of Firearms in China," *Isis*, XXXVI (1945–46), 114-123, 250-251. On the use of gunpowder for firearms by the Sung Chinese against Mongol invaders in the 13th century.

341

Wang Ling. "On the Invention and Use of Gunpowder and Firearms in China," *Isis*, XXXVII (1947), 160-178. Data on Sung military technology, supplementary to "The Early Development of Firearms in China" by Goodrich and Feng.

342

Kuwabara Jitsuzo. "On P'u Shou-keng," *Memoirs of the Research Department of The Toyo Bunko*, II (1928), 1-79; VII (1935), 1-104. A compendium of miscellany on Arab trade with China in T'ang and especially Sung times, focused on a family of Arab origin that gained official control of foreign trade at Canton and, later, at Ch'üan-chou in Fukien.

343

Minorsky, V. (trans.) *Sharaf Al-Zaman Tahir Marvazi on China, the Turks and India*. London: Luzac, 1942. An early 12th century Arabic description of life and trading conditions in China (pp. 13-29); cf. some technical notes by Chou Yi-liang in *Harvard Journal of Asiatic Studies*, IX (1945–47), 13-23.

344

Hirth, Friedrich and W. W. Rockhill (trans.). *Chau Ju-kua*. St. Petersburg: Imperial Academy of Sciences, 1911. An annotated translation of *Chu-fan-chih* ("Treatise on the Barbarians"), an early 13th century Chinese description of overseas countries and of the various spices and other produce that China obtained from abroad; with an introduction on the historical development of East-West sea trade and its status in Sung times.

345

Enoki, K. "Some Remarks on the Country of Ta-ch'in as Known to the Chinese under the Sung," *Asia Major*, IV (1954), 1-19. On 12th century Chinese geographic knowledge of the Near East, identifying "Ta-ch'in" as the Abassid Caliphate at Bagdad; with translations of some Chinese accounts.

346

Wada Sei. "The Philippine Islands as Known to the Chinese Before the Ming Period," *Memoirs of the Research Department of The Toyo Bunko*, IV (1929), 121-166. A survey of Chinese references to the Philippine and nearby islands in the Sung and Yüan periods.

Bureaucratic factionalism in Sung times

347

Williamson, H. R. *Wang An-shih, Chinese Statesman and Educationalist of the Sung Dynasty*. 2 vols. London: Arthur Probsthain, 1935–37. The most comprehensive description of Wang An-shih's controversial reform program of the 1080's; vol. 2 offers special essays on Wang's time, his literary influence, and his forerunners in the realm of fiscal reform, as well as translations of many of his literary essays.

348

Liu, James T. C. *Reform in Sung China: Wang An-shih (1021–1086) and his New Policies*. Cambridge: Harvard University Press, 1959. (Harvard East Asian Studies, 3). A brief and generally sympathetic reappraisal, from a modern behavioral science approach, of one of traditional China's most controversial political reformers; especially valuable for its interpretive analyses of political thought and bureaucratic behavior in Wang's time.

349

Lin Yutang. *The Gay Genius: The Life and Time of Su Tung-po*. New York: John Day, 1947. A detailed biography of a great 11th century litterateur-statesman, who was one of the leading antagonists of the reformer Wang An-shih; strongly biassed against Wang, but gives a reliable, colorful panorama of life among the Sung élite.

350

Liu, James T. C. "An Early Sung Reformer: Fan Chung-yen," in *Chinese Thought and Institutions* (J. K. Fairbank, ed.; Chicago: University of Chicago Press, 1957), pp. 104-131. An analysis of a struggle between "idealistic" and "career-minded" bureaucrats over administrative reforms in the 1040's that was a prelude to the great Wang An-shih controversy of the next generation.

351

Buriks, Peter. "Fan Chung-yen's Versuch einer Reform des chinesischen Beamtenstaates in den Jahren 1043-44," *Oriens Extremus*, III (1956), 57-90, 153-184. The most detailed modern analysis of abortive political reforms of the 1040's.

352

Rogers, Michael C. "Factionalism and Koryo Policy under the Northern Sung," *Journal of the American Oriental Society*, LIX (1959), 16-23. On suggestions in the 1040's that Sung ally with Korea against the Ch'i-tan "barbarians," with relevance to the factional struggle of Fan Chung-yen's time. Cf. Rogers' subsequent article, "Sung-Koryo Relations: Some Inhibiting Factors," *Oriens*, XI (1958), 194-202, for the continuation of the controversy about relations with Korea in the 1070's, with reference to the program of Wang An-shih.

353

Fischer, J. "Fan Chung-yen (989–1052): Das Lebensbild eines chinesischen Staatsmannes," *Oriens Extremus*, II (1955), 74-85. On a political reformer of the 1040's; especially valuable for its account of the Sung war with the western, Tangutan state of Hsi Hsia.

354

Lin Yutang. *A History of the Press and Public Opinion in China*. Chicago: University of Chicago Press, 1936. Chap. 6, "Student Petitions in Sung," is a collection of historical episodes dealing with public criticism of corrupt or unpopular officials.

THE AGE OF
RENEWED INVASIONS

Liao, 907–1125

Chin, 1125–1234

Yüan, 1260–1368

Throughout the T'ang period (618–907), the northern frontier of China had been threatened successively by T'u-chüeh (Turk), Uighur, and Kirchiz nomads, all of the Turkic language family. Then, in the last T'ang years, a proto-Mongol people called Ch'i-tan (Khitan) founded a new nomad empire in Mongolia and encroached upon the northern part of the North China plain, occupying the region of modern Peking. During the Five Dynasties period (907–960) their Liao state cowed the North China governments, and even the Sung emperors, after vainly trying to expel the Ch'i-tan from China Proper, resignedly paid them annual tribute. At last the Liao state, which had never significantly adopted Chinese ways, was overthrown from the rear in 1125, whereupon a group of Ch'i-tan refugees migrated westward and established a short-lived Central Asian empire called Kara Khitai (whence the name Cathay). Liao power in Mongolia was destroyed by a more sedentary people, the Tungusic - speaking and proto - Manchu Jurchen, emerging from the woodlands of modern Manchuria. Though at first allied with Sung to the south, the Jurchen after crushing Liao immediately turned against Sung, conquered the whole Yellow River valley, and even campaigned south of the Yangtze River before an uneasy peace was arranged, with a frontier cutting across Central China between the two great river valleys. Concurrently, while the Jurchen state, called Chin (Kin), dominated the North China plain, a Tibetan-speaking people known as Tangutans dominated northwestern China with their Hsi Hsia state (Tangutia). Both the Jurchen and the Tangutans adopted many Chinese ways, and they eventually found themselves vainly defending the North China frontier against a new threat from the rear, the Mongols of Chingis Khan. Perhaps the most warlike people of Asian history, the Mongols between 1206 and 1279 created a vast Eurasian empire that stretched from the Pacific to the Mediterranean. In the process Chin, Hsi Hsia, Kara Khitai, and finally Sung were crushed. For the Chinese corner of the empire Kubilai Khan in 1260 founded a Chinese-style Yüan dynasty. Under Mongol rule the Chinese suffered from social discrimination, economic exploitation, and in general the most ruthless tyranny of their history. But the Pax Mongolica that overspread Eurasia served to introduce new influences from the West: cotton cultivation, Roman Catholic missions, and numerous foreign adventurers and technicians, of whom the Venetian merchant Marco Polo was representative. The Mongols did not rule China prudently, and their vigor rapidly waned. Chinese rebels seriously challenged them in the 1340's and 1350's, and in 1368 a great rebel coordinator drove them out of China Proper and set about reestablishing the disrupted native tradition.

Recommended general histories: Reischauer and Fairbank, chap. 7; Grousset, chaps. 25-27; Goodrich, chap. 6.

The Khitan and Jurchen

355

Wittfogel, Karl A. and Feng Chia-sheng. *History of Chinese Society: Liao (907–1125).* Philadelphia: American Philosophical Society, 1949. (Transactions of the American Philosophical Society, new series, XXXVI). A monumental compendium on the Khitan people and their Liao dynasty, in a topical analysis, fully documented; the basic source on this aspect of Chinese history and not likely to be superseded. Contains a special appendix on the Central Asian branch of the Khitan empire, called Kara Khitai.

356

Chavannes, Édouard. "Voyageurs chinois chez les Khitan et les Joutchen," *Journal Asiatique,* 9th series, IX (1897), 377-429; XI (1898), 361-439. A detailed, authoritative study of 12th century Chinese relations with the Khitan and Jurchen peoples.

357

Barthold, V. V. *Turkestan down to the Mongol Invasion,* trans. by H. A. R. Gibb. 2d ed. rev. London: Luzac, 1958. Pp. 323-380 on the Khitan empire in Central Asia (Kara Khitai); authoritative, with emphasis on political history.

358

Barthold, V. V. *Four Studies on the History of Central Asia,* trans. by V. and T. Minorsky. 2 vols. of a projected 3. Leiden: E. J. Brill, 1956–58. Vol. 1, pp. 26-30 and 100-110 on the late Khitan empire in Turkestan called Kara Khitai.

359

Tamura Jitsuzo. "The Civilization of the Liao Empire," in *Akten des vierundzwansigsten Internationalen Orientalisten-Kongresses München, 1957* (Herbert Franke, ed.; Wiesbaden: Franz Steiner, 1959).

360

Kates, G. N. "A New Date for the Origins of the Forbidden City," *Harvard Journal of Asiatic Studies,* VII 1942–43), 180-202. On the origin and history of the imperial palace at Peking in Jurchen times.

361

Harlez, C. de (trans.). *L'histoire de l'empire du Kin.* Louvain: Charles Peeters, 1887. The only substantial contribution in a Western language to the history of the Jurchen Chin dynasty; translated from the chronicle *Aisin-Gurun-I-Suduri Bithe,* in Manchu.

The Mongols in general

362

Miller, Robert J. "A Selective Survey of Literature on Mongolia," *American Political Science Review,* XLVI (1952), 849-866. A useful introductory review of authoritative materials on the history and modern circumstances of the various Mongol peoples.

363

Prawdin, Michael (pseud. of Michael Charol). *The Mongol Empire: Its Rise and Legacy,* trans. by Eden and Cedar Paul. London: Allen and Unwin, 1940. Probably the most readable general account of Mongol history, though not based on original scholarship and weak in its treatment of the Mongols in China.

364

Martin, Henry Desmond. *The Rise of Chingis Khan and his Conquest of North China.* Baltimore: Johns Hopkins Press, 1950. An authoritative analysis of Chingis Khan's consolidation of power in Mongolia and his campaigns against Hsi Hsia and the Chin empire; especially valuable for its data on Mongol military organization and techniques.

365

Howorth, Henry H. *History of the Mongols, from the 9th to the 19th Century.* 4 parts in 5 vols. London: Longmans Green, 1876–1927. The most comprehensive chronicle of Mongol history throughout Eurasia now available; a standard reference.

366

Vladimirtsov, Boris I. *The Life of Chingis-Khan,* trans. by Prince D. S. Mirsky. London: Routledge, 1930. Readable and authoritative; based on original sources but without documentation.

367

Grousset, René. *L'empire des steppes.* Paris: Payot, 1948. Pp. 243-486 offer an authoritative general history of the Mongols from their origins to the last decades of the 14th century.

368

Boyle, John Andrew (trans.) *The History of the World Conqueror by 'Ala-ud-Din 'Ata-Malik Juvaaini.* 2 vols. Cambridge: Harvard University Press, 1958. Fully annotated translation of a Persian biography of Chingis

Khan by Juvaini (1226–83), a Mongol-appointed governor of Bagdad and a visitor at the Mongol capital, Karakorum; emphasizes Mongol conquests in southwest Asia but attempts to deal with the Mongol empire as a whole; a basic source on early Mongol history.

369

Lamb, Harold. *Genghis Khan, the Emperor of All Men.* New York: Robert McBride, 1927; paperbound reprint, New York: Bantam Books, 1960. A popular and somewhat romanticized biography of Chingis Khan, with addenda about other aspects of Mongol history.

370

Vladimirtsov, B. *La régime social des Mongols: le féodalisme nomade,* trans. by Michel Carsow. Paris: Adrien-Maisonneuve, 1948. On the organization and evolution of Mongol society from the 11th century to the 17th, with a brief epilogue about modern times; comprehensive and authoritative.

371

Pelliot, Paul. *Histoire secrète des Mongols: restitution du texte Mongol et traduction francaise des chapitres I à VI.* Paris: Adrien-Maisonneuve, 1949. (Oeuvres posthumes de Paul Pelliot, I). The most authoritative, but incomplete, presentation of a basic source on Chingis Khan: *Yüan-ch'ao pi-shih,* a 13th century chronicle known only in a Chinese version of the 14th century.

372

Haenisch, Erich (trans.). *Die geheime Geschichte der Mongolen.* Leipzig: Otto Harrassowitz, 1948. A complete translation of *Yüan-ch'ao pi-shih,* with brief annotations.

373

Pelliot, Paul and Louis Hambis (trans.). *Histoire des campagnes de Gengis Khan: Cheng-wou ts'in-tcheng lou.* Tome 1. Leiden: E. J. Brill, 1951. Profusely annotated, incomplete translation of an early Chinese chronicle of the conquests of Chingis and his son Ogodai *(Sheng-wu Ch'in-cheng lu),* itself a transcription from a Mongol original.

374

Schurmann, H. F. "Mongolian Tributary Practices of the Thirteenth Century," *Harvard Journal of Asiatic Studies,* XIX (1956), 304-389. A detailed, technical study of fiscal obligations imposed by the Mongols on all subjugated peoples, from China to Persia and Russia.

375

Grousset, René. *L'empire Mongol (1re phase).* Paris: E. de Boccard, 1941. An authoritative general history of the Mongols from their origins into the 14th century.

376

Vernadsky, George and Michael Karpovich. *A History of Russia.* Vol. 3: *The Mongols and Russia,* by George Vernadsky. New Haven: Yale University Press, 1953. A standard reference on the early Mongol conquests in Russian Turkestan and on the history and culture of Russia under domination of the "Golden Horde."

377

Pelliot, Paul. *Notes sur l'histoire de la horde d'or.* Paris: Adrien-Maisonneuve, 1949. (Oeuvres posthumes de Paul Pelliot, II). A collection of highly technical notes, indispensable for serious study of the Mongols in Russia.

378

Iwamura Shinobu. "Mongol Invasion of Poland in the Thirteenth Century," *Memoirs of the Research Department of The Toyo Bunko,* X (1938), 103-157. On the Mongol assaults of 1241 and 1259; with translations and reproductions of relevant Polish texts in Latin.

379

Barthold, V. V. *Turkestan down to the Mongol Invasion,* trans. by H. A. R. Gibb. 2d ed. rev. London: Luzac, 1958. Pp. 381-462: a detailed, authoritative history of Mongol conquests in Central Asia.

380

Barthold, V. V. *Four Studies on the History of Central Asia,* trans. by V. and T. Minorsky. 2 vols. of a pro-

jected 3. Leiden: E. J. Brill, 1956-58. Vol. 1, pp. 32-53 and 110-137 on early Mongol conquests in Russian Turkestan; vol. 2 on the later Mongol empire in Turkestan, with special reference to Ulugh-Beg, a grandson of Tamerlane.

381

D'Ohsson, C. *Histoire des Mongols, depuis Tchinguiz-khan jusqu'à Timour Bey ou Tamerlan.* 4 vols. Amsterdam: Les Frères Van Cleef, 1834-35. A panoramic study of the history of the Mongols from their beginnings into the 14th century, based on Chinese and Near Eastern sources; cannot be relied on in detail, but not wholly superseded.

382

Blake, Robert P. and Richard N. Frye. "History of the Nation of the Archers (The Mongols)," *Harvard Journal of Asiatic Studies,* XII (1949), 269-399. Reproduction and annotated translation of a 13th century Armenian history of early Mongol conquests in southwest Asia, by Grigor of Akanc.

383

Gibb, H. A. R. (trans.) *Ibn Battuta: Travels in Asia and Africa, 1325-54.* London: Routledge, 1929. Selected observations of a famous Islamic traveler, whose work is a basic source on Mongol history in Western Asia.

384

Tucci, Giuseppe. *Tibetan Painted Scrolls.* 2 vols. Rome: La Libreria dello Stato, 1949. Vol. 1 includes detailed, authoritative data on Tibetan-Mongol-Chinese relations during the Yüan period.

385

Vernadsky, George. "The Scope and Contents of Chingis Khan's *Yasa,*" *Harvard Journal of Asiatic Studies,* III (1938), 337-360. On the basic law code of the Mongols, interpreted as an imperial system of law created to facilitate Chingis Khan's planned world conquest.

386

Bretschneider, E. *Mediaeval Researches from Eastern Asiatic Sources.* 2 vols. London: Kegan Paul, 1910. A miscellany of annotated translations from Chinese sources, mostly about the Mongols and their relations with Central Asia; not wholly superseded.

387

Krader, Lawrence. "Feudalism and the Tatar Polity of the Middle Ages," *Comparative Studies in Society and History,* I (1958-59), 76-99. On the social and political institutions of the Mongols, with a good review of modern interpretations.

388

Bouvat, Lucien. *L'empire Mongol (2ème phase).* Paris: E. de Boccard, 1927. On the successors of the early Mongol empire in Russian Turkestan and India: Tamerlane and the Moghuls.

389

Hung, William. "The Transmission of the Book Known as *The Secret History of the Mongols,*" *Harvard Journal of Asiatic Studies,* XIV (1951), 433-492. On the textual history of *Yüan-ch'ao pi-shih;* technical.

390

Clauson, Gerard. "The hP'ags-pa Alphabet," *Bulletin of the School of Oriental and African Studies,* London University, XXII (1959), 300-323. On a phonetic writing system devised by a Lamaist monk for the Mongols to use as a universal script.

391

Poppe, Nicholas and John R. Krueger. *The Mongolian Monuments in hP'ags-pa Script.* Wiesbaden: Otto Harrassowitz, 1957. Includes a general discussion of the universal writing system tentatively adopted by the Mongols.

General East-West relations in Mongol times

392

Hudson, Geoffrey F. *Europe and China: A Survey of Their Relations from the Earliest Times to 1800.* London:

Edward Arnold, 1931; paperbound reprint, Boston: Beacon Press, 1961. Chap. 6 excellently summarizes East-West relations during the period of Mongol supremacy in China.

393

Komroff, Manuel (ed.). *Contemporaries of Marco Polo.* New York: Liveright, 1928. Includes the travel accounts of Pope Innocent IV's envoy to Kuyuk Khan at Karakorum in 1245–47, John of Pian de Carpine; of King Louis IX's envoy to Mangu Khan at Karakorum in 1253–55, William of Rubruck; and of a Franciscan missionary in Yüan China in the 1320's, Odoric of Pordenone. Derived principally from the translations of W. W. Rockhill and Henry Yule, and without annotations.

394

Dawson, Christopher (ed.). *The Mongol Mission.* New York: Sheed and Ward, 1955. New translations, mostly by "a nun of Stanbrook Abbey," of travel accounts and letters about the Mongols and China by John of Plano Carpini (1245–47) and his companion Brother Benedict the Pole, by William of Rubruck (1253–55), by John of Monte Corvino and Andrew of Perugia (both early 14th century), etc. — all basic sources on the Mongol epoch. Not fully annotated.

395

Olschki, Leonardo. *Marco Polo's Precursors.* Baltimore: Johns Hopkins Press, 1943. A general, compact survey of medieval Europe's knowledge of Asia, of the European background of 13th century exploration eastward, and of missionary and mercantile missions to the Mongols prior to Marco Polo.

396

Budge, E. A. Wallis (trans.). *The Monks of Kublai Khan, Emperor of China.* London: The Religious Tract Society, 1928. On two 13th century Chinese of the Nestorian faith who set out as pilgrims to the Holy Land and prospered, one becoming Mar Yaballaha III, patriarch of the whole Nestorian church, and the other (Bar Sauma) a distinguished church envoy to Rome and Paris. A full translation of a Syriac account, with detailed prolegomena about Nestorianism and its history in China.

397

Montgomery, James A. (trans.). *The History of Yaballaha III.* New York: Columbia University Press, 1927. Partial translation of a Syriac account of Mar Yaballaha III and Bar Sauma; better annotated than Budge's translation.

398

Moule, Arthur C. *Christians in China before the Year 1550.* London: Society for Promoting Christian Knowledge, 1930. An authoritative survey of Christian missions and activities, especially of the Mongol era, with extracts from Marco Polo and other Chinese and European sources; chap. 4 on the Nestorian patriarch Mar Yaballaha III.

399

Olschki, Leonardo. *Guillaume Boucher, a French Artist at the Court of the Khans.* Baltimore: Johns Hopkins Press, 1946. On a Parisian artist-engineer, captured at Belgrade in 1242, who was in the service of the Mongols at Karakorum into the 1250's; with useful data about the sophisticated cultural life of the Mongol court.

400

Yule, Henry (ed.). *Cathay and the Way Thither, being a Collection of Medieval Notices of China.* New ed. rev. by Henri Cordier. 4 vols. London: The Hakluyt Society, 1913–16. Includes travel accounts and letters about the Mongols and China by Odoric of Pordenone (the 1320's), John of Montecorvino (early 14th century), Andrew Bishop of Zayton (early 14th century), John of Marignolli (the 1340's), and Ibn Batuta (the 1340's); and extracts from Rashid ed-Din's "History of the Mongols" (ca. 1300).

401

Pelliot, Paul. *Les Mongols et la papauté.* 3 parts. Paris: A. Picard, 1923–31. Includes translations of documents regarding Mongol-Rome relations in the 13th and early 14th centuries, among them some letters of Mar Yaballaha III; originally published as a series of articles in *Revue de L'Orient Chrétien,* 1922–31.

402

Rockhill, William W. (trans.) *The Journey of William of Rubruck to the Eastern Parts of the World, 1253–55.* London: The Hakluyt Society, 1900. Friar William's own detailed account of his mission to Mangu Khan's court at Karakorum for King Louis IX of France, a basic source on early Mongol history and customs; with two short notices of the mission of Friar John of Pian de Carpine to Kuyuk Khan on behalf of Pope Innocent IV in 1245–47. Still the most authoritative translations.

Marco Polo

403

Collis, Maurice. *Marco Polo.* New York: New Directions, 1960. A popular retelling of Marco Polo's travels and observations, based principally on the translation by Moule and Pelliot and the notes of Sir Henry Yule.

404

Hart, Henry H. *Venetian Adventurer: Being an Account of the Life and Times and of the Book of Messer Marco Polo.* Stanford: Stanford University Press, 1942; paperbound reprint, New York: Bantam Books, 1956. A reliable biography for the general reader, especially attempting to analyze Polo's personality; with useful data on the European background.

405

Moule, Arthur C. and Paul Pelliot (trans.). *Marco Polo: The Description of the World.* 2 vols. of a projected 3. London: Routledge, 1938. The most authoritative English translation, a composite from various editions of the original work. Vol. 2 reproduces a Latin text discovered at Toledo in 1932. A planned 3d vol. will be devoted to notes and addenda, chiefly by Pelliot.

406

Yule, Henry (ed.). *The Book of Ser Marco Polo.* 3d ed. rev. by Henri Cordier. 2 vols. Reprinted London: John Murray and New York: Scribner, 1929. The most thoroughly annotated version of Polo's travel account now available; should be used in conjunction with Cordier's extra volume of notes and with the Moule-Pelliot translation.

407

Cordier, Henri. *Ser Marco Polo: Notes and Addenda.* London: John Murray, 1920. Miscellaneous data supplementary to the Yule edition.

408

Marsden, William (trans.). *The Travels of Marco Polo.* New York: Dell Laurel Books, 1961. A paperbound reissue of a classical English rendering, first published in 1818; with a brief introduction by F. W. Mote.

409

Latham, Ronald E. (trans.) *The Travels of Marco Polo.* London: Penguin Books, 1958. A popular, complete translation based on the annotated edition of L. F. Benedetto.

410

Olschki, Leonardo. *Marco Polo's Asia,* trans. by John A. Scott. Berkeley: University of California Press, 1961. A thorough and authoritative critique of Marco Polo's presentation of the Asia of his time.

411

Power, Eileen. *Medieval People.* Garden City, N. Y.: Doubleday Anchor Books, 1955. Pp. 37-72 on the life, travels, and influence on Marco Polo, in popular style.

China under the Mongols

412

Schurmann, Herbert F. (trans.) *Economic Structure of the Yüan Dynasty*. Cambridge: Harvard University Press, 1956. (Harvard-Yenching Institute Studies, XVI). Annotated translations of *Yüan-shih* treatises on economic and fiscal policies of the Mongol government in China, with useful introductions to all sections.

413

Franke, Herbert A. *Geld und Wirtschaft in China unter der Mongolen-herrschaft: Beitrage zur Wirtschaftsgeschichte der Yüan-zeit*. Leipzig: Otto Harrassowitz, 1949. A detailed analysis of the Yüan monetary system, especially emphasizing the Mongols' inflationary experiments with paper money; with many statistical tables.

414

Mote, Frederick W. "Confucian Eremitism in the Yüan Period," in *The Confucian Persuasion* (A. F. Wright, ed.; Stanford: Stanford University Press, 1960), pp. 202-240. On the reaction of some Confucian scholars to Mongol dominance, with special reference to the notable litterateur Liu Yin (1249–93).

415

Ratchnevsky, Paul. *Un code des Yuan*. Paris: Ernest Leroux, 1937. A fully annotated, technical translation of parts of the Yüan dynasty law code, from the *Yüan-shih;* an indispensable guide to Yüan governmental institutions.

416

Lo Jung-pang. "The Controversy over Grain Conveyance during the Reign of Qubilai Qaqan, 1260–94," *Far Eastern Quarterly*, XIII (1953–54), 263-285. On the extension of the Grand Canal to its final length (Hang-chou to Peking) and the development of both canal and coastal fleets to haul Yangtze valley grain to North China.

417

Serruys, Henry. "Remains of Mongol Customs during the Early Ming," *Monumenta Serica*, XVI (1957), 137-190. On the penetration of Mongol influences into Chinese culture, as reflected in governmental institutions, clothing, marriage customs, etc., of the early Ming period; with much relevance to Yüan China.

418

Cleaves, Francis W. (trans.) "The Biography of Bayan of the Barin in the *Yüan shih*," *Harvard Journal of Asiatic Studies*, XIX (1956), 185-303. On one of the greatest Mongol generals, Kubilai Khan's commander-in-chief in the assault on Southern Sung, 1274–76; highly technical, with full annotations.

419

Lo Jung-pang. "The Emergence of China as a Sea Power during the Late Sung and Early Yüan Periods," *Far Eastern Quarterly*, XIV (1954–55), 489-503. Notes the rapidity with which the Mongols developed sea power.

420

Cleaves, Francis W. (trans.) "The Sino-Mongolian Inscription of 1362 in Memory of Prince Hindu," *Harvard Journal of Asiatic Studies*, XII (1949), 1-133. The first of a series of highly technical annotated translations of Yüan dynasty documents of considerable historical value. Cf. other translations by Cleaves in subsequent volumes of *Harvard Journal of Asiatic Studies*.

421

Franke, Herbert. "Ahmed, ein beitrag zur Wirtschaftsgeschichte chinas unter Qubilai," *Oriens*, II (1949), 222-236. On a controversial Near Easterner who became Kubilai Khan's chief economic and fiscal adviser and was murdered in 1282.

422

Olbricht, Peter. *Das Postwesen in China unter der Mongolenherrschaft im 13. und 14. Jahrhundert*. Wiesbaden: Otto Harrassowitz, 1954. A technical study of the administration of postal relays and transport systems in Yüan China.

423

Franke, Herbert. "Could the Mongol Emperors Read and Write Chinese?" *Asia Major*, III (1952–53), 28-41. On the gradual acculturation of the Yüan rulers through education.

424

Sansom, George. *A History of Japan to 1334*. Stanford: Stanford University Press, 1958. Pp. 438-459 on Kubilai Khan's attempts to conquer Japan and their effects on Japanese history; cf. Sansom's *Japan: A Short Cultural History* (rev. ed.; New York: Appleton-Century-Crofts, 1943), pp. 309-326.

425

Tsunoda Ryusaku (trans.). *Japan in the Chinese Dynastic Histories: Later Han Through Ming Dynasties,* ed. by L. C. Goodrich. South Pasadena: P. D. and Ione Perkins, 1951. Pp. 73-105: an annotated translation of the account of Japan in the *Yüan-shih,* especially valuable as a record of Kubilai Khan's attempted conquest of Japan.

426

Tregonning, K. G. "Kublai Khan and South-east Asia," *History Today*, VII (1957), 163-170. A general survey of the background, the progress, and the consequences of Mongol military adventures in Burma, Indo-china, and Java in the late 13th century.

427

Groeneveldt, W. P. "The Expedition of the Mongols against Java in 1293 A.D.," *China Review*, IV (1875–76), 246-254. A standard reference, not yet superseded, on a lesser-known Mongol adventure overseas.

428

Franke, Herbert (trans.). *Beitrage zur Kulturgeschichtechinas unter der Mongolenherrschaft: Das Shan-kü sin-hua des Yang Yü*. Wiesbaden: Franz Steiner, 1956. Translations from *Shan-chü hsin-hua*, a 14th century scholar's notebook of miscellany *(pi-chi);* a valuable source for Yüan dynasty social and intellectual history.

429

Tullock, Gordon. "Paper Money – a Cycle in Cathay," *Economic History Review*, IX (1956–57), 393-407. A general survey of the history of paper money in China from T'ang to Ming times, with special reference to the Mongol period.

430

Chü Ch'ing-yüan. "Government Artisans of the Yüan Dynasty," in *Chinese Social History* (E-tu Zen Sun and John de Francis, ed.; Washington: American Council of Learned Societies, 1956), pp. 234-246. On the estimated 400,000 industrial laborers employed in government factories by the Mongol rulers.

431

Hucker, Charles O. "The Yüan Contribution to Censorial History," *Bulletin of the Institute of History and Philology, Academia Sinica*, extra vol. no. 4 (1960), 219-227. Suggests that the Mongol emperors played a creative role in making China's traditional government more authoritarian by strengthening and centralizing its surveillance apparatus.

432

Grousset, René. *L'empire des steppes*. Paris: Payot, 1948. Pp. 352-397 an authoritative survey of the history of the Mongols in China.

433

Goodrich, L. Carrington. "Westerners and Central Asians in Yuan China," in *Oriente Poliana* (Rome: Instituto Italiano per il Medio ed Estremo Oriente, 1957), pp. 1-21. On the adoption of Chinese, and especially Confucian, ways of life by non-Mongol foreigners in Yüan times.

434

Demiéville, Paul. "La situation religieuse en Chine au temps de Marco Polo," in *Oriente Poliana* (Rome: Instituto Italiano per il Medio ed Estremo Oriente, 1957), pp. 193-234. On struggles for influence among Buddhists, Taoists, and Lamaists under Kubilai Khan, with some reference to the status of Confucianism, Islam, and Christianity.

435

Moule, Arthur C. *Quinsai, with Other Notes on Marco Polo.* Cambridge: Cambridge University Press, 1957. Miscellaneous notes on the history, the layout, the sights, the customs, etc., of the great city Hang-chou (Quinsai), as explications of Marco Polo's references to it.

436

Chavannes, Édouard. "Inscriptions et pièces de chancellerie chinoises de l'époque Mongole," *T'oung Pao,* V (1904), 357-447; VI (1905), 1-42. Useful technical studies of Yüan documents, indispensable for the serious student.

437

Waley, Arthur (trans.). *The Travels of an Alchemist.* London: Routledge, 1931. Translation of a biography of the Chinese Taoist master Ch'ang-ch'un, whom Chingis Khan summoned to his camp in western Asia in 1222-23 for religious instruction, by his disciple Li Chih-ch'ang. Includes useful descriptions of the people and customs of Central Asia; with introductory comments by Waley about medieval Taoist thought and influence.

438

Balazs, Étienne. "Marco Polo dans la capitale de la Chine," in *Oriente Poliana* (Rome: Instituto Italiano per il Medio ed Estremo Oriente, 1957), pp. 133-154. On city life in China in Polo's time, with special reference to Hang-chou.

439

Riasanovsky, V. A. "Mongol Law and Chinese Law in the Yuan Dynasty," *Chinese Social and Political Science Review,* XX (1936-37), 266-289. An analysis of *Yüan tien-chang,* the Yüan dynasty law code, revealing its dominant reliance on the T'ang code and very minor influences from the customary law of the Mongols.

440

Hambis, Louis (trans.). *Le chapitre CVIII du Yuan Che: les fiefs attribués aux membres de la famille impériale et aux ministres de la cour Mongole d'apres l'histoire Chinoise officielle de la dynastie Mongole.* Tome I. Leiden: E. J. Brill, 1954.

441

Hambis, Louis (trans.). *Le chapitre CVII du Yuan Che: les genealogies impériales Mongoles dans l'histoire Chinoise officielle de la dynastie Mongole.* Leiden: E. J. Brill, 1945.

INDIAN SUMMER OF THE EMPIRE

Ming, 1368-1644

Ch'ing, 1644-1912

The century of Mongol dominance in China was ended by Chu Yüan-chang, a commoner who succeeded in consolidating divisive rebel forces into a nationalistic revolution and in 1368, proclaiming a new native dynasty called Ming, drove the disorganized and demoralized Mongols back into Mongolia. Chu and his successors, consciously trying to recapture the glories of T'ang times, created a stable, prosperous, and militarily strong China that once again dominated East Asia, freer from serious outside threats than at any time since the early T'ang

period. In the early 1400's tribute-seeking Chinese fleets roamed as far as Java, the coasts of India, the Persian gulf, and even the east coast of Africa. Korea became a loyal tributary, and Japan eagerly sought trading opportunities on the mainland. The long-unused Grand Canal was reopened, the Great Wall was rebuilt, city walls went up everywhere, and the beautiful modern city of Peking was planned and constructed. Neo-Confucian philosophy, though somewhat reinterpreted, became the unchallenged orthodoxy. Painting and poetry in traditional styles were practised assiduously. Scholarship flourished. The short story, the novel, and the drama became important literary genres. New ceramic styles appeared and became prized items of export trade. Portuguese, Dutch, and Spanish established mercantile factories on the south coast. Roman Catholic missionaries, inactive in China since the Mongol period, reappeared late in the 16th century under the leadership of Matteo Ricci and soon won a place of respect and influence. For two centuries Ming China thrived busily. Then in the early 1600's intense bureaucratic partisanship began to paralyze the government and the Tungusic-speaking Manchu "barbarians" of the far northeast began encroaching on the Manchurian provinces. In 1644 the central government dramatically collapsed, and Manchu leaders promptly took it over, establishing a Ch'ing dynasty over the Ming governmental machinery. Ming loyalists resisted in South China and Formosa until 1683, and for a time during the 1670's other anti-Manchu nationalists seriously challenged the new dynasty. But, on the whole, the transition from Ming to Ch'ing rule was remarkably smooth. Ming trends in cultural development persisted almost undisrupted. Under two particularly able and unusually long-lived Manchu emperors, K'ang-hsi (1661-1722) and Ch'ien-lung (1735-1796), China attained a level of power, prestige, and prosperity that was probably unparalleled in its history. The Manchus crushed newly resurgent Mongols, subjugated Tibet and Chinese Turkestan (Sinkiang), and defied and humiliated predatory Europeans. In peace and prosperity — and partly because of the introduction of such new crops from the West as maize, sweet potatoes, and peanuts — China's population surged from perhaps 100 million in 1600 to about 300 million in 1800. But the Manchus had become even more dedicated than the Chinese to preserving the traditional Chinese values and ways, and on the eve of the 19th century the national mood was one of rather ominous contentment and conservatism.

Recommended general histories: Reischauer and Fairbank, chaps. 8-9; Fitzgerald, parts 6-7; Grousset, pp. 258-302; Goodrich, chaps. 7-8; Eberhard, pp. 243-285.

Ming

442

Franke, Wolfgang. *Preliminary Notes on the Important Chinese Literary Sources for the History of the Ming Dynasty (1368–1644).* Chengtu: 1948. (Studia Serica Monographs, Series A, No. 2). An invaluable reference guide for the specialist; cf. addenda and corrigenda in *Studia Serica,* IX (1950), 33-41.

443

Franke, Wolfgang. "Der gegenwärtige Stand der Forschung zur Geschichte Chinas im 15. und 16. Jahrhundert," *Saeculum,* VII (1956), 413-441. A bibliographic essay on Chinese, Japanese, and Western writings about Ming China; with a valuable, detailed list arranged by topics.

* * *

444

Hucker, Charles O. *The Traditional Chinese State in Ming Times (1368–1644).* Tucson: University of Arizona Press, 1961. A general interpretive description of the organization, personnel, societal relations, functions, and ideology of the Ming state system.

445

Grimm, Tilemann. *Erziehung and Politik im konfuzianischen China der Ming-zeit (1364–1644).* Wiesbaden: Otto Harrassowitz, 1960. (Mitteilungen der Gesellschaft für Natur- und Völkerkunde Ostasiens, XXXV B). A detailed historical study of state schools, semi-official "private academies," and their utilization for civil service recruitment in Ming times, with statistical tables.

446

Friese, Heinz. *Das Dienstleistungs-System der Ming-zeit.* Wiesbaden: Otto Harrassowitz, 1959. (Mitteilungen der Gesellschaft für Natur- und Völkerkunde Ostasiens, XXXV A). An authoritative, technical analysis of the Ming dynasty's corvée system, with details of types of labor assignments, of classifications of citizens from whom labor was required, of organization and direction of the labor forces, of abuses and reforms in the system, etc.

447

Hucker, Charles O. "Governmental Organization of the Ming Dynasty," *Harvard Journal of Asiatic Studies,* XXI (1958), 1-66. A technical description of the agencies of the Ming government and their major functions.

448

Liang Fang-chung. *The Single-whip Method of Taxation in China,* trans. by Wang Yü-ch'üan. Cambridge: Harvard University Press, 1956. A general study of the Ming fiscal system, emphasizing a tax reform instituted in the 16th century.

449

Grimm, Tilemann. "Das Neiko der Ming-zeit, von den Anfängen bis 1506," *Oriens Extremus,* I (1954), 139-177. On the early history and organization of the Ming dynasty Grand Secretariat, with a sociological analysis of the grand secretaries who shaped it.

450

Hucker, Charles O. "The Traditional Chinese Censorate and the New Peking Regime," *American Political Science Review,* XLV (1951), 1041-1057. Includes a general description of the Ming government's censorial apparatus, with statistical analyses of its personnel and its activities during the 1420's.

451

Wild, Norman. "Materials for the Study of the Ssu I Kuan," *Bulletin of the School of Oriental and African Studies,* London University, XI (1943–46), 617-640. On the history and functions of the Ming government's College of Translators, which handled communications to and from tributary states; cf. Paul Pelliot, "Le Sseu-yi-Kouan et le Houei-t'ong-kouan," *T'oung Pao,* XXXVIII (1948), 207-290, for a technical study of the same subject.

452

Franke, Wolfgang. "Zur Grundsteuer in China während der Ming-Dynastie (1368-1644)," *Zeitschrift für vergleichende Rechtswissenschaft,* LVI (1953), 93-103. A general history of the land tax system throughout the Ming period.

453

Grimm, Tilemann. "War das China der Ming-Zeit totalitär," *Nachrichten der Gesellschaft für Natur- und Völkerkunde Ostasiens,* No. 79-80 (1956), 30-36. A brief but informative essay on state control of education in Ming times.

* * *

454

Feuerwerker, Albert. "From 'Feudalism' to 'Capitalism' in Recent Historical Writing from Mainland China," *Journal of Asian Studies,* XVIII (1958-59), 107-115. A critical discussion of communist studies suggesting that the Ming dynasty was a period of "incipient capitalism" and thus an important turning point in China's economic history.

455

Levenson, Joseph R. "The Amateur Ideal in Ming and Early Ch'ing Society: Evidence from Painting," in *Chinese Thought and Institutions* (J. K. Fairbank, ed.; Chicago: University of Chicago Press, 1957), pp. 320-341. An interpretation of the Ming intellectual "style" as being "antivocational, retrospective humanism in learning"; with special reference to the ideal of the gentleman-painter.

456

Sun, E-tu Zen and John de Francis (trans.). *Chinese Social History.* Washington: American Council of Learned Societies, 1956. Includes 5 articles on socioeconomic aspects of Ming life: "Local Tax Collectors in the Ming Dynasty" and "The 'Ten-Parts Tax System of Ming," by Liang Fang-chung; "Price Control and Paper Currency in Ming," by Li Chien-nung; "The Ming System of Merchant Colonization," by Wang Ch'ung-wu; and "Frontier Horse Markets in the Ming Dynasty," by Hou Jen-chih.

457

Lo Jung-pang. "The Decline of the Early Ming Navy," *Oriens Extremus,* V (1958-59), 149-168. Suggests that political decay, social unrest, economic dislocations, and above all a change from dynamism toward lethargy in the national character account for the abrupt decline of China's maritime vigor following the overseas expeditions of Cheng Ho in the first decades of the 15th century.

458

Parsons, James B. "A Case History of Revolt in China: The Late Ming Rebellion of Chang Hsien-chung," *Oriens Extremus,* III (1956), 81-93. An analysis of the career of one of the great rebels who hastened the collapse of the Ming dynasty. Cf. two related articles by Parsons: "Overtones of Religion and Superstition in the Rebellion of Chang Hsien-chung," *Sinologica,* IV (1955), 170-177; and "The Culmination of a Chinese Peasant Rebellion: Chang Hsien-chung in Szechwan, 1644-46," *Journal of Asian Studies,* XVI (1956-57), 387-400.

459

Chang Yü-ch'üan. "Wang Shou-jen as a Statesman," *Chinese Social and Political Science Review,* XXIII (1939–40), 30-99, 155-259, 319-375, 473-517. A detailed biographical study of a great 16th century governor and military commander who is best known as a Neo-Confucian philosopher under the name Wang Yang-ming.

460

Ku Chieh-kang. "A Study of Literary Persecution during the Ming," trans. by L. C. Goodrich. *Harvard Journal of Asiatic Studies,* III (1938), 254-311. A catalogue of despotic aberrations on the part of Ming emperors, with special reference to the harsh reactions of the first emperor to suspected slanders.

461

Hucker, Charles O. "The Tung Lin Movement of the Late Ming Period," in *Chinese Thought and Institutions* (J. K. Fairbank, ed.; Chicago: University of Chicago Press, 1957), pp. 132-163. A general survey of a politico-philosophical reform movement of the late 16th and early 17th centuries, which was finally destroyed by the powerful eunuch Wei Chung-hsien in the 1620's; with analyses of the social and institutional environment.

462

Franke, Wolfgang. "Yü Ch'ien, Staatsmann and Kriegs-minister, 1398-1457," *Monumenta Serica*, XI (1946), 87-122. On one of the most controversial figures of Ming history, who gained almost dictatorial power following a Chinese defeat by the Mongols in 1449; cf. addenda entitled "Ein Document Prozess gegen Yü Ch'ien im Jahr 1457," *Studia Serica*, VI (1947), 193-208, concerning the legal proceedings that rationalized Yü's execution.

463

Mote, Frederick W. "Notes on the Life of T'ao Tsung-i," *Silver Jubilee Volume of the Zinbun-Kagaku-Kenkyu-syo*, Kyoto University (Kyoto: 1954), pp. 279-293. On an unorthodox 14th century scholar who refused to take office under the newly-established Ming dynasty.

464

Hucker, Charles O. "Confucianism and the Chinese Censorial System," in *Confucianism in Action* (D. S. Nivison and A. F. Wright, ed.; Stanford: Stanford University Press, 1959), pp. 182-208. The attitudes and behavior of Ming dynasty surveillance and remonstrance officials analyzed according to Confucian and Legalist value systems, with comments on the theoretical foundations of the traditional censorial institutions.

465

Pelliot, Paul. "Le Hoja et le Sayyid Husain de l'histoire des Ming," *T'oung Pao*, XXXVIII (1948), 81-292. A monumental miscellany about the entry of the Portuguese into Ming China, with valuable data on the character and habits of the eccentric 16th century emperor Wu-tsung and on eminent personages of this time.

466

Krafft, Barbara. "Wang Shih-chen (1526-1590): Abriss seines Lebens," *Oriens Extremus*, V (1958-59), 169-201. On one of the most influential scholars and historians of the Ming era.

467

Busch, Heinrich. "The Tung-lin shu-yüan and its Political and Philosophical Significance," *Monumenta Serica*, XIV (1949-55), 1-163. A technical study of a reform movement of the late 16th and early 17th centuries, associated with a private academy in Kiangsu province; emphasizes its philosophical aspect.

468

Franke, Wolfgang. "Chinesische Feldzüge durch die Mongolei im frühen 15. Jahrhundert," *Sinologica*, III (1951-53), 81-88. A brief interpretive summary of five Chinese military expeditions against the Mongols conducted by the third Ming emperor in the early 15th century; for greater detail, see Franke's "Yung-lo's Mongolei-Feldzüge," *Sinologische Arbeiten*, III (1945), 1-54.

469

Chan, D. B. "The Problem of the Princes as Faced by the Ming Emperor Hui (1399-1402)," *Oriens*, XI (1958), 183-193. On the background of the rebellion of the Prince of Yen, who became the third Ming emperor.

470

Crawford, Robert B., Harry M. Lamley, and Albert B. Mann. "Fang Hsiao-ju in the Light of Early Ming Society," *Monumenta Serica*, XV (1956), 303-327. On the life and political philosophy of a statesman who was put to death in 1402 by the third Ming emperor, with a study of the despotic character of early Ming government.

471

Seuberlich, Wolfgang. "Kaisertrue oder auflehnung? Eine Episode aus der Ming-zeit," *Zeitschrift der Deutschen Morgenländischen Gesellschaft*, CII (1952), 304-314. On a censorial official who in 1517 won a battle of wills with the emperor Wu-tsung, with comments on the nature of imperial despotism in Ming times.

472

Sprenkel, O. B. van der. "High Officials of the Ming," *Bulletin of the School of Oriental and African Studies*, London University, XIV (1952), 87-114. A statistical study of career patterns in the Ming bureaucracy; includes a suggested scheme for periodizing Ming history on this basis.

473

Ho Ping-ti. "The Introduction of American Food Plants into China," *American Anthropologist*, LVII (1955), 191-201. On the basis of Chinese references, suggests that peanuts, sweet potatoes, and maize were introduced to China in the middle or earlier years of the 16th century.

474

Serruys, Henry. "Remains of Mongol Customs during the Early Ming," *Monumenta Serica*, XVI (1957), 137-190. On the penetration of Mongol influences into Chinese culture, as reflected in governmental institutions, clothing, marriage customs, etc., of the early Ming period; and on early Ming nationalistic efforts to stamp out such influences.

475

Maspero, Henri. "Comment tombe une dynastie Chinoise: la chute des Ming," in Henri Maspero, *Melanges posthumes sur les religions et l'histoire de la Chine*, vol. 3 (Paris: Civilisations du Sud, 1950), pp. 209-225. A narrative survey of the last decade of Ming history, in popular terms.

476

Hucker, Charles O. (trans.) "Su-chou and the Agents of Wei Chung-hsien," in *Silver Jubilee Volume of the Zinbun-Kagaku-Kenkyusyo*, Kyoto University (Kyoto: 1954), pp. 224-256. An annotated translation of a contemporary account of the arrest and trial of the official Chou Shun-ch'ang by police agents of a eunuch dictator in 1626 and of a popular uprising that ensued.

477

Backhouse, Edmund and J. O. P. Bland. *Annals and Memoirs of the Court of Peking*. Boston: Houghton Mifflin, 1914. An episodic, subjective, undocumented review of China's political history from the 16th century to the end of the Manchu era; a famous, standard reference, still useful for general background, but not to be relied on for detail.

478

Lin Yutang. *A History of the Press and Public Opinion in China*. Chicago: University of Chicago Press, 1936. Chap. 7, "Eunuchs, Censors and Tunglin Scholars in Ming," is a general survey of official protests against eunuch corruption and related governmental abuses.

479

Wu, K. T. "Ming Printing and Printers," *Harvard Journal of Asiatic Studies*, VII (1943), 203-260. A general survey, including data on color printing and movable type.

480

Sprenkel, O. B. van der. "Population Statistics of Ming China," *Bulletin of the School of Oriental and African Studies*, London University, XV (1953), 289-326. A detailed, technical study of Ming census registration procedures and findings; with many statistical charts.

481

Vanderstappen, Harrie. "Painters at the Early Ming Court (1368-1435) and the Problem of a Ming Painting Academy," *Monumenta Serica*, XV (1956), 259-302; XVI (1957), 315-346. A detailed compendium of information about officially-sponsored painters, with much biographical data.

482

Collis, Maurice. *The Great Within*. London: Faber and Faber, 1941. Part 1, "The Ruin of the Great Ming," is a popular and somewhat dramatized narrative of the last Ming decades, the fall of Ming, and the struggle of Ming loyalists in the South; not authoritative.

483

Jansé, O. R. T. "Notes on Chinese Influences in the Philippines in pre-Spanish times," *Harvard Journal of Asiatic Studies*, VIII (1944-45), 34-62. A report of archaeological excavations, valuable for findings of Ming ceramics; with many illustrations.

484

Gaspardone, Émile. "La supplique aux Ming de Le Lo'i," *Silver Jubilee Volume of the Zinbun-Kagaku-Kenkyusyo*, Kyoto University (Kyoto: 1954), pp. 158-166. On Ming China's intervention in Indo-china in the early decades of the 15th century

*   *   *

485

Duyvendak, J. J. L. *China's Discovery of Africa*. London: Arthur Probsthain, 1949. A brief summary of the circumstances that led to the sending of Chinese fleets to the east African coast in the early 15th century under a famous Moslem eunuch, Cheng Ho, who in six or perhaps seven voyages established Chinese naval supremacy throughout the South China Sea, the Indian Ocean, and the Persian Gulf.

486

Duyvendak, J. J. L. "The True Dates of the Chinese Maritime Expeditions in the Early Fifteenth Century," *T'oung Pao*, XXXIV (1938), 341-412. A detailed, technical study of the dates and itineraries of the Indian Ocean voyages made by the Ming dynasty's great eunuch admiral, Cheng Ho.

487

Pelliot, Paul. "Les grandes voyages maritimes chinois au début du XVe Siècle," *T'oung Pao*, XXX (1933), 237-452. The most comprehensive accounts of the maritime expeditions of Cheng Ho; cf. Pelliot's addenda in *T'oung Pao*, XXXI (1935), 274-314, and XXXII (1936), 210-222.

488

Duyvendak, J. J. L. *Ma Huan Re-examined*. Amsterdam: Noord-Hollandsche, 1933. A Chinese report of the maritime expeditions of the early 15th century; a technical analysis.

489

Tsunoda Ryusaku (trans.). *Japan in the Chinese Dynastic Histories: Later Han Through Ming Dynasties*, ed. by L. C. Goodrich. South Pasadena: P. D. and Ione Perkins, 1951. Pp. 106-161: an annotated translation of the notice on Japan in the *Ming-shih*, a basic source for Chinese-Japanese relations during the Ming period; on Japanese raids along China's coasts, on trading relations, on the Chinese-Japanese war in Korea in the 1590's.

490

Wang Yi-t'ung. *Official Relations between China and Japan*, 1368-1549. Cambridge: Harvard University Press, 1953. (Harvard-Yenching Institute Studies, IX). A technical, authoritative study of the Ming government's attempts to impose tributary status on Japan so as to halt coastal raiding by Japanese pirate fleets.

491

Sansom, George. *A History of Japan, 1334-1615*. Stanford: Stanford University Press, 1961. Pp. 352-362 on the Chinese-Japanese war in Korea during the 1590's.

492

Kuno, Yoshi S. *Japanese Expansion on the Asiatic Continent*. Vol. 1. Berkeley: University of California Press, 1937. Pp. 61-178 give a detailed, authoritative account of Japanese piracy and diplomatic relations throughout the Ming period and of the Sino-Japanese war in Korea in the 1590's; based on Japanese materials.

493

Griffis, William E. *Corea, the Hermit Nation*. 6th rev. ed. New York: Scribner, 1902. Chaps. 12-20 give a detailed history of the Chinese-Japanese war in Korea in the 1590's.

494

Stramigioli, Giuliana. "Hideyoshi's Expansionist Policy on the Asiatic Mainland," *Transactions of the Asiatic Society of Japan*, 3d series, III (1954), 74-116. On the Japanese background and conduct of the Sino-Japanese war in Korea in the 1590's, entirely from Japanese sources and the Japanese point of view.

495

Rockhill, William W. *China's Intercourse with Korea from the Fifteenth Century to 1895*. London: Luzac, 1905. A standard reference.

*   *   *

496

Lin, T. C. "Manchurian Trade and Tribute in the Ming Dynasty," *Nankai Social and Economic Quarterly*, IX (1936), 855-892. An analysis of Chinese theories and practices used in dominating the proto-Manchu peoples of Manchuria.

497

Lin, T. C. "Manchuria in the Ming Empire," *Nankai Social and Economic Quarterly*, VIII (1935), 1-43. A study of Chinese military establishments and colonial organization in the far northeast.

498

Serruys, Henry. *Sino-Jurced Relations during the Yung-lo Period (1403–1424)*. Wiesbaden: Otto Harrassowitz, 1955. On early Ming military establishments in the far northeast and relations with the proto-Manchu inhabitants; highly technical.

499

Pokotilov, D. *History of the Eastern Mongols during the Ming Dynasty from 1368 to 1634*, trans. by Rudolph Löwenthal. Chengtu: 1947. (Studia Serica Monographs, Series A, No. 1.) An authoritative Russian study; cf. the addenda and corrigenda by Wolfgang Franke published as Studia Serica Monographs, Series A, No. 3 (1949).

500

Howorth, Henry Hoyle. *History of the Mongols, from the 9th to the 19th Century*. 4 vols. in 5. London: Longmans, Green, 1876–1927. Vol. 1 includes histories of the various Mongol groups and their relations with China in Ming times.

501

Grousset, René. *L'empire des steppes*. Paris: Payot, 1948. Pp. 486-546, 568-622: an authoritative survey of Mongol history and of Mongol-Chinese relations in Ming times.

502

Serruys, Henry. "Chinese in Southern Mongolia during the Sixteenth Century," *Monumenta Serica*, XVIII (1959), 1-95. An enlightening analysis of Chinese-Mongol relations, with special emphasis on the activities of Chinese soldiers and civilians who lived among the Mongols and in some cases "became Mongols."

503

Serruys, Henry. "Were the Ming Against the Mongols' Settling in North China?" *Oriens Extremus*, VI (1959–60), 131-159.

504

Serruys, Henry. "The Mongols of Kansu during the Ming," *Mélanges Chinois et Bouddhiques*, X (1955), 215-346. A detailed, authoritative study; includes information about both official and unofficial Chinese-Mongol relations.

505

Serruys, Henry (trans.). "Pei-lou fong-sou: les coutumes des esclaves septentrionaux," *Monumenta Serica*, X (1945), 117-208. Annotated translation of Hsiao Taheng's *Pei-lu feng-su*, a contemporary Chinese description of Mongol customs and Chinese-Mongol relations of the second half of the 16th century. Cf. the same author's *Geneological Tables of the Descendants of Dayan-Qan* ('s-Gravenhage: Mouton, 1958), a greatly expanded version of Hsiao's tables of 16th century Mongol rulers.

506

Serruys, Henry. "Notes on a Few Mongolian Rulers of the 15th Century," *Journal of the American Oriental Society,* LXXVI (1956), 82-90. Attempts to identify and date some early Ming Mongol khans.

507

Bretschneider, E. *Mediaeval Researches from Eastern Asiatic Sources.* Vol. 2. London: Kegan Paul, 1888. Pp. 139-332, "Chinese Intercourse with the Countries of Central and Western Asia during the Fifteenth and Sixteenth Centuries," includes annotated translations from Chinese sources about the Mongols, the peoples of Turkestan, and even about the Arabic and West European nations; not yet wholly superseded.

Early Ch'ing

508

Hummel, Arthur W. (ed.) *Eminent Chinese of the Ch'ing Period (1644–1912).* 2 vols. Washington: Government Printing Office, 1943–44. A detailed biographical dictionary of some 800 notable Chinese, Manchus, and Mongols, with excellent indexes; the single most valuable reference for general Chinese history of the Ch'ing era.

509

Michael, Franz. *The Origin of Manchu Rule in China.* Baltimore: Johns Hopkins Press, 1942. A standard reference on the rise of the Manchus to power in the far northeast and their subsequent conquest of China Proper; an institutional analysis.

510

Hsieh Pao-chao. *The Government of China (1644–1911).* Baltimore: Johns Hopkins Press, 1925. A readable, interpretive description of the Ch'ing governmental system; one of the best general introductions to the scope and rationale of traditional Chinese political organization.

511

Goodrich, L. Carrington. *The Literary Inquisition of Ch'ien-lung.* Baltimore: Waverly Press, 1935. A detailed, authoritative analysis of 18th century efforts to destroy writings that were considered subversive of Manchu authority and prestige; with valuable data on the compilation of a gigantic compendium of Confucian literature, *Ssu-k'u ch'üan-shu.*

512

Nivison, David S. "Ho-shen and His Accusers: Ideology and Political Behavior in the Eighteenth Century," in *Confucianism in Action* (D. S. Nivison and A. F. Wright, ed.; Stanford: Stanford University Press, 1959), pp. 209-243. On a notoriously corrupt Manchu favorite of the Ch'ien-lung emperor, credited traditionally with setting the Ch'ing dynasty on its decline.

513

Fairbank, John K. and Teng Ssu-yü. *Ch'ing Administration: Three Studies.* Cambridge: Harvard University Press, 1960. (Harvard-Yenching Institute Studies, XIX.) A collection of three technical articles from the *Harvard Journal of Asiatic Studies* (vols. IV, V, VI) relating to administrative practices of the Manchu era: "On the Transmission of Ch'ing Documents," "On the Types and Uses of Ch'ing Documents," and "On the Ch'ing Tributary System."

514

Liang Ch'i-ch'ao. *Intellectual Trends in the Ch'ing Period (1644–1912),* trans. by Immanuel C. Y. Hsü. Cambridge: Harvard University Press, 1959. (Harvard East Asian Studies, II.) A standard Chinese study of the intellectual history of the Manchu era, in an authoritative translation.

515

Waley, Arthur. *Yuan Mei, Eighteenth Century Chinese Poet.* New York: Macmillan, 1956; paperbound reprint, New York: Grove Press, 1956. An authoritative but readable biography of a "lovable, witty, generous, affectionate, hot-tempered, wildly prejudiced man;" of great usefulness in the study of early Ch'ing intellectual life.

516

Petech, Luciano. *China and Tibet in the Early Eighteenth Century.* Leiden: E. J. Brill, 1950. An authoritative study of the establishment of a Chinese protectorate over Tibet between 1705 and 1751, based on both Chinese and Tibetan sources.

517

Wilhelm, Hellmut. "The Po-hsüeh Hung-ju Examination of 1679," *Journal of the American Oriental Society,* LXXI (1951), 60-66. On early Manchu attempts to appease Chinese scholars and entice them into government service.

518

Giles, Herbert A. *China and the Manchus.* Cambridge: Harvard University Press, 1912. A very brief resumé of the history of the Ch'ing dynasty, in popular style.

519

Wada Sei. "Some Problems Concerning the Rise of T'aitsu, the Founder of the Manchu Dynasty," *Memoirs of the Research Department of The Toyo Bunko,* XVI (1957), 35-73.

520

Fairbank, John K. *Ch'ing Documents: An Introductory Syllabus.* 2d rev. ed. Cambridge: Harvard University Press, 1959. A technical reader for students of Chinese; with useful introductory information about Ch'ing administrative practices.

521

Ho Ping-ti. "The Salt Merchants of Yang-chou: a Study of Commercial Capitalism in Eighteenth-century China," *Harvard Journal of Asiatic Studies,* XVII (1954), 130-168. Includes much data on administration of the salt monopoly in early Ch'ing times.

522

Ma Feng-ch'en. "Manchu-Chinese Social and Economic Conflicts in Early Ch'ing," in *Chinese Social History* (E-tu Zen Sun and John de Francis, ed.; Washington: American Council of Learned Societies, 1956), pp. 333-351. On land enclosure, enslavement, and other conflicts and their gradual adjustment.

523

Harcourt-Smith, Simon. "The Emperor Ch'ien Lung, 1735–1799," *History Today,* V (1955), 164-173. A brief "appreciation" of one of China's greatest emperors, with general comments on his reign, his court, and his Jesuit tutors and companions.

524

Keene, Donald R. (trans.) *The Battles of Coxinga.* London: Taylors Foreign Press, 1951. Includes a general survey of the career of a Ming-loyalist raider who harassed the Ch'ing empire's coast in the 17th century (Cheng Ch'eng-kung, or Koxinga). Cf. R. A. B. Ponsonby-Fane, "Koxinga: Chronicles of the Tei Family," *Transactions and Proceedings of the Japan Society,* London, XXXIV (1937), 65-132.

526

Hsieh Kuo-chen. "Removal of Coastal Population in the Early Tsing Period," trans. by T. H. Chen. *Chinese Social and Political Science Review,* XV (1930–31), 559-596. On a strategic measure adopted by the Manchus to frustrate the coastal raids of Koxinga and other Ming loyalists.

527

Malone, Carroll. *History of the Peking Summer Palaces under the Ch'ing Dynasty*. Urbana: University of Illinois, 1934. Contains much useful information about court life under the Manchus, the activities of European architects and decorators in 18th century China, etc.

528

Ho, Alfred K. L. "The Grand Council in the Ch'ing Dynasty," *Far Eastern Quarterly*, XI (1951–52), 167-182. On the establishment of the *Chün-chi-ch'u*, the highest ranking advisory body in the Ch'ing government, in 1729; its organization, procedures, and personnel.

529

Li Tieh-tseng. *The Historical Status of Tibet*. New York: King's Crown Press, 1956. Chaps. 2-4 summarize Chinese-Tibetan relations in the Manchu era.

530

Tucci, Giuseppe. *Tibetan Painted Scrolls*. 2 vols. Rome: La Libreria dello Stato, 1949. Vol. 1 includes detailed, authoritative data on Tibetan-Mongol-Chinese relations during Ming and early Ch'ing times.

531

Howorth, Henry Hoyle. *History of the Mongols, from the 9th to the 19th Century*. 4 vols. in 5. London: Longmans, Green, 1876–1927. Vol. 1 includes histories of the various Mongol groups and their relations with China in Ch'ing times.

532

Baddeley, John F. *Russia, Mongolia, China*. 2 vols. London: Macmillan, 1919. A standard source on Chinese-Mongol-Russian relations in the 17th century, based largely on the narratives and reports of Russian diplomatic emissaries to China and the Mongol khans.

533

Hedin, Sven. *Jehol, City of Emperors*. New York: Dutton, 1933. Contains much readable information on the personalities and times of the K'ang-shi and, especially, Ch'ien-lung emperors.

534

Fang Chaoying. "A Technique for Estimating the Numerical Strength of the Early Manchu Military Forces," *Harvard Journal of Asiatic Studies*, XIII (1950), 192-215. A useful description and statistical analysis of the early Ch'ing military organization.

535

Chen Shao-Kwan. *The System of Taxation in China in the Tsing Dynasty, 1644–1911*. New York: Columbia University Press, 1914. A general descriptive study.

536

Cammann, Schuyler. "The Panchen Lama's Visit to China in 1780: an Episode in Anglo-Tibetan Relations," *Far Eastern Quarterly*, IX (1949–50), 3-19.

537

Hibbert, Eloise T. *K'ang Hsi, Emperor of China*. London: Kegan Paul, 1942. A popular biography of the great 17th-18th century monarch; not to be relied on for scholarly purposes.

538

Grantham, A. E. *Manchu Monarch: an Interpretation of Chia Ch'ing*. London: Allen and Unwin, 1934. A popular, undocumented account of the reign of the Chia-ch'ing emperor (1796–1820), including data on the corrupt Manchu favorite Ho-shen and on the British mission under Lord Amherst in 1816; not authoritative, but still useful.

539

Backhouse, Edmund and J. O. P. Bland. *Annals and Memoirs of the Court of Peking*. Boston: Houghton Mifflin, 1914. An episodic, subjective, undocumented review of China's political history from the 16th century to the end of the Manchu era; a famous, standard reference, still useful for general background, but not to be relied on for detail.

540

Grousset, René. *L'empire des steppes*. Paris: Payot, 1948. Pp. 486-546, 568-622 provide an authoritative survey of Mongol history and of Mongol-Chinese relations in Ch'ing times.

541

Brunnert, H. S. and V. V. Hagelstrom. *Present Day Political Organization of China*. Rev. by N. Th. Kolessoff. Trans. by A. Beltchenko and E. E. Moran. Shanghai: Kelly and Walsh, 1912. A standard manual of Ch'ing governmental agencies, including the innovations of the dynasty's last years.

542

Mayers, William Frederick. *The Chinese Government*. 3d ed. rev. by G. M. H. Playfair. Shanghai: Kelly and Walsh, 1897. A technical manual of Chinese governmental titles in the Ch'ing dynasty.

543

Staunton, George T. (trans.) *Ta Tsing Leu Lee*. London: T. Cadell and W. Davies, 1810. Partial translation of the Ch'ing dynasty law code, *Ta Ch'ing lü-li*.

544

Rockhill, William W. *China's Intercourse with Korea from the Fifteenth Century to 1895*. London: Luzac, 1905. A standard reference.

Early modern Chinese-Western relations

545

Rowbotham, Arnold H. *Missionary and Mandarin: The Jesuits at the Court of China*. Berkeley: University of California Press, 1942. A standard, detailed reference for Jesuit history in China from Matteo Ricci on; authoritative but entertaining.

546

Gallagher, Louis J. (trans.) *China in the Sixteenth Century: The Journals of Matthew Ricci: 1583–1610*. New York: Random House, 1953. The standard English-language source on Matteo Ricci; contains both Ricci's invaluable, detailed description of Ming life and institutions and his account of the history of the early Jesuit missionary activities in China. An earlier version of Gallagher's translation of the former section was published under the title *The China That Was* (Milwaukee: Bruce Publishing Co., 1942).

547

Boxer, C. R. "Jesuits at the Court of Peking, 1601-1775," *History Today*, VII (1957), 580-589. A brief evaluation of the history and importance of the Jesuit endeavors in China.

548

Latourette, Kenneth Scott. *A History of Christian Missions in China*. New York: Macmillan, 1929. Includes a general account of Catholic activities in China during Ming and early Ch'ing times; a standard reference.

549

Cronin, Vincent. *The Wise Man from the West*. New York: Dutton, 1955; paperbound reprint, New York: Doubleday, 1957. A popular, pious retelling of the biography of Matteo Ricci.

550

D'Elia, Pasquale M. (ed.) *Fonti Ricciane*. 3 vols. Rome: La Libreria dello Stato, 1942–49. A monumental sourcebook of original documents concerning Matteo Ricci and the activities of the Jesuit missions in China through 1615.

551

D'Elia, Pasquale M. "La rèprise des missions Catholiques en Chine à la fin des Ming," *Cahiers d'Histoire Mondiale*, V (1959–60), 679-700. An Italian authority's evaluation of Jesuit history and influence from Ricci to the fall of the Ming dynasty.

552

Rosso, Antonio Sisto. *Apostolic Legations to China of the Eighteenth Century*. South Pasadena: P. D. and Ione

1948. A collection of documents pertaining to the "Rites controversy" of the late 17th and early 18th centuries, which resulted in a great restriction of Catholic missionary activity in China.

553

Bernard, Henri. *Matteo Ricci's Scientific Contribution to China*, trans. by E. C. Werner. Peiping: Henri Vetch, 1935. A standard reference on the introduction of European knowledge into Ming China.

554

Prandi, Fortunato (trans.). *Memoirs of Father Ripa during 13 Years Residence at the Court of Peking in the Service of the Emperor of China*. London: J. Murray, 1844. An entertaining eyewitness account of Chinese life in the reign of the K'ang-hsi emperor, by Father Matteo Ripa.

555

Pfister, Aloys. *Notices biographiques et bibliographiques sur les Jesuites de l'ancienne mission de Chine, 1552–1773*. 2 vols. Shanghai: Mission Catholique, 1932–34. (Variétés Sinologiques, 59-60). An encyclopedic sourcebook of data on all Jesuits active in China during the Ming and early Ch'ing periods.

*   *   *

557

Boxer, Charles Ralph. *Fidalgos in the Far East, 1550-1770*. The Hague: Nijhoff, 1948. An entertaining but authoritative history of the Portuguese settlement at Macao.

558

Hudson, Geoffrey F. *Europe and China: A Survey of Their Relations from the Earliest Times to 1800:* London: Edward Arnold 1931; paperbound reprint, Boston: Beacon Press, 1961. Chaps. 6-10 provide an excellent general survey of European approaches to and relations with China in Ming and early Ch'ing times and of Chinese influence in Europe.

559

Sansom, George B. *The Western World and Japan*. New York: Knopf, 1950. Part 1, "Europe and Asia," contains a thoughtful interpretive discussion of the European background of early modern imperialistic expansion and of the "interaction of cultures" that resulted, by a distinguished historian of Japan; with much relevance to early modern European relations with China.

560

Morse, Hosea Ballou. *The Chronicles of the East India Company Trading to China, 1635–1834*. 5 vols. Oxford: Clarendon Press, 1926–29. The voluminous standard reference on the famous "John Company's" relations with China; based entirely on official company records, many of which are quoted extensively.

561

Greenberg, Michael. *British Trade and the Opening of China, 1800–42*. Cambridge University Press, 1951. Based principally on archives of the dominant British firm Jardine Matheson and Co., of Canton; with much information about Chinese trading practices.

562

Chang T'ien-tse. *Sino-Portugese Trade from 1514 to 1644*. Leiden: E. J. Brill, 1934. The standard reference for the first modern European contacts with China; cf. the detailed critique by Paul Pelliot in *T'oung Pao*, XXXI (1935), 58-94.

563

Pritchard, Earl H. *Anglo-Chinese Relations during the Seventeenth and Eighteenth Centuries*. Urbana: University of Illinois Press, 1930. A comprehensive study of an important period of "spectacular political and diplomatic events," based principally on fresh research in British archives.

564

Pritchard, Earl H. *The Crucial Years of Early Anglo-Chinese Relations, 1750-1800*. Pullman: Washington State College, 1936. An authoritative analysis, with valuable comparisons of the socioeconomic backgrounds of the two nations.

565

Chang Teh-ch'ang. "Maritime Trade at Canton during the Ming Dynasty," *Chinese Social and Political Science Review*, XVII (1933–34), 264-282. Should be used as a supplement to Chang T'ien-tse's *Sino-Portuguese Trade from 1514 to 1644*.

566

Cammann, Schuyler. *Trade Through the Himalayas*. Princeton: Princeton University Press, 1951. An authoritative study of 18th century Chinese-British relations in Tibet.

567

Pritchard, Earl H. "Private Trade between England and China in the Eighteenth Century (1680–1833)," *Journal of the Economic and Social History of the Orient*, I (1957–58), 108-137, 221-256. On the conditions and amounts of private trading permitted on the East India Company's ships, with many statistical tables.

568

Hsü, Immanuel C. Y. "The Secret Mission of the Lord Amherst on the China Coast, 1832," *Harvard Journal of Asiatic Studies*, XVII (1954), 231-252. On an exploratory mission along China's southeastern coast that revealed China's military weakness to the British before the Opium War; notes the increasing difficulties of Chinese-English trading relations and the developing pressures for change.

569

Braga, José Maria. *The Western Pioneers and Their Discovery of Macao*. Macao: Imprensa Nacional, 1949. A general study of Portuguese relations with China up to the settlement at Macao in the 1550's.

570

Danton, George H. *The Culture Contacts of the United States and China*. New York: Columbia University Press, 1931. A survey of Sino-American mercantile, missionary, and other relations between 1784 and 1844.

571

Dulles, Foster Rhea. *The Old China Trade*. Boston: Houghton Mifflin, 1930. The mercantile details of Sino-American relations up to 1844, in popular presentation.

572

Greenbie, Sydney and Marjorie Greenbie. *Gold of Ophir: The China Trade in the Making of America*. Rev. ed. New York: Wilson-Erickson, 1937. The influence of the China trade in America between the American Revolution and Civil War, in popular terms.

573

Boxer, C. R. (ed.) *South China in the Sixteenth Century*. London: Hakluyt Society, 1953. Annotated translations of three detailed Portuguese and Spanish eyewitness descriptions of Ming China in the period 1550-1575, with excellent introductory material on early Portuguese and Spanish relations with China in general.

574

Reichwein, Adolf. *China and Europe*. New York: Alfred A. Knopf, 1925. An extensive analysis of the impact of Chinese culture on 18th century Europe: in painting, ceramics, textiles, architecture, landscaping, furniture, and especially in the thought of such leaders of the Enlightenment as Leibniz, Wolff, Voltaire, Quesnay, the Encyclopaedists, Goethe, etc.

575

Appleton, William W. *A Cycle of Cathay*. New York: Columbia University Press, 1951. A survey of English references to China in the 17th and 18th centuries, with an analysis of Chinese influences on English arts and tastes.

576

Liu Hsüan-ming. "Russo-Chinese Relations up to the Treaty of Nerchinsk," *Chinese Social and Political Science Review,* XXIII (1939–40), 391-440. On the background of China's first treaty with a modern European power; cf. V. S. Frank, "The Territorial Claims of the Sino-Russian Treaty of Nerchinsk, 1869," *Pacific Historical Review,* XVI (1947), 256-270.

577

Le May, G. H. L. "Two British Embassies to China: 1793 and 1816," *History Today,* II (1952), 479-486. A brief general account and evaluation of the unfruitful and somewhat humiliating missions of Lord Macartney and Lord Amherst to the Manchu court.

578

Staunton, George. *An Authentic Account of an Embassy from the King of Great Britain to the Emperor of China.* 2 vols. and extra folio volume of plates. London: G. Nicol, 1797; often republished. A detailed narrative of the Macartney mission to the court of Ch'ien-lung in 1793, by the official secretary of the mission; with many observations about Chinese life in general.

579

Ellis, Henry. *Journal of the Proceedings of the Late Embassy to China.* London: J. Murray, 1817. The basic source on the fruitless mission of Lord Amherst to China in 1816.

580

Lamb, Alistair. "Tibet in Anglo-Chinese Relations, 1767–1842," *Journal of the Royal Asiatic Society,* 1957, 161-176; 1958, 26-43. On Britain's early effort to open China through the Himalayan policies of British India.

581

Boxer, C. R. "The Manila Galleon: 1565–1815," *History Today,* VIII (1958), 538-547. A brief summary of Spain's early system of exchanging Mexican silver for Chinese silk through Manila. For greater detail, see W. L. Schurz's *The Manila Galleon* (New York: Dutton, 1939; paperbound reprint by same publisher, 1959).

582

Kammerer, Albert. *La découverte de la Chine par les Portugais au XVIème siècle et la cartographie des Portulans.* Leiden: E. J. Brill, 1944. A detailed, highly technical study of Portuguese contacts and establishments in Ming China; should be used to supplement Chang T'ien-tse's *Sino-Portuguese Trade from 1514 to 1644.*

583

Fu Lo-shu. "The Two Portuguese Embassies to China during the K'ang-hsi Period," *T'oung Pao,* XLIII (1954–55), 75-94. On the missions of Manuel de Saldanha in 1670 and Bento Pereyra de Faria in 1678, concerning Portuguese trading arrangements in China; cf. addenda by Luciano Petech in *op. cit.,* XLIV (1956), 227-241.

584

Braga, José Maria. *China Landfall, 1513.* Hongkong: K. Weiss, 1956. A detailed study, of somewhat uneven quality, of the first Portuguese to reach Canton, Jorge Alvares; with background data on Sino-Portuguese relations generally.

585

Campbell, William. *Formosa under the Dutch Described from Contemporary Records with Explanatory Notes and a Bibliography of the Island.* London: Kegan Paul, 1903. A voluminous compendium of source materials concerning the Dutch occupation of Taiwan and its later conquest by Koxinga in the 17th century; a standard reference.

586

Mancall, Mark. "China's First Missions to Russia, 1729–1731," *Papers on China* (Harvard University Committee on Regional Studies), IX (1955), 75-110. On Chinese efforts to counter the rising power of the western Mongols (Zungars) in Central Asia.

587

Volker, T. *Porcelain and the Dutch East India Company.* Leiden: E. J. Brill, 1954. Includes a detailed documentary account of Dutch trading activities in China and Taiwan in Ming times; based on original Dutch sources.

588

Maverick, Lewis A. *China, a Model for Europe.* San Antonio: Paul Anderson Co., 1946. A study of Chinese influence on the physiocratic thinkers of Europe in the 17th and 18th centuries, including a translation of Francois Quesnay's admiring description of the "benevolent despotism" of China, *Le despotisme de la Chine* (1767).

589

Pritchard, Earl H. "The Kotow in the Macartney Embassy to China in 1793," *Far Eastern Quarterly,* II (1942–43), 163-203. A detailed evaluation of conflicting English, Russian, and Chinese evidence as to whether or not Lord Macartney performed the humiliating k'ou-t'ou prostration in court audience, concluding that he did not; with notes on all foreign missions to the Chinese court from 1520 to 1840.

590

Collis, Maurice. *The Great Within.* London: Faber and Faber, 1941. An episodic, dramatized narrative of Sino-Western relations up to the Opium War; based entirely on secondary sources, especially Backhouse and Bland's *Annals and Memoirs of the Court of Peking.*

591

Hyma, Albert. *A History of the Dutch in the Far East.* Ann Arbor: George Wahr Publishing Co., 1953. Includes a brief account of Dutch activities in late Ming China.

592

Collis, Maurice. *The Grand Peregrination, Being the Life and Adventures of Fernao Mendes Pinto.* London: Faber and Faber, 1949. A popular retelling of the adventures in China of a 16th century European, who apparently never visited China at all.

593

Cogan, Henry (trans.). "The Voyages and Adventures of Fernao Mendes Pinto," in *Portuguese Voyages, 1498–1663* (C. D. Ley, ed.; New York: Dutton, 1947), pp. 79-236. The probably apocryphal tales of a Portuguese adventurer in China during the 1540's.

594

Mendoza, Juan Gonzalez de. *The History of the Great and Mighty Kingdom of China,* trans. by R. Parke, ed. by G. T. Staunton. 2 vols. London: The Hakluyt Society, 1853–54. A detailed description of life in late Ming China and of early Western-Chinese contacts by a Spanish Augustinian monk who visited the coast in 1580 and supplemented his eyewitness observations with study of all prior accounts; first published in 1585. Rare, but a useful companion to Ricci's account.

595

Cortesao, Armando (trans.). *The Suma Oriental of Tome Pires.* 2 vols. London: The Hakluyt Society, 1944. Includes an account of what the Portuguese had learned of the wealth and trade of Ming China by 1515; suggests that "with ten ships the (Portuguese) Governor of India who took Malacca could take the whole of China along the sea-coast" (I, 123).

596

Mundy, Peter. *The Travels of Peter Mundy in Europe and Asia, 1608–1667.* Vol. 3, Part 1. London: The Hakluyt Society, 1919. The earliest Englishman's account of travels in China, narrating a visit to the Macao-Canton area in 1637; illustrated with pencil drawings.

THE NINETEENTH CENTURY

The 19th century marks the beginning of China's agonizing transition from its traditional Confucian, agrarian, imperial order to a new "modern" order, the ultimate nature of which was still not clearly determined by mid-20th century. The old regime had been at its power zenith in the 18th century but in the 19th did not respond effectively to new conditions and dissolved ingloriously. The Ch'ing dynasty of the Manchus faced challenges both from within and from without. On the domestic scene population growth outran China's agricultural resources. New ideas and techniques began undermining the traditional social system. Governmental corruption, inaction, and inability to cope with international problems revived long-dormant anti-Manchu nationalism. Gathering strength in local outbreaks of the 1830's and 1840's, growing discontent erupted in 1850 in the most devastating upheaval of human history, the Taiping Rebellion, which wracked South and Central China for fifteen years and perhaps cost 30 million lives. Simultaneously North China was ravaged by roving bandits called the Nien rebels, and soon Moslem Chinese of the far west rose in a separate rebellion. The Ch'ing government, with the support of able Chinese leaders such as Tseng Kuo-fan who rallied to defend the Confucian social order, managed at great cost to put down these challenges from within. It even survived humiliating aggressions on the part of the newly-industrialized European powers — the Opium War of 1839−42 and Anglo-French punitive expeditions in 1856−58 and 1859−60. In the 1870's and 1880's, under the leadership of the empress dowager Tz'u-hsi, the government braked the deterioration notably, and China seemed on the verge of recovering its old resiliency and its dignity among the nations. But the scorned neighbor and sometime tributary, Japan, was beating China dramatically in the race to modernize; and when a quarrel developed over the status of Korea, Chinese forces were easily and humiliatingly defeated in the Sino-Japanese War of 1894−95. The western powers promptly moved in to divide China among themselves as they had recently divided Africa. In the face of this threat, the Chinese tried reforms without success and then were swept up in a paroxysm of fanatic anti-foreign reaction, the Boxer Rebellion of 1900. Discredited both at home and abroad, the Ch'ing government drifted inexorably toward its end—and the end of the whole millenia-old imperial tradition—in 1911−12.

Introductory references: standard textbooks on the Far East

597
Clyde, Paul H. The Far East. 3d ed. Englewood Cliffs, N. J.: Prentice-Hall, 1958.

598
Michael, Franz H. and George E. Taylor. *The Far East in the Modern World.* New York: Holt, 1956.

599
Vinacke, Harold M. *A History of the Far East in Modern Times.* 6th ed. New York: Appleton-Century-Crofts, 1959.

600
MacNair, H. F. and Donald F. Lach. *Modern Far Eastern International Relations.* 2d ed. New York: Van Nostrand, 1955.

600a
Latourette, K. S. *A Short History of the Far East.* Rev. ed. New York: Macmillan, 1951.

601
Cameron, Meribeth E. and others. *China, Japan and the Powers.* New York: Ronald Press, 1952.

602
Peffer, Nathaniel. *The Far East.* Ann Arbor: University of Michigan Press, 1958.

603
Crofts, Alfred and Percy Buchanan. *A History of the Far East.* New York: Longmans, Green, 1958.

General

604
Li Chien-nung. *The Political History of China, 1840−1928,* trans. by Teng Ssu-yü and Jeremy Ingalls. Princeton: Van Nostrand, 1956. The most detailed, authoritative narrative now available, written in 1948 as a textbook for Chinese college students; incorporates many important documents.

605
Hummel, Arthur W. (ed.) *Eminent Chinese of the Ch'ing Period (1644−1912).* 2 vols. Washington: Government Printing Office, 1943−44. A detailed biographical dictionary of some 800 notable Chinese, Manchus, and Mongols, with excellent indexes; the single most valuable reference for general Chinese history of the Ch'ing era.

606
Latourette, Kenneth Scott. *The Chinese, Their History and Culture.* 3d ed. rev. New York: Macmillan, 1946. Chaps. 10-11 survey general history in the 19th century.

607
Teng Ssu-yü and John K. Fairbank. *China's Response to the West.* 2 vols. Cambridge: Harvard University Press, 1954. A documentary history of China's political reactions to the challenge of the West from 1839 on. Vol. 2, *A Research Guide for . . .,* is devoted to notes, glossaries, and bibliographies.

608
Fairbank, John King. *The United States and China.* Rev. ed. Cambridge: Harvard University Press, 1958. A standard introductory reference on modern China, including an analysis of traditional Chinese society and culture and the impact of the Western world in the 19th century.

609
Harris, Richard. "China Under the Empress Dowager," *History Today,* VII (1957), 662-671. A survey of the career of the empress dowager Tz'u-hsi, who effectively governed China from 1861 to her death in 1908; for the general reader.

610
Bland, J. O. P. and E. Backhouse. *China under the Empress Dowager.* Philadelphia: Lippincott, 1910. A voluminous standard reference on the life and times of the empress dowager Tz'u-hsi, who dominated Chinese political life from 1861 until her death in 1908, based partly on personal knowledge and partly on Chinese sources (some questionable), but not adequately annotated.

611
Hussey, Harry. *Venerable Ancestor: The Life and Times of Tz'u Hsi, 1835−1908, Empress of China.* New York: Doubleday, 1949. A highly readable and friendly biography of the famous empress dowager, based in part on the diaries and reminiscences of people who knew her; not in a scholarly approach.

612
Der Ling, Princess. *Son of Heaven.* New York: Appleton-Century, 1935. A romanticized biography of the emperor Kuang-hsü, who sponsored the reform movement of 1898, by a long-time lady in waiting upon the empress dowager Tz'u-hsi; representative of a long list of

memoirs about the last Manchu years by the same author, including *Old Buddha, Imperial Incense, Two Years in the Forbidden City, Kowtow,* and *Lotus Petals* (all New York: Dodd, Mead, 1924–33).

613

Backhouse, Edmund and J. O. P. Bland. *Annals and Memoirs of the Court of Peking.* Boston: Houghton Mifflin, 1914. An episodic, subjective, undocumented review of China's political history from the 16th century to the end of the Manchu era; a famous, standard reference, still useful for general background, but not to be relied on for detail.

* * *

614

Papers on China. Cambridge: Harvard University Committee on Regional Studies (since 1957, Center for East Asian Studies), 1947–. An annual collection of Harvard seminar papers, mimeographed for private distribution; contain many excellent studies, especially of late 19th and early 20th century history.

615

Journal of the North China Branch, Royal Asiatic Society. 1858–1948. Published quarterly in Shanghai; an excellent source for contemporary views and reports on 19th century China.

616

The Chinese Repository. Canton: 1832–1851. A journal containing articles in English about Chinese history and current events; a valuable source, principally for Western relations with China.

The Taiping Rebellion and its suppression

617

Wright, Mary Clabaugh. *The Last Stand of Chinese Conservatism: The T'ung-chih Restoration, 1862–1874.* Stanford: Stanford University Press, 1957. (Stanford Studies in History, Economics, and Political Science, XIII.) A monumental study of vigorous but eventually unfruitful efforts to rehabilitate the Confucian state and society after the ravages of the Taiping Rebellion; a most important contribution to the understanding of China's agonizing transition from traditional to modern status.

618

Teng Ssu-yü. *New Light on the History of the Taiping Rebellion.* Cambridge: Harvard University Press, 1950. A survey of some historical problems relating to the Taiping era, in the form of a bibliographical essay on new publications in China and elsewhere; a useful introduction for the informed student.

619

Taylor, George E. "The Taiping Rebellion: Its Economic Background and Social Theory," *Chinese Social and Political Science Review,* XVI (1932–33), 545-614. A standard reference on the revolutionary socioeconomic program of the Taiping movement and on its origins.

620

Li Chien-nung. *The Political History of China, 1840–1928,* trans. by Teng Ssu-yü and Jeremy Ingalls. Princeton: Van Nostrand, 1956. Pp. 47-94 provide a detailed narrative of the Taiping Rebellion and the Ch'ing dynasty's efforts to suppress it.

621

Hail, William J. *Tseng Kuo-fan and the Tai Ping Rebellion.* New Haven: Yale University Press, 1927. A standard reference.

622

Linebarger, Paul M. A., Djang Chu, and Ardath W. Burks. *Far Eastern Governments and Politics: China and Japan.* 2d ed. Princeton: Van Nostrand, 1956. Pp. 102-119 give a useful description of the organization and policies of the Taiping government.

623

Anderson, Flavia. *The Rebel Emperor.* London: Gollancz, 1958. A "historical reconstruction" or novelized account of the life of Hung Hsiu-ch'üan, the vision-driven leader of the Taiping Rebellion; not for scholarly use, but reliable for the general facts.

624

Boardman, Eugene P. *Christian Influence upon the Ideology of the Taiping Rebellion, 1851–1864.* Madison: University of Wisconsin Press, 1952. An analysis of the ideology of the Taiping movement, including a general survey of its history. Cf. the author's article of the same title in *Far Eastern Quarterly,* X (1950–51), 115-124.

625

Meadows, Thomas Taylor. *The Chinese and Their Rebellions.* Stanford: Academic Reprints, 1953. An analytical account of the early history of the Taiping Rebellion by a well-informed and unusually perceptive Englishman, based on his first-hand experience in China in the 1850's; originally published in 1856. Cf. John K. Fairbanks "Meadows on China: a Centennial Review," *Far Eastern Quarterly,* XIV (1954–55), 365-371.

626

Lindley, Augustus ("Lin-le"). *Ti-Ping Tien-Kwoh; the History of the Ti-Ping Revolution.* 2 vols. London: Day and Son, 1866. A contemporary, highly sympathetic account of the Taiping Rebellion, coupled with a denunciation of British intervention against it, by an Englishman who served in the Taiping forces from 1860 to 1864; remains one of the best sources on the customs and personalities of the Taiping movement.

627

Callery, J. M. and Melchior Yvan. *History of the Insurrection in China,* trans. by John Oxenford. New York: Harper, 1853. A chronicle of the Taiping Rebellion through 1852 by two staff members of the French embassy in China; a basic source.

628

Abend, Hallett E. *The God From the West.* Garden City, N.Y.: Doubleday, 1947. A popular biography of Frederick Townsend Ward, an American who founded the anti-Taiping "Ever Victorious Army" in Shanghai and led it successfully for two years until fatally wounded in 1862.

629

Gregory, John S. "British Intervention Against the Taiping Rebellion," *Journal of Asian Studies,* XIX (1959–60), 11-24. A modern reappraisal of British motives for helping to suppress the Taiping Rebellion, suggesting that British policy was less cynical and imperialistic than is usually indicated in historical interpretations.

630

Michael, Franz. "Military Organization and Power Structure of China During the Taiping Rebellion," *Pacific Historical Review,* XVIII (1949), 469-483. On the shift from centralism to regionalism in Chinese administrative organization that resulted from efforts to suppress the Taiping Rebellion.

631

Laai, Yi-faai. "River Strategy: a Phase of the Taiping's Military Development," *Oriens,* X (1952), 302–329.

632

Yap, P. M. "The Mental Illness of Hung Hsiu-ch'üan, Leader of the Taiping Rebellion," *Far Eastern Quarterly,* XIII (1953–54), 287-304. A psychiatrist's evaluation of the visions that made a failed examination candidate into a great pseudo-Christian revolutionary leader.

633

Wilhelm, Hellmut. "The Background of Tseng Kuo-fan's Ideology," *Asiatische Studien,* III (1949), 90-100. On the moral and political revitalization of Confucianism in the mid-19th century.

634

So Kwan-wai, E. P. Boardman, and Ch'iu P'ing. "Hung Jen-kan, Taiping Prime Minister, 1859–1864," *Harvard Journal of Asian Studies,* XX (1957), 262-294. On the most Westernized Taiping leader, an advocate of economic change and industrial development.

635

Shih, Vincent Y. C. "The Ideology of the Taiping T'ien Kuo," *Sinologica*, III (1951), 1-15. A brief analytical evaluation of the revolutionary religious, moral, socioeconomic, political, and military programs of the Taiping movement.

636

Shih, Vincent Y. C. "Interpretations of the Taiping T'ien-Kuo by Noncommunist Chinese Writers," *Far Eastern Quarterly*, X (1950–51), 248-256. On the range of modern interpretations, from the Taiping as a traditional peasant revolt to the Taiping as a proto-communist social revolution.

637

Wu, James T. K. "The Impact of the Taiping Rebellion Upon the Manchu Fiscal System," *Pacific Historical Review*, XIX (1950), 265-275. On the financial aspects of the development of regional autonomy in Chinese administration during the era of the Taiping Rebellion.

638

Hsia Nai. "The Land Tax in the Yangtze Provinces before and after the Taiping Rebellion," in *Chinese Social History* (E-tu Zen Sun and John de Francis, ed.; Washington: American Council of Learned Societies, 1956), pp. 361-382. On fiscal abuses before, and fiscal reforms after, the great mid-century rebellion.

639

Boulger, Demetrius C. *Life of Gordon*. 2 vols. London: Unwin, 1896. A standard, authorized biography of Charles George Gordon ("Chinese Gordon"), who commanded the "Ever-victorious Army" that helped the Manchu government suppress the Taiping Rebellion; only vol. 1 deals with his career in China.

Other rebellions and reforms

640

Chiang Siang-tseh. *The Nien Rebellion*. Seattle: University of Washington Press, 1954. A thorough analysis of the history and character of a rebel movement that ravaged North China from 1853 to 1868, sometimes in cooperation with the Taiping Rebellion, and of the Ch'ing government's difficulties in exterminating it.

641

Bales, William L. *Tso Tsung-t'ang*. Shanghai: Kelly and Walsh, 1937. A standard biography of one of China's greatest generals, especially noted for his reconquest of Sinkiang in the 1870's from Moslem rebels.

642

Fairbank, John King. "Patterns behind the Tientsin Massacre," *Harvard Journal of Asiatic Studies*, XX (1957), 480-511. An interpretive analysis of Chinese-Western, and especially gentry-missionary, frictions that lay behind an anti-Christian outburst in 1870.

643

Chu Wen-djang. "The Immediate Cause of the Moslem Rebellion in North-west China in 1862," *Central Asiatic Journal*, III (1958), 309-316. Attributes the beginning of a great revolt to a quarrel between some Moslems and some Chinese over the purchase of bamboo poles.

644

Broomhall, Marshall. *Islam in China: a Neglected Problem*. London: Morgan and Scott, 1910. Pp. 123-163 give a detailed account of the mid-century Moslem uprisings against the Manchus in Yunnan and Central Asia.

645

Chang Ch'u (Djang Chu). "War and Diplomacy over Ili," *Chinese Social and Political Science Review*, XX (1936–37), 369-392. Includes much data on the mid-century Moslem rebellion of Yakoob Beg in Central Asia.

*   *   *

646

Cameron, Meribeth E. *The Reform Movement in China, 1898–1912*. Stanford: Stanford University Press, 1931. (Stanford University Publications, University Series: History, Economics, and Political Science, vol. III, no. 1). An authoritative scholarly analysis of the 1898 efforts by K'ang Yu-wei and others to modernize the Chi'ing government and of subsequent constitution-making and army-building undertakings of the empress dowager Tz'u-hsi.

647

Powell, Ralph. *The Rise of Chinese Military Power, 1895–1912*. Princeton: Princeton University Press, 1955. A detailed analysis of the military reforms undertaken and accomplished during the last years of the Manchu empire, especially by such leaders as Chang Chih-tung and Yüan Shih-k'ai.

648

Levenson, Joseph R. *Confucian China and its Modern Fate: The Problem of Intellectual Continuity*. Berkeley: University of California Press, 1958. Highly interpretive essays on China's intellectual history under the impact of the West, with special emphasis on reform movements of the late Ch'ing decades.

649

Thompson, L. G. (trans.) *Ta T'ung Shu: The One-World Philosophy of K'ang Yu-wei*. London: Allen and Unwin, 1958. Includes a useful introduction on the life of the great 1898 reformer.

650

Chang Chih-tung. *China's Only Hope*, trans. by S. I. Woodbridge. New York: Young People's Missionary Movement, 1907. A prescription for China's domestic and foreign ills originally published in 1898 by one of the most influential late Ch'ing officials, an advocate of gradual reform.

651

Hsiao Kung-chuan. "Weng T'ung-ho and the Reform Movement of 1898," *Tsing Hua Journal of Chinese Studies*, I (1957), 111-243. A detailed, authoritative analysis of reasons for the failure of the 1898 reforms attempted by K'ang Yu-wei and others, focused on the role of a high minister who was one of the reform program's early sponsors.

652

Ho Ping-ti. "Weng T'ung-ho and the 'One Hundred Days of Reform'," *Far Eastern Quarterly*, X (1950–51), 125-135. On the controversial role played by a high minister in the 1898 reform movement of K'ang Yu-wei and others.

*   *   *

653

Tan, Chester C. *The Boxer Catastrophe*. New York: Columbia University Press, 1955. An authoritative study of the background, the origins, the progress, and the consequences of the anti-Western Boxer Rebellion of 1900.

654

Fleming, Peter. *The Siege at Peking*. New York: Harper, 1959. A lively popular account of the assault on the foreign legations during the Boxer Rebellion of 1900.

655

Wu Yung. *The Flight of an Empress*. London: Faber and Faber, 1937. The memoirs of a traditional Chinese official who accompanied the empress dowager Tz'u-hsi in her flight from and return to Peking in 1900-01 in consequence of the Boxer Rebellion, with much data on the empress as a person; in an English rendering by Ida Pruitt.

Foreign relations

656

Maki, John M. (ed.) *Selected Documents: Far Eastern International Relations, 1689–1951*. Seattle: University of Washington Press, 1957. Chaps. 2 and 5-7 provide documentary sources on China's international relations during the 19th century.

657

Walker, Richard L. (ed.) *China and the West: Cultural Collision.* New Haven: Far Eastern Publications, Yale University, 1956. A collection of documentary sources, chaps. 2-4 dealing with 19th century foreign relations.

658

MacNair, Harley F. (ed.) *Modern Chinese History: Selected Readings.* Shanghai: Commercial Press, 1923; reprinted in 2 vols., Taipei: Commercial Press, 1957. A compendium of sources on China's international relations from the early 1800's into the 1920's.

659

MacMurray, John V. A. (ed.) *Treaties and Agreements With and Concerning China.* Vol. I. New York: Oxford University Press, 1921. A monumental sourcebook on China's foreign relations from 1894 to 1911.

* * *

660

Fairbank, John King. *Trade and Diplomacy on the China Coast.* 2 vols. Cambridge: Harvard University Press, 1953. A detailed, authoritative analysis of the establishment of the "Treaty Port system" between 1842 and 1854.

661

Hsü, Immanuel C. Y. *China's Entrance into the Family of Nations: the Diplomatic Phase, 1858–1880.* Cambridge: Harvard University Press, 1960. (Harvard East Asian Studies, 5). A general survey of the first establishment of foreign legations in Peking and of Chinese legations abroad; with a useful appendix listing all major Chinese and foreign diplomatic appointees.

662

Morse, Hosea Ballou. *The International Relations of the Chinese Empire.* 3 vols. London: Longmans, Green, 1910–18. The standard reference for China's relations with the modern Western powers up to the fall of the Ch'ing dynasty.

663

Allen, G. C. and Audrey G. Donnithorne. *Western Enterprise in Far Eastern Economic Development: China and Japan.* London: Allen and Unwin, 1954. On the impact of foreign merchants, engineers, and financiers on Chinese economic practices and developments in the 19th and 20th centuries.

664

Langer, William L. *The Diplomacy of Imperialism, 1890–1902.* 2 vols. New York: Knopf, 1935. A standard, detailed reference on European diplomacy, with special reference to China's international relations from the Sino-Japanese war of 1894–95 through the Boxer Rebellion of 1900.

665

Fairbank, John K. "Synarchy under the Treaties," in *Chinese Thought and Institutions* (J. K. Fairbank, ed.; Chicago: University of Chicago Press, 1957), pp. 204-231. On foreign participation in Chinese government under the "Treaty Port system" and its gradual decline with the rise of Chinese nationalism.

666

Biggerstaff, Knight. "Secret Correspondence of 1867–1868: Views of Leading Chinese Statesmen Regarding the Further Opening of China to Western Influence," *Journal of Modern History*, XXII (1950), 122-136. An analysis of views presented to the Tsung-li yamen (China's foreign office) by Tseng Kuo-fan, Tso Tsung-t'ang, Li Hung-chang and others; emphasizes the ignorance of the world that they display.

667

Morse, Hosea Ballou. *The Trade and Administration of China.* 3d rev. ed. London: Longmans, Green, 1920. A standard descriptive and statistical account of the fiscal administration, domestic trade, and foreign trade of China; especially useful in reference to the 19th century situation.

668

Hu Sheng. *Imperialism and Chinese Politics, 1840–1925.* Peking: Foreign Languages Press, 1955. A Marxist interpretation of imperialist aggression against China and of Chinese "tools" of foreign impeerialism.

* * *

669

Waley, Arthur. *The Opium War Through Chinese Eyes.* London: Allen and Unwin, 1958. A collection of anecdotal material about the Opium War from an unofficial point of view and mostly from Chinese diaries, autobiographies, etc.; with special reference to the era of Lin Tse-hsü, the famous "opium commissioner" at Canton whose confiscation of foreign opium stores precipitated the war.

670

Kuo Pin-chia. *A Critical Study of the First Anglo-Chinese War.* Shanghai: Commercial Press, 1935. A standard reference on the causes and progress of the Opium War, based on Chinese sources.

671

Teng Ssu-yü. *Chang Hsi and the Treaty of Nanking, 1842.* Chicago: University of Chicago Press, 1944. Analysis of a participant's behind-the-scenes account of the Chinese-British negotiations that terminated the Opium War, incorporating an annotated translation of his *Fu-i jih-chi;* with an excellent annotated bibliography on the Opium War.

672

Collis, Maurice. *Foreign Mud.* New York: Knopf, 1947. A popular but generally reliable account of the opium trade at Canton in the 1830's and the consequent Opium War between China and Britain, 1839–42.

673

Wright, Stanley F. *Hart and the Chinese Customs.* Belfast: Mullan, 1950. A monumental compendium of data about the development of China's foreign-controlled customs service from the 1850's until the end of the Manchu empire — one of the most remarkable aspects of synarchy, or Chinese-foreign cooperation in Chinese administration. Written by a former Chinese customs commissioner, the book focuses on the career of Sir Robert Hart (1835–1911), long-time Inspector General of Customs and a prime mover in the introduction of Western administrative techniques into China.

674

Fox, Grace E. *British Admirals and Chinese Pirates, 1832–1869.* London: Kegan Paul, 1940. A history of British naval activities along the China coast from 1832 to 1869, based principally on files of the British Admiralty; with many statistical appendices.

675

Smith, David Bonner and E. W. R. Lumby. *The Second China War, 1856–1860.* London: Navy Records Society, 1954. A documentary history, based on official British records.

676

Sun, E-tu Zen. *Chinese Railways and British Interests, 1898–1911.* New York: King's Crown Press, 1954. A case study of China's difficulties in dealing with financial and commercial pressures from abroad.

677

Pelcovits, Nathan A. *Old China Hands and the Foreign Office.* New York: Institute of Pacific Relations, 1948. On the conflict between mercantile and diplomatic views in shaping Britain's 19th century policy toward China.

678

Lamb, Alistair. *Britain and Chinese Central Asia.* London: Kegan Paul, 1960. A detailed history of Chinese-British-Russian relations in Sinkiang and Tibet from 1767 to 1905.

679

Endacott, G. B. *A History of Hong Kong*. London: Oxford University Press, 1958. Emphasizes 19th century developments from the point of view of the English Governors.

680

Fleming, Peter. *Bayonets to Lhasa*. New York: Harper, 1961. A popular but generally reliable study of England's Younghusband expedition into Tibet in 1904.

681

Nolde, John J. "The 'False Edict' of 1849," *Journal of Asian Studies*, XX (1960–61), 299-315. On a Chinese-British controversy over the right of foreigners to reside at Canton and how a Chinese official bluffed the British into a diplomatic defeat.

682

Lubbock, Basil. *The Opium Clippers*. Boston: Lauriat, 1933. A rambling, romanticized compendium of data about the foreign trade along the China coast from the 1820's into the 1860's, with special reference to the opium trade from India; with many illustrations from drawings.

683

Hunter, William C. *The 'Fan Kwae' at Canton before Treaty Days, 1825–1844, by an Old Resident*. Shanghai: Kelly and Walsh, 1911. An entertaining eyewitness account of the life and tribulations of the foreign settlement at Canton up to the Opium War.

684

Ouchterlony, John. *The Chinese War*. 2d ed. London: Saunders and Otley, 1844. A detailed report by a participant of British military activities during the Opium War, 1839–42, with many illustrations drawn by the author.

* * *

685

Swisher, Earl (trans.). *China's Management of the American Barbarians*. New Haven: Far Eastern Publications, Yale University, 1953. (Monographs of the Far Eastern Association, 2.) A voluminous compendium of selections about Chinese-American relations, 1841–61, from *Ch'ou-pan i-wu shih-mo*, the official Chinese record of foreign affairs; with abundant introductory material.

686

Dulles, Foster Rhea. *China and America*. Princeton: Princeton University Press, 1946. Chaps. 1-8 deal with the 19th century; a good general survey.

687

Pressman, Harvey. "Hay, Rockhill, and China's Integrity: A Reappraisal," *Papers on China* (Harvard University Center for East Asian Studies), XIII (1959), 61-79. On the background and evolution of the American Open Door Policy toward China, enunciated in 1899.

688

Vevier, Charles. "The Open Door: an Idea in Action, 1906–1913," *Pacific Historical Review*, XXIV (1955), 49-62. A reappraisal of American policy toward China from John Hay to Woodrow Wilson, suggesting that the "open door" idea was used "to justify an attempt at American financial supremacy in China and Manchuria."

689

Dennett, Tyler. *Americans in Eastern Asia*. New York: Macmillan, 1922; reprinted New York: Barnes and Noble, 1941. A standard reference on official American policies toward and relations with China (and Korea and Japan) during the 19th century; thorough, detailed, and documented.

690

Clyde, Paul H. (ed.) *United States Policy toward China*. Durham, N.C.: Duke University Press, 1940. A collection of documents concerning American policy toward China from 1839 to 1939, principally of the 19th century.

691

Christy, Arthur (ed.). *The Asian Legacy and American Life*. New York: John Day, 1945. Ten essays on Chinese and other Asian contributions to American (and, in general, Western) life — in art, in agriculture, in literature, in religion, etc.

692

Campbell, Charles S., Jr. *Special Business Interests and the Open Door Policy*. New Haven: Yale University Press, 1951. (Yale Historical Publications, 53.) A monographic analysis of the American commercial pressures that played a role in developing the "Open Door" policy statements of 1899.

693

La Fargue, Thomas E. *China's First Hundred*. Pullman: State College of Washington, 1942. On the first group of Chinese students sent to American colleges in the 1870's.

694

Griffin, Eldon. *Clippers and Consuls*. Ann Arbor: Edwards Brothers, 1938. A comprehensive, thoroughly documented report of American trade and consular activities in East Asia from 1845 to 1860, especially emphasizing the China trade.

695

Lubbock, Basil. *The China Clippers*. Glasgow: Brown, 1922. A rambling, romanticized history of the American clipper ships sailing to China from the 1850s to the 1870's.

696

Yung Wing. *My Life in China and America*. New York: Holt, 1909. The autobiography of China's first American-trained college graduate (B.A. Yale, 1854), who organized a government-sponsored effort to educate Chinese in the United States during the 1870's.

* * *

697

Nelson, M. Frederick. *Korea and the Old Orders in Eastern Asia*. Baton Rouge: Louisiana State University Press, 1945. Includes an analysis of Chinese-Japanese-Korean relations in the 19th century.

698

Lin, T. C. "Li Hung-chang: His Korean Policies, 1870–1885," *Chinese Social and Political Science Review*, XIX (1935–36), 202-233. On the early stage of modern Chinese-Japanese rivalries in Korea.

699

Clyde, Paul Hibbert. *International Rivalries in Manchuria*. 2d ed. rev. Columbus: Ohio State University Press, 1928. A standard reference on Chinese-Japanese-Russian relations in Manchuria from 1894 to 1922.

700

Rockhill, William W. *China's Intercourse with Korea from the Fifteenth Century to 1895*. London: Luzac, 1905. A standard reference, with a detailed narrative of the Sino-Japanese War of 1894–95.

* * *

701

Malenzemoff, Andrew. *Russian Far Eastern Policy, 1881–1904*. Berkeley: University of California Press, 1958. A detailed study of Russo-Japanese rivalries in Korea and Manchuria.

702

Dallin, David J. *The Rise of Russia in Asia*. New Haven: Yale University Press, 1949. Includes a survey of Russian-Chinese relations from the mid-1800's up to 1931.

703

Wu, Aitchen K. *China and the Soviet Union*. New York: John Day, 1950. Part 1 provides a thorough general survey of Chinese-Russian relations in Manchu times.

704

Chang Ch'u (Djang Chu). "War and Diplomacy over Ili," *Chinese Social and Political Science Review*, XX (1936–37), 369-392. On Russian penetration of Eastern Asia, the mid-century Moslem rebellion of Yakoob Beg, and Chinese-Russian rivalries in Sinkiang.

THE NATIONALIST ERA, 1912-

The 20th century effort to create a modern Chinese republic, following the collapse of the old regime in 1911–12, has been hampered by successive confrontations of antagonistic, divisive forces. The Ch'ing empire was overthrown by idealistic republican revolutionaries led by Sun Yat-sen, and their Kuomintang or Nationalist Party was for a decade the only group in China that had a reasonably promising program for progress. But Sun, until his death in 1925, was frustrated by having no military power. Warlords stole the fruits of the revolution from him, and the Peking government that they established won international recognition and support. These events sowed the seeds of despair among many Chinese about the suitability for China of Western-style republicanism. The international debacle of World War I, and particularly its diplomatic consequences, added to the Chinese disillusionment. Genuinely popular nationalistic agitation exploded in the "May 4th Movement" of 1919, and the consequent intellectual ferment spawned the formation of a Chinese Communist Party in 1921. It also revitalized the Kuomintang, which set up a precarious regional government of its own at Canton and undertook to militarize itself. To this end, beginning in 1923, it collaborated with the Chinese Communist Party and welcomed Comintern advisers. In 1926, under Sun's disciple Chiang Kai-shek, Nationalist forces began a successful march to the north that toppled the stagnant Peking administration in 1927. Chiang broke up the Kuomintang-Communist alliance and crushed subsequent Communist Party efforts at armed subversion. A new national government at Nanking inaugurated a broad program of modernization and industrialization. But Japan interfered, first by occupying the Manchurian provinces in 1931 and then by mounting a campaign to subjugate all China in 1937. Chiang Kai-shek became a symbol of national resistance; even the Communist Party joined the Kuomintang in a nominal and mutually-distrustful united front. But Nationalist forces had to fall back ever farther southward and westward. Despite help from world allies during the latter years of the war, Nationalist Party morale and effectiveness steadily deteriorated. Meantime, the Chinese Communist Party gained much ground and sympathy by effective guerrilla activity, and the defeat of Japan by allied powers in 1945 brought with peace the danger of rampant civil war in China. Efforts by the United States to bring about a new Kuomintang-Communist accord failed, and civil war began in 1948. Nationalist forces again fell back, and finally in 1949 the Nationalist government abandoned the mainland and settled in a prearranged sanctuary, the island of Formosa. There Chiang Kai-shek maintained the semblance of a national government, effected economic and administrative reforms, rebuilt Nationalist military strength with American aid, and waited for an opportunity to resume the Kuomintang program on the mainland.

Introductory references

705
Clyde, Paul H. *The Far East.* 3d ed. Englewood Cliffs, N.J.: Prentice-Hall, 1958.

706
Michael, Franz H. and George E. Taylor. *The Far East in the Modern World.* New York: Holt, 1956.

707
Vinacke, Harold M. *A History of the Far East in Modern Times.* 6th ed. New York: Appleton-Century-Crofts, 1959.

708
MacNair, Harley F. and Donald F. Lach. *Modern Far Eastern International Relations.* 2d ed. New York: Van Nostrand, 1955.

709
Latourette, Kenneth Scott. *A Short History of the Far East.* Rev. ed. New York: Macmillan, 1951.

710
Cameron, Meribeth E. and others. *China, Japan and the Powers.* New York: Ronald Press, 1952.

711
Buss, Claude. *The Far East.* New York: Macmillan, 1955.

712
Peffer, Nathaniel. *The Far East.* Ann Arbor: University of Michigan Press, 1958.

713
Greene, Fred. *The Far East.* New York: Rinehart, 1957.

714
Crofts, Alfred and Percy Buchanan. *A History of the Far East.* New York: Longmans, Green, 1958.

General

715
Boorman, Howard L. (ed.) *Men and Politics in Modern China: Preliminary 50 Biographies.* New York: Columbia University, 1960. A preliminary selection from a comprehensive biographical dictionary of 20th century China being prepared by the Columbia University Modern China Project.

716
Perleberg, Max. *Who's Who in Modern China.* Hong Kong: Ye Olde Printerie, 1954. More than 2000 brief biographical notes on people active in China's public affairs from 1911 through 1953, with many useful appendices including histories of the political parties, etc.

717
Fairbank, John K. and Liu Kwang-ching. *Modern China: A Bibliographical Guide to Chinese Works, 1898–1937.* Cambridge: Harvard University Press, 1950. (Harvard-Yenching Institute Studies, I.) A voluminous, annotated, classified list of important books and periodicals in the Chinese language; an indispensable reference for the serious student.

718
China Year Book, ed. by H. G. W. Woodhead. 20 vols. 1912–1939. An irregular yearbook of historical information and statistical data published in New York until 1919, in Tientsin until 1929, and by the North China Daily News in Shanghai until its termination; a useful reference of the almanac sort.

719

Journal of the North China Branch, Royal Asiatic Society. 1858-1948. Published quarterly in Shanghai; a good source for contemporary views and reports on republican China.

720

Chinese Social and Political Science Review. 1916-37. Published quarterly by the Chinese Social and Political Science Association; a good source for contemporary views and reports on republican China.

721

Papers on China. Cambridge: Harvard University Committee on Regional Studies (since 1957, Center for East Asian Studies), 1947-. An annual collection of Harvard seminar papers, mimeographed for private distribution; contain many excellent studies of the republican era.

* * *

722

Latourette, Kenneth Scott. *A History of Modern China.* London: Penguin Books, 1954. A dispassionate resumé of 20th century history in the setting of its historical and cultural background; a good factual introduction, abstaining from interpretive analyses.

723

Fairbank, John King. *The United States and China.* Rev. ed. Cambridge: Harverd University Press, 1958. A standard introductory reference on modern China, including an analysis of the history, the institutions, and the international relations of the republican period.

724

Rowe, David Nelson. *Modern China: A Brief History.* Princeton: Van Nostrand, 1959. A paperbound resumé of 20th century history, with numerous documentary appendices; condemns both American policy in the 1940's and the Chinese communist movement.

725

Latourette, Kenneth Scott. *The Chinese, Their History and Culture.* 3d ed. rev. New York: Macmillan, 1946. Chap. 12 surveys 20th century history up into World War II.

726

Linebarger, Paul M.A., Djang Chu, and Ardath W. Burks. *Far Eastern Governments and Politics: China and Japan.* 2d ed. Princeton: Van Nostrand, 1956. Chaps. 6-7 provide authoritative discussions of political life in mainland China from 1912 to 1949.

727

Levenson, Joseph R. *Confucian China and Its Modern Fate: The Problem of Intellectual Continuity.* Berkeley: University of California Press, 1958. Highly interpretive essays on China's intellectual history under the impact of the West, noting the rise of nationalism and, later, the appeal of communism.

728

Hughes, E. R. *The Invasion of China by the Western World.* New York: Macmillan, 1938. A general, authoritative analysis of the impact of Western ideas and techniques on Chinese life during the 19th and, especially, the early 20th century; emphasizes intellectual concerns.

729

Ch'ien Tuan-sheng. *The Government and Politics of China.* Cambridge: Harvard University Press, 1950. Provides a detailed analysis of political life during the republican era; very critical of the nationalist leadership.

730

Michael, Franz. "The Fall of China," *World Politics,* VIII (1955-56), 296-306. A general interpretive survey of China's modern history, from imperial times to the communist conquest, emphasizing the role of the Soviet Union in undermining the nationalist government and the binding ties between communist China and the U.S.S.R.; a review of recent literature.

731

Holcombe, Arthur N. *The Spirit of the Chinese Revolution.* New York: Knopf, 1930. An analysis of the democratic, communist, Christian, militaristic, capitalistic, and scientific aspects of the broad social revolution in China during the 1920's.

732

De Francis, John. *Nationalism and Language Reform in China.* Princeton: Princeton University Press, 1950. A history of efforts to alphabetize Chinese writing, with good discussions of the political implications and difficulties of the movement in the 20th century.

* * *

733

Stuart, John Leighton. *Fifty Years in China.* New York: Random House, 1954. The memoirs of an American educational missionary who was the organizer and president of Yenching University of Peking from 1918 through 1941 and U. S. ambassador to China from 1946 to 1952.

734

Powell, John B. *My Twenty-five Years in China.* New York: Macmillan, 1945. Autobiographical account by the editor of the *China Weekly Review* of Shanghai, covering the period from 1917 into World War II; with many valuable sidelights on Chinese public affairs.

735

Gale, Esson M. *Salt for the Dragon.* East Lansing: Michigan State College Press, 1953. The autobiography of an American who lived in China, with some interruptions, from 1908 to 1945, chiefly as a foreign official of China's salt revenue administration.

736

Sues, Ilona Ralf. *Shark's Fins and Millet.* Garden City, N. Y.: Garden City Publishing Co., 1945. A Swiss woman's highly personal and anecdotal account of her experiences in China from the early 1930's into the late 1930's as a League of Nations representative, moving in the highest circles of both nationalist and communist areas.

737

Chao, Buwei Yang. *Autobiography of a Chinese Woman,* rendered in English by Yuenren Chao. New York: John Day, 1947. An intensely personal account of life among China's intellectuals in the 20th century, by the wife of an eminent Chinese linguist.

738

Hume, Edward H. *Doctors East, Doctors West.* New York: Norton, 1946. Autobiography of an American medical missionary in Central China, 1905-26.

739

Chiang Monlin. *Tides From the West.* New Haven: Yale University Press, 1947. The autobiography of a distinguished Chinese educator-official who has been Minister of Education and chairman of the Joint Committee on Rural Reconstruction; a reference for Kuomintang history from the revolution into World War II.

740

Gould, Randall. *China in the Sun.* Garden City, N. Y.: Doubleday, 1946. A Shanghai editor's account of his experiences in China from the 1920's through World War II, including useful sidelights on many public affairs and a sympathetic appraisal of nationalist China's plans and problems at the end of the war. Notable in that it pays little attention to the post-war communist problem.

741

Dunlap, Albert M. *Behind the Iron Curtain.* Washington: Public Affairs Press, 1956. The journal of an American doctor who spent 40 years in Peking and Shanghai from early republican days until the communist conquest, with comments on important events.

The Warlord era

742

Li Chien-nung. *The Political History of China, 1840–1928,* trans. by Teng Ssu-yü and Jeremy Ingalls. Princeton: Van Nostrand, 1956. The most detailed, authoritative narrative now available, written in 1948 as a textbook for Chinese college students; incorporates many important documents.

743

MacNair, Harley Farnsworth. *China in Revolution.* Chicago: University of Chicago Press, 1931. A well-informed political history of China from 1911 to 1931.

744

Houn, Franklin W. *Central Government of China, 1912–1928.* Madison: University of Wisconsin Press, 1957. A detailed, scholarly analysis of the organization and operations of the Peking government from Yüan Shih-k'ai's time until the Kuomintang's conquest of North China; a valuable study of the little-known warlord period of republican development.

745

Powell, Ralph L. *The Rise of Chinese Military Power, 1895–1912.* Princeton: Princeton University Press, 1955. A thorough analysis of attempts to modernize China's military forces during the last Ch'ing dynasty years; especially valuable for its data on the early career of Yüan Shih-k'ai and as background for understanding the rise of warlordism in 20th century China.

746

Gillin, Donald G. "Portrait of a Warlord: Yen Hsi-shan in Shansi Province, 1911–1930," *Journal of Asian Studies,* XIX (1959–60), 289-306. A critical analysis and evaluation of the career and reform policies of one of the most progressive of the military governors who dominated North China prior to the unification under Chiang Kai-shek.

747

Weisshart, Herbert. "Feng Yü-hsiang: His Rise as a Militarist and His Training Programs," *Papers on China,* VI (Cambridge: Harvard University Committee on International and Regional Studies, 1952; privately distributed), 75-111. A seminar paper on the "Christian general" who was one of the dominant warlords of North China in the 1920's and on his social reforms.

748

Iriye Akira. "Chang Hsüeh-liang and the Japanese," *Journal of Asian Studies,* XX (1960–61), 33-43. An analysis of the political calculations that brought subordination of the Manchurian provinces to the nationalist government in 1928.

749

Levenson, Joseph R. *Liang Ch'i-ch'ao and the Mind of Modern China.* Cambridge: Harvard University Press, 1953. A critical biography of a progressive thinker and propagandist who was a dominant influence in intelleclectual currents of the early 20th century decades.

750

The Sino-Japanese Negotiations of 1915; Japanese and Chinese Documents and Chinese Official Statement. Washington: Carnegie Endowment for International Peace, 1921. Translations of both Japanese and Chinese official texts relating to Japan's "21 demands," an attempt during World War I to establish a Japanese protectorate over much of China.

751

Bland, J. O. P. *China, Japan and Korea.* New York: Scribner, 1921. Includes much authoritative information on China in the time of Yüan Shih-k'ai.

752

Bland, J. O. P. *Recent Events and Present Policies in China.* London: Heinemann, 1912. A well-informed eyewitness account of the collapse of the Manchu regime and the establishment of the first republican government in 1911–12, with many photographic illustrations.

753

Johnston, Reginald F. *Twilight in the Forbidden City.* London: Appleton-Century, 1934. An intimate account of the life of the Manchu imperial family from the time of the 1911 revolution until its final expulsion from the Peking palace in 1924, with much relevance to political developments of the area; by an Englishman who served as tutor and confidant of the last emperor, P'u-yi, throughout the "Twilight" period.

* * *

754

Chow Tse-tsung. *The May Fourth Movement: Intellectual Revolution in Modern China.* 2 vols. Cambridge: Harvard University Press, 1960. A detailed analysis of philosophical, literary, and socio-political ferment in early republican China, leading to and spreading from 1919 demonstrations against the Versailles Treaty negotiations. Cf. the review article by J. R. Levenson, "The Day Confucius Died," in *Journal of Asian Studies,* XX (1960–61), 221-226.

755

Hu Shih. *The Chinese Renaissance.* Chicago: University of Chicago Press, 1934. A good introduction to the intellectual history of the early republican period; an early evaluation of the New Culture Movement that sprang up in the first republican decade, by one of its prime movers.

756

Teng Ssu-yü and John K. Fairbank. *China's Response to the West.* 2 vols. Cambridge: Harvard University Press, 1954. Includes a documentary history of the May 4th Movement of 1919, including its background and its consequences up to 1923.

757

Franke, Wolfgang. *Chinas kulturelle Revolution: die Bewegung vom 4 Mai 1919.* Munich: R. Oldenbourg, 1957. A very brief interpretation, in popular style, of the background, content, and aftermath of the intellectual revolution associated with the May 4th Movement of 1919; by a distinguished Sinologist.

The Kuomintang: leaders and coming to power

758

Jansen, Marius B. *The Japanese and Sun Yat-sen.* Cambridge: Harvard University Press, 1954. (Harvard Historical Monographs, XXVII) An intensive analysis of the support Sun Yat-sen and other Chinese nationalists received from the 1890's to 1917 from Japanese nationalists interested in Asian unity against Western imperialism.

759

Sharman, Lyon. *Sun Yat-sen, His Life and Its Meaning.* New York: John Way, 1934. The standard biography.

760

Chen, Stephen and Robert Payne. *Sun Yat-sen, a Portrait.* New York: John Day, 1934. The standard biography.

761

Hsüeh Chün-tu. "Sun Yat-sen, Yang Ch'ü-yün, and the Early Revolutionary Movement in China," *Journal of Asian Studies,* XIX (1959–60), 307-318. On the competing personalities and the activities of the republican revolutionary group in its earliest days, from 1895 to 1900.

762

Linebarger, Paul. *Sun Yat Sen and the Chinese Republic.* New York: Century, 1925. A biography by an American lawyer who knew Dr. Sun intimately and served the Kuomintang in various advisory and legal capacities from the time of the 1911 revolution; based in part on Dr. Sun's own reminiscences told to the author.

763

Sun Yat-sen. *Memoirs of a Chinese Revolutionary.* Taipei: China Cultural Service, 1953. Dr. Sun's evaluation of the early history and apparent failure of the national revolution, first published in 1918.

764

Sun Yat-sen. *San Min Chu I: The Three Principles of the People,* trans. by F. W. Price, ed. by L. T. Chen. Shanghai: Commercial Press, 1929. The standard English translation of Sun Yat-sen's lectures setting forth the basic Kuomintang doctrines; the canonical statement of principles of the revolutionary party.

765

Hsü, Leonard Shihlien (comp. and trans.). *Sun Yat-sen: His Political and Social Ideals.* Los Angeles: University of Southern California Press, 1933. Translations of *San-min chu-i,* Dr. Sun's autobiography, and other of Dr. Sun's writings which form the Kuomintang canon; with a biography of Dr. Sun by the translator emphasizing the development of his political thinking.

766

Glick, Carl. *Double Ten.* New York: Whittlesey House, 1945. On the support of Chinese in America for Sun Yat-sen's republican revolution, as told by Captain Ansel O'Banion, who trained revolutionary troops in California.

* * *

767

Hahn, Emily. *Chiang Kai-shek.* New York: Doubleday, 1955. A balanced biography of the nationalist generalissimo up to the communist conquest of mainland China; unauthorized, but generally sympathetic.

768

Chiang Kai-shek. *Soviet Russia in China: a Summing-up at Seventy.* New York: Farrar, Straus, and Cudahy, 1957. The nationalist generalissimo's own story of his public life and interpretation of the events of his time, suffused with a determination to reestablish Kuomintang control of mainland China.

769

Hsiung Shih-i. *The Life of Chiang Kai-shek.* London: Davies, 1948. An authorized and very admiring biography.

770

Chiang Kai-shek. *China's Destiny,* trans. by Wang Chung-hui. New York: Macmillan, 1947. The authorized translation of Chiang's diagnosis of modern China's troubles (heaping much blame on the unequal treaties) and his prescriptions for restoring China's power and prosperity, with a sympathetic introduction by Lin Yutang.

771

Chiang Kai-shek. *China's Destiny, and Chinese Economic Theory,* trans. by Philip Jaffe. New York: Roy, 1947. An unauthorized translation of Chiang's evaluation of China's problems and prospects, with an introduction by the translator that is highly critical of the Kuomintang's "reactionary" thinking and practices.

772

Chiang Kai-shek. *The Collected Wartime Messages of Generalissimo Chiang Kai-shek, 1937–1945.* 2 vols. New York: John Day, 1946. Official texts compiled by the Chinese Ministry of Information.

* * *

773

Wright, Mary C. "From Revolution to Restoration: the Transformation of Kuomintang Ideology," *Far Eastern Quarterly,* XIV (1954–55), 515-532. A general interpretation of the Kuomintang's failure in mainland China, suggesting that under Chiang Kai-shek, the once-revolutionary party became an uncompromising, backward-looking defender of traditional Confucian morality and failed to offer any promise of fundamental improvement in the economic lot of the people at large.

774

Liu, F. F. *A Military History of Modern China, 1924–1949.* Princeton: Princeton University Press, 1956. In-

cludes a study of how the Kuomintang developed a party army in the 1920's and used it to establish the nationalist government.

775

North, Robert C. *Kuomintang and Chinese Communist Elites.* Stanford: Stanford University Press, 1952. (Hoover Institute Studies, series B, No. 8) An analysis of the backgrounds and careers of the leaders of both nationalist and communist parties with brief histories of changing currents evidenced in the leadership of the two parties from their origins.

776

MacFarquhar, Roderick L. "The Whampoa Military Academy," *Papers on China,* IX (Cambridge: Harvard University Committee on Regional Studies, 1955; privately distributed), 146-172. A seminar paper on the organization, operation, and influence of "the Kuomintang West Point" in the 1920's.

777

Bertram, James M. *First Act in China.* New York: Viking, 1938. A British journalist's account of the kidnapping of Chiang Kai-shek by his own troops at Sian in December, 1936, and of the Kuomintang-communist negotiations preceding and following his release that led to a united front against Japanese aggression; based on first-hand experience in Sian during the kidnapping incident.

778

Snow, Edgar. *Red Star over China.* Rev. ed. New York: Random House, 1944. A journalist's eyewitness account of the Chinese communist movement in 1936–37, with much data on the kidnapping of Chiang Kai-shek at Sian in 1936 and the communist role in his release; cf. the author's later addenda, *Random Notes on Red China, 1936–1945* (Cambridge: Harvard University Press, 1957) for more material on the Sian incident.

779

Thomson, James C., Jr. "Communist Policy and the United Front in China, 1935–1936," *Papers on China,* XI (Cambridge: Harvard University Center for East Asian Studies, 1957; privately distributed), 99-148. On the kidnapping and release of Chiang Kai-shek in 1936 at Sian, in the light of a policy controversy between the Chinese Communist Party and the Comintern.

780

Selle, Earl Albert. *Donald of China.* New York: Harper, 1948. A journalistic biography of William Henry Donald, an Australian newsman who became an intimate and influential adviser to Sun Yat-sen and Chiang Kai-shek; based on deathbed interviews with Donald and told from his point of view.

781

Hahn, Emily. *The Soong Sisters.* Garden City, N. Y.: Doubleday, 1941. A biographical study, in a popular style and an admiring tone, of Charlie Soong, an American-educated Chinese merchant, and his three remarkable and influential daughters, who became the wives of Sun Yat-sen, Chiang Kai-shek, and H. H. Kung; a reliable if somewhat romanticized depiction of life among the upper classes in republican China.

782

Hsieh Ping-ying. *Autobiography of a Chinese Girl,* trans. by Tsui Chi. London: Allen and Unwin, 1948. The story of a girl soldier in the Kuomintang campaigns against the warlords in the late 1920's.

783

Linebarger, Paul M. A. *The China of Chiang Kai-shek: A Political Study.* Boston: World Peace Foundation, 1941. A detailed, authoritative description of the governmental institutions, ideology, and procedures of the nationalist government during the 1930's, with discussions of the roles of the Kuomintang, the Chinese Communist Party, and Japanese puppet governments.

784

Misselwitz, Henry Francis. *The Dragon Stirs*. New York: Harbinger, 1941. An American journalist's reminiscences about the establishment of Kuomintang control throughout China in 1927–29, difficulties with Chinese communism, and some of the notable Chinese and foreign personalities of the era.

War with Japan and Kuomintang decline
785

Storry, G. R. "The Mukden Incident of September 18-19, 1931," *St. Antony's Papers*, II (London: Chatto and Windus, 1957), 1-12. A reappraisal of the opening of the Sino-Japanese War, based on evidence given at the Tokyo war crimes trials.

786

Ferrell, R. H. "Mukden Incident, September 18-19, 1931," *Journal of Modern History*, XXVII (1955), 66-72. Another reappraisal of the incident that "provoked" Japan to occupy far northeastern China in the first act of World War II, taking into account testimony given at the war-crimes trials in 1946-48.

787

Willoughby, Westel W. *The Sino-Japanese Controversy and the League of Nations*. Baltimore: John Hopkins Press, 1935. A voluminous, semi-documentary history of Japanese aggression in Manchuria and Shanghai in 1931–32 on the basis of the ineffectual League of Nations inquiry; with historical background.

788

Hudson, Manley O. (ed.) *The Verdict of the League: China and Japan in Manchuria*. Boston: World Peace Foundation, 1933. The official text of the League of Nations' denunciation of Japanese aggression in Manchuria, with notes, an introduction, and some appendices.

789

Koo, V. K. Wellington. *Memoranda Presented to the Lytton Commission*. 2 vols. New York: The Chinese Cultural Society, 1932. The official Chinese version and interpretation of Japan's 1931 aggression in Manchuria, presented to the League of Nations' investigatory body; reproduces many documents.

790

Kawakami, K. K. *Manchoukuo, Child of Conflict*. New York: Macmillian, 1933. A Japanese newspaperman's apologia for the Japanese occupation of Manchuria.

791

Young, C. Walter. *Japan's Special Position in Manchuria*. Baltimore: Johns Hopkins Press, 1931. An authoritative study of Japan's economic interests in far northeastern China on the eve of its aggressive occupation; based on field research and approaching the subject in the light of international law. Also see two other, simultaneously-published books by Young, *The International Legal Status of the Kwantung Leased Territory* and *Japanese Jurisdiction in the South Manchuria Railway Areas;* the 3 volumes form a series generally entitled *Japan's Jurisdiction and International Legal Position in Manchuria*.

792

Taylor, George E. *The Struggle for North China*. New York: Institute of Pacific Relations, 1940. An analytical, authoritative history of Japan's encroachment on China's sovereignty in North China from 1937 to 1940, centered on the history of the provisional government at Peking.

793

Wang Ching-chun. *Japan's Continental Adventure*. London: Allen and Unwin, 1940. A survey of the Japanese aggression in China from 1931 to 1939.

794

MacNair, Harley Farnsworth. *The Real Conflict Between China and Japan*. Chicago: University of Chicago Press, 1938. A perceptive and authoritative essay on the underlying ideological and psychological differences that have made Chinese-Japanese relations a recurring problem in the 20th century.

795

Quigley, Harold Scott. *Far Eastern War, 1937–1941*. Boston: World Peace Foundation, 1942. On the progress of Japan's aggression in China up to Pearl Harbor, emphasizing the international negotiations resulting from it rather than its military aspects.

796

Jones, Francis C. *Manchuria since 1931*. London: Royal Institute of International Affairs, 1949. A broad analysis of Japanese policies and problems in occupied Manchuria from 1931 through World War II, with a brief concluding survey of the resumption of Chinese control in postwar years.

797

Bisson, T. A. *Japan in China*. New York: Macmillan, 1938. An interpretive analysis of Japanese aggression in China from 1931 through 1937 and of China's response to it.

*   *   *

798

Liu, F. F. *A Military History of Modern China, 1924–1949*. Princeton: Princeton University Press, 1956. A dispassionate, well-informed study of how Chiang Kai-shek built the Kuomintang's military power, fought the Japanese, and eventually lost the mainland to the communists; suggests that nationalist China was undone by Chiang's loyal reliance upon a clique of often unprogressive and unaggressive officers trained largely by himself in the 1920's.

799

White, Theodore H. and Annalee Jacoby. *Thunder Out of China*. New York: William Sloane Associates, 1946. Probably the single most influential American book about the deterioration of the nationalist government during the last years of World War II; a first-hand report by journalists.

800

Belden, Jack. *China Shakes the World*. New York: Harper, 1949. A journalist's first-hand account of the nationalist-communist civil war from 1946 to 1949, generally sympathetic toward the new regime and rather bitterly contemptuous of the old; a very influential book.

801

Chang, Carsun. *The Third Force in China*. New York: Bookman Associates, 1952. A detailed political history of China from the nationalist revolution of 1911 to the communist conquest of the mainland, concentrating especially on the period of World War II and thereafter; by the organizer and leader of an anti-communist, Kuomintang-persecuted "third force" (the Democratic-Socialist Party) that was active in China from 1931 on. Critical of Chiang Kai-shek, critical in great detail of American wartime and post-war policy toward China, and most especially critical of the Chinese communist movement and the Soviet Union's support of it.

802

Peck, Graham. *Two Kinds of Time*. Boston: Houghton, Mifflin, 1950. An American's highly personal and perceptive account of life in China during World War II; very critical of the Kuomintang.

803

Clubb, O. Edmund. "Chiang Kai-shek's Waterloo: The Battle of the Hwai-Hai," *Pacific Historical Review*, XXV (1956), 389-399. An analysis of the defeat of nationalist troops by the Chinese communists north of Nanking in January, 1949; emphasizes poor generalship and general incompetence on the part of the nationalists.

804

Carlson, Evans Fordyce. *Twin Stars of China*. New York: Dodd, Mead, 1941. A first-hand account by a U.S. Marine officer of China's struggle with Japan in the early years of World War II, including observations of both the nationalist and the communist efforts; highly personal, with many photographic illustrations.

805

Epstein, Israel. *The Unfinished Revolution in China.* Boston: Little, Brown, 1947. A journalist's analytical study of China in wartime and during the post-World War II civil war; highly disapproving of the Kuomintang and American policy toward China.

806

Rowe, David Nelson. *China Among the Powers.* New York: Harcourt, Brace, 1945. A general appraisal of China's political and economic situation at the end of World War II and of its prospects in the world community.

807

Rosinger, Lawrence K. *China's Wartime Politics, 1937–1944.* Princeton: Princeton University Press, 1944. On changes in political organization, personnel, and policies; with some documentary appendices.

Sino-American relations to 1949

808

Griswold, A. Whitney. *The Far Eastern Policy of the United States.* New York: Harcourt, Brace, 1938. A standard, authoritative history of American policy toward China and other Far Eastern countries in the 20th century up to the mid-1930's; a basic reference.

809

Clyde, Paul H. (ed.) *United States Policy toward China.* Durham, N.C.: Duke University Press, 1940. A collection of documents; chaps. 36-43 represent the pre-nationalist republican period, chaps. 44-46 the American response to Japanese aggression in China up to 1939.

810

Dulles, Foster Rhea. *China and America.* Princeton: Princeton University Press, 1946. A good general survey; chaps. 9-18 deal with the 20th century.

811

Fifield, Russell H. *Woodrow Wilson and the Far East.* New York: Crowell, 1952. A detailed, authoritative study of the special claims on Manchuria that Japan advanced during World War I and of the role of American diplomacy in handling "the Shantung question."

812

Borg, Dorothy. *American Policy and the Chinese Revolution, 1925–1928.* New York: Institute of Pacific Relations, 1947. A detailed monographic study, emphasizing diplomatic activity as well as policy, and congressional and editorial opinion.

813

Christopher, James W. *Conflict in the Far East.* Leiden: E. J. Brill, 1950. A reappraisal, in rather emotional and condemnatory terms, of America's diplomatic role in the early stages of the Sino-Japanese conflict, from 1928 to 1933.

814

Curry, Roy Watson. *Woodrow Wilson and Far Eastern Policy, 1913–1921.* New York: Bookman Associates, 1957. A sympathetic, scholarly study of Wilson's difficulties.

815

Hull, Cordell. *The Memoirs of Cordell Hull.* 2 vols. New York: Macmillan, 1948. An invaluable source on American policies and attitudes toward China from 1933 through World War II.

* * *

816

Stilwell, Joseph W. *The Stilwell Papers.* New York: Sloane, 1948. The personal diary of the controversial, bitterly outspoken American commander of the Chinese war theater from early 1942 to late 1944; very uncompli-

mentary to the Chinese in general and to Chiang Kai-shek in particular.

817

Romanus, Charles F. and R. Sunderland. *Stilwell's Mission to China* and *Stilwell's Command Problems.* Washington: Department of the Army, 1953 and 1956. Official military histories of "Vinegar Joe" Stilwell's controversy-burdened service as chief of staff for Chiang Kai-shek, 1942–44.

818

Chennault, Claire L. *Way of a Fighter: the Memoirs of Claire Lee Chennault.* New York: Putnam, 1949. Highly personal account of the organization and activities of the Flying Tigers (later the U.S. 14th Air Force) in support of China's war against Japanese aggression; especially bitter toward General Stilwell.

* * *

819

Feis, Herbert. *The China Tangle.* Princeton: Princeton University Press, 1953. A balanced, remarkably dispassionate analysis of "The American Effort in China from Pearl Harbor to the Marshall Mission" (subtitle); a standard reference on Sino-American relations at a critical time.

820

United States Department of State. *United States Relations with China.* Washington: 1949. (Department of State Publication 3573.) The famous American "white paper" on China: a voluminous documentary history of official American relations with China, especially during World War II and up to 1949; a justification of the U.S. government's decision not to intervene against the ever more powerful Chinese communist movement.

821

Latourette, Kenneth Scott. *The American Record in the Far East, 1945–1951.* New York: Macmillan, 1952. A dispassionate, neutral account of United States relations with China from the end of World War II through the beginning of the Korean War.

822

Utley, Freda. *The China Story.* Chicago: Regnery, 1951. An angry denunciation of communist influence on American policy toward China during and after World War II; suggests that China was lost to communism because communist influence in the American government sabotaged military aid for the Kuomintang; supports Senator McCarthy's charges against Owen Lattimore, etc.

823

Koen, Ross Y. *The China Lobby in American Politics.* New York: Macmillan, 1960. An unsympathetic study of those groups in American politics which during the 1950's blamed the Roosevelt and Truman administrations for the loss of China to communism.

Other foreign relations of the republican era

824

Levi, Werner. *Modern China's Foreign Policy.* Minneapolis: University of Minnesota Press, 1953. An authoritative interpretive study of the aims and the domestic determinants of foreign policy during the republican era.

825

Fishel, Wesley R. *The End of Extraterritoriality in China.* Berkeley: University of California Press, 1952. A detailed history of international negotiations through the 20th century about revision of the "unequal treaties," leading to the renunciation of all extraterritorial privileges by the Western powers in 1943; with many documentary appendices.

826

China Institute of International Affairs. *China and the United Nations.* New York: Carnegie Endowment for International Peace, 1959. A history of nationalist China's participation in the United Nations, by a panel of professors from Taiwan.

827

MacMurray, John V. A. (ed.) *Treatises and Agreements With and Concerning China.* Vol. II. New York: Oxford University Press, 1921. A monumental sourcebook on China's foreign relations from 1912 to 1919.

828

Carnegie Endowment for International Peace. *Treaties and Agreements with and Concerning China, 1919–29.* Washington: 1929.

829

Ch'en Yin-ching (ed.). *Treaties and Agreements Between the Republic of China and Other Powers, 1929–54.* Washington: Sino-American Publication Service, 1957.

830

Maki, John M. (ed.) *Selected Documents: Far Eastern International Relations, 1689–1951.* Seattle: University of Washington Press, 1957. Chaps. 12, 16-18 and 22-23 provide documentary sources on China's international relations during the early republican and the nationalist periods.

831

MacNair, Harley F. (ed.) *Modern Chinese History: Selected Readings.* Shanghai: Commercial Press, 1923; reprinted in 2 vols., Taipei: Commercial Press, 1957. A compendium of source materials, especially emphasizing international relations; chaps. 15-17 deal with the early republican period to 1922.

832

Walker, Richard L. (ed.) *China and the West: Cultural Collision.* New Haven: Far Eastern Publications, Yale University, 1956. A collection of documentary sources, chap. 5 dealing with foreign relations and domestic policies of the nationalist era.

833

Young, C. Walter. *The International Relations of Manchuria.* Chicago: University of Chicago Press, 1929. A voluminous digest of treaties, etc., relating to far northeastern China, covering the period from 1895 to 1929.

*   *   *

834

Dallin, David J. *Soviet Russia and the Far East.* New Haven: Yale University Press, 1948. Includes authoritative interpretations of Chinese-Russian relations from 1931 through World War II.

835

Beloff, Max. *Soviet Policy in the Far East, 1944–1951.* London: Oxford University Press, 1953. Includes a balanced, critical study of the USSR's role in the nationalist-communist shift of power in China.

836

Degras, Jane (ed.). *Soviet Documents on Foreign Policy.* 3 vols. London: Oxford University Press for the Royal Institute of International Affairs, 1951–53. Documents covering the period 1917–41, arranged in chronological order; with intermittent relevance to Sino-Soviet relations.

837

Wu, Aitchen K. *China and the Soviet Union.* New York: John Day, 1950. A general survey of Sino-Soviet relations during the republican era.

838

Wei, Henry. *China and Soviet Russia.* Princeton: Van Nostrand, 1956. A detailed analysis of Sino-Soviet relations from 1917 into the early 1950's, with many documentary appendices; from the point of view of the nationalist government, but generally objective.

839

Cheng Tien-fong. *A History of Sino-Russian Relations.* Washington: Public Affairs Press, 1957. Especially detailed on the 20th century; from the point of view of nationalist China.

840

Whiting, Allen S. and Sheng Shih-ts'ai. *Sinkiang: Pawn or Pivot?* East Lansing: Michigan State University Press,

1958. An authoritative analysis of Sino-Soviet rivalries in Central Asia from 1933 to 1949; the second part offers the personal memoirs of General Sheng Shih-ts'ai, a Chinese agent in the struggle.

841

Tang, Peter S. H. *Russian and Soviet Policy in Manchuria and Outer Mongolia, 1911–1931.* Durham, N.C.: Duke University Press, 1959. A comprehensive, authoritative, well documented study of two important aspects of modern Chinese-Russian relations.

842

Hudson, G. F. "The Sino-Soviet Alliance Treaty of 1945," *St. Antony's Papers,* II (London: Chatto and Windus, 1957), 13-33. A reappraisal of the attitudes of the great powers toward China during the last years of World War II.

*   *   *

843

Friedman, Irving S. *British Relations with China, 1931–39.* New York: Institute of Pacific Relations, 1940. Analytical and authoritative.

844

Friters, Gerald M. *Outer Mongolia and Its International Position.* Baltimore: Johns Hopkins Press, 1949. Includes data on Sino-Mongolian relations during the republican era.

845

Ma Ho-t'ien. *Chinese Agent in Mongolia,* trans. by John de Francis. Baltimore: Johns Hopkins Press, 1949. An account of the activities and observations of a Chinese governmental representative in Outer Mongolia, 1926–27.

Nationalist China in Taiwan

846

Barnett, A. Doak. *Communist China and Asia.* New York: Council on Foreign Relations, 1960; paperbound reprint New York: Vintage Books, 1961. Chap. 13 provides a detailed discussion of conditions in Taiwan and American policy toward nationalist China.

847

Walker, Richard L. "Taiwan's Development as Free China," *Annals of the American Academy of Political and Social Science,* 321 (January 1959), 122-135. A broad, sympathetic evaluation of political, social, and economic achievements during the 1950's within nationalist China, with an appraisal of its continuing problems.

848

Whiting, Allen S. "The United States and Taiwan," in *The United States and the Far East* (New York: The American Assembly, Columbia University, 1956), pp. 173-201. A brief, balanced essay on the political, economic, and military status of nationalist China in the 1950's, with special emphasis on Sino-American commitments and problems.

849

China Yearbook, 1959–1960. Taipei: China Publishing Co., 1960. An almanac-like compendium of historical and statistical data about life in nationalist China. Published annually, but originally issued irregularly under the title *China Handbook,* beginning with a 1937-43 edition (New York: Macmillan).

850

Riggs, Fred W. *Formosa under Chinese Nationalist Rule.* New York: Macmillan, 1952. On the reestablishment of Chinese control in Taiwan, 1946–50.

851

Linebarger, Paul M.A., Djang Chu, and Ardath W. Burks. *Far Eastern Governments and Politics: China and Japan.* 2d ed. Princeton: Van Nostrand, 1956. Chap. 8 is an authoritative discussion of political conditions in Taiwan under the nationalists.

852

Harvey, Richard. "The United States and the Legal Status of Formosa," *World Affairs Quarterly,* XXX (1959–60),

134-153. A detailed, legalistic analysis of the status of Formosa in international law and the problems raised by the lack of any treaties recognizing Chinese sovereignty there.

853
Phillips, Claude S., Jr. "The International Legal Status of Formosa," *Western Political Quarterly*, X (1957), 276-289. Notes that the status of Formosa is dependent entirely on political rather than legal (treaty) bases.

THE COMMUNIST ERA, 1921-

Establishment of the People's Republic of China with its capital at Peking on October 1, 1949, culminated a struggle that had begun with the founding of the Chinese Communist Party in 1921. Under instructions from the Comintern, the party had collaborated with the Kuomintang from 1923 to 1927. Then, having been purged and outlawed by Chiang Kai-shek, it had engineered a series of urban uprisings which, it hoped, might rally the working class against the capitalist-supported, West-oriented nationalists. These failed ignominiously, and during the early 1930's party dominance had passed to Mao Tse-tung and others who had concurrently been developing peasant-based rural soviets in the hinterlands of southeast China. Campaigns by the nationalist government to exterminate this state within a state finally drove Mao's small Red Army out of its stronghold in 1934. By 1936, after a disastrous Long March westward and northward, the remnants had regrouped at Yenan in Shensi province. The Sino-Japanese War of 1937–45, during which there was an unstable new Kuomintang-communist alliance, gave the party new life. By guerrilla tactics, its Red Army came to control much of North China behind Japanese lines, and the party gained prestige and support among the peasantry by moderate land redistribution policies. After the defeat of Japan in 1945, the Communist Party felt strong enough to challenge the war-weary Kuomintang for control of all China, and civil war resulted in a decisive Communist victory in 1949. With Mao Tse-tung its dominant figure, the new regime embarked upon a drastic overhauling of Chinese society — to substitute nationalism for familism and regionalism, to substitute Maoism (a reinterpretation of Marxist-Leninist doctrines) for traditional values, to collectivize and then communalize agriculture, and to create a modern industrial establishment in the quickest possible time. In 1950–53 the Peking government sent so-called volunteers to fight United Nations forces in Korea, and through the 1950's it persistently denounced American influence in the Far East and threatened to destroy the Nationalist government on Formosa. In 1958–59 it ruthlessly reasserted traditional Chinese authority in Tibet and quarreled with

India about Indo-Tibetan borders. From the beginning, the regime received substantial aid from the Soviet Union, and in turn it gave aid and inspiration to Communist movements in Japan, Korea, Southeast Asia, Africa, and even Latin America.

Introductory references

854
Clyde, Paul H. *The Far East*. 3d ed. Englewood Cliffs, N.J.: Prentice-Hall, 1958.

855
Michael, Franz H. and George E. Taylor. *The Far East in the Modern World*. New York: Holt, 1956.

856
Vinacke, Harold M. *A History of the Far East in Modern Times*. 6th ed. New York: Appleton-Century-Crofts, 1959.

857
MacNair, Harley F. and Donald F. Lach. *Modern Far Eastern International Relations*. 2d ed. New York: Van Nostrand, 1955.

858
Buss, Claude. *The Far East*. New York: Macmillan, 1955.

859
Greene, Fred. *The Far East*. New York: Rinehart, 1957.

860
Crofts, Alfred and Percy Buchanan. *A History of the Far East*. New York: Longmans, Green, 1958.

861
Peffer, Nathaniel. *The Far East*. Ann Arbor: University of Michigan Press, 1958.

Chinese communist leaders

862
North, Robert C. *Kuomintang and Chinese Communist Elites*. Stanford: Stanford University Press, 1952. (Hoover Institute Studies, series B, no. 8.) An analysis of the backgrounds and careers of the leaders of both nationalist and communist parties; with brief histories of changing currents evidenced in the leadership of the two parties from their origins.

863
Payne, Robert. *Mao Tse-tung, Ruler of Red China*. London: Secker and Warburg, 1950. The only full-scale biography, but undocumented; a sympathetic effort principally to trace Mao's intellectual development.

864
Smedley, Agnes. *The Great Road: The Life and Times of Chu Teh*. New York: Monthly Review Press, 1956. A detailed, highly admiring biography of the Chinese Red Army's organizer and commander in chief, based on his own reminiscences taken just after World War II; by perhaps the West's greatest sympathizer of the Chinese communist movement.

865
MacFarquhar, Roderick. "The Leadership in China; Succession to Mao Tse-tung," *World Today*, XV (1959), 310-323. An appraisal of the significance of Mao Tse-tung's yielding the chairmanship of the communist government to Liu Shao-ch'i in 1959, with speculations about possible post-Mao struggles for power.

866
Hsiao Yü ("Siao-yu"). *Mao Tse-tung and I were Beggars*. Syracuse: Syracuse University Press, 1959. The memoirs of one of Mao's boyhood schoolmates, dealing principally with the period 1912–18; with historical commentary by R. C. North.

867

Wales, Nym (pseud. of Helen Foster Snow). *Red Dust.* Stanford: Stanford University Press, 1952. A collection of 24 autobiographies of leading Chinese communist soldiers, scholars, doctors, actors, women, etc., told to the author in 1937; with an introductory survey of Chinese communist history by R. C. North.

868

Mao Tse-tung. *Selected Works of Mao Tse-tung.* 4 vols. New York: International Publishers, 1954–56. An officially-sanctioned English version of most of the communist leader's most important writings, constituting guides to the best orthodox thinking.

Pre-1949 communist history

869

North, Robert C. *Moscow and Chinese Communists.* Stanford: Stanford University Press, 1953. An excellent, authoritative history of the Chinese communist movement from its origins to its conquest of the whole mainland, with special relevance to its relations with the Soviet Union.

870

Schwartz, Benjamin I. *Chinese Communism and the Rise of Mao.* Cambridge: Harvard University Press, 1951. An authoritative study of the tortuous history of the Comintern's efforts to control the revolution in China through the 1920's and early 1930's until the eventual and unorthodox rise of Mao Tse-tung to the leadership of the Chinese Communist Party; a basic reference.

871

Brandt, Conrad, Benjamin Schwartz and John K. Fairbank. *A Documentary History of Chinese Communism.* Cambridge: Harvard University Press, 1952. (Russian Research Center Studies, 6.) An invaluable sourcebook of materials on the history of the Chinese communist movement from 1918 to 1950, specially emphasizing the period up to 1945; with detailed introductory information and a general history of the movement.

872

Brandt, Conrad. *Stalin's Failure in China, 1924–27.* Cambridge: Harvard University Press, 1958. (Russian Research Center Studies, 31.) An authoritative reappraisal of Chinese history during the period of Kuomintang-communist collaboration.

873

Wint, Guy. *Dragon and Sickle.* New York: Praeger, 1959. A brief general interpretation of how communism gained control of mainland China; in popular style, but objective and well informed.

874

McLane, Charles B. *Soviet Policy and the Chinese Communists, 1931–1946.* New York: Columbia University Press, 1958. An authoritative interpretation, based most importantly on Russian sources, of changing Soviet attitudes toward the Chinese communist movement during a period when the Moscow government officially supported Chiang Kai-shek.

875

Wilbur, C. Martin and Julie Lien-ying How (ed.). *Documents on Communism, Nationalism, and Soviet Advisers in China, 1918–1927.* New York: Columbia University Press, 1956. A collection of documents seized in a raid on the Peking office of the Soviet military attaché in 1927; a valuable sourcebook on the Kuomintang-communist collaboration of the 1920's, from the communist — and especially the Soviet Union — point of view.

876

Compton, Boyd (trans.). *Mao's China: Party Reform Documents, 1942–44.* Seattle: University of Washington Press, 1952. Efforts by Mao Tse-tung, Liu Shao-ch'i, and others to impose Marxist-Leninist orthodoxy upon all Chinese communists in preparation for all-out civil war with the nationalist government.

877

Wittfogel, Karl A. "The Legend of Maoism," *The China Quarterly,* no. 1 (January-March 1960), 72-86; no. 2 (April-June 1960), 16-34. Argues that Mao Tse-tung, in the early years of his leadership of the Chinese Communist Party, did not depart significantly from Marxist-Leninist orthodoxy; cf. response by Benjamin Schwartz in no. 2, pp. 35-43, and further controversial comment in no. 4 (October-December 1960), pp. 88-101.

878

Isaacs, Harold Robert. *The Tragedy of the Chinese Revolution.* Rev. ed. Stanford: Stanford University Press, 1951. A study of the Kuomintang-communist collaboration of the 1920's, with addenda about the later history of the communist movement including its eventual conquest of the mainland; by an admirer of Trotsky. Equally denounces the Kuomintang, the Comintern, and Maoism.

879

Daniels, Robert Vincent. "The Chinese Revolution in Russian Perspective," *World Politics,* XIII (1960–61), 210-230. An interpretive appraisal of the communist revolution in China in comparison with original Marxism and with Stalinist Russia.

880

Whiting, Allen Suess. *Soviet Policies in China, 1917–1924.* New York: Columbia University Press, 1954. An analytical, authoritative study, with several documentary appendices.

881

Seton-Watson, Hugh. *From Lenin to Khruschev: the History of World Communism.* New York: Praeger, 1960. A standard reference, including good summaries of Chinese communist development by periods, and its relations with the world communist movement.

882

Kennedy, Malcolm. *A History of Communism in East Asia.* New York: Praeger, 1957. Includes a general, interpretive history of the Chinese communist movement from its beginnings to 1955.

883

Eudin, Xenia J. and Robert C. North. *Soviet Russia and the East, 1920–1927.* Stanford: Stanford University Press, 1957. An authoritative documentary history; basic on the early history of the Chinese Communist Party and on the nationalist-communist collaboration of the 1920's.

884

Fischer, Louis. *The Soviets in World Affairs: a History of the Relations Between the Soviet Union and the Rest of the World, 1917–1929.* 2 vols. Princeton: Princeton University Press, 1951. A standard reference, including information about Soviet influence on the early development of the Chinese communist movement.

885

Hu Shih. "China in Stalin's Grand Strategy," *Foreign Affairs,* XXIX (1950–51), 11-40. A review of Russian influence on the history of the Chinese Communist Party from 1924 to 1949 and on Kuomintang history during the 1920's; from a distinctly hostile point of view.

886

Thomson, James C., Jr. "Communist Policy and the United Front in China, 1935–1936," *Papers on China,* XI (Cambridge: Harvard University Center for East Asian Studies, 1957; privately distributed), 99-148. A seminar paper on an important policy controversy between the Chinese Communist Party and the Comintern, culminating in the kidnapping and release of Chiang Kai-shek at Sian in 1936.

887

Gelder, Stuart (ed.). *The Chinese Communists.* London: Gollancz, 1946. A collection of writings by and about Chinese communists (Mao Tse-tung, Israel Epstein, Chu Teh, Michael Lindsay, William Band and others) collected in wartime by an English journalist; with an introduction denouncing the Kuomintang.

888

Roy, M. N. *Revolution and Counter-revolution in China.* Calcutta: Renaissance Publishers, 1946. A history of Chinese politics in the 20th century, especially focusing on the Kuomintang-communist collaboration of the 1920's and its rupture in 1927; by an Indian Marxist who was Comintern representative in China in 1926–27. Rather contemptuous of the subsequent development of peasant-based communism under Mao Tse-tung.

889

T'ang Leang-li. *Suppressing Communist-Banditry in China.* Shanghai: China United Press, 1934. A history of the nationalist government's campaigns to exterminate Chinese communism between 1927 and 1934, with a brief history of the communist movement prior to 1934 and a description of the organization and life of the Chinese soviets; a semi-official apologia for the nationalist government.

890

Yakhontoff, Victor A. *The Chinese Soviets.* New York: Coward-McCann, 1934. An early study of the communist movement in China up to 1933, with much data on the state of the soviets organized in Southeast China after 1927 by Mao Tse-tung and Chu Teh; written without benefit of direct contact with the Chinese communists.

891

Mao Tse-tung. *China's New Democracy.* New York: New Century, 1945. Mao's 1941 statement of policy, proposing a coalition of all classes in a communist-led but not communist-dominated social revolution.

* * *

892

Snow, Edgar. *Red Star over China.* Rev. ed. New York: Random House, 1944. A classical eyewitness account by an informed journalist of the condition of the Chinese communist movement in 1936-37, including interviews with leaders of the movement about its earlier history; sympathetic, but not uncritical. Cf. Snow's *Scorched Earth* (2 vols. London: V. Gollancz, 1941) for data on Chinese communism during the early years of World War II; and *Random Notes on Red China, 1936–1945* (Cambridge: Harvard University Press, 1957) for miscellaneous addenda.

893

Band, Claire and William Band. *Two Years with the Chinese Communists.* New Haven: Yale University Press, 1948. A detailed personal account by an American couple of their life among communist guerrilla forces of North China following their escape from Peking after the Japanese attack on Pearl Harbor; perhaps the most objective Western account of the communist movement during wartime.

894

Forman, Harrison. *Report from Red China.* New York: Holt, 1945. An American journalist's account of his visit to Yenan in 1944; sympathetic, but fairly objective reporting of his personal observations and conversations.

895

Stein, Gunther. *The Challenge of Red China.* New York: Whittlesey House, 1945. Another journalist's account of his visit to Yenan in 1944; highly sympathetic to the Chinese communists and highly critical of the nationalist government.

896

Belden, Jack. *China Shakes the World.* New York: Harper, 1949. A journalist's first-hand account of the civil war from 1946 to 1949, much of it devoted to reporting observations within the communist-controlled areas.

897

Payne, Robert. *Journey to Red China.* London: Heinemann, 1947. A sympathetic, anecdotal account of a visit among the Chinese communists in the interval between World War II and the Kuomintang-communist civil war.

898

Sues, Ilona Ralf. *Shark's Fins and Millet.* Garden City, N. Y.: Garden City Publishing Co., 1945. A Swiss woman's highly personal and anecdotal account of her experiences in China from the early 1930's into the late 1930's as a League of Nations representative; includes first-hand descriptions of life in communist-controlled areas (and among the communist leaders) during the time of the nationalist-communist united front against Japanese aggression.

899

Smedley, Agnes. *Battle Hymn of China.* New York: Knopf, 1943. A detailed account of experiences in China from 1928 to 1941, with much first-hand data about the communist guerrilla effort in the early years of World War II; by the Chinese communist movement's most influential Western sympathizer.

900

Strong, Anna Louise. *The Chinese Conquer China.* Garden City, N. Y.: Doubleday, 1949. A description of the Chinese communist movement by a dedicated Western sympathizer; representative of several influential works by Miss Strong.

* * *

901

Ch'en Kung-po. *The Communist Movement in China,* ed. by C. Martin Wilbur. New York: East Asian Institute of Columbia University, 1960. (East Asian Institute Series, 7). The earliest known report on the founding of the Chinese Communist Party by a participant, written as a master's thesis at Columbia University in 1924 and incorporating several important documents; privately distributed.

902

Ho Kan-chih. *A History of the Modern Chinese Revolution.* Peking: Foreign Languages Press, 1959. A voluminous, detailed history of China from 1919 to 1956 according to the official interpretation of the People's Republic, with emphasis on the history of the Chinese Communist Party and with biographical sketches of both communist and nationalist personages.

903

Ch'en Po-ta. *Notes on Ten Years of Civil War, 1927–1936.* Peking: Foreign Languages Press, 1954. A brief narrative written in 1944, eulogizing Mao Tse-tung's creative use of Marxism-Leninism in early Chinese communist development.

904

Chen Ch'ang-feng. *On the Long March with Chairman Mao.* Peking: Foreign Languages Press, 1959. Brief, adulatory memoirs by a Chinese communist officer about his early days as orderly and bodyguard for Mao Tse-tung, 1930-36; with an appendix summarizing political development during the Long March.

905

Liao Kai-lung. *From Yenan to Peking.* Peking: Foreign Languages Press, 1954. An officially sanctioned political history of China from the end of the Sino-Japanese war in 1945 through 1953.

The People's Republic: general

906

United States Consulate-General, Hong Kong. *Current Background,* 1950–. A basic research tool on communist China, containing statistical compilations, tabulations of other kinds of data, and translations of speeches, reports, and other documents; issued irregularly in mimeographed form and privately distributed by the U. S. Department of State. Accompanying translations series, issued more regularly and more voluminously, include *Survey of the China Mainland Press* (1950–) and *Extracts from China Mainland Magazines* (1956–).

907

The China Quarterly. London: Congress for Cultural Freedom, 1960-. A scholarly quarterly devoted exclusively to the study of communist China; with useful chronicles of current events and translations of important contemporary documents.

908

Asian Survey. Berkeley; University of California Institute of International Studies, 1961-. Published monthly as a successor to *Far Eastern Survey;* regularly includes brief articles on contemporary developments in China.

909

Contemporary China. Hong Kong: Hong Kong University Press, 1955-. An English-language journal devoted almost exclusively to the study of communist China, including articles, translations of important current documents, chronologies of events, and current bibliographic notes; published biennially.

910

Communist China. Kowloon: Union Research Institute, 1955-. An annual collection of essays on varied aspects of life and developments in mainland China; issued in mimeograph form.

*   *   *

911

"Communist China and Continuing Coexistence." Special issue of *Current History,* December 1960 (vol. 39, no. 232). Six authoritative essays on political conditions, economic development, and international relations.

912

"Red China: The First Ten Years," *The Atlantic,* December 1959 (vol. 204, no. 6), pp. 39-109. A special symposium of articles on various aspects of mainland China's development during the 1950's by specialists, together with selected Chinese poems, stories, and plays; an excellent, generally authoritative survey for the general reader.

913

"Contemporary China and the Chinese." Special issue of *Annals of the American Academy of Political and Social Science,* January 1959 (vol. 321). An excellent, general, balanced introduction for the informed reader to the whole panorama of the contemporary Chinese scene—communist, nationalist, and overseas; consisting of 14 documented studies by authorities, edited by Howard L. Boorman.

914

"Report on Communist China." Special issue of *Current History,* December 1958 (vol. 35, no. 208). Seven essays by specialists on domestic developments and Sino-Soviet relations.

915

"Communist China: A Special Report." Special issue of *The New Republic,* May 13, 1957 (vol. 136, no. 19). Ten essays for the general reader by authoritative specialists—on political controls and problems, brainwashing, industrialization, collectivization, etc.

916

"Communist China in World Politics." Special issue of *Journal of International Affairs,* vol. XI, no. 2 (1957). A symposium of 10 authoritative articles by specialists on the political and economic development of communist China and its relations with the Soviet Union, the rest of Asia, and the United States as of 1957.

917

"Report on China." Special issue of *Annals of the American Academy of Political and Social Science,* vol. 277 (September 1951). An early appraisal, in authoritative essays by specialists, of the historical background, the political structure, the socioeconomic policies, and the foreign policy of the Peking regime; ed. by H. Arthur Steiner.

918

"Asia and Future World Leadership." Special issue of *Annals of the American Academy of Political and So-*

cial Science, July 1958 (vol. 318). On social, economic, political, intellectual, and military conditions and prospects of the whole of Asia, in a series of general articles; with constant references to communist China.

*   *   *

919

Barnett, A Doak. *Communist China and Asia.* New York: Council on Foreign Relations, 1960; paperbound reprint New York: Vintage Books, 1961. A thorough, authoritative, balanced analysis of the rise of the People's Republic of China to world power, considered as a threat to its Asian neighbors and a challenge to American policy; suggests an approach toward normalized American relations with both Chinas.

920

Fairbank, John King. *The United States and China.* Rev. ed. Cambridge: Harvard University Press, 1958. Includes an authoritative discussion of the communist conquest of China, the aims and achievements of the People's Republic, and the historic patterns and contemporary problems of American policy toward China; a standard introductory reference, with an interpretive approach.

921

Guillermaz, Jacques. *La Chine populaire.* Paris: Presses Universitaires de France, 1959. An excellent brief survey of the history of Chinese communism from its beginnings and of the government, society, and economy of mainland China in the 1950's; undocumented and in popular style, but reliable and objective.

922

Wint, Guy. *Common Sense about China.* New York: Macmillan, 1960. A brief interpretation of why communism won China and how it is transforming Chinese life, by an objective and well-informed newspaperman; a good introduction for the general reader.

923

The Challenge of Communist China. Minneapolis: University of Minnesota Center for International Relations and Area Studies, 1960. A symposium of 4 articles about mainland China's internal problems and foreign affairs and about American policy toward China presented by specialists at a 1960 conference.

924

Rowe, David Nelson. *Modern China: A Brief History.* Princeton: Van Nostrand, 1959. Includes a very brief appraisal of communist China during the 1950's, in a condemnatory tone.

925

Barnett, A. Doak. "The United States and Communist China," in *The United States and the Far East* (New York: The American Assembly, Columbia University, 1956), pp. 105-171. An excellent brief resumé of the communist conquest of mainland China, the political and economic techniques and achievements of the Peking regime, and the problems and prospects of Sino-American relations in the 1950's.

926

Walker, Richard L. "Communist China: Power and Prospects." Special issue of *The New Leader,* October 20, 1958. A general, unsympathetic survey for the general reader.

927

Walker, Richard L. *China Under Communism.* New Haven: Yale University Press, 1955. A comprehensive history of communist China from 1949 through 1953, arranged by topics; thoroughly documented and annotated, but in an angrily denunciatory tone.

928

Taylor, George E. "On the Nature of Communist Rule in China," *World Politics,* IX (1956–57), 140-147. A highly denunciatory review of the Chinese communists' "cruel animal cunning" in playing power politics; a survey of some recent publications.

929

Callis, Helmut G. *China Confucian and Communist*. New York: Holt, 1959. Chaps. 16-24 survey political and economic conditions in communist China and its international relations.

930

Linebarger, Paul M. A., Djang Chu, and Ardath W. Burks. *Far Eastern Governments and Politics: China and Japan*. 2d ed. Princeton: Van Nostrand, 1956. Chap. 9 summarizes the political organization, policies, and general political conditions of China under communism.

931

Rostow, W. W. and others. *The Prospects for Communist China*. New York: Wiley, 1954. A broad, dispassionate analysis of the political and economic power of the communist regime after its early years of mainland control, with sober calculations of its future potential and problems; includes a useful comprehensive bibliography.

932

Shabad, Theodore. *China's Changing Map*. New York: Praeger, 1956. A detailed description of political organization and economic life in communist China, with surveys of its various regions.

933

Fitzgerald, Charles Patrick. *Revolution in China*. New York: Praeger, 1952. An analysis, in a broad historical framework, of the transition from nationalist to communist control in mainland China; a relatively favorable view of the new regime and a very unfavorable view of the Kuomintang.

934

Tang, Peter S. H. *Communist China Today*. 2 vols. New York: Praeger, 1957–58. An encyclopedic, somewhat speculative survey for the general reader, dealing with both domestic and foreign policies; strongly critical in tone. Vol. 2 provides translations of documents and a long chronological table.

935

Kuo Pin-chia. *China: New Age and New Outlook*. New York: Alfred A. Knopf, 1956. A sympathetic appraisal of the historical background and the general achievements of communist China, with special emphasis on China's drive to attain international status as a great power.

936

Daniels, Robert V. (ed.) *A Documentary History of Communism*. New York: Random House, 1960. Chap. 8, "Communism in the Far East" (pp. 282-393), is overwhelmingly devoted to the writings of Mao Tse-tung, Liu Shao-ch'i, and other Chinese communists, mainly excerpted from *A Documentary History of Chinese Communism* by Brandt and others, but continued into 1958.

937

Walker, Richard L. (ed.) *China and the West: Cultural Collision*. New Haven: Far Eastern Publications, Yale University, 1956. A collection of documentary sources, chap. 6 dealing with the techniques of communist control in China and chap. 7 dealing with communist China's views toward and relations with the United States.

938

Boorman, Howard L. "The Study of Contemporary Chinese Politics: Some Remarks on Retarded Development," *World Politics*, XII (1959–60), 585-599. An assessment of the problems, achievements, and the challenges of American scholarship regarding communist China.

939

Lindbeck, John M. "Research Materials on Communist China; United States Government Sources," *Journal of Asian Studies*, XVIII (1958–59), 357-363. Reviews resources on communist China that are available in various agencies of the U. S. federal government; a useful research aid.

* * *

940

Chen, Theodore H. E. *Thought Reform of the Chinese Intellectuals*. Hong Kong: Hong Kong University Press, 1960. A detailed, authoritative history of anti-intellectual programs pursued by the Chinese communists during the 1950's, with special emphasis on the period of mass confessions by professional people (1950-52) and the "bloom-contend" movement of 1956-57.

941

MacFarquhar, Roderick. *The Hundred Flowers Campaign and the Chinese Intellectuals*. New York: Praeger, 1960. A study of communist Chinese thought control in 1957-58, including translations of invited criticisms that provoked "ideological remolding;" interprets the "bloom-contend' (free criticism) movement as a "colossal mistake" by Mao Tse-tung. With an epilogue by G. F. Hudson.

942

Lifton, Robert. *Thought Reform and the Psychology of Totalism*. New York: Norton, 1961. A readable, interpretive analysis by a psychiatrist of Chinese "brainwashing" based on the case histories of both Westerners and Chinese who have been subjected to it, with attempts to provide psychological explanations of their experiences; probably the best work on the subject now available. Cf. Lifton's article, "Thought Reform of Chinese Intellectuals: A Psychiatric Evaluation," in *Journal of Asian Studies*, XVI (1956–57), 75-88.

943

Schein, Edgar and others. *Coercive Persuasion*. New York: Norton, 1961. A thoroughly documented history of Chinese thought reform; not as readable as Lifton's book, and less stimulating in its psychological interpretations.

944

Hawtin, Elise. "The 'Hundred Flowers Movement' and the Role of the Intellectaul in China: Fei Hsiao-t'ung, a Case History," *Papers on China*, XII (Cambridge: Harvard University Center for East Asian Studies, 1958; privately distributed), 147-198. A seminar paper on the sudden shift from free criticism to ideological remolding in the Peking regime's relations with intellectuals in 1957, as reflected in the case of an eminent anthropologist.

945

Johnson, Chalmers A. "An Intellectual Weed in the Socialist Garden: the Case of Ch'ien Tuan-sheng," *China Quarterly*, no. 6 (April-June 1961), 29-52. A detailed analysis of the 1957 confessions of a Harvard-educated political scientist during the "ideological remolding" that followed the "bloom-contend" movement.

946

Hunter, Edward. *Brain-washing in Red China*. New York: Vanguard Press, 1951. A journalist's account, based on 1950-51 interviews with Chinese who had experienced thought-reform during the initial communist domination of the mainland, with special reference to its use in schools and colleges.

947

Johnson, Chalmers A. *Communist Policies Toward the Intellectual Class*. Kowloon: Union Research Institute, 1959. A critical analysis of thought control in mainland China during the 1950's, with background on general intellectual history of the 20th century.

* * *

948

Hudson, G. F., A. V. Sherman, and A. Zauberman. *The Chinese Communes: a Documentary Review and Analysis of the "Great Leap Forward."* London: Soviet Survey, 1959. Three well-informed essays on communist China's dramatic efforts at social and economic reorganization in 1958-59.

949

Whiting, Allen S. *China Crosses the Yalu: the Decision to Enter the Korean War.* New York: Macmillan, 1960. Suggests that the Soviet Union planned North Korea's aggression in June, 1950, and that Red China intervened in October because Chinese-American communications were ineffective.

950

"Science in China," *China Quarterly,* no. 6 (April-June 1961), 91-169. Four articles presented to a symposium on the sciences in communist China sponsored by the American Association for the Advancement of Science in December 1960: "The Organization and Development of Science" by John M. H. Lindbeck, "Agricultural Science and its Application" by Ralph W. Phillips and Leslie T. C. Kuo, "Genetics" by C. C. Li, and "Medicine and Public Health" by William Y. Chen; with a brief report on the AAAS symposium as a whole by Betty Feinberg.

951

Wright, Mary C. "The Chinese Peasant and Communism," *Pacific Affairs,* XXIV (1951), 256-265. An evaluation of why the Chinese communist movement relied heavily on peasant support, why the peasants reponded sympathetically, and why China's development under communism seems likely to be largely at peasant expense.

952

Schwartz, Benjamin. "The Intelligentsia in Communist China: a Tentative Comparison," *Daedalus,* LXXXIX (1960), 604-621. On the intellectual background and the present status on China's educated elite, in contrast to the intelligentsia of mid-19th century Russia.

953

Hinton, Harold C. "Intra-Party Politics and Economic Policy in Communist China," *World Politics,* XII (1959-60), 509-524. An analysis of personalities and groups in the People's Republic leadership, with special reference to progress of the "Great Leap Forward" in economic development in 1958-59.

954

Barnett, A. Doak. "The Inclusion of Communist China in an Arms-Control Program," *Daedalus,* LXXXIX (1960), 831-845. On Chinese progress in nuclear-fission developments and its significance for the world's military situation.

955

Welch, Holmes. "Buddhism under the Communists," *China Quarterly,* no. 6 (April-June 1961), 1-14. On the revision of Buddhist organizations and activities during the 1950's; predicts that Chinese Buddhism will soon be dead.

956

Skinner, G. William. "Aftermath of Communist Liberation in the Chengtu Plain," *Pacific Affairs,* XXIV (1951), 61-76. An analysis of the social, economic, and political programs of the communists in newly conquered Szechwan province and of local reactions to them.

957

Ting Li. *Militia of Communist China.* Kowloon: Union Research Institute, 1954. On the military organization of mainland Chinese under communism for social control and economic production as well as for military purposes.

958

Tang Chu-kuo. *The Student Anti-communist Movement in Peiping.* Taipei: Asian Peoples' Anti-Communist League, 1960. An undocumented refugee account of discontent among mainland intellectuals in 1957; representative of a long series of propagandistic exposés of mainland conditions sponsored by the nationalist government on Taiwan.

959

Shih Ch'eng-chih. *People's Resistance in Mainland China, 1950-55.* Kowloon: Union Research Institute, 1956. On the extent, the nature, and the methods of anti-communist subversion within the People's Republic; with a rather subjective anti-communist approach.

960

Hunter, Edward. *The Black Book on Red China.* New York: The Bookmailer, 1958. An angry denunciation of the Peking government for oppressing China's neighbors, Christian missionaries, and the Chinese people at large; representative of many publications sponsored and distributed by an American group called "The Committee of One Million (Against the Admission of Communist China to the United Nations)."

Personal accounts

961

Eskelund, Karl. *The Red Mandarins: Travels in Red China.* London: Redman, 1959. A highly personal account of a visit in mainland China in 1956 by a Danish journalist with prior experience in China and his Chinese wife; an objective, perceptive report of how communism has changed people's lives. One of the better books by recent visitors.

962

Fitzgerald, Charles Patrick. *Flood Tide in China.* London: Cresset Press, 1958. A new appraisal of communist China by an authority on China's traditional history and culture; antagonistic toward nationalist China, American policy in the Far East, and the notion of a possible "two Chinas" development, and generally sympathetic to the aims of the Peking regime. Based in part on a visit in China in 1956.

963

Guillain, Robert. *600 Million Chinese,* trans. by Mervyn Savill. New York: Criterion, 1957. A critical, personal report of life in communist China by a French journalist who visited the mainland in 1955 and judged it in the light of his experience in pre-communist China; one of the more objective, and one of the most readable, traveler's accounts.

964

Yen, Maria (pseud.). *The Umbrella Garden.* New York: Macmillan, 1954. A first-hand account, by a not unduly embittered refugee, of the communist takeover in Peking in 1949, with special reference to life at National Peking University; in very readable style.

965

Moraes, Frank. *Report on Mao's China.* New York: Macmillan, 1953. An objective, critical description of life in communist China by an influential Indian newspaper editor, based on a visit in 1952 against a background of service in China as a war correspondent in 1944-45.

966

Hutheesing, Raja. *The Great Peace.* New York: Harper, 1953. A critical, disillusioned account of conditions in mainland China by an Indian journalist, based on two visits in 1951 and 1952.

967

Clark, Gerald. *Impatient Giant, Red China Today.* New York: McKay, 1959. An English journalist's account of his visit to mainland China in 1958, with special data on the early commune development; admiring and rather superficial.

968

Rickett, Allyn and Adele Rickett. *Prisoners of Liberation.* New York: Cameron, 1957. An American couple's account of their "brain-washing" during more than 3 years of detention in mainland China, which seems to have made a lasting impression.

969

Lapwood, Ralph and Nancy Lapwood. *Through the Chinese Revolution.* London: Spalding and Levy, 1954. A generally sympathetic account of the establishment of the communist regime, based on residence in Peking from 1948 to 1952; by long-time English missionaries.

970

Panikkar, K. M. *In Two Chinas.* London: Allen and Unwin, 1955. An objective, personal account of the experiences of India's ambassador to China from 1948 to 1952.

971

Schuman, Julian. *Assignment China.* New York: Whittier Books, 1956. A fairly objective, though intensely personal, eyewitness report on China in 1947–53 by a Western journalist.

972

Stevenson, William. *The Yellow Wind.* London: Cassell, 1959. A Canadian journalist's account of his visits to mainland China and some of its neighboring states in 1954–57; generally hostile and wary.

973

Tennien, Mark A. *No Secret is Safe Behind the Bamboo Curtain.* New York: Farrar, Straus & Young, 1952. An American Maryknoll priest's account of his treatment, and that of Christianity in general, by the Chinese communists between 1948 and 1952; with much data on communist techniques in persecution.

974

Martinson, Harold H. *Red Dragon over China.* Minneapolis: Augsburg Publishing House, 1956. A missionary's bitter denunciation of the communist take-over in China, including case studies of numerous persons who have suffered at communist hands.

975

Kinmond, William. *No Dogs in China: A Report on China Today.* New York: T. Nelson, 1957. A Canadian journalist's account of his visit to mainland China in 1956; objective but rather superficial.

976

Boyd-Orr, Lord and Peter Townsend. *What's Happening in China?* Garden City, N. Y.: Doubleday, 1959. A report on conditions in mainland China in the fall of 1958; based on a brief visit by admiring Britishers.

977

Bodde, Derk. *Peking Diary: a Year of Revolution.* New York: Schuman, 1951. A distinguished American Sinologist's perceptive record of his residence in Peking from August, 1948, to October, 1949—the era of the establishment of communist control; a generally sympathetic appraisal of the new order.

978

Sprenkel, Otto B. van der (ed.). *New China: Three Views.* New York: John Day, 1951. Long essays by Robert Guillain, Michael Lindsay, and the editor on the establishment of the communist regime in mainland China in 1948–49, based on first-hand observation and long prior experience and training; generally sympathetic.

Foreign relations: general

979

Steiner, H. Arthur. *The International Position of Communist China.* New York: Institute of Pacific Relations, 1958. A brief, authoritative interpretation of the major themes and basic principles of mainland China's relations with the rest of the world, and their sometimes drastic changes, during the 1950's.

980

Whiting, Allen S. *"Foreign Policy of Communist China,"* in *Foreign Policy in World Affairs* (R. Macridis, ed.; Englewood Cliffs, N. J.: Prentice-Hall, 1958), pp. 264-294. An authoritative analysis of communist China's foreign policy during the 1950's: its formation processes, its ideological bases, and its content.

981

"Communist China's Foreign Policy." Special issue of *Current History,* December 1957 (vol. 33, no. 196). Six authoritative essays on mainland China's relations with the Soviet Union, Britain, nationalist China, Southeast Asia, Japan, and the United States.

982

Chin, Calvin S. K. *A Study of Chinese Dependence Upon the Soviet Union for Economic Development as a Factor in Communist China's Foreign Policy.* Kowloon: Union Research Institute, 1959. Includes analyses of China's changing foreign policies during the 1950's and especially of the "hate America" campaigns.

983

Levi, Werner. *Modern China's Foreign Policy.* Minneapolis; University of Minnesota Press, 1953. The historical background and early development of foreign policy under the communist regime, with special reference to China's attitudes toward its Asian neighbors.

984

Lindsay, Michael (Lord Lindsay of Birker). *China and the Cold War.* Melbourne: Melbourne University Press, 1955. A bitter criticism of communist China's foreign policies during the 1950's by an Englishman who had been a sympathetic co-worker in the communist guerrilla movement during World War II.

985

Thomas, S. B. *Communist China and Her Neighbors.* Toronto: Canadian Institute of International Affairs, 1955. On communist China's political, social, and economic organization, and especially on its relations with the Soviet Union and neighboring Asian countries.

986

Armstrong, Hamilton Fish. "Thoughts Along the China Border; Will Neutrality Be Enough?" *Foreign Affairs,* XXXVIII (1959–60), 238-260. A speculative commentary on reactions in South and Southeast Asia to the possible threat of an expansive communist China.

987

Lu Yu-sun. *Programs of Communist China for Overseas Chinese.* Kowloon: Union Research Institute, 1956. A brief analysis of communist China's many-sided relations with overseas Chinese, principally in Southeast Asia.

988

Halpern, A. M. "The Chinese Communist Line on Neutralism," *China Quarterly,* no. 5 (January-March 1961), 90-115. An intensive analysis of communist China's changing attitudes toward its Asian neighbors from 1957 through 1960.

989

Elegant, Robert S. *The Dragon's Seed.* New York: St. Martin's Press, 1959. On the influence of the Peking government on the overseas Chinese of Southeast Asia, with special reference to Singapore and Malaya; in a journalistic and highly personal style, but well informed.

990

Hinton, Harold C. *China's Relations with Burma and Vietnam; a Brief Survey.* New York: Institute of Pacific Relations, 1958. Emphasizes the 1950's, but has brief historical backgrounds.

991

Wilbur, C. Martin. "Japan and the Rise of Communist China," in Hugh Borton and others, *Japan between East and West* (New York: Council on Foreign Relations, 1957), pp. 199-239. An authoritative survey of Sino-Japanese relations and of official and unofficial Japanese attitudes toward China, during the 1950's.

992

Rupen, Robert A. "Outer Mongolia, 1957–1960," *Pacific Affairs,* XXXIII (1960), 126-143. Includes an assessment of Chinese communist activity and influence among the Mongols.

993

Alba, Victor. "The Chinese in Latin America," *China Quarterly,* no. 5 (January-March 1961), 53-61. A brief survey and evaluation of communist China's propaganda activities in Latin America during the late 1950's.

994

Katzenbach, E. L., Jr., and Gene Z. Hanrahan. "Revolutionary Strategy of Mao Tse-tung," *Political Science Quarterly,* LXX (1955), 321-340. On the background and development of Mao's military thinking and its possible consequences in China's international relations.

995

Brook, David. *The U. N. and the China Dilemma.* New York: Vantage Press, 1956. A brief analytical discussion of the problems posed for the United Nations by the question of Chinese representation.

Relations with Tibet and India

996

Patterson, George N. "China and Tibet: Background to the Revolt," *China Quarterly,* no. 1 (Jan.-March 1960), 87-102. A general analysis of Chinese-Tibetan conflicts during the 1950's.

997

Miller, Beatrice D. "The Web of Tibetan Monasticism," *Journal of Asian Studies,* XX (1960–61), 197-203. An analysis of Lamaism as an organizational network, with explanations of communist China's difficulty in controlling it.

998

Ginsburgs, George. "Peking-Lhasa-New Delhi," *Political Science Quarterly,* LXXV (1960), 338-354. On Sino-Indian relations concerning Tibet and border problems.

999

Connell, John. "The India-China Frontier Dispute," *Journal of the Royal Central Asian Society,* XLVII (1960) 270-285. A review of Chinese-Tibetan-Indian relations in the late 1950's from the point of view of the Republic of India but critical of Prime Minister Nehru as an "appeaser."

1000

India, Ministry of External Affairs. *White Paper: Notes, Memoranda and Letters Exchanged and Agreements Signed between the Governments of India and China, 1954–1959.* New Delhi: Government of India, 1959. A basic source on Chinese activities in Tibet and on Sino-Indian border disputes; supplemented by *White Paper No. II, covering the critical period September-November 1959* (New Delhi: 1959).

1001

Tibet and the Chinese People's Republic. Geneva: International Commission of Jesuits, 1960. A documented charge that Tibet, as an independent sovereign state, has been subjected to unprovoked aggression and genocide by communist China, presented to the International Commission of Jurists by its Legal Inquiry Committee on Tibet; based on interviews with Tibetan refugees and documents.

1002

Fisher, Margaret W. and Joan V. Bondurant (ed.). *Indian Views of Sino-Indian Relations.* Berkeley: Institute of International Studies, University of California, 1956. (Indian Press Digests—Monograph Series, No. 1) A collection of official statements and privately pulished observations reflecting opinion about China in India from 1951 into 1955, with commentary.

1003

Sen, Chanakya. *Tibet Disappears.* New York: Asia Publishing House, 1960. A "documentary history" of communist China's activities in Tibet and its border dispute with India into 1959; the documents are almost entirely Indian.

1004

Gilbert, Rodney (ed.). *Genocide in Tibet.* New York: American-Asian Educational Exchange, 1959. A brief compilation of statements by Tibetans and from the mainland Chinese press about the extension of Chinese power in Tibet during the 1950's, based principally on information gathered by an International Commission of Jurists with headquarters in Geneva, with propagandistic illustrative drawings and editorial comment; representative of many anti-Peking materials issued by the publisher, an organization dedicated to supporting anti-communism in Asia.

Relations with the Soviet Union

1005

Lindsay, Michael (Lord Lindsay of Birker). "Is Cleavage between Russia and China Inevitable?" *Annals of the American Academy of Political and Social Science,* vol. 336 (July 1961), 53-61. A speculative analysis of Sino-Soviet tensions in 1960–61, suggesting little likelihood of an open rupture.

1006

Lowenthal, Richard. "Diplomacy and Revolution: The Dialectics of a Dispute," *China Quarterly,* no. 5 (January-March 1961), 1-24. A survey of intensifying Sino-Soviet differences regarding strategies for world revolution in 1959-60, concluding that world communism has become polycentric rather than monolithic. Cf. the full text of a policy declaration adopted by a conference of 81 communist parties in Moscow in December 1960, which follows on pp. 25-52.

1007

Brzezinski, Zbigniew. "Political Developments in the Sino-Soviet Bloc," *Annals of the American Academy of Political and Social Science,* vol. 336 (July 1961), 40-52. An analysis of recent trends within the communist world, emphasizing growing diversity and division of labor.

1008

Brzezinski, Zbigniew. "The Organization of the Communist Camp," *World Politics,* XIII (1960-61), 175-209. An authoritative analysis of the institutional organization of the world communist bloc and of its dynamics; a valuable framework within which to consider Soviet-Chinese relations.

1009

Bradbury, John. "Sino-Soviet Competition in North Korea," *China Quarterly,* no. 6 (April-June 1961), 15-28. An analysis of North Korea's support of China from 1958 through 1960 in ideological disputes between China and the Soviet Union.

1010

Halpern, A. M. "Communist China and Peaceful Co-existence," *China Quarterly,* no. 3 (July-September 1960), 16-31. An analysis of Chinese attitudes in a 1960 Chinese-Soviet dispute about peaceful co-existence and the inevitability of war between the communist and capitalist worlds.

1011

Whiting, Allen S. "Contradictions in the Moscow-Peking Axis," *Journal of Politics,* XX (1958), 127-161. An authoritative analysis of Sino-Soviet policy differences as regards Poland, Hungary, Tito, etc.; notes communist China's growing autonomy within the communist bloc.

1012

Boorman, Howard L. and others. *Moscow-Peking Axis: Strengths and Strains.* New York: Council on Foreign Relations, 1957. Authoritative analyses of Sino-Soviet relations into the middle 1950's by Boorman, Alexander Eckstein, Philip E. Mosely, and Benjamin Schwartz; a good background for study of the sharpened differences of views within the world communist bloc of the late 1950's and early 1960's.

1013

Beloff, Max. *Soviet Policy in the Far East, 1944–1951.* London: Oxford University Press, 1953. Largely devoted to U.S.S.R. relations with China during the civil war of the middle 1940's and after establishment of a communist regime in Peking in 1949; authoritative.

American policy toward communist China

1014

Whelan, Joseph G. "The U. S. and Diplomatic Recognition: The Contrasting Cases of Russia and Communist

China," *China Quarterly,* no. 5 (January-March 1961), 62-89. A broad analysis of factors affecting the problem of American recognition of communist China, in contrast with those affecting recognition of the Soviet Union in 1933.

1015

Seligman, Eustace and Richard L. Walker. *Should the United States Change its China Policy?* New York: Foreign Policy Association, May-June 1958. (Headline Series, 129) A confrontation of two diametrically opposed arguments on American policy regarding the diplomatic recognition of communist China and its admission into the United Nations.

1016

United States Foreign Policy: Asia. Washington: Government Printing Office, 1959. ("Studies prepared at the request of the Committee on Foreign Relations, United States Senate, by Conlon Associates Ltd., No. 5") Pp. 119-155: "Communist China and Taiwan," by Robert A. Scalapino, provides a resumé of mainland China's domestic development and foreign policies during the 1950's, a speculative evaluation of its potential for the future, and a recommendation that the United States adopt a policy of "exploration and negotiation" looking toward eventual recognition of and normal relations with the People's Republic on the mainland as well as the nationalist Republic on Taiwan.

1017

Fairbank, John K. *Communist China and Taiwan in United States Foreign Policy.* Storrs, Conn.: University of Connecticut, 1960. (4th annual Brien McMahon Lecture) A brief reappraisal of American policy toward China since 1941 and speculations about future Sino-American relations, with particular reference to the American need of fostering a democratic and independent nationalist government in Taiwan.

1018

Brecht, Arnold. "Fairness in Foreign Policy: The Chinese Issue," *Social Research,* XXVIII (1961), 95-105. A call for a reappraisal of American policy toward China, with a survey of problems concerning both U. S. diplomatic recognition and U.N. membership.

1019

Clough, Ralph N. "United States China Policy," *Annals of the American Academy of Political and Social Science,* 321 (January 1959), 20-28. A brief but authoritative and balanced exposition of American policy toward China in the 1950's by an official of the U. S. Department of State.

1020

Dulles, John Foster. *Our Policies toward China.* Washington: Department of State, 1957. (Department of State Press Release No. 393) An authoritative statement and justification of the American policy of nonrecognition toward communist China in the 1950's.

1021

Wright, Quincy. "The Chinese Recognition Problem," *American Journal of International Law,* XLIX (1955), 320-338. A technical, authoritative discussion of United States relations with nationalist China and communist China from a legal point of view.

INTELLECTUAL AND AESTHETIC PATTERNS

Balance and variety are the outstanding characteristics of China's heritage in intellectual and aesthetic fields. Music alone never attracted serious attention and lagged in development. In all other realms—in religion and philosophy, art and architecture, literature, and even science and technology—

China has had a long record of remarkable accomplishments which throughout history have exerted seminal influences on other cultures of East Asia and in modern times have been increasingly admired in the West. Moreover, the Chinese mind has been almost equally as adept at theory as at practice, especially productive in metaphysics, literary criticism, and the theory of art.

RELIGION AND PHILOSOPHY

General

In general, Chinese thinking about life has characteristically been rational and sceptical, conservative in the sense of being sanctioned by precedents, polytheistic rather than monotheistic, this-worldly rather than other-worldly, and concerned principally with defining a satisfying and secure way of life for the individual in close harmony with society and the universe at large. However, widely variant and uncharacteristic notions have been tolerated and at times even fanatically championed. The underlying, highly eclectic folk religion has always concentrated on guiding man's efforts to influence, for his own immediate practical good, the various natural and spiritual forces that are assumed to surround and dominate him. On a more sophisticated plane, the program of earnest moral and social action called Confucianism has been paramount since early times and throughout most of Chinese history has been the orthodox, state-espoused ideology. One native competitor, the quietistic individualism known as Taoism, has had a strong complementary appeal; and Buddhism, imported from India, rapidly became an integral element of Chinese life. Buddhism was, in fact, the most vital intellectual force in China from the 3rd to the 9th centuries. Both Taoism and Buddhism eventually lost their early importance and in recent centuries have been more nearly aspects of the folk religion than creative philosophies. Other importations of traditional times —Islam, Christianity, even Judaism—developed zealous supporters in China but never had widespread influence. In the 20th century various modern systems of thought, notably including Marxism, have flooded in from the West; but their acceptance has been hindered by the resilience of Confucian attitudes and the persistence of folk superstitions, so that China perhaps remains the least Westernized in outlook of the major Far Eastern nations.

Special reference aids

1022

Chan Wing-tsit. *An Outline and Annotated Bibiography of Chinese Philosophy.* New Haven: Yale University Far Eastern Publications, 1959. A most useful reference guide: a graded, annotated list of books and articles, arranged by topics.

1023

Chan Wing-tsit. "A Bibliography of Chinese Philosophy," *Philosophy East and West,* III (1953–54), 241-256. A selective, graded reading list; cf. the author's "Chinese Philosophy: A Bibliographical Essay," *op. cit.,* pp. 337-357, a discussion of sources and interpretations.

Brief introductory surveys

1024

Noss, John B. *Man's Religions.* Rev. ed. New York: Macmillan, 1956. Pp. 294-398 provide a carefully studied and well balanced survey of the history and major characteristics of Chinese folk religion, Taoism, and Confucianism.

1025

Chan Wing-tsit. "The Story of Chinese Philosophy," in *Philosophy East and West* (C. A. Moore, ed.; Princeton: Princeton University Press, 1944), pp. 24-68. A general overview of the main patterns of Chinese thought and its development, by an authority; cf. the same author's "The Spirit of Oriental Philosophy," *op. cit.,* pp. 137-167.

1026

Creel, H. G. "Chinese Philosophy," in *History of Philosophical Systems* (V. Ferm, ed.; Ames, Iowa: New Students Outline Series, 1958; originally published New York: Philosophical Library, 1950), pp. 44-56. A very brief interpretive overview of the major ancient schools of thought: Confucianism, Moism, Taoism, and Legalism.

1027

MacNair, Harley F. (ed.) *China.* Berkeley: University of California Press, 1946. Part 3 contains excellent, authoritative summations of China's religious and philosophical traditions: "Chinese Thought" by Hu Shih (pp. 221-230), "Folk Religion" by Lewis Hodous (231-244), "Confucianism" by John K. Shryock (245-253), "Neo-Confucianism" by Chan Wing-tsit (254-265), "Taoism" by Homer H. Dubs (266-289), "Buddhism" by Clarence H. Hamilton (290-300), "Christianity" by K. S. Latourette (301-311), and "Trends in Contemporary Philosophy" by Chan Wing-tsit (312-330). Also see "Dominant Ideas" by Derk Bodde (18-28) for some of the basic themes and problems of traditional Chinese throught in general.

1028

Smith, Huston. *The Religions of Man.* New York: Harper, 1958; paperbound reprint New York: Mentor Books, 1959. Chaps. 4-5: a popular, generally reliable interpretation of the thought of Confucius and the Taoists, their influences on later Chinese life, and some of their early rivals. Chap. 3 surveys the basic concepts of Buddhism, dealing with the Ch'an (Zen) school as well as other Mahayana movements in China.

1029

Bodde, Derk. "Harmony and Conflict in Chinese Philosophy," in *Studies in Chinese Thought* (A. F. Wright, ed.; Chicago: University of Chicago Press, 1953), pp. 19-80. An analytical survey of traditional Chinese thought about the cosmos, about history, about good and evil, etc., suggesting some characteristics of a common world view that seems to underlie all Chinese philosophies.

1030

Mei, Y. P. "Man and Nature in Chinese Philosophy," in *Indiana University Conference on Oriental-Western Literary Relations* (Horst Frenz and G. L. Anderson, ed; Chapel Hill: University of North Carolina Press, 1955), pp. 151-160. On some basic characteristics of Chinese thought: an absorbing interest in man, an appreciation of nature, and a realization of the affinity between man and nature.

1031

Yang, C. K. "The Functional Relationship between Confucian Thought and Chinese Religion," in *Chinese Thought and Institutions* (J. K. Fairbank, ed.; Chicago: University of Chicago Press, 1957) pp. 269-290. On the predominant rationalism of Chinese thought and its accommodations with various religious movements of Chinese history.

1032

Liebenthal, Walter. "On Trends in Chinese Thought," in *Silver Jubilee Volume of the Zinbun-Kagaku-Kenyusyo,* Kyoto University (Kyoto: 1954), pp. 262-278. A brief overview of the development of Chinese thought throughout history, of its main themes and problems, and of modern efforts to define the basic Chinese spirit.

1033

Schwartz, Benjamin. "The Intellectual History of China: Preliminary Reflections," in *Chinese Thought and Institutions* (J. K. Fairbank, ed.; Chicago: University of Chicago Press, 1957), pp. 15-30. Suggestions about possible theoretical approaches to the study of China's intellectual history.

1034

Jurji, E. J. (ed.) *The Great Religions of the Modern World.* Princeton: Princeton University Press, 1947. Includes brief surveys of the basic attitudes and modern status of Buddhism. (A. K. Reischauer), Confucianism, and Taoism (both by Lewis Hodous); somewhat outdated in scholarship.

1035

Burtt, Edwin A. *Man Seeks the Divine.* New York: Harper, 1957. Part 2 includes general analyses of Chinese religious attitudes and chapters interpreting Confucianism, Toaism, and Buddhism; by an authority on comparative religion.

1036

Ross, Floyd H. and Tynette Hills. *The Great Religions by Which Men Live.* Greenwich, Conn.: Fawcett Publications, 1956. Section 2 on Buddhism; section 3 on Toaism and Confucianism. General surveys on the basic attitudes and historical evolutions of the religions and philosophies; in popular, simple terms but rather well done.

1037

Gould, William D. and others. *Oriental Philosophies.* 3d ed. rev. New York: Russell F. Moore Co., 1951. Chaps. 7-10: brief but reliable evaluations of Confucius, Mencius, Lao-tzu, and Chuang-tzu, with excerpts from standard translations.

1038

Bouquet, A. C. *Comparative Religion.* 5th ed. London: Penguin Books, 1956. Pp. 175-191: a critical but very brief overview of all religio-philosophical schools in China.

1039

Finegan, Jack. *The Archeology of World Religions.* Princeton: Princeton University Press, 1952. Chaps. 6-7: extensive discussions of the origins and historical developments of Confucianism and Taoism, with emphasis on the historical contexts, up into the period of the Sung dynasty.

1040

Champion, Selwyn Gurney and Dorothy Short (ed.). *Readings from World Religions.* Boston: Beacon Press, 1951; paperbound reprint Greenwich, Conn.: Fawcett, 1959. Chaps. 6-7 survey Taoism and Confucianism, appending brief selections from standard translations of basic texts; somewhat uncritical.

1041

Braden, Charles S. *The World's Religions.* Rev. paperbound ed. New York: Abingdon Press, 1954. Includes very brief discussions of Confucianism, Taoism, and Chinese Buddhism; somewhat uncritical.

1042

Gaer, Joseph. *How the Great Religions Began.* Rev. ed. New York: Signet Key Books, 1958. Includes brief discussions of early Confucianism and early Taoism; very uncritical, and in a dramatic, staccato style. Not recommended for any scholastic use.

General histories and anthologies

1043

Fung Yu-lan. *A Short History of Chinese Philosophy,* ed. by Derk Bodde, New York: Macmillan, 1948; paperbound reprint, 1960. A substantial, comprehensive, and well-balanced history and explication of China's philosophical developments from earliest times into the 20th century, by one of China's most eminent philosophers and historians of philosophy of modern times.

1044

Creel, Herrlee G. *Chinese Thought from Confucius to Mao Tse-tung.* Chicago: University of Chicago Press, 1953; paperbound reprint New York: Mentor Books, 1960. A brief introduction to the various Chinese systems of thought and their historical development, by a distinguished specialist on ancient Chinese culture at the University of Chicago. Highly readable, more interpretive than Fung Yu-lan, but disproportionately brief and episodic in its treatment of the post-classical era.

1045

De Bary, W. T., Chan Wing-tist, and Burton Watson. *Sources of Chinese Tradition.* New York: Columbia University Press, 1960. A monumental survey of China's intellectual history, compiled originally for use at Columbia University; primarily a collection of sources in new and authoritative translations, but with well-informed introductions.

1046

Fung Yu-lan. *A History of Chinese Philosophy,* trans. by Derk Bodde. 2 vols. Princeton: Princeton University Press, 1952–53. The most comprehensive history in English; a standard reference.

1047

Fung Yu-lan. *The Spirit of Chinese Philosophy.* London: Kegan Paul, 1947. A brief but authoritative interpretation of Chinese philosophical development throughout history, in the end introducing a new system urged by the author, himself one of 20th century China's leading philosophers.

1048

Needham, Joseph. *Science and Civilisation in China.* Vol. 2. Cambridge: Cambridge University Press, 1956. One of the more voluminous surveys of China's intellectual history, especially emphasizing the view that Taoism represents a progressive, scientific attitude whereas Confucianism represents a conservative, moralistic attitude that stifled scientific thought; highly theoretical and controversial. Cf. extensive critiques of Needham's methods and biases by C. C. Gillespie in *American Scientist,* XLV (1957), 169-176, and by A. F. Wright in *American Historical Review,* LXII (1956–57), 918-920, and in *Pacific Affairs,* XXXIV (1961), 77-79. Also note Chan Wing-tsit's "Neo-Confucianism and Chinese Scientific Thought," *Philosophy East and West,* VI (1956–57), 309-332, for a defense of the Confucian tradition against Needham's interpretation.

1049

Lin Mousheng. *Men and Ideas.* New York: John Day, 1942. A survey of Chinese intellectual history for the general reader, emphasizing "political thought" in a broad definition.

1050

Hughes, E. R. and K. Hughes. *Religion in China.* London: Hutchinson's University Library, 1950. A brief survey of the history of Confucianism, Taoism, Buddhism, Islam, and Christianity in China, with a concluding chapter about the religious condition of China in the 20th century.

1051

Hughes, E. R. *Chinese Philosophy in Classical Times.* New York: Dutton Everyman's Library, 1942. An an-
thology of original, authoritative translations of selected passages from all the ancient schools, with a general introduction surveying the history of ancient Chinese thought in its social and historical context and brief special introductions for all the schools represented.

1052

Soothill, W. E. *The Three Religions of China.* 3d ed. London: Oxford University Press, 1929. An authoritative introductory survey of Confucianism, Taoism, and Buddhism and their roles in Chinese life, with chapters on "The Idea of God," "Cosmological Ideas," "Moral Ideals," "The Official Cult," "Private Religion," etc.

1053

Forke, Alfred. *Geschichte der alten chinesischen Philosophie; Geschichte der mittelalterlichen chinesischen Philosophie; Geschichte der neueren chinesischen Philosophie.* Hamburg: Friederichsen, 1927, 1934, 1938. Three substantial volumes comprising the most detailed history in any Western language; a monumental standard reference, but superseded in many aspects.

1054

Maspero, Henri. *Mélanges posthumes sur les religions et l'histoire de la Chine.* Vol. 1: *Les religions chinoises.* Paris: Civilisations du Sud, 1950. An authoritative survey of China's religio-philosophical development throughout history.

1055

Liang Ch'i-ch'ao. *History of Chinese Political Thought During the Early Tsin Period,* trans. by L. T. Chen. New York: Harcourt, Brace, 1930. A general evaluation of all the various schools of ancient Chinese philosophy prior to the 3d century B.C. Ch'in dynasty, by a noted 20th century scholar-philosopher; with special reference to socio-political implications of the philosophies.

1056

Wei, Francis C. M. *The Spirit of Chinese Culture.* New York: Scribner, 1947. A readable and reliable general introductory survey of China's religio-philosophical tradition, dealing with the history and basic concepts of Confucianism, Taoism, and Buddhism and giving special attention to the problems of instituting Christianity successfully among the Chinese; by an eminent Chinese educator and Christian convert.

1057

Lin Yutang. *The Wisdom of China and India.* New York: Modern Library, 1942. Includes mostly original, but not always complete, translations of Lao-tzu, Chuang-tzu, Mencius, Mo-tzu, Confucius, and the *Doctrine of the Mean (Chung-yung);* without scholarly trappings, but generally reliable.

1058

Browne, Lewis (ed.). *The World's Great Scriptures.* New York: Macmillan, 1946; paperbound reprint, 1961. Includes unusually extensive selections from basic Confucian, Taoist, and Moist texts, but not all from standard translations.

1059

Groot, Jan J. M. de. *The Religious System of China.* 6 vols. Leiden: E. J. Brill, 1892–1910. A compendium of information about the characteristics and histories of China's various religio-philosophical schools; not to be relied on for scholarly purposes except in regard to demonology and other aspects of modern popular religion.

1060

Ballou, R. O. (ed.) *The Bible of the World.* New York: Viking Press, 1939. Parts 2-4 give extensive selections from translations of basic Buddhist, Confucian, and Taoist texts, though not always from standard translations; a somewhat abbreviated paperbound version, by the same editor, is *The Viking Portable Library World Bible* (New York: Viking Press, 1944)

1061

Smith, Ruth (ed.). *The Tree of Life.* New York: Viking Press, 1942. Chaps. 5-6 include brief selections from standard translations of the major Confucian and Taoist texts.

Special studies

1062

Hsü, Francis L. K. *Americans and Chinese: Two Ways of Life*. New York: Henry Schuman, 1953. An ambitious attempt to analyze the social psychology or national character of the Chinese, especially emphasizing the influence of polytheism in Chinese thinking in contrast to monotheism in American thinking; unavoidably susceptible to dispute over details, but interesting.

1063

Fairbank, John K. (ed.) *Chinese Thought and Institutions*. Chicago: University of Chicago Press, 1957. Articles by 13 specialists on various aspects of China's intellectual and institutional history; a symposium from a 1954 conference of the Committee on Chinese Thought.

1064

Wright, Arthur F. (ed.) *Studies in Chinese Thought*. Chicago: University of Chicago Press, 1953. Articles by nine specialists, on various aspects of traditional Chinese thought and intellectual history; a symposium from a 1952 conference of the Committee on Chinese Thought.

1065

Northrup, F. S. C. *The Meeting of East and West*. New York: Macmillan, 1946; paperbound reprint 1960. A highly theoretical, wide-ranging analysis of the intellectual and aesthetic essences of world cultures, suggesting that Far Eastern cultures as a whole, including China's, share a common aesthetic attitude toward the cosmos—"the undifferentiated aesthetic continuum." Infltential and provocative, but not to be relied on for descriptive detail as regards China.

1066

Needham, Joseph. *Science and Civilisation in China*. Vol. 2. Cambridge: Cambridge University Press, 1956. Pp. 518-583, "Human Law and the Laws of Nature in China and the West": a detailed analysis of the "organic" world view of traditional China in contrast with traditional Western theology; previously published in *Journal of the History of Ideas*, XII (1951), 3-30, 194-230.

1067

Bodde, Derk. "Evidence for 'Laws of Nature' in Chinese Thought," *Harvard Journal of Asiatic Studies*, XX (1957), 709-727. Suggests that "at least a few early Chinese thinkers viewed the universe in terms strikingly similar to those underlying the Western concept of 'laws of nature'."

1068

Mei, Y. P. "Some Observations on the Problem of Knowledge Among the Ancient Chinese Logicians," *Tsing Hua Journal of Chinese Studies*, I (1956), 114-121. On "the nature of the knowing experience and the nature and functions of names," with reference to Mo-tzu, the Logicians, Chuang-tzu, and Hsün-tzu.

1069

Reichelt, Karl. *Meditation and Piety in the Far East*. New York: Harper, 1954. Essays on aspects of the meditative tradition in China, including references to Buddhism, Taoism, and Confucianism; by a long-time missionary.

1070

Marcus, John T. "Time and the Sense of History: West and East," *Comparative Studies in Society and History*, III (1960–61), 123-139. On conceptions of time, history, and progress in the evolution of China's worldview under the impact of Western values; with analysis of China's traditional "history-consciousness."

1071

Groot, J. J. M. de. *Sectarianism and Religious Persecution in China*. 2 vols. Amsterdam: Johannes Müller, 1903–

04. A compendium of translations and essays about governmental efforts throughout history to control or suppress Buddhism, Taoism, Christianity, secret societies, etc., with special reference to the T'ang, Ming, and Ch'ing periods.

1072

Graham, A. C. " 'Being' in Western Philosophy Compared with Shih/Fei and Yu/Wu in Chinese Philosophy," *Asia Major*, VII (1959), 79-112. A technical case study of the extent to which the Chinese language has influenced Chinese thought.

Folk religion

All Chinese philosophies and religions have contributed elements to, have borrowed premises from, and in popular expression have been hard to distinguish from basic folk attitudes that can be traced back to the very dawn of Chinese history. These principally include a somewhat mechanistic conception of the universe. It is assumed that the universe is self-perpetuating and dominated by natural forces which are symbolized by the dragon. All things are created by, and essentially consist of, two complementary, interacting impulses or principles: *Yang* (positive, light, strong, male, etc.) and *Yin* (negative, dark, weak, female, etc.). Over all presides a non-anthropomorphic but nevertheless vaguely personalized Heaven; and the universe is peopled with an infinite number of benevolent spirits and malevolent demons, toward which the traditional Chinese attitude has been rather unawed and businesslike. Among these, notably, are ancestral spirits, for the human soul is thought to be eternal. Man's self-interest dictates that he win the support of benevolent spirits, defend himself against malevolent demons, and refrain from disrupting the orderly operations of natural forces in general. To this end, the Chinese follows a somewhat ritualized daily routine, engages in regular ceremonies intended to honor and sustain the spirits of his ancestors, uses offerings and charms to arouse or appease other spirits and demons, and consults about important matters with professional or semi-professional practitioners of divination, exorcism, and prognostication.

1073

Hsü, Francis L. K. *Americans and Chinese: Two Ways of Life*. New York: Henry Schuman, 1953. An ambitious theoretical attempt to generalize about the national character of China in contrast to that of America, with special emphasis on the basic religious outlooks of the two cultures; an interesting and readable introduction to Chinese attitudes on the relations between gods and men.

1074

Hsü, Francis L. K. *Under the Ancestors' Shadow*. New York: Columbia University Press, 1948. An anthropological field report on a Yunnan town, with special emphasis on beliefs and practices relating to ancestor worship and other aspects of modern folk religion.

1075

Reichelt, Karl L. *Religion in Chinese Garment*, trans. by Joseph Tetlie. New York: Philosophical Library, 1951. An authoritative survey of animistic folk religion in modern China, with descriptions of Confucian, Taoist, and Budhist contributions to it; by a Norwegian missionary of long experience with the Chinese.

1076

Bodde, Derk (trans.). *Annual Customs and Festivals in Peking*. Peking: Henri Vetch, 1936. A handbook on some aspects of folk religion in the 19th century: the *Yen-ching sui-shih chi* by Tun Li-ch'en; annotated.

1077

Eberhard, Wolfram. *Chinese Festivals*. New York: Henry Schuman, 1952. A brief catalogue of the religious festivals of traditional China, from a sociological point of view.

1078

Elliott, A. J. A. *Chinese Spirit Medium Cults in Singapore*. London: Royal Anthropological Institute, 1955. A useful introduction of Chinese folk religion practices in general.

1079

Hsü, Francis L. K. *Religion, Science and Human Crises*. London: Routledge and Kegan Paul, 1952. A detailed anthropological study of the reaction to a cholera epidemic among the Chinese of a Yunnan town, throwing much light on the basic concepts and practices of modern folk religion.

1080

Shryock, John K. *Temples of Anking and their Cults: A Study of Modern Chinese Religion*. Paris: 1931. A field study of modern religious practices in the capital of Anhwei province, with detailed descriptions of the temples, their gods, and related religious matters; illustrated.

1081

Waley, Arthur. *The Nine Songs: A Study of Shamanism in Ancient China*. London: Allen and Unwin, 1955. Translations of nine poems from the pre-Han collection *Ch'u-tz'u*, with an introduction and commentaries about the South China shamanistic tradition from which they emerged.

1082

Burkhardt, V. R. *Chinese Creeds and Customs*. Hong Kong: South China Morning Post, 1954. A brief descriptive survey of traditional Chinese festivals and other aspects of folk religion, with illustrations.

1083

MacCulloch, John Arnott (ed.). *The Mythology of All Races*. Vol. 8: *Chinese and Japanese*. Boston: Archaeological Institute of America, 1937. Chaps. 1-16 provide an authoritative survey of many folk religion beliefs by John C. Ferguson, with many illustrations.

1084

Hodous, Lewis. *Folkways in China*. London: Probsthain, 1929. A catalogue of festivals and other folk-religion observances and customs, based on long observation and done in the style of a raconteur.

1085

Werner, Edward T. C. *Myths and Legends of China*. New York: Brentano's, 1922. A standard reference on the beliefs and practices of popular religion.

1086

Werner, Edward T. C. *A Dictionary of Chinese Mythology*. Shanghai: Kelly and Walsh, 1932. A standard reference work on the gods, demons, etc., of popular religion.

1087

Larousse Encyclopedia of Mythology. New York: Prometheus Press, 1959. Pp. 393-411, by Wu I-tai (Ou-I-Tai), present a general survey of the gods of popular religion (including Buddhism), with many illustrations.

1088

Groot, J. J. M. de. *The Religion of the Chinese*. New York: Macmillan, 1910. A general survey of Chinese popular religion, noting the religious aspects and contributions of Confucianism, Taoism, and Buddhism.

1089

Bredon, Juliet and Igor Mitrophanow. *The Moon Year*. Shanghai: Kelly and Walsh, 1927. A description of popular festivals and the customs associated with them, arranged month by month.

1090

Groot, J. J. M. de. *The Religious System of China*. 6 vols. Leiden: E. J. Brill, 1892–1910. A compendium of information about demonology and other aspects of modern popular religion; should not be relied on for the history of Chinese religions and philosophies.

1091

Doré, Henri. *Manuel des supersitions chinoises*. 2d ed. Shanghai: Mission Catholique, 1936. A catalogue of Chinese superstitions and general practices of popular religion, arranged according to broad topics.

1092

Doré, Henri. *Researches into Chinese Superstitions*, trans. by M. Kennelly and others. 13 vols. Shanghai: Tusewei Press, 1914-38. A monumental, voluminous compendium of information about Chinese folk religion in modern times, with numerous illustrations.

1093

Harvey, Edwin Deeks. *The Mind of China*. New Haven: Yale University Press, 1933. A detailed, personal report on the characteristics and practices of Chinese popular religion, with special attention to notions about the soul, various fetishes, astrology, etc.

1094

Morgan, H. T. *Chinese Symbols and Superstitions*. South Pasadena: P. D. and Ione Perkins, 1942. A description of common Chinese design symbols and the superstitions associated with them.

1095

Willoughby-Mead, Gerald. *Chinese Ghouls and Goblins*. New York: Stokes, 1928. An introduction to modern Chinese folk religion, and especially to its demonology and symbolism; with translations of numerous folk tales about the supernatural.

Confucianism

Confucianism is a code of conduct, rooted in family relationships but prescribing broadly for all social and political relationships, that is intended to foster individual and social well-being by subordinating all aspects of life to a universal moral order ordained by a willful but impersonal Heaven. It imposes on the individual a heavy sense of moral responsibility and advocates earnest efforts at moral regeneration. For society at large it advocates rule by men of moral merit, steeped in the wisdom of the ancients and the lessons of the past. Though some characteristic Confucian attitudes can be traced back to such early paragons as the Duke of Chou of the 12th century B.C., the doctrines were first expounded in a somewhat systematic way by K'ung Ch'iu (Confucius, 550–471 B.C.), who was perhaps China's first professional teacher. His aphoristic sayings, known as the *Lun-yü* ("Analects"), were quite unsystematically collected by disciples after his death. Other early Confucian thinkers of note include Meng-tzu (Mencius, 371–289 B.C.) and Hsün-tzu (fl. 3rd century B.C.). In addition to their writings, the *Hsiao-ching* ("Classic of Filial

Piety") is considered an early canon. Under the Former Han dynasty (202 B.C.–A.D. 9) Confucian doctrines became the official ideology of the newly-emerged imperial state, but in a form that borrowed emphases from the rival schools of Taoism and Legalism and was notably more authoritarian than the original doctrines. This so-called Imperial Confucianism, systematized by the Former Han interpreter Tung Chung-shu (179–104 B.C.), underwent further changes of emphasis from period to period in Chinese history. In Sung times (960–1279) it was wholly reinterpreted in response to the challenge of Buddhism, in the process actually absorbing some elements from Buddhism. The resulting Neo-Confucianism buttresses the moral values of original Confucianism with an elaborate metaphysical system. Among variant Neo-Confucian schools, that of the synthesizer Chu Hsi (1130–1200) has provided the predominant Chinese philosophical current into the 20th century.

Confucianism in general

1096

Creel, H. G. *Confucius the Man and the Myth.* New York: John Day, 1949; paperbound reprint New York: Harper, 1960, under the title *Confucius and the Chinese Way.* A comprehensive, authoritative, and readable analysis of the life and times of Confucius, his thought and its transformation into an authoritarian state-supported orthodoxy, and the influence of Confucianism in modern times in both China and the West; perhaps overemphasizes the democratic qualities of Confucian thought.

1097

Wright, Arthur F. (ed.) *The Confucian Persuasion.* Stanford: Stanford University Press, 1960. Essays by 10 specialists, on different aspects of Confucianism as a way of life throughout history; symposium from conferences of the Committee on Chinese Thought, 1957–58.

1098

Nivison, David S. and Arthur F. Wright (ed.). *Confucianism in Action.* Stanford: Stanford University Press, 1959. Essays by 11 specialists, on Confucian elements in family and bureaucratic life and on Confucianism in Japan; symposium from conferences of the Committee on Chinese Thought, 1957-58.

1099

Liu Wu-chi. *A Short History of Confucian Philosophy.* Baltimore: Penguin Books, 1955. A practitioner's enthusiastic interpretation of the meaning and history of Confucianism, sometimes more admiring than critical.

1100

Graham, A. C. "Confucianism," in *Concise Encyclopedia of Living Faiths* (R. C. Zaehner, ed.; New York: Hawthorne Books, 1959), pp. 365-384. A brief authoritative introduction to the history and principal doctrines of Confucianism.

1101

Cheng T'ien-hsi. *China Moulded by Confucius.* London: Stevens, 1947. A wide-ranging, well informed discussion of Chinese culture as a whole, revealing what it means to be a conservative Confucian in modern times.

1102

Schwartz, Benjamin. "Some Polarities in Confucian Thought," in *Confucianism in Action* (D. S. Nivison and A. F. Wright, ed.; Stanford: Stanford University Press, 1959), pp. 50-62. On "self-cultivation and the ordering of society," "knowledge and action," etc., as characteristic Confucian problems.

1103

Chan Wing-tsit. "The Evolution of the Confucian Concept *Jen*," *Philosophy East and West,* IV (1954–55), 295-319. An evaluation of modern scholarly controversies concerning the meaning and significance to Confucian thought in general of a term used by all Confucians ("goodness"? "perfect virtue"? "benevolence"? "love"? etc.).

1104

Dubs, Homer H. "The Development of Altruism in Confucianism," *Philosophy East and West,* I (1951), 48-55. On a Moist contribution to the development of Confucian ethics.

1105

Herbert, Edward (pseud. of E. H. Kenney). *A Confucian Notebook.* London: John Murray, 1950; paperbound reprint New York: Grove Press, 1960. (Wisdom of the East Series) Miscellaneous brief essays on various aspects of early Confucian thought and history and some of the rival schools.

1106

Weber, Max. *The Religion of China,* trans. by Hans H. Gerth. Glencoe, Ill.: Free Press, 1951. Includes an analysis of imperial Confucianism from a highly theoretical, sociological point of view; not to be relied on for descriptive detail.

1107

Dubs, Homer H. "The Archaic Royal Jou Religion," *T'oung Pao,* XLVII (1958), 217-259. A technical study of religious aspects of Chou ("Jou") dynasty thought, suggesting that until the time of Hsün-tzu there was a clear belief in a supreme "high-god" *(ti),* even on Confucius' part, and *t'ien* ("Heaven") was synonymous.

1108

Dubs, Homer H. "The Rise of Philosophy in China before Confucius," in *Akten des vierundzwansigsten Internationalen Orientalisten-Kongresses München, 1957* (Herbert Franke, ed.; Wiesbaden: Franz Steiner, 1959).

1109

Hsü, Leonard Shihlien. *The Political Philosophy of Confucianism.* London: Routledge, 1932. A rather traditionalistic and uncritical presentation of the socio-political implications of early Confucian (perhaps preferably "early Chinese") thought.

1110

Rowbotham, A. H. "The Impact of Confucianism on Seventeenth Century Europe," *Far Eastern Quarterly,* IV (1944–45), 224-242. A balanced evaluation of Confucian influence on the European Enlightenment.

* * *

1111

Chen, Ivan. *The Book of Filial Duty.* London: John Murray, 1920. (Wisdom of the East Series) A complete translation of the *Hsiao-ching,* "The Classic of Filial Piety," a work probably of Han date that became a basic ethical text for later Confucians.

1112

Müller, Max (ed.). *Sacred Books of the East.* Vol. 1. Oxford: Clarendon Press, 1879. Includes an authoritative translation by James Legge of the *Hsiao-ching.*

Confucius

Recommended general histories: Creel: *Chinese Thought,* chap. 3; Fung: *Short History,* chap. 4; de Bary: *Sources,* chap. 2; Fung: *History,* I, chap. 4.

1113

Creel, H. G. *Confucius the Man and the Myth.* New York; John Day, 1949; paperbound reprint New York: Harper, 1960, under the title *Confucius and the Chinese Way.* A comprehensive, authoritative, and readable analysis of the life, times, thought, and influence of Confucius; perhaps overemphasizes the democratic qualities of his thought.

1114

Kaizuka Shigeki. *Confucius*, trans, by G. Bownas. New York: Macmillan, 1956. A brief study of the life and teachings of Confucius, in a somewhat traditionalistic analysis.

1115

Hamburger, Max. "Aristotle and Confucius: A Comparison," *Journal of the History of Ideas*, XX (1959), 236-249. On the inseparability of ethics and politics, the doctrine of the mean, humanism, social order, the importance of education, etc.; a general interpretive comparison. Cf. Hamburger's earlier article on the same theme, "Aristotle and Confucius: A Study in Comparative Philosophy," *Philosophy*, XXXI (1956), 324-357, in which he refutes a common analogy between Confucius and Socrates, Mencius and Plato, and Hsün-tzu and Aristotle.

1116

Taam Cheuk-woon. "On Studies of Confucius," *Philosophy East and West*, III (1953–54), 147-165. A critical review of translations and biographies of Confucius.

1117

Sinaiko, Herman L. "The Analects of Confucius," in *Approaches to the Oriental Classics* (W. T. de Bary, ed.; New York: Columbia University Press, 1959), pp. 142-152. An evaluation of the significance of the *Analects* for general education purposes in the United States.

1118

Collis, Maurice. *The First Holy One*. New York: Knopf, 1948. A popular study of Confucius' life, teachings, and influence, based entirely on secondary materials; not to be used for scholarly purposes.

1119

Doeblin, Alfred. *The Living Thoughts of Confucius*. New York: David McKay, 1940; paperbound reprint Greenwich, Conn.: Fawcett, 1959. A popular introduction to Confucius and his thought, supplemented by selections from the *Lun-yü* and other Confucian classics (from Legge's translations, without credit); not authoritative and not recommended for any scholarly use.

* * *

1120

Waley, Arthur (trans.). *The Analects of Confucius*. London: Allen and Unwin, 1938. The most often recommended modern translation, with critical textual and historical annotations and authoritative introductory discussions of some of the most important terms and ideas that appear in the text.

1121

Legge, James (trans.). *The Chinese Classics*. 2d ed. rev. Vol. 1. Oxford: Clarendon Press, 1893. (Being reprinted by Hong Kong University Press, 1961.) Includes an authoritative, annotated translation of the *Analects* and reproduces the Chinese text; remains a standard reference for scholarly purposes.

1122

Soothill, W. E. (trans.) *The Analects of Confucius*. London: Oxford University Press, 1937. (The World's Classics series.) A standard, authoritative translation with a biographical introduction and very limited annotations; useful in contrast to the renderings of Legge and Waley.

1123

Ware, James R. (trans.) *The Sayings of Confucius*. New York: Mentor Books, 1955. A complete, reliable translation, with an introduction but without annotations.

1124

Lin Yutang (trans.). *The Wisdom of Confucius*. New York: Modern Library, 1938. A complete translation of the *Analects*, rearranged by topics; supplemented with a translation of the biography of Confucius in Ssu-ma Ch'ien's *Shih-chi* and translations from Mencius and

other early Confucian writings; with a long introduction about the major characteristics of Confucian thought.

1125

Giles, Lionel (trans.). *The Sayings of Confucius*. London: John Murray, 1907; paperbound reprint New York: Grove Press, 1961. (Wisdom of the East Series.) Translations of most of the sections of the *Lun-yü*, rearranged according to broad topics; with brief annotations.

1126

Kramers, R. P. (trans.) *K'ung Tzu Chia Yü: The School Sayings of Confucius*. Leiden: E. J. Brill, 1950. The first 10 sections (*chüan* 1-2) of an early collection of anecdotes about Confucius, probably compiled in the 3d century A.D. and of dubious reliability; with detailed philological annotations and a long, technical introduction about the origin and significance of the work.

Mencius

Recommended general histories: Fung: *Short History*, chap. 7; Creel: *Chinese Thought*, chap. 5; Fung: *History*, I, chap. 6.

1127

Chang, Carsun. "The Significance of Mencius," *Philosophy East and West*, VIII (1958–59), 37-48. A reappraisal of Mencius' importance in the history of Confucianism, suggesting that he was more influential than Confucius and noting some analogies between Mencius' thought and that of Plato and Kant.

1128

Richards, I. A. *Mencius on the Mind*. London: Kegan Paul, 1932. An analysis of Mencius' interpretation of human psychology by a noted English semanticist; speculative but stimulating.

1129

Dubs, Homer H. "Mencius and Sün-dz On Human Nature," *Philosophy East and West*, VI (1956–57), 213-222. The influence on subsequent Chinese thought of the difference of opinion between Mencius and Hsün-tzu as to whether human nature is inherently good or bad.

1130

Sargent, G. E. "Le debat entre Meng-tseu et Siun-tseu sur 'la nature humaine'," *Oriens Extremus*, III (1956), 1-17. On one of the great disagreements in early Confucianism: Mencius' belief that human nature is essentially good as against Hsün-tzu's belief that it is inherently bad.

* * *

1131

Ware, James R. (trans.) *The Sayings of Mencius*. New York: Mentor Books, 1960. A complete, reliable translation, but without annotations; the introduction includes representative selections from Mencius' philosophical predecessors for comparative purposes.

1132

Waley, Arthur. *Three Ways of Thought in Ancient China*. New York: Macmillan, 1939; paperbound reprint Garden City, N.Y.: Doubleday Anchor Books, 1956. Part 2 is an authoritative introduction to Mencius, incorporating many substantial translations.

1133

Legge, James (trans.). *The Chinese Classics*. 2d ed. rev. Vol. 2. Oxford: Clarendon Press, 1895. (Being reprinted by Hong Kong University Press, 1961.) An authoritative, annotated translation of the book of Mencius; remains a standard reference for scholarly purposes.

1134

Lyall, Leonard A. (trans.) *Mencius*. London: Longmans, Green, 1932. A standard, complete translation; should be consulted for contrast with Ware's rendering.

1135

Giles, Lionel (trans.). *The Book of Mencius*. London: John Murray, 1942. (Wisdom of the East Series.) Incomplete, but reliable.

Hsün-tzu

Recommended general histories: Fung: *Short History*, chap 13; Creel: *Chinese Thought*, chap. 7; Fung: *History*, I, chap. 12.

1136

Dubs, Homer H. *Hsüntze, the Moulder of Ancient Confucianism*. London: Probsthain, 1927. A comprehensive study of the life and thought of Hsün-tzu, ancient champion of a "realistic" and somewhat authoritarian brand of Confucianism as opposed to the "idealistic" version of Mencius; critical and authoritative.

1137

Dubs, Homer H. (trans.) *The Works of Hsüntze*. London: Probsthain, 1928. The only substantial translation from the Hsün-tzu in a Western language, though not complete.

1138

Dubs, Homer H. "Mencius and Sun-dz On Human Nature," *Philosophy East and West*, VI (1956–57), 213-222. The influence on subsequent Chinese thought of the difference of opinion between Mencius and Hsün-tzu as to whether human nature is inherently good or bad.

Neo-Confucianism

Recommended general histories: Fung: *Short History*, chaps. 23-26; de Bary: *Sources*, chaps. 18-22; Fung: *History*, II, chaps. 10-16.

1139

Chang, Carsun. *The Development of Neo-Confucian Thought*. New York: Bookman Associates, 1957. A detailed general study of the development of Neo-Confucianism in T'ang and Sung times, incorporating many brief translations; interpretive, repeatedly showing contrasts and comparisons with Western thought.

1140

De Bary, W. T. "Some Common Tendencies in Neo-Confucianism," in *Confucianism in Action* (D. S. Nivison and A. F. Wright, ed.; Stanford: Stanford University Press, 1959), pp. 25-49. On what is "Confucian" about various Chinese and Japanese schools of thought in recent centuries, and why Confucianism has lost its former influence.

1141

Kimura Eiichi. "The New Confucianism and Taoism in China and Japan from the Fourth to the Thirteenth Centuries A.D.," *Cahiers d'Histoire Mondiale*, V (1959–60), 801-829. A brief, interpretive resumé of medieval Chinese intellectual history with reference to the development from Confucian scholasticism *(ching-hsüeh)* into Neo-Confucianism.

1142

De Bary, W. T. "A Reappraisal of Neo-Confucianism," in *Studies in Chinese Thought* (A. F. Wright, ed.; Chicago: University of Chicago Press, 1953), pp. 81-111. Emphasizes the political concerns that animated the Sung founders of Neo-Confucianism.

1143

Chan Wing-tsit. "The Neo-Confucian Solution of the Problems of Evil," *Bulletin of the Institute of History and Philology, Academia Sinica*, XXVIII (1957), 773-791. A case study of the process by which Neo-Confucians of the Sung dynasty created a metaphysical justification for a traditional Confucian ethical concept.

1144

Chan Wing-Tsit. "Neo-Confucianism and Chinese Scientific Thought," *Philosophy East and West*, VI (1956–57), 309-332. On the scientific spirit in Neo-Confucianism; with special reference to the writings of Joseph Needham and Hu Shih.

1145

Nivison, David S. "Protest against Conventions and Conventions of Protest," in *The Confucian Persuasion* (A. F. Wright, ed.; Stanford; Stanford University Press, 1960), pp. 177-201. How Neo-Confucians since T'ang times have expressed dissatisfaction with the established values of their society, and especially with the standardization of education associated with the civil service examination system.

1146

Mote, Frederick W. "Confucian Eremitism in the Yüan Period," in *The Confucian Persuasion* (A. F. Wright, ed.; Stanford: Stanford University Press, 1960), pp. 202-240. Includes a general discussion of Confucian, Taoist, and Neo-Confucian views on withdrawal from society.

* * *

1147

Bruce, J. P. *Chu Hsi and His Masters*. London: Probsthain, 1923. A standard reference on the development of Neo-Confucianism in Sung times and its culmination in the synthesis of Chu Hsi.

1148

Bruce, J. P. (trans.) *The Philosophy of Human Nature, by Chu Hsi*. London: Probsthain, 1922. Extensive selections from Chu Hsi's collected works, concerning his psychological analysis of the human condition.

1149

Graham, A. C. *Two Chinese Philosophers, Ch'eng Ming-tao and Ch'eng Yi-ch'uan*. London: Lund Humphries, 1958. An excellent explication of two great 11th century molders of Neo-Confucianism, Ch'eng Hao and Ch'eng I, secondary in importance only to Chu Hsi.

1150

Pulleyblank, Edwin G. "Neo-Confucianism and Neo-Legalism in T'ang Intellectual Life, 755–805," in *The Confucian Persuasion* (A. F. Wright, ed.; Stanford: Stanford University Press, 1960), pp. 77-114. On the conflicts of moralism and rationalism after the An Lu-shan rebellion, setting the stage for Sung Neo-Confucianism.

1151

Le Gall, Stanislas. *Le philosophe Tchou Hi, sa doctrine, son influence*. 2d ed. Shanghai: Mission Catholique, 1923. (Variétés Sinologiques, 6.) A general, critical study of the great synthesizer of Sung Neo-Confucianism; should be used as a contrast to Bruce's *Chu Hsi and His Masters*.

1152

Sargent, G. E. *Tchou Hi contre le Bouddhisme*. Paris: Imprimerie Nationale, 1955; reprinted in *Mélanges de l'Institut des Hautes Études Chinoises*, I (1957), 1-156. Reproduction and translation of Chu Hsi's essays attacking Buddhism, with an introduction.

1153

Chow Yih-ching. *La philosophie morale dans le Neo-Confucianisme*. Paris: Presses Universitaires de France, 1954. An authoritative study of the philosophy of Chou Tun-i (1017–73), one of the early shapers of Sung Neo-Confucianism; with selected translations from his works.

1154

Graf, Olaf (trans.). *Dschu Hsi: Djin-si Lu, die sungkonfuzianische Summa*. 3 vols. Tokyo: Sophia University Press, 1953. (Monumenta Nipponica Monographs, 12.) A German translation of *Chin-ssu lu*, Chu Hsi's synthesis of his Neo-Confucian doctrines; with detailed introductory interpretations.

* * *

1155

Huang Siu-chi. *Lu Hsiang-shan, a Twelfth Century Chinese Idealist Philosopher*. New Haven: American Oriental Society, 1944. A brief but critical and authoritative study of a contemporary of Chu Hsi who founded a competing, "idealistic" school of Neo-Confucianism; with an excellent introductory discussion of the history of Neo-Confucianism in general and a brief evaluation of the great 16th century intuitive idealist Wang Yang-ming, in whom Lu's influence culminated.

1156

Chang, Carsun. "Wang Yang-ming's Philosophy," *Philosophy East and West*, V (1955–56), 3-18. A brief, nontechnical interpretation of the idealism of the great Ming dynasty Neo-Confucian, with an assessment of his influence in both China and Japan.

1157

Henke, Frederick G. *The Philosophy of Wang Yang-ming*. Chicago: Open Court Publishing Co., 1916. A selective translation of the teachings of the 15th-16th century Neo-Confucian who was the most serious challenger of orthodox Chu Hsi-ism in Ming times.

1158

Nivison, David S. "The Problem of 'Knowledge' and 'Action' in Chinese Thought Since Wang Yang-ming," in *Studies in Chinese Thought* (A. F. Wright, ed.; Chicago: University of Chicago Press, 1953), pp. 112-145. On related notions that 'knowing' implies 'doing' and 'doing' implies 'knowing' among certain Chinese thinkers from the 16th century to Sun Yat-sen and Mao Tse-tung, with special detail on Chang Hsüeh-ch'eng (1738–1801).

1159

Hucker, Charles O. "The Tung Lin Movement of the Late Ming Period," in *Chinese Thought and Institutions* (J. K. Fairbank, ed.; Chicago: University of Chicago Press, 1957), pp. 132-163. On an anti-Wang Yang-ming reform movement of the late 16th and early 17th centuries, with emphasis on its political activism.

1160

Busch, Heinrich. "The Tung-lin shu-yüan and its Political and Philosophical Significance," *Monumenta Serica*, XIV (1949–55), 1-163. On a conservative philosophical movement of the late 16th and early 17th centuries, reacting against the "intuitive" radicalism of Wang Yang-ming's followers.

1161

Hucker, Charles O. "Confucianism and the Chinese Censorial System," in *Confucianism in Action* (D. S. Nivison and A. F. Wright, ed.; Stanford: Stanford University Press, 1959), pp. 182-208. An analysis of the mixed Confucian-Legalist ideology that constituted "imperial Confucianism" in Ming times.

1162

Wang Tch'ang-tche. *La philosophie morale de Wang Yang-ming*. Paris: P. Geunther, 1936. (Variétés Sinologiques, 63.) A thorough analysis of Wang Yang-ming's doctrine of "moral intuition" or "intuitive knowledge," which differentiates his thinking from that of the orthodox, Chu Hsi school of Neo-Confucianism.

* * *

1163

Liang Ch'i-ch'ao. *Intellectual Trends in the Ch'ing Period (1644–1912)*, trans. by Immanuel C. Y. Hsü. Cambridge: Harvard University Press, 1959. (Harvard East Asian Studies, II) Includes much data on Confucian movements of the Manchu period, especially the "Han Learning" movement.

1164

De Bary, William Theodore. "Chinese Despotism and the Confucian Ideal: A Seventeenth-Century View," in *Chinese Thought and Institutions* (J. K. Fairbank, ed.; Chicago: University of Chicago Press, 1957), pp. 163-203. An analytical summary of a socio-political critique by an eminent Neo-Confucian scholar: Huang Tsung-hsi's *Ming-i Tai-fang Lu*.

1165

Freeman, Mansfield. "The Ch'ing Dynasty Criticism of Sung Politico-philosophy," *Journal of the North China Branch, Royal Asiatic Society*, LIX (1928), 78-110. On early Ch'ing reappraisals of Chu Hsi-ism.

1166

Freeman, Mansfield. "The Philosophy of Tai Tung-yüan," *Journal of the North China Branch, Royal Asiatic Society*, LXIV (1933), 50-71. On the Neo-Confucian Tai

Chen (1724–77), generally considered the most creative thinker of Ch'ing times.

1167

Freeman, Mansfield. "Yen Hsi Chai, a 17th Century Philosopher," *Journal of the North China Branch, Royal Asiatic Society*, LVII (1926), 70-91. On the Neo-Confucian Yen Yüan, an early Chinese pragmatist.

Confucianism as a state cult

Recommended general histories: de Bary: *Sources*, chap. 12; Fung: *Short History*, chaps. 17-18; Fung: *History*, I, chaps. 14-15, II, chaps. 1-3.

1168

Shryock, John K. *The Origin and Development of the State Cult of Confucius*. New York: Century, 1932. A detailed, authoritative analysis of the history of Confucianism as a state-sponsored, semi-religious system of public ceremonies from the death of Confucius into the 20th century republican era; with brief descriptive comments about later Confucian thinkers and two especially useful chapters on the emergence of state-sponsored Confucianism in Han times: "Han Wu Ti and the Confucian Triumph" (3) and "Tung Chung-shu on the Art of Government" (4).

1169

Dubs, H. H. "The Victory of Han Confucianism," in Dubs' translation of *The History of the Former Han Dynasty, by Pan Ku*, vol. 2 (Baltimore: Waverly Press, 1944), pp. 341-353. On the adoption of Confucianism as the official orthodoxy by Emperor Wu in the 2d century B.C., under the influence of Tung Chung-shu.

1170

Chan Wing-tsit. "Confucianism," in *Living Schools of Religion* (V. Ferm, ed.; Ames, Iowa: New Students Outline Series, 1958; originally published New York: Philosophical Library, 1948, under the title *Religion in the Twentieth Century*), pp. 97-111. A survey of Confucianism in its religious aspects: worship of Heaven, ancestors, and Confucius himself.

1171

Johnston, Reginald F. *Confucianism and Modern China*. New York: Appleton-Century, 1935. Especially on Confucianism as a semi-official religious system or system of public morality, with particular reference to the 20th century.

1172

Williams, E. T. "The State Religion of China during the Manchu Dynasty," *Journal of the North China Branch, Royal Asiatic Society*, XLIV (1913), 11-45. Detailed description of the ceremonies associated with the worship of Heaven and other rituals of state Confucianism.

1173

Tjan Tjoe Som. *Po Hu T'ung: The Comprehensive Discussions in the White Tiger Hall*. 2 vols. Leiden: E. J. Brill, 1949–52. Translation of a report of a court-sponsored conference on the classics in A.D. 79, with a long technical introduction; a major contribution toward understanding the world-view and intellectual life of Han China.

1174

Groot, J. J. M. de. *Sectarianism and Religious Persecution in China*. 2 vols. Amsterdam: Johannes Müller, 1903–04. A compendium of translations and essays about governmental efforts throughout history to control or suppress Buddhism, Taoism, Christianity, secret societies, etc., with special reference to the T'ang, Ming, and Ch'ing periods.

1175

Harlez, Charles Joseph de. *La religion et les cérémonies impériales de la Chine moderne*. Brussels: 1893. A voluminous description of Confucianism as an official cult under the Ch'ing dynasty; based on the *Ta Ch'ing chi-li*.

Taoism

Taoism has many obscurities and contradictions, which feed continuing scholarly controversies about its nature and meaning. Basically, it is a quietistic creed that opposes any form of artificial interference with the natural course of the universe, even government and especially "do-goodism." The Taoist inclination is toward eremitism, individualistic spontaneity, and rather mystical harmonizing with nature, of which Tao ("The Way") is the impersonal prime mover. Taoism's principal philosophic text, *Tao-te ching,* is a semi-poetic and very obscure tract attributed to a legendary sage called Lao-tzu (6th century B.C.?). It is China's most translated work of literature. Other early philosophic texts include the more discursive and anecdotal writings of Chuang-tzu (ca. 369-ca. 286 B.C.) and fragments of questionable authenticity attributed to Lieh-tzu (5th century B.C.?) and Yang Chu (4th century B.C.?). The naturalistic quietism of these writings has appealed to Chinese of all periods and at an early time became absorbed into the prevailing world-view of the educated classes, as a kind of individualistic and mystical counterweight against the society-oriented and rational Confucianism that predominated. It contributed to the formation of Ch'an or Zen Buddhism and influenced both literature and landscape painting. What remained as a separate tradition was a form of Taoism devoted chiefly to magic and pseudo-science, organized monastically under a Taoist church hierarchy. This later Taoism was associated with yoga exercises, alchemical experiments, and popular rebellions. The diviners and demon-exorcisers who have been its principal practitioners in modern times have almost monopolized Chinese folk religion.

Taoism in general

1176

Welch, Holmes. *The Parting of the Way: Lao Tzu and the Taoist Movement.* Boston: Beacon Press, 1957. Taoist principles and history interpreted for modern Americans; generally serious, but not overly technical. Though dependent on secondary sources and at times speculative and highly fanciful (e.g., in suggesting what Lao-tzu might have to say to 20th century sophisticates), perhaps the most satisfactory introduction to the Taoist movement as a whole for the general reader.

1177

Eichhorn, Werner. "Taoism," in *Concise Encyclopedia of Living Faiths* (R. C. Zaehner, ed.; New York: Hawthorne Books, 1959), pp. 385-401. A brief authoritative introduction to the doctrines, history, and influence of Taoism.

1178

Lin Tung-chi. "The Chinese Mind: Its Taoist Substratum," *Journal of the History of Ideas,* VIII (1947), 259-272. An interpretive essay on the Taoist spirit of individualism, its pervasive influence on Chinese character, and its differences from Western individualism; suggests that the Chinese are "socially Confucian and individually Taoist." Especially lauds the Taoist "returnist" — who despite his Taoist scepticism becomes a staunch crusader

in society and "the highest type of personality to which Chinese culture is capable of giving birth."

1179

Creel, H. G. "What is Taoism," *Journal of the American Oriental Society,* LXXVI (1956), 139-152. Differentiates two essentially separate creeds in Taoism: (1) Philosophic Taoism, developing from an original naturalistic mysticism that might be called Contemplative Taoism into a Purposive Taoism concerned with methods of acquiring power over natural forces and mankind; and (2) a later Hsien Taoism, or Religious Taoism, devoted to the search for physical immortality. For the same theme, cf. Creel's article "On Two Aspects in Early Taoism," in *Silver Jubilee Volume of the Zinbun-Kagaku-Kenkyusyo,* Kyoto University (Kyoto: 1954), pp. 43-53.

1180

Hail, William James. "Taoism," in *Living Schools of Religion* (V. Ferm, ed.; Ames, Iowa: New Students Outline Series, 1958; originally published New York: Philosophical Library, 1948, under the title *Religion in the Twentieth Century*), pp. 83-93. A general survey, emphasizing the magico-religious aspects of modern Taoism.

1181

Herbert, Edward (pseud. of E. H. Kenney). *A Taoist Notebook.* London: John Murray, 1955; paperbound reprint New York: Grove Press, 1960. (Wisdom of the East Series.) Notes or essays on various aspects of Taoist thought.

1182

Mote, Frederick W. "Confucian Eremitism in the Yüan Period," in *The Confucian Persuasion* (A. F. Wright, ed.; Stanford: Stanford University Press, 1960), pp. 202-240. Includes an analysis of traditional Taoist views on withdrawal from society.

1183

Weber, Max. *The Religion of China,* trans. by Hans H. Gerth. Glencoe, Ill.: Free Press, 1951. Includes an analysis of Taoism from a highly theoretical, sociological point of view; not to be relied on for descriptive detail.

* * *

1184

Legge, James (trans.). *The Texts of Taoism.* New York: Julian Press, 1959. Authoritative, complete translations of Lao-tzu, Chuang-tzu, and a Sung dynasty "Tractate of Actions and Their Retributions" *(T'ai-shang kan-ying p'ien);* reprinted from *Sacred Books of the East* (Max Müller, ed.), vols. 39-40 (Oxford: Clarendon Press, 1891), with a new introduction about the background and meaning of early Taoism and its relation to later Ch'an Buddhism, by D. T. Suzuki.

Lao-tzu

Recommended general histories: Fung: *Short History,* chap. 9; Fung: *History,* I, chap. 8; de Bary: *Sources,* chap. 4; Creel: *Chinese Thought,* chap. 6.

1185

Waley, Arthur (trans.). *The Way and Its Power: A Study of the Tao Te Ching and Its Place in Chinese Thought.* New York: Macmillan, 1934; paperbound reprint New York: Grove Press, 1958. A standard translation, giving a somewhat magico-mystical interpretation; with a long, authoritative introduction on the philosophical context of early China out of which Taoism emerged.

1186

Duyvendak, J. J. L. (trans.) *Tao Te Ching: The Book of the Way and Its Virtue.* London: John Murray, 1954. (Wisdom of the East Series.) A complete translation with a somewhat philological emphasis, giving a predominantly rationalistic interpretation; well annotated.

1187

Ch'u Ta-Kao (trans.). *Tao Te Ching.* 5th ed. London: Allen and Unwin, 1959. A standard, fluent, very influential translation, representing some rearrangements in the text in accordance with the modern edition of Ch'en Chu.

1188

Welch, Holmes. *The Parting of the Way: Lao Tzu and the Taoist Movement.* Boston: Beacon Press, 1957. Parts 1-2 discuss the problem of Lao-tzu's historicity and the basic concepts of the *Tao-te ching.*

1189

Legge, James (trans.). *The Texts of Taoism.* New York: Julian Press, 1959. Includes an authoritative, complete translation of the *Tao-te ching.*

1190

Lin Yutang (trans.). *The Wisdom of Laotse.* New York: Modern Library, 1948. Complete translation giving a rationalistic interpretation; cf. Lin's *The Wisdom of China and India* (New York: Modern Library, 1942), pp. 579-624.

1191

Carus, Paul (trans.). *The Canon of Reason and Virtue.* Chicago: Open Court, 1945. A standard English rendering of the *Tao-te ching,* with reproduction of the Chinese text and brief annotations.

1192

Erkes, Eduard (trans.). *Ho-Shang-Kung's Commentary on Lao-Tse.* Ascona, Switzerland: Artibus Asiae, 1958. A translation of the *Tao-te ching* as modified by a Taoist commentary of the 2d century A.D., presenting the text as Taoist practitioners understand and use it.

1193

Giles, Lionel (trans.). *The Sayings of Lao Tzu.* London: John Murray, 1905; repeatedly reissued. (Wisdom of the East Series.) A translation of the *Tao-te ching* rearranged under topical headings, with a brief introduction but no annotations.

1194

Blakney, R. B. (trans.) *The Way of Life: Lao Tzu.* New York: Mentor Books, 1955. An annotated, not too literal translation, with a long introduction about principal Taoist concepts and terms; emphasizes a mystical interpretation.

1195

Bahm, Archie J. *Tao Teh King by Lao Tzu Interpreted as Nature and Intelligence.* New York: Frederick Ungar, 1958. The latest of numerous attempts to render the *Tao-te ching* into English without reference to the Chinese original (an "interpretation" rather than a translation), with a clear and often persuasive discussion of what the author believes early Taoist terms must have meant; should be used with caution.

Chuang-tzu

Recommended general histories: Fung: *Short History,* chap. 10; Fung: *History,* I, chap. 10; de Bary: *Sources,* chap. 4; Creel: *Chinese Thought,* chap. 6.

1196

Legge, James (trans.). *The Texts of Taoism.* New York: Julian Press, 1959. Includes an authoritative, complete translation of the *Chuang-tzu.*

1197

Waley, Arthur. *Three Ways of Thought in Ancient China.* New York: Macmillan, 1939; paperbound reprint Garden City, N.Y.: Doubleday Anchor Books, 1956. Part 1 is an authoritative introduction to Chuang-tzu, incorporating many substantial translations.

1198

Giles, Herbert A. (trans.) *Chuang Tzu: Mystic, Moralist, and Social Reformer.* 2d ed. rev. London: B. Quaritch, 1926. A complete, standard translation of the most poetic and imaginative of the Taoists.

1199

Fung Yu-lan (trans.). *Chuang Tzu.* Shanghai: Commercial Press, 1933. Extensive selections in an original, author-

itative translation, interspersed with explanations by a Taoist of the 3d-4th centuries A.D., Kuo Hsiang, and with a full exposition of the thought of Kuo Hsiang as a combination of naturalism and mysticism.

1200

Lin Yutang. *The Wisdom of China and India.* New York: Modern Library, 1942. Pp. 625-694, "Chuangtse, Mystic and Humorist," offers almost complete translations of 11 of the *Chuang-tzu's* 33 chapters; derived from the rendering of Giles, but with many original touches.

1201

Giles, Lionel (ed.). *Musings of a Chinese Mystic.* London: John Murray, 1906; repeatedly reissued. (Wisdom of the East Series.) An introduction to the thought of Chuang-tzu, with extensive selections from the translation by H. A. Giles.

Other early Taoist writings

1202

Forke, Anton (trans.). *Yang Chu's Garden of Pleasure.* New York: Dutton, 1912. (Wisdom of the East Series.) A translation of the section on Yang Chu in the book of Lieh-tzu, with an introductory discussion of Yang Chu's hedonism by Hugh Cranmer-Byng. Cf. Fung Yu-lan's *A Short History of Chinese Philosophy* (New York: Macmillan, 1948; paperbound reprint 1960), chap. 7; and Fung's *A History of Chinese Philosophy,* vol. 1 (Princeton: Princeton University Press, 1952), chap. 7.

* * *

1203

Graham, A. C. (trans.) *The Book of Lieh-tzu.* London: John Murray, 1961. (Wisdom of the East Series.) A complete translation, with introduction.

1204

Giles, Lionel (trans.). *Taoist Teachings from the Book of Lieh Tzu.* 2d ed. London: John Murray, 1947. (Wisdom of the East Series.) An authoritative translation, omitting the section devoted to Yang Chu.

* * *

1205

Morgan, Evan (trans.). *Tao the Great Luminant.* London: Kegan Paul, 1935. Translations from the *Huai-nan-tzu,* an eclectic philosophical work of the 2d century B.C., with strong Taoist tinges.

Later Taoism

Recommended general histories: Fung: *Short History,* chaps. 18-20; Fung: *History,* II, chaps. 5-6; de Bary: *Sources,* chap. 14.

1206

Welch, Holmes. *The Parting of the Way: Lao Tzu and the Taoist Movement.* Boston: Beacon Press, 1957. Part 3 is the most comprehensive general account available in English of magico-religious Taoism in medieval and modern times; dependent on secondary sources, but reliable.

1207

Kimura Eiichi. "The New Confucianism and Taoism in China and Japan from the Fourth to the Thirteenth Centuries A.D.," *Cahiers d'Histoire Mondiale,* V (1959–60), 801-829. A brief, interpretive resumé of medieval Chinese intellectual history, with reference to the gradual evolution of Taoism as a popular religion.

1208

Balazs, Étienne. "La crise sociale et la philosophie politique à la fin des Han," *T'oung Pao,* XXXIX (1949–50), 83-131. On the intellectual ferment of the last Han decades; pp. 116-131 on Chung-ch'ang T'ung, a Taoist poet and visionary reformer.

1209

Levy, Howard S. "Yellow Turban Religion and Rebellion at the End of Han," *Journal of the American Oriental Society,* LXXVI (1956), 214-227. Analysis of a magico-

religious Taoist movement that disrupted the last decades of the Later Han period.

1210

Maspero, Henri. *Mélanges posthumes sur les religions et
l'histoire de la Chine.* Vol. 2: *Le Taoisme.* Paris: Civilisations du Sud, 1950. A detailed study of Neo-Taoism
in late Han and post-Han times, by an authority.

1211

Holzman, Donald. "Les Sept Sages de la Foret des Bambous et la société de leur temps," *T'oung Pao,* XLIV
(1956), 317-346. On the social and intellectual ferment
of 3d century China, reflected by a famous group of
free spirits.

1212

Chang Chung-yuan. "Introduction to Taoist Yoga," *Review of Religion,* XX (1956), 131-148. On breath-con-
trol and similar energy-concentrating techniques adopted
and advocated by Neo-Taoists in post-Han times.

1213

Holzman, Donald. *La vie et la pensée de Hi K'ang (223-
262).* Leiden: E. J. Brill, 1957. On an eccentric philosopher-poet (Hsi K'ang) who was a leader of the "pure
chat" Neo-Taoist movement of the 3d century, with annotated translations of some of his writings; authoritative.

1214

Kaltenmark, Max (trans.). *Le Lie-sien tchouan.* Peking:
Centre d'Études Sinologiques de Pékin, 1953. Annotated
translation of *Lieh-hsien chuan,* a collection of ancedotes
about the magical prowess of ancient Taoist immortals,
traditionally attributed to the Former Han scholar Liu
Hsiang (77-6 B.C.).

1215

T'ang Yung-t'ung. "Wang Pi's New Interpretation of the
I Ching and Lun Yü," trans. by Walter Liebenthal. *Harvard Journal of Asiatic Studies,* X (1947), 124-161. On
"the first and greatest of the Neo-Taoists" (3d century)
and his cosmological system; technical.

1216

Giles, Lionel (trans.). *A Gallery of Chinese Immortals.*
London: John Murray, 1948. (Wisdom of the East
Series.) Biographical notes about Taoist marvel-workers translated or paraphrased from various sources, principally including a 3d century compendium about Taoist
magicians called *Lieh-hsien chuan* and a similar compendium of the 4th century called *Shen-hsien chuan,* by
Ko Hung; includes a section on the "8 Immortals" of
the Taoist tradition.

1217

Wilhelm, Richard (trans.). *The Secret of the Golden Flower:
a Chinese Book of Life,* rendered into English by Cary
F. Baynes. London: Kegan Paul, 1942. A manual of
Taoist yoga attributed to Lü Yen of the 8th century,
with a commentary by C. G. Jung relating Taoist yoga
to some themes of modern psychology.

1218

Waley, Arthur (trans.). *The Travels of an Alchemist.* London: Routledge, 1931. Translation of a biography of the
Chinese Taoist master Ch'ang-ch'un, whom Chingis Khan
summoned across Central Asia in 1222-23 for religious
instruction, with useful introductory comments about
medieval Taoist thought and influence.

1219

Demiéville, Paul. "La situation religieuse en Chine au
temps de Marco Polo," in *Oriente Poliana* (Rome: Instituto Italiano per il Medio ed Estremo Oriente, 1957),
pp. 193-234. On Buddhist-Taoist struggles for influence
at the court of Kubilai Khan in the 13th century.

Other early native philosophies

After Han times (202 B.C.–A.D. 220), despite
widespread eclecticism, all Chinese thinkers considered themselves Confucians, Taoists, or Bud-

dhists. But in the earlier formative age, when Confucianism and Taoism were emerging as the dominant native currents of thought, there were numerous competing schools, including logicians, meta-
physicians, diplomatic theorists, and military stra-
tegists. Among the more important schools was
Moism, founded by a onetime Confucian called
Mo-tzu (Micius, fl. 5th century B.C.). His highly
disciplined organization, which retained a separate
identity into Han times, preached utilitarianism and
universal love, was strongly theistic, and excelled in
dialectics. Another important movement was Legalism, a decidedly authoritarian and even Machiavel-
lian strain of political thinking associated principally with Kung-sun Yang (Lord Shang, d. 338
B.C.) and Han Fei (d. 233 B.C.). Legalism never
became an organized school, but its principles
guided the short-lived Ch'in dynasty (221-207
B.C.) and subsequently were partly incorporated
into Imperial Confucianism. A noteworthy independent thinker of the Han period was Wang
Ch'ung (A.D. 27-100), a startlingly shrewd but uninfluential iconoclast who devoted himself to expos-
ing superstition and humbug.

Moism and the logicians

Recommended general histories: Fung: *Short History,*
chaps. 5, 8, 11; Creel: *Chinese Thought,* chap. 4; Fung:
History, I, chaps. 5, 7, 9, 11; de Bary: *Sources,* chaps. 3, 5.

1220

Mei, Y. P. *Motse, the Neglected Rival of Confucius.* London: Probsthain, 1934. A scholarly and authoritative analysis of the life, times, thought, and influence of Mo-
tzu, early China's great advocate of universal love, utilitarianism, and defensive warfare.

1221

Mei, Y. P. (trans.) *The Ethical and Political Works of
Motse.* London: Probsthain, 1929. An authoritative, an-
notated translation of more than half of the Mo-tzu.
Extensive selections from Mei's translation are repro-
duced in Lin Yutang's *The Wisdom of China and India*
(New York: Random House, 1942), pp. 785-810.

1222

Perleberg, Max (trans.). *The Works of Kung-sun Lung-tzu.*
Hong Kong: 1952. The works of a dialectician of the
3d century B.C., most famous for his sophistries concerning "a white horse is not a horse," in a complete,
authoritative translation.

1223

Tomkinson, L. (trans.) "The Social Teachings of Meh
Tse," *Transactions of the Asiatic Society of Japan,* 2d
series, IV (1927), 3-179. A very substantial selection
from the book of Mo-tzu in an unannotated translation,
with a brief introduction on the philosopher and the history of his school.

1224

Holth, Sverre. *Micius.* Shanghai: Commercial Press, 1935.
A brief interpretation of the thought and influence of
Mo-tzu; undocumented.

1225

Dubs, Homer H. "The Development of Altruism in Confucianism," *Philosophy East and West,* I (1951), 48-55.
On a Moist contribution to the development of Confucian ethics.

Legalism

Recommended general histories: Fung: *Short History*, chap. 14; Creel: *Chinese Thought*, chap. 8; Fung: *History*, I, chap. 13; de Bary: *Sources*, chap. 7.

1226

Waley, Arthur. *Three Ways of Thought in Ancient China.* New York: Macmillan, 1939; paperbound reprint Garden City, N.Y.: Doubleday Anchor Books, 1956. Part 3 is an authoritative introduction to the Legalist school ("The Realists"), incorporating many substantial translations from Han Fei.

1227

Duyvendak, J. J. L. (trans.) *The Book of Lord Shang.* London: Probsthain, 1928. The writings of a 4th century B.C. prime minister of Ch'in who instituted the harshly authoritarian state controls that strengthened the far western state for its ultimate conquest of all China; with a useful, authoritative introduction about the school of Legalist thought.

1228

Liao, W. K. (trans.) *The Complete Works of Han Fei Tzu.* 2 vols. London: Probsthain, 1939–59. The most carefully systematic explanation of the Legalist point of view, by a 3d century B.C. noble who at one time studied under the Confucian Hsün-tzu.

1229

Bodde, Derk. *China's First Unifier: A Study of the Ch'in Dynasty as Seen in the Life of Li Ssu, 280?–208 B.C.* Leiden: E. J. Brill, 1938. On Legalism in practice during the Ch'in dynasty.

1230

Creel, Herrlee G. "The Meaning of *Hsing Ming*," in *Studia Serica Bernhard Karlgren Dedicata* (Copenhagen: Ejnar Munksgaard, 1959), pp. 199-211. On a doctrine of personnel control and testing that was associated with Legalist administrative techniques.

1231

Pulleyblank, Edwin G. "Neo-Confucianism and Neo-Legalism in T'ang Intellectual Life, 755–805," in *The Confucian Persuasion* (A. F. Wright, ed.; Stanford: Stanford University Press, 1960), pp. 77-114. Reveals the persistence of rationalistic Legalist attitudes long after the disappearance of Legalism as a recognized school.

1232

Hucker, Charles O. "Confucianism and the Chinese Censorial System," in *Confucianism in Action* (D. S. Nivison and A. F. Wright, ed.; Stanford: Stanford University Press, 1959), pp. 182-208. On Legalist vestiges in the "imperial Confucianism" of Ming times.

1233

Maverick, Lewis (ed.). *Economic Dialogues in Ancient China: Selections from the Kuan-Tzu*, trans. by T'an Po-fu and Wen Kung-wen. Carbondale, Ill.: 1954. Proto-Legalist ideas about socioeconomic state controls, probably written in the 3d century B.C. but attributed to Kuan Chung, a statesman of the 7th century B.C.; the translation is unfortunately not authoritative.

1234

Sah Mong-wu. "The Impact of Hanfeism on the Earlier Han Censorial System," *Chinese Culture*, I (1957), 75-111. A study of how Legalistic principles persisted in the governmental institutions and practices of the Former Han dynasty.

Wang Ch'ung and others

Recommended general histories: Creel: *Chinese Thought*, chap. 9; Fung: *History*, II, chap. 4; de Bary: *Sources*, chap. 11.

1235

Forke, Alfred (trans.). *Lun Heng.* 2 vols. London: Luzac, 1907. The complete works ("Critical Essays") of a famous but uninfluential debunker of superstitions and all-round sceptic, Wang Ch'ung of the 1st century A.D.

1236

Shryock, J. K. (trans.) *The Study of Human Abilities: The Jen Wu Chih of Liu Shao.* New Haven: American Oriental Society, 1937. On a behavioral scientist of the 3d century, whose work "might be called applied psychology of character;" with a useful introductory discussion of intellectual developments from pre-Han into post-Han times.

Buddhism

Chinese Buddhism is of the Mahayana variety. That is, it lays great stress on the moral life of laymen and the merciful benevolence of saints (Bodhisattvas), in contrast to the Hinayana or Theravada Buddhism that prevails in Southeast Asia, which emphasizes a strict monastic regimen and somber self-reliance. After a long development in India, Buddhism by the 2nd century A.D. had gained a foothold in China, where its doctrines about rebirth (*samsara*), causality (*karma*), and ultimate salvation (*nirvana*) were indeed novel. Its pageantry and iconography, its monastic sanctuaries from life's harassments, and its promises of glorious paradises for dead devotees attracted an eager popular audience; and its moral, psychological, and metaphysical analyses won respectful attention from the ruling classes. Between the 3rd and 9th centuries Buddhism became a thoroughly Chinese movement and a vigorously creative one, spawning new sects of all kinds that carried the Buddhist message on into Korea and Japan. Some were popular sects (Ching-t'u, Chen-yen), promising extravagant paradises in exchange for relatively effortless worship of messianic Bodhisattvas; they eventually found their level alongside, and intermingled with, the traditional folk religion. Others were meditative sects of an intensely intellectual nature (T'ien-t'ai and Ch'an, known to the West chiefly by its Japanese name Zen); these reinspired and reshaped all of China's intellectual and aesthetic traditions and contributed importantly to the dominant Chinese world-view. However, after the reinvigoration of Confucian thought in the 11th and 12th centuries, Buddhism lost most of its dynamic creativity and became at best a subordinate element in China's intellectual life.

World Buddhism in general

1237

Conze, Edward. *Buddhism: Its Essence and Development.* Oxford: Cassirer, 1951; paperbound reprint New York: Harper, 1959. A standard, comprehensive introduction to world Buddhism, without much special reference to China.

1238

Burtt, E. A. (ed.) *The Teachings of the Compassionate Buddha.* New York: Mentor Books, 1955. A sourcebook of readings in Buddhist scriptures, with reliable introductory statements on the history and practices of of Buddhism, including the Chinese sects; a good general introduction.

1239

Hamilton, Clarence H. (ed.) *Buddhism, a Religion of Infinite Compassion*. New York: Liberal Arts Press, 1952. A sourcebook of Buddhism teachings, including some Chinese texts, with authoritative introductory matter.

1240

Takakusu Junjiro. *The Essentials of Buddhism Philosophy*. 2d ed. Honolulu: 1949. A standard reference on the beliefs of the various Mahayana sects, from a Japanese point of view but reliable as regards Chinese Buddhism.

1241

Grimm, George. *The Doctrine of the Buddha*. 2d rev. ed. Berlin: Akademie-Verlag, 1958. A standard interpretation of the original Buddhist teachings in India by a German authority; detailed and somewhat technical.

1242

Thomas, E. J. *The History of Buddhist Thought*. London: Kegan Paul, 1933; reprinted 1951. A standard reference on the general development of Buddhist philosophy from its origins, with some reference to the Chinese sects.

1243

Bahm, Archie J. *Philosophy of the Buddha*. London: Rider, 1958. A reinterpretation of the original Buddha's concepts; a stimulating but not standard introduction to Buddhist ideas in general.

1244

Humphreys, Christmas. *Buddhism*. Harmondsworth, England: Penguin Books, 1951. An enthusiastic general survey of the history, the teachings, and the present status of world Buddhism, including data on the Chinese sects, by the founder of the Buddhist Society of London.

* * *

1245

Bibliographie Bhouddique. Paris: P. Guenther, 1928–. The most comprehensive bibliography on Buddhism throughout the world, issued serially in annual volumes; vol. 27 (issued 1958) extends coverage through 1954. Supplemented by Hanayama Shinsho, *Bibliography on Buddhism* (Tokyo: Hokuseido Press, 1961), on pre-1928 literature.

History of Buddhism in China: general

Recommended general histories: Fung: *Short History*, chap. 21; Fung: *History*, II, chaps. 7-9; de Bary: *Sources*, chaps. 15-17.

1246

Tsukamoto Zenryu. "Buddhism in China and Korea," trans. by Leon Hurvitz, in *The Path of the Buddha: Buddhism Interpreted by Buddhists* (K. W. Morgan, ed.; New York: Ronald Press, 1956), pp. 182-236. A brief but authoritative survey of the coming of Buddhism to China, the development of new Chinese sects, and the status and practices of Chinese Buddhism in the 20th century.

1247

Wright, Arthur F. "Buddhism and Chinese Culture: Phases of Interaction," *Journal of Asian Studies*, XVII (1957–58), 17-42. Suggests a 4-way periodization of Buddhist history in China: a Period of Preparation from about A.D. 65 to 317, then a Period of Domestication from 317 to 589, then a Period of Acceptance and Independent Growth from 589 to about 900, and finally a Period of Appropriation from about 900 to the present.

1248

Robinson, Richard H. "Buddhism: in China and Japan," in *Concise Encyclopedia of Living Faiths* (R. C. Zaehner, ed.; New York: Hawthorne Books, 1959), pp. 321-347. A reliable and lucid survey of the history, sects, and major beliefs and practices of Chinese Buddhism.

1249

Wright, Arthur F. *Buddhism in Chinese History*. Stanford: Stanford University Press, 1959. An authoritative interpretive essay on the general history of Buddhism in China and its influence on Chinese society and culture.

1250

Zürcher, E. *The Buddhist Conquest of China: The Spread and Adaptation of Buddhism in Early Medieval China*. 2 vols. Leiden: E. J. Brill, 1959. The most thorough, authoritative, and up to date account of the early Buddhist movements in China, with special emphasis on notable monks and communities in South and Central China in the 4th and 5th centuries; somewhat technical, but indispensable.

1251

Tsukamoto Zenryu. "The Early Stages of the Introduction of Buddhism into China," *Cahiers d'Histoire Mondiale*, V (1959–60), 546-572. A distinguished authority's reinterpretation of the history of Chinese Buddhism up to the 5th century, emphasizing its close ties with India.

1252

Liebenthal, Walter. "Chinese Buddhism During the 4th and 5th Centuries," *Monumenta Nipponica*, XI (1955), 44-83. Analyzes how various Chinese social classes reacted to Buddhism and describes the succession of disputes and debates that marked early Buddhist history in China.

1253

Gernet, Jacques. *Les aspects économiques du Bouddhisme dans la société chinoise du Ve au Xe siècle*. Saigon: École Francaise d'Extrème-Orient, 1956. An important contribution to the study of medieval Buddhism, analyzing the number of people absorbed into monasteries, their accumulation of wealth, and the extent and influence of their economic activities in the fields of commerce, trade, and industry. Cf. long review articles by A. F. Wright in *Journal of Asian Studies*, XVI (1956–57), 408-414, and by D. C. Twitchett in *Bulletin of the School of Oriental and African Studies*, London University, XIX (1957), 526-549.

1254

Hu Shih. "The Indianization of China," in *Independence, Convergence, and Borrowing in Institutions, Thought, and Art* (Cambridge: Harvard University Press, 1937), pp. 219-247. An interpretive survey of the broad impact of Buddhism on Chinese culture and of China's changing responses to it, suggesting four stages: (1) mass borrowing, (2) resistance and persecution, (3) domestication, and (4) appropriation.

1255

Chan Wing-tsit. "Transformation of Buddhism in China," *Philosophy East and West*, VII (1957–58), 107-116. On the influence of traditional Chinese humanism on the development of Chinese Buddhism.

1256

Demiéville, Paul. "La penetration du Bouddhisme dans la tradition philosophique chinoise," *Cahiers d'Histoire Mondiale*, III (1956–57), 19-38. An authoritative, interpretive review of Buddhist influence on Chinese thought in the post-Han centuries.

1257

Eliot, Charles. *Hinduism and Buddhism: An Historical Sketch*. Vol. 3. Reprint ed. New York: Barnes and Noble, 1954. Pp. 223-335 provide a standard history of Buddhism in China, noting the various Chinese sects in historical sequence and describing the 20th century status of the religion.

1258

Reichelt, Karl L. *Truth and Tradition in Chinese Buddhism*, trans. by K. van Wagenen Bugge. Rev. ed. Shanghai: Commercial Press, 1934. A standard, detailed history of Chinese Buddhism from its origins, with studies of its major beliefs and practices and an assessment of its 20th century condition; of somewhat outdated and uncritical scholarship.

1259

Bagchi, Prabodh Chandra. *India and China: A Thousand Years of Cultural Relations.* 2d ed. New York: Philosophical Library, 1951. Emphasizes the introduction of Buddhism to China.

1260

Chou Hsiang-kuang. *A History of Chinese Buddhism.* Allahabad: Indo-Chinese Literature Publications, 1955. A general, detailed survey; in a somewhat traditionalistic and uncritical approach, and in often poor English.

History of Buddhism in China: special studies

1261

Mather, Richard. "The Conflict of Buddhism with Native Chinese Ideologies," *Review of Religion*, XX (1955), 25-3*1*. A brief interpretive analysis on ideological grounds.

1262

Tsukamoto Zenryu. "The Sramana Superintendent T'anyao and his Time," trans. by G. E. Sargent. *Monumenta Serica*, XVI (1957), 363-396. On the revival of Buddhism and its institutionalization under state sponsorship in the 5th century, following its first major persecution.

1263

Twitchett, Denis. "Monastic Estates in T'ang China," *Asia Major*, V (1955-56), 123-146. A detailed, technical study of the extent and economic influence of land ownership by Buddhist establishments and of government efforts to regulate and control it.

1264

Wright, Arthur F. "Biography and Hagiography: Huichiao's *Lives of Eminent Monks*," in *Silver Jubilee Volume of the Zinbun-Kagaku-Kenkyusyo*, Kyoto University (Kyoto: 1954), pp. 383-432. A critical study of a famous 6th century compendium of biographies of Buddhist monks, noting Buddhism's introduction of alien standards of conduct into the Chinese tradition.

1265

Ch'en, Kenneth. "On Some Factors Responsible for the Anti-Buddhist Persecution under the Pei-ch'ao," *Harvard Journal of Asiatic Studies*, XVII (1954), 261-273. Reflections on why Buddhists were sometimes forcefully suppressed by the northern dynasties (Pei-ch'ao) whereas they were subjected only to debates and intellectual arguments under the southern dynasties, in terms of social and political differences between North and South China from the 4th to 6th centuries.

1266

Ch'en, Kenneth. "The Economic Background of the Huich'ang Suppression of Buddhism," *Harvard Journal of Asiatic Studies*, XIX (1956), 67-105. An analysis of the causes of the T'ang government's drastic suppression of organized Buddhism in 845, emphasizing the disruption of T'ang state revenues by tax-exempt church estates; has much data on the economic aspects of medieval Buddhist monasteries.

1267

Yang Lien-sheng. "Buddhist Monasteries and Four Money-raising Institutions in Chinese History," in Yang's book *Studies in Chinese Institutional History* (Cambridge: Harvard University Press, 1961), pp. 198-215; reprinted from *Harvard Journal of Asiatic Studies*, XIII (1950), 174-191. On the economic activities of medieval monasteries, with special reference to pawnshops, mutual financing associations, auction sales, and sales of lottery tickets.

1268

Wright, Arthur F. "Fu I and the Rejection of Buddhism," *Journal of the History of Ideas*, XII (1951), 33-47. On an early T'ang warning about the danger of Buddhism to the Confucian state system.

1269

Chou Yi-liang. "Tantrism in China," *Harvard Journal of Asiatic Studies*, VIII (1944-45), 241-332. On a form of Buddhism emphasizing magic-working, which flourished in T'ang and Sung China; with translations of biographies of three Tantric monks and numerous appendices. Technical.

1270

Suzuki, Beatrice Lane. *Mahayana Buddhism*. 2d ed. London: Marlowe, 1948. A brief untechnical discussion of the basic doctrines and practices of the Chinese form of Buddhism.

1271

Duyvendak, J. J. L. *A Chinese "Divina Commedia."* Leiden: E. J. Brill, 1952. On the Chinese Buddhist conception of Hell as reflected in a 16th century tale of a visit to Hell.

1272

Demiéville, Paul. "La situation religieuse en Chine au temps de Marco Polo," in *Oriente Poliana* (Rome: Instituto Italiano per il Medio ed Estremo Oriente, 1957), pp. 193-234. On Buddhist and Lamaist influence at the court of Kubilai Khan in the 13th century, with special reference to Buddhist-Taoist controversies.

* * *

1273

Beal, Samuel (trans.). *The Life of Hiuen-Tsiang by the Shaman Hwui Li.* New ed. London: Kegan Paul, 1911. A disciple's biography of the great Chinese Buddhist pilgrim of the 7th century, Hsüan-tsang (600-664); the preface includes information about the late 7th century pilgrim I-ching.

1274

Liebenthal, Walter. "The World Conception of Chu Tao-shen," *Monumenta Nipponica*, XII (1956-57), 65-103 and 241-268. A detailed, technical analysis of the thought of an influential Buddhist monk of the 4th century, with translations.

1275

Link, Arthur E. "Shih Seng-yu and his Writings," *Journal of the American Oriental Society*, LXXX (1960), 17-43. A technical study of the intellectual environment and the writings of an eminent Buddhist monk (d. 518).

1276

Robinson, Richard H. "Mysticism and Logic in Seng-chao's Thought," *Philosophy East and West*, VIII (1958-59), 99-120. On an important 4th-5th century Buddhist thinker.

1276A

Mather, Richard. "The Landscape Buddhism of the Fifth-century Poet Hsieh Ling-yün," *Journal of Asian Studies*, XVIII (1958-59), 67-79. On the fusion of Buddhist ideas into early "landscape poetry."

1277

Wu Chi-yu. "A study of Han-shan," *T'oung Pao*, XLV (1957), 392-450. A technical study of the life of a 7th century Buddhist poet, with translations of some of his poems.

* * *

1278

Blofeld, John. *The Jewel in the Lotus.* London: Sidgwick and Jackson, 1948. A general discussion of modern Chinese Buddhism.

1279

Callahan, Paul E. "T'ai Hsü and the New Buddhist Movement," *Papers on China*, VI (Cambridge: Harvard University Committee on International and Regional Studies, 1952; privately distributed), 149-188. A seminar paper on revitalization of Buddhism through national organization in the 20th century, emphasizing the life and work of the greatest modern Buddhist leader (d. 1947).

Ch'an (Zen) Buddhism

Recommended general histories: Fung: *Short History*. chap. 22; Fung: *History*, II, chap 9; de Bary: *Sources*, chap. 17.

1280

Watts, Alan W. *The Way of Zen*. New York: Pantheon Books, 1957; paperbound reprint New York: Mentor Books, 1959. Probably the most readable and stimulating introduction to the history and practice of Zen Buddhism; authoritative.

1281

Suzuki, D. T. *Zen Buddhism*. Garden City, N. Y. Doubleday, 1956. A paperbound collection of essays on Zen history and practice by a Zen master who has become the doctrine's most learned and persuasive interpreter to the West, edited by William Barrett. An excellent, authoritative introduction. For more detailed presentations, see the works by Suzuki from which the essays were selected: *Essays in Zen Buddhism, First Series; The Zen Doctrine of No-Mind; Essays in Zen Buddhism, Second Series; Essays in Zen Buddhism, Third Series;* and *Studies in Zen* (all London: Rider, 1949–55).

1282

Chang Chen-chi. *The Practice of Zen*. New York: Harper, 1959. A good introduction for Westerners, with some selected translations about the lives of old Chinese masters. One chapter previously published as an article entitled "The Nature of Ch'an (Zen) Buddhism," in *Philosophy East and West*, VI (1956–57), 333-355.

1283

Hu Shih. "Ch'an (Zen) Buddhism in China: Its History and Method," *Philosophy East and West*, III (1953–54), 3-24. Disputes Suzuki's interpretation of Zen as being so irrational and illogical that it is beyond "human understanding."

1284

Dumoulin, Heinrich. *The Development of Chinese Zen after the Sixth Patriarch*, trans. by Ruth F. Sasaki. New York: First Zen Institute of America, 1953. A brief history of Ch'an Buddhism during T'ang and Sung times, with appended translations and abundant indices, etc.

1285

Benoit, Hubert. *The Supreme Doctrine*. New York: Pantheon Books, 1955; paperbound reprint New York: Viking, 1959. A French psychiatrist's explanation of his own Zen-inspired "revelation" of what the human condition is and how it can be improved; an often stimulating presentation of what might be called applied Zen for Westerners, but not a scholarly exposition of Zen history and thought.

1286

Blofeld, John (trans.). *The Zen Teaching of Huang Po on the Transmission of Mind*. New York: Grove Press, 1959. Complete translation of some of the basic Chinese Ch'an teachings, by a 9th century master; with a brief introductory history of the Ch'an movement.

1287

Senzaki Nyogen and Ruth S. McCandless. *Buddhism and Zen*. New York: Philosophical Library, 1953. A simplified introduction to the theory and practice of Zen Buddhism, with translations and explications of some of the early Chinese teachings.

1288

Suzuki, D. T. *Mysticism, Christian and Buddhist*. New York: Harper, 1957. A brief collection of essays on Zen mysticism, especially contrasting it with the mysticism of Meister Eckhart.

1289

Humphreys, Christmas. *Zen Buddhism*. London: Allen and Unwin, 1949. An enthusiastic general survey of the meaning and significance of Zen, based principally on the work of Suzuki and Watts.

1290

Wong, Mou-lam (trans.). *The Sutra of Wei Lang*, newly ed. by Christmas Humphreys. London: Luzac, 1944. The teachings of one of the greatest Chinese Ch'an masters, best known as Hui-neng (638-713).

1291

Suzuki, D. T. (ed.) *Manual of Zen Buddhism*. Paperbound reprint. New York: Grove Press, 1960. A miscellaneous collection of Zen prayers and canonical texts, with illustrations.

Some Chinese Buddhist texts

1292

Soothill, William Edward (trans.). *The Lotus of the Wonderful Law*. Oxford: Clarendon Press, 1930. An abbreviated rendering of the *Miao-fa lien-hua ching*, one of the basic sources of Mahayana (especially T'ien-t'ai) teachings. See a summary and evaluation of this text by Chan Wing-tsit in *Approaches to the Oriental Classics* (W. T. de Bary, ed.; New York: Columbia University Press, 1959), pp. 153-165.

1293

Suzuki, D. T. (trans.) *The Lankavatara Sutra*. London: Routledge and Kegan Paul, 1956. One of the basic canons of Mahayana, and especially Chinese, Buddhism, translated from the original Sanscrit version (pre-4th century).

1294

Price, A. F. (trans.). *The Diamond Sutra, or the Jewel of Transcendental Wisdom*. 2d ed. London: Buddhist Society, 1955. One of the basic texts of Chinese Buddhism, in the version of the 5th century missionary to China, Kumarajiva.

1295

Liebenthal, Walter (trans.). *The Book of Chao*. Peiping: Catholic University, 1948. The *Chao-lun*, a Chinese Buddhist classic by Seng-chao (384-414); with an analysis of Seng-chao's importance in the history of Chinese thought, based in part on the research of T'ang Yung-t'ung.

1296

Hurvitz, Leon (trans.). *Wei Shou: Treatise on Buddhism and Taoism*. Kyoto: Jinbunkagaku Kenkyusho, Kyoto University, 1956. An annotated translation of a 6th century Chinese treatise on the early history of Buddhism in China, from the *Wei-shu*, and of Japanese notes by Tsukamoto Zenryo.

1297

Robinson, Richard (trans.). *Chinese Buddhist Verse*. London: John Murray, 1954. (Wisdom of the East Series) A selection of Buddhist hymns, with an introduction on the history, style, and techniques of this aspect of the Chinese poetic tradition.

Islam, Judaism and Christianity in China

Several Near Eastern religions — Manichaeism, Mazdaism, Islam, Judaism, and Christianity — had been introduced into China by T'ang times (618–907), and Islam and Christianity have been increasingly important in modern times. Moslem communities of Arab traders existed in south coastal cities as early as the 8th century. Later, and especially beginning in the Mongol period, Islam infiltrated China from Central Asia. In modern times the several million Chinese Moslems who chiefly inhabit the western provinces of Sinkiang, Yunnan, and Kansu have been recognized as an important cultural (actually, "racial") minority. Chinese Jews maintained a synogogue in the north Chinese city of K'ai-feng from the 8th into the 19th centuries and during their early history in

China were established in several cities; but the community was never large and by the 20th century had dissolved. Christianity was first introduced in 632 in the heretical Nestorian form, and Nestorian influence persisted for several centuries. Roman Catholic missionary activity began in the 13th century as a consequence of European concern about the Mongols but soon ceased, to be renewed more vigorously in the 16th century as one aspect of modern European expansion. In the 17th century the Jesuits gained extraordinary favor and influence in China and fostered great interest among Europeans in things Chinese ("Chinoiserie"). But Catholic progress in China was hampered by bitter disputes among competing orders, which provoked papal intervention and Chinese antagonism. Protestant missionary activity began in the 19th century and proved notably influential in educational and medical fields. However, all Christian work in China has been impeded by Chinese scepticism and eclecticism and by the rise of Chinese nationalism, and no Near Eastern religion has ever had Buddhism's success in appealing to the population at large or influencing the native intellectual tradition.

1298

Hughes, E. R. and K. Hughes. *Religion in China.* London: Hutchinson's University Library, 1950. Chap. 6 briefly surveys the history of Islam in China.

1299

Broomhall, Marshall. *Islam in China: a Neglected Problem.* London: Morgan and Scott, 1910. A voluminous work on the history and early 20th century status of Moslems in China; the only substantial study of the subject.

1300

Drake, F. S. "Mohammedanism in the T'ang Dynasty," *Monumenta Serica,* VIII (1943), 1-40. On the earliest Chinese contacts with Moslems and on the earliest Moslem communities in China.

* * *

1301

White, William Charles (comp.). *Chinese Jews.* 3 vols. Toronto: University of Toronto Press, 1942. A monumental compendium of data about the Jewish community at K'ai-feng in Honan province, including historical articles by various scholars, translations of inscriptions, and genealogical registers, etc.; with photographic illustrations.

* * *

1302

Moule, Arthur C. *Christians in China Before the Year 1550.* London: Society for Promoting Christian Knowledge, 1930. A standard reference on early Christian activities in China, especially noting the history of the Nestorian heresy.

1303

Saeki, P. Yoshiro. *The Nestorian Documents and Relics in China.* 2d ed. Tokyo: Maruzen, 1951. A monumental sourcebook of data on the history of Nestorian Christianity in China.

1304

Budge, E. A. Wallis (trans.). *The Monks of Kublai Khan, Emperor of China.* London: The Religious Tract Society, 1928. On two 13th century Chinese of the Nestorian faith who set out as pilgrims to the Holy Land and prospered, one becoming Mar Yaballah III, patriarch of the whole Nestorian church, and the other

(Bar Sauma) a distinguished church envoy to Rome and Paris. A full translation of a Syriac account, with detailed prolegomena about Nestorianism and its history in China.

1305

Montgomery, James A. (trans.). *The History of Yaballaha III.* New York: Columbia University Press, 1927. Partial translation of a Syriac account of Mar Yaballaha III and Bar Sauma; better annotated than Budge's translation.

* * *

1306

Latourette, Kenneth Scott. *A History of Christian Missions in China.* New York: Macmillan, 1929. The standard reference, from earliest times into the 1920's.

1307

Rowbotham, Arnold H. *Missionary and Mandarin: The Jesuits at the Court of China.* Berkeley: University of California Press, 1942. A standard, detailed reference for Jesuit history in China from Matteo Ricci on; authoritative but entertaining.

1308

Varg, Paul A. *Missionaries, Chinese, and Diplomats.* Princeton: Princeton University Press, 1958. A critical history of American Protestant missionary activities in China from 1890 to 1952.

1309

Hughes, E. R. *The Invasion of China by the Western World.* New York: Macmillan, 1938. Chap. 2, "The Missionary Influence," surveys the impact of Christianity on traditional Chinese life during the 19th and early 20th centuries.

1310

Cohen, Paul A. "The Anti-Christian Tradition in China," *Journal of Asian Studies,* XX (1960–61), 169-180. A survey of disdainful attitudes among China's intellectuals toward Christianity from the 17th century into the 1950's.

1311

Boardman, Eugene P. *Christian Influence upon the Ideology of the Taiping Rebellion, 1851–1864.* Madison: University of Wisconsin Press, 1952. A study of the Christian documents available to the Taiping leaders and their use of them in their writings. Cf. Boardman's brief article with the same title in *Far Eastern Quarterly,* X (1950–51), 115-124.

1312

Liu Kwang-ching. "Early Christian Colleges in China," *Journal of Asian Studies,* XX (1960–61), 71-78. On the establishment, curricula, and influence of church-sponsored colleges between 1882 and 1911.

1313

Boxer, C. R. "Jesuits at the Court of Peking, 1601-1775," *History Today,* VII (1957), 580-589. A brief evaluation of the history and importance of the Jesuit endeavors in China, for the general reader.

* * *

1314

Dawson, Christopher (ed.). *The Mongol Mission.* New York: Sheed and Ward, 1955. On Christian contacts with the Mongols and China in the 13th and 14th centuries; new translations, mostly by "a nun of Stanbrook Abbey," concerning John of Plano Carpini, William of Rubruck, John of Monte Corvino, Andrew of Perugia, etc., not fully annotated.

1315

Komroff, Manuel (ed.). *Contemporaries of Marco Polo.* New York: Liveright, 1928. Popular, unannotated renderings of standard accounts of Christian contacts with the Mongols and China in the 13th and 14th centuries; concerning John of Plano Carpini, William of Rubruck, and Odoric of Pordenone.

1316

Rockhill, William W. (trans.) *The Journey of William of Rubruck to the Eastern Parts of the World, 1253–55.*

London: The Hakluyt Society, 1900. The standard translations concerning William of Rubruck and John of Plano Carpini, 13th century Christian envoys to the courts of Mangu and Kuyuk Khan.

1317

Yule, Henry (ed.). *Cathay and the Way Thither, being a Collection of Medieval Notices of China.* New ed. rev. by Henri Cordier. 4 vols. London: The Hakluyt Society, 1913-16. A standard reference on Christian contacts with the Mongols and China in the 14th century; authoritative, annotated translations concerning Odoric of Pordenone, John of Montecorvino, Andrew Bishop of Zayton, John of Marignolli, etc.

1318

Pelliot, Paul. *Les Mongols et la papauté.* 3 parts. Paris: A. Picard, 1923-31. An authoritative study of Mongol-Rome relations in the 13th and 14th centuries, incorporating many documents; originally published as a series of articles in *Revue de l'Orient Chrétien,* 1922-31.

* * *

1319

Gallagher, L. J. (trans.) *China in the Sixteenth Century: The Journals of Matthew Ricci, 1583-1610.* New York: Random House, 1953. The second part contains Ricci's own account of the development of the Jesuit mission in Ming China; a basic source.

1320

Cronin, Vincent. *The Wise Man from the West.* New York: Dutton, 1955. Paperbound reprint New York: Doubleday, 1957. A popular, pious retelling of the biography of Matteo Ricci.

1321

Rosso, Antonio Sisto. *Apostolic Legations to China of the Eighteenth Century.* South Pasadena: P. D. and Ione Perkins, 1948. A collection of documents pertaining to the Rites Controversy of the late 17th and early 18th centuries, which resulted in a great restriction of Catholic missionary activity in China.

1322

D'Elia, Pasquale M. "La réprise des missions Catholiques en Chine à la fin des Ming," *Cashiers d'Histoire Mondiale,* V (1959-60), 679-700. An Italian authority's evaluation of Jesuit history and influence from Ricci to the fall of the Ming dynasty.

1323

Pfister, Aloys. *Notices biographiques et bibliographiques sur les Jésuites de l'ancienne mission de Chine, 1552-1773.* 2 vols. Shanghai: Mission Catholique, 1932-34. (Variétés Sinologiques, 59-60) An encyclopedic sourcebook of data on all Jesuits of the old China establishment.

1324

D'Elia, Pasquale M. (ed.) *Fonti Ricciane.* 3 vols. Rome: La Libreria dello Stato, 1942-49. A monumental sourcebook of original documents concerning Matteo Ricci and the activities of the Jesuit missions in China through 1615.

1325

Dehergne, Joseph. "Les chrétientés de Chine de la periode Ming (1581-1650)," *Monumenta Serica,* XVI (1957), 1-136. A detailed catalogue, province by province and place by place, of early Christian establishments and communities and their modern remains.

China's intellectual reaction to the Modern West

On an intellectual plane, China's response to the impact of the modern West was first one of rather haughty indifference and then came to be dominated by an effort to cling to the essence that makes China uniquely Chinese while half-heartedly advocating those aspects of Western institutions and philosophy that were judged necessary for China's national survival. The decay of the old political order at the beginning of the 20th century and the concurrent rise in prestige of Westernized Japan induced more determined study of Western ideas. Inspired by visits of Bertrand Russell and John Dewey after World War I, but generally quite unselective, Chinese zealously explored and championed all the variant currents of contemporary European and American thinking. For most, the appeal of traditional Chinese values remained strong. But in the 1930's and 1940's socialistic and communistic ideas became steadily more dominant in intellectual circles, and after the communist conquest of the mainland in 1949 Marxism-Leninism, as interpreted by Mao Tse-tung, became the official orthodoxy and a prescribed subject of study and discussion for all Chinese.

Recommended general histories: de Bary: *Sources,* chaps. 24-29; Fung: *Short History,* chap. 27; Creel: *Chinese Thought,* chap. 12.

1326

Teng Ssu-yü and John K. Fairbank. *China's Response to the West.* 2 vols. Cambridge: Harvard University Press, 1954. A documentary history of China's intellectual reactions to the challenge of the West from 1839 into the 20th century; an invaluable reference.

1327

Hughes, E. R. *The Invasion of China by the Western World.* New York: Macmillan, 1938. A general, authoritative description of changes in traditional Chinese life during the 19th and 20th centuries under the impact of the West, with special reference to social and intellectual aspects.

1328

Briere, O. *Fifty Years of Chinese Philosophy, 1898-1950,* trans. by L. G. Thompson. London: Allen and Unwin, 1956. A brief, objective survey of major thinkers and philosophical movements of the 20th century, showing the gradual trend away from native "idealism" toward Western-derived "materialism" and the dominance of Marxist concepts from about 1930 on; originally published in October, 1949, as an article in *Bulletin de l'Université d'Aurore* (Shanghai).

1329

Levenson, Joseph R. *Confucian China and its Modern Fate: The Problem of Intellectual Continuity.* Berkeley: University of California Press, 1958. Highly interpretive essays on China's traditional intellectual patterns and their changes in the 19th and 20th century under the impact of the West and the rise of nationalism.

1330

Chan Wing-tsit. "Modern Trends in Chinese Philosophy and Religion," in *Modern Trends in World Religions* (Chicago: Open Court, 1959), pp. 193-216. An authoritative, brief interpretation of modern developments in Chinese philosophy up into the 1950's.

1331

Chan Wing-tsit. *Religious Trends in Modern China.* New York: Columbia University Press, 1953. An authoritative study of the 20th century status of Confucianism, Taoism, Buddhism, Islam, Christianity, and folk religion; principally emphasizes syncretist movements.

* * *

1332

Wilhelm, Hellmut. "The Problem of Within and Without, A Confucian Attempt in Syncretism," *Journal of the History of Ideas,* XII (1951), 48-60. On 19th century attempts to rationalize a combination of traditional and Western ideas for the sake of modernizing China.

1333

Swisher, Earl. "Chinese Intellectuals and the Western Impact, 1838-1900," *Comparative Studies in Society and History,* I (1958-59), 26-37. On China's difficulties in adjusting to the Western pressures in the 19th century, with special reference to the thought of Lin Tse-hsü, Tseng Kuo-fan, and Chang Chih-tung.

1334

Liang Ch'i-ch'ao. *Intellectual Trends in the Ch'ing Period (1644-1912),* trans. by Immanuel C. Y. Hsü. Cambridge: Harvard University Press, 1959. (Harvard East Asian Studies, II) A study of traditional thought under the impact of modern Western ideas, by an active participant in the struggle to find a new ideological basis for Chinese life.

1335

Levenson, Joseph R. *Liang Ch'i-ch'ao and the Mind of Modern China.* Cambridge: Harvard University Press, 1953. A critical, somewhat psychoanalytical study of one of the great intellectual leaders of early 20th century China; with relevance to the agonizing transitions among all intellectuals from traditional to "modern" thinking.

1336

Levenson, Joseph F. "'History' and 'Value': The Tensions of Intellectual Choice in Modern China," in *Studies in Chinese Thought* (A. F. Wright, ed.; Chicago: University of Chicago Press, 1953), pp. 146-194. A highly interpretive analysis of the struggle between cultural nationalists and advocates of Western values in the 19th and 20th centuries, with special reference to Tseng Kuo-fan (1811-72), K'ang Yu-wei (1858-1927) and the "old text" and "new text" schools of learning, and the appeal of communism.

1337

Chang Chih-tung. *China's Only Hope, trans. by S. I.* Woodbridge. New York: Young People's Missionary Movement, 1907. A prescription for China's ills published in 1898 by one of the most influential late Ch'ing officials, an advocate of gradual reform. The book, *Ch'üan-hsüeh p'ien* ("Exhortation to Learn"), is an outstanding representation of the common 19th century view in China that, whereas Western technology should be adopted for its utilitarian value, the basic Chinese "essence" should be retained.

1338

Hsiao Kung-ch'üan. "K'ang Yu-wei and Confucianism," *Monumenta Serica,* XVIII (1959), 96-212. A detailed, authoritative appraisal of the scholarship and classical interpretations of the last of the great Confucians, best known as leader of the political reform movement of 1898.

1339

Thompson, L. G. (trans.) *Ta T'ung Shu: The One-World Philosophy of K'ang Yu-wei.* London: Allen and Unwin, 1958. A utopian vision of a world commonwealth to come, by the last of the great Confucian philosopher-reformers, completed in 1902; an annotated translation, not quite complete, with a useful introduction on K'ang's life and thought.

1340

Oka Takishi. "The Philosophy of T'an Ssu-t'ung," *Papers on China* (Harvard University Committee on Regional Studies), IX (1955), 1-47. On one of the most radical pro-Western reformers of the late Ch'ing period, a martyr of the 1898 reform movement; with a summary and analysis of his "A Study of Benevolence" (*Jen-hsüeh*).

1341

Talbott, Nathan. "T'an Ssu-t'ung and the Ether," in *Studies on Asia, 1960* (R. K. Sakai, ed.; Lincoln: University of Nebraska Press, 1960), pp. 20-34. A brief discussion of some metaphysical aspects in the philosophy of a martyred 1898 reformer.

* * *

1342

Huang Sung-k'ang. *Lu Hsün and the New Culture Movement of Modern China.* Amsterdam: Djambatan, 1957. A scholarly, authoritative analysis of intellectual history in the 20th century, with special emphasis on the role of the satirist and critic Lu Hsün.

1343

Hu Shih. *The Chinese Renaissance.* Chicago: University of Chicago Press, 1934. A good introduction to the intellectual history of the early 20th century; an evaluation of the New Culture Movement, by one of its prime movers.

1344

Chow Tse-tsung. "The Anti-Confucian Movement in Early Republican China," in *The Confucian Persuasion* (A. F. Wright, ed.; Stanford: Stanford University Press, 1960), pp. 288-312. On the struggle between Confucian reformers such as K'ang Yu-wei and iconoclasts, especially in association with the May Fourth Movement of 1919.

1345

Fung Yu-lan. *The Spirit of Chinese Philosophy.* London: Kegan Paul, 1947. Includes a new philosophical system proposed by the author, one of 20th century China's leading philosophers and historians of philosophy.

1346

Chan Wing-tsit. "Hu Shih and Chinese Philosophy," *Philosophy East and West,* VI (1956-57), 3-12. An appreciation of one of the most influential 20th century Chinese philosopher-scholars, especially noting his championship of John Dewey's pragmatism.

1347

Levenson, Joseph R. "Ill Wind in the Weil-field: The Erosion of the Confucian Ground of Controversy," in *The Confucian Persuasion.* (A. F. Wright, ed.; Stanford: Stanford University Press, 1960), pp. 268-287. How an ancient theory about equalized land holdings (the well-field system) has been revived as a focal point of politico-conomic controversy among 20th century intellectuals.

1348

Scalapino, Robert A. and Harold Schiffrin. "Early Socialist currents in the Chinese Revolutionary Movement," *Journal of Asian Studies,* XVIII (1958-59), 321-342. On socialistic influences in the thought of Sun Yat-sen and Liang Ch'i-ch'ao at the beginning of the 20th century.

1349

Schiffrin, Harold. "Sun Yat-sen's Early Land Policy," *Journal of Asian Studies,* XVI (1956-57), 549-564. On Sun's early advocacy of "equilization of land rights," derived from Henry George's land value taxation theory; cf. Harold Schiffrin and Pow-key Sohn, "Henry George on Two Continents: A Comparative Study in the Diffusion of Ideas," *Comparative Studies in Society and History,* II (1959-60), 85-109.

* * *

1350

Mao Tse-tung. *Selected Works of Mao Tse-tung.* 4 vols. New York: International Publishers, 1954-56. The officially-sanctioned English version of most of Mao's most important writings, constituting guides to the best orthodox thinking for Chinese communists.

1351

Liu Shao-ch'i. *How to be a Good Communist.* Peking: Foreign Languages Press, 1951. A basic text on the ethical views of the Chinese Communist Party.

1352

Ch'en, Theodore H. E. *Thought Reform of the Chinese Intellectuals.* Hong Kong: University Press, 1960. A detailed, authoritative history of communist China's attemps during the 1950's to impress the Marxist-Maoist ideology upon the professional classes.

1353

Nivison, David S. "Communist Ethics and Chinese Tradition," *Journal of Asian Studies*, XVI (1956–57), 51-74. On some canons of morality according to the Chinese Communist Party in comparison with traditional Confucian ethics.

1354

Wright, Arthur F. "Struggle versus Harmony, Symbols of Competing Values in China," *World Politics*, VI, (1953–54), 31-44. A contrast of traditional Chinese views with those of the Chinese communist movement.

1355

Schwartz, Benjamin. "Ch'en Tu-hsiu and the Acceptance of the modern West," *Journal of the History of Ideas*, XII (1951), 61-74. On the strongly Western-oriented thinking of a founder of the Chinese Communist Party.

1356

Johnson, Chalmers A. *Communist Policies Toward the Intellectual Class*. Kowloon: Union Research Institute, 1959. A critical analysis of thought-control in mainland China during the 1950's, with special reference to philosophical and literary spheres; with background on the general intellectual and literary history of the 20th century.

SCIENCE AND TECHNOLOGY

Scientific attitudes among the Chinese were traditionally dominated by a concern for obtaining practical benefits from an understanding of the natural universe. Abstract and experimental interests in nature were not encouraged by the prevalent ideology of imperial times. Astronomical studies and calendarical calculations, which were highly developed at the dawn of Chinese history, consequently led principally into such pseudo-sciences as astrology, geomacy, numerology, and horoscopy, all of which came to be flourishing aspects of traditional Chinese life. But there were notable developments of applied sciences, especially in the medical arts (diagnosing from the pulse, therapeutics, acupuncture) and the invention of such things as the compass, printing, and gunpowder. By the 19th century, however, China had lagged far behind the West in technology as well as science; and both political and socioeconomic problems have gravely hampered China's 20th century efforts to close this gap. Since 1949 the Peking government, with a "walk on two legs" policy, has been encouraging the maintenance of traditional technology while, at the same time, trying desperately to introduce the latest scientific techniques of the Western world.

1357

Needham, Joseph. *Science and Civilization in China*. 3 vols. of a projected 7. Cambridge: Cambridge University Press, 1954–58. A monumental compendium on China's traditional science and technology. Vol. 1 surveys China's historical evolution with particular reference to the progress of science and the interchange of ideas with the Near East and the West. Vol. 2 surveys traditional Chinese thought, especially emphasizing the scientific implications of Taoism. Vol. 3 gives a detailed history of mathematics, astronomy, meteorology, geography, cartography, geology, seismology, and mineralogy. Subsequent volumes are scheduled to deal with physics, engineering, and technology (4); chemistry and industrial chemistry (5); biology, agriculture, and medicine (6); and "the social background" (7). Especially note vol. 2, pp. 216-345: "The Fundamental Ideas of Chinese Science" and pp. 346-395: "The Pseudo-Sciences and the Sceptical Tradition." But note warnings about some of Needham's methods and about his ideological biases in extensive reviews by C. C. Gillespie in *American Scientist*, XLV (1957), 169-176, and by A. F. Wright in *American Historical Review*, LXII (1956-57). 918-920, and in *Pacific Affairs*, XXXIV (1961), 77-79.

1358

Yabuuchi Kiyoshi. "The Development of the Sciences in China from the 4th to the End of the 12th Century," *Cahiers d'Historie Mondiale*, IV (1958), 330-347. A valuable brief survey of medieval Chinese developments in mathematics, astronomy, medical arts, agricultural techniques, printing, paper-making, cartography, gunpowder and magnetism.

1359

Hughes, E. R. *The Invasion of China by the Western World*. New York: Macmillan, 1938. Chap. 5 surveys the impact of Western science and medicine on traditional Chinese attitudes during the 19th and early 20th centuries and China's tentative efforts to modernize in this regard in the republican era.

1360

Li Ch'iao-p'ing. *The Chemical Arts of Old China*. Easton, Pa.: Journal of Chemical Education, 1948. A detailed history of chemistry in China, with much useful information on metallurgy, ceramic industries, the industrial processing of agricultural products, and technology in general.

1361

Needham, Joseph. *The Development of Iron and Steel Technology in China*. London: The Newcomen Society, 1958. A brief but thorough review, based on original Chinese sources; notes the use of cast iron in the 4th century B.C., the making of steel in the 2d century B.C., etc.

1362

Li Shu-hua. "The South-Pointing Carriage and the Mariner's Compass," *Tsing Hua Journal of Chinese Studies*, I (1956), 63-113. On the development in the 3d century and thereafter of direction-pointing mechanical devices and the appearance of the magnetic compass in Chinese navigation in the 11th century.

1363

Hashimoto, M. "Origin of the Compass," *Memoirs of the Research Department of The Toyo Bunko*, I (1926), 69-92. A detailed study of historical references to "south-pointing chariots" and other compass-like instruments of China's ancient and medieval times; concludes that the magnetic needle and navigation by compass were in use in China not later than the 11th century.

1364

Bodde, Derk. "The Chinese Cosmic Magic Known as Watching for the Ethers," in *Studia Serica Bernhard Karlgren Dedicata* (Copenhagen: Ejnar Munksgaard, 1959), pp. 14-35. Surveys the history of one Chinese pseudo-science: the attempt, with pitch-pipes, to gauge the alternation of *yang* and *yin* forces from season to season, from Han into Ming times.

1365

Cammann, Schuyler. "The Evolution of Magic Squares in China," *Journal of the American Oriental Society*, LXXX (1960), 116-124. On the history and uses of numerical diagrams, an aspect of traditional China's mathematical pseudo-science.

1366

Bernard, Henri. *Matteo Ricci's Scientific Contribution to China,* trans. by E. C. Werner. Peiping: Henri Vetch, 1935. A standard reference on the introduction of European knowledge into Ming China.

1367

Winter, H. J. J. *Eastern Science.* London: Murray, 1952. (Wisdom of the East Series) Very brief and inadequate comments on the history of Chinese science are scattered throughout, but especially in chap. 2.

1368

Siu, R. G. H. *The Tao of Science: An Essay on Western Knowledge and Eastern Wisdom.* Cambridge, Mass.: The Technology Press, 1957. Includes some references to traditional Chinese attitudes toward science, but is principally a vague philosophical pleading for a combination of Western scientific method with Oriental "no-knowledge" to produce "philosopher-executives" to direct future research.

* * *

1369

Carter, Thomas F. *The Invention of Printing in China and its Spread Westward.* Rev. by L. C. Goodrich. New York: Columbia University Press, 1955. A standard reference on the history of Chinese technology as regards paper-making, printing, and book-making, with special emphasis on the devolpment of woodblock printing during T'ang, Five Dynasties, and especially Sung times.

1370

Wu, K. T. "Ming Printing and Printers," *Harvard Journal of Asiatic Studies,* VII (1943), 203-260. Has important data on the Chinese development of color printing and movable type.

1371

Wu, K. T. "Chinese Printing Under Four Alien Dynasties (916–1368 A.D.)," *Harvard Journal of Asiatic Studies,* XIII (1950), 447-523. A technical survey of printing techniques under the Liao, Hsi Hsia, Chin, and Yüan dynasties.

* * *

1372

Wong, K. Chimin and Wu Lien-teh. *History of Chinese Medicine.* 2d ed. Shanghai: National Quarantine Service, 1936. A detailed study of traditional medical ideas, practices, and practioners and of the introduction and influence of Western scientific methods in recent centuries; a monumental and indispensable compendium.

1373

Hume, Edward H. *The Chinese Way in Medicine.* Baltimore: Johns Hopkins Press, 1940. A general survey of the religio-philosophical background, the history, the techniques, and the medicines of traditional Chinese physicians.

1374

Veith, Ilza (trans.). *Huang Ti Nei Ching Su Wen: The Yellow Emperor's Classic of Internal Medicine.* Baltimore: Williams and Wilkins, 1949. The most prestigeful handbook on traditional Chinese medical arts, dating from pre-Han or early Han times, in a partial and "rough" translation, with useful introductory comments on the major medical techniques the work speaks of; with illustrations.

1375

Huard, Pierre A. and Wong Ming. *La medecine chinoise au cours des siècles.* Paris: R. Dacosta, 1959. A general survey; authoritative.

1376

Snapper, Isidore. *Chinese Lessons to Western Medicine.* New York: Interscience Publications, 1941. On the activities of the Peking Union Medical College in the 1930's, with special reference to its treatment of various diseases among the Chinese.

* * *

1377

Dubs, Homer H. "The Beginnings of Chinese Astronomy," *Journal of the American Oriental Society,* LVIII (1958), 295-300. On the purposes and techniques of Chinese astronomy from earliest times into the Han era. For an earlier, more detailed study, cf. Henri Maspero, "L'astronomie chinoise avant les Han," *T'oung Pao,* XXVI (1929), 267-356.

1378

Needham, Joseph, Wang Ling, and Derek J. Price. *Heavenly Clockwork.* London: Cambridge University Press, 1960. A history of Chinese technology in the field of clepsydras, armillaries, and power-driven astronomical models, with special reference to the engineering feats of Su Sung (1020-1101); fully illustrated.

1379

D'Elia, Pasquale M. *Galileo in China.* Cambridge: Harvard University Press, 1960. A brief study of the Jesuits' dissemination of Galileo's discoveries in 17th century China, with translations of many relevant texts and comments on the contemporary status of China's indigenous astronomy.

1380

Needham, Joseph. *Chinese Astronomy and the Jesuit Mission: An Encounter of Cultures.* London: The China Society, 1958. A brief evaluation of the impact of modern Western astronomy on China's scientific knowledge in the 17th century; with illustrations.

1381

Yabuuti Kiyoshi. "Indian and Arabian Astronomy in China," in *Silver Jubilee Volume of the Zinbun-Kagaku-Kenkyusyo,* Kyoto University (Kyoto: 1954), pp. 585-603. On the introduction and influence of Hindu and Arabian astronomical techniques in China during the T'ang, Yüan, and Ming dynasties.

1382

Dubs, H. H. (trans.) *The History of the Former Han Dynasty, by Pan Ku.* 3 vols. Baltimore: Waverly Press, 1938–55. The appendices include detailed information about lunar and solar eclipses recorded in Former Han times and about Han calendrical calculations.

* * *

1383

Goodrich, L. C. and Feng Chia-sheng. "The Early Development of Firearms in China," *Isis,* XXXVI (1945–46), 114-123, 250-251. On the use of gunpowder for firearms by the Sung Chinese against Mongol invaders in the 13th century.

1384

Wang Ling. "On the Invention and Use of Gunpowder and Firearms in China," *Isis,* XXXVII (1947), 160-178. Data on Sung military technology, supplementary to "The Early Development of Firearms in China" by Goodrich and Feng.

1385

Lo Jung-pang. "The Emergence of China as a Sea Power during the Late Sung and Early Yüan Periods," *Far Eastern Quarterly,* XIV (1954–55), 489-503. Summarizes rapid developments in naval technology and firearms in 13th-century China.

ART AND ARCHITECTURE

No aspect of Chinese civilization has been more studied and admired in the West than art, and China has often been acclaimed the most gifted nation of the world in this realm. Its earliest known masterpieces are ornate ritual vessels in bronze that were produced in Shang and early Chou times (to about the 8th century B.C.); they have been called the most exquisite bronzes ever produced anywhere. Other plastic arts reached their peaks of development later. A relatively minor one is the carving of jade into small animal and geometric forms, in which the Chinese have excelled throughout history. Their ceramic art includes an earthenware tradition that is most notably represented by human and animal figurines of the T'ang dynasty (618–907) and a porcelain tradition that reached its peak with lustrous monochrome wares of the Sung era (960–1279) and brilliant polychrome wares of Ming times (1368–1644). Sculpture in wood and stone flourished especially under Buddhist influence and especially in the T'ang period. Among its most striking products are monumental figures of animals both real and mythical, of the Buddha and various Bodhisattvas, and of Taoist deities. Of all the arts, however, painting has had greatest esteem among the Chinese, who came to consider skills in painting and literature to be complementary attributes of any educated man. From a very early time calligraphy was considered a major art form, closely allied to the composition of poetry; and from this eventually developed a tradition of calligraphy-like painting of bamboo shoots, which many claim to be China's most superb artistic achievement. Chinese paintings also include multi-hued water color representations of animals, birds, and flowers, but less portraiture than in the Western tradition. Most admired in the West have been China's monochrome, misty landscapes with figures, which originated in the Sung dynasty. Reflecting both Buddhist and Taoist influences, they suggest man's involvement with and subordination to the universe at large. In all arts, there is a distinctive and readily recognizable Chinese style — in the use of form and line and color and in the choice of subject matter. It has greatly influenced arts in the modern West but has not been significantly influenced by the West in return. The traditional Chinese art forms persist.

In architecture the Chinese have had an equally impressive and influential tradition, the finest extant representative being the imperial palace enclosure (the "Forbidden City") in Peking. Important characteristics include tthe predominant use of wood rather than stone or bricks for building, the use of pillars and beams as basic structural units, lavish coloring of all surfaces with paints and roof tiles, elaborate carved and sculptured decorations, curving roofs with upturned corners, and strictly axial dispositions in architectural groupings. Pagodas and other kinds of towers abound, but the dominance of horizontal lines gives to all Chinese buildings a dignified air of harmonizing with the surrounding landscape. Artificial landscaping has always been considered an essential corollary of architectural construction, and Chinese gardens have been imitated all over the world.

Journals specializing in Chinese art

1386
Archives of the Chinese Art Society of America. New York: 1945–.

1387
Artibus Asiae. Dresden and Ascona: 1925–.

1388
Oriental Art. London: 1948–.

1389
Bulletin of the Musem of Far Eastern Antiquities. Stockholm: 1929–.

1390
Far Eastern Ceramic Bulletin. Cambridge, Mass.: 1948–.

1391
Transactions of the Oriental Ceramic Society. London: 1921–.

1392
Ars Asiatica. Brussels: 1914–35.

1393
Revue des Arts Asiatiques. Paris: 1924–42.

The arts in general

1394
Sickman, Laurence and Alexander Soper. *The Art and Architecture of China.* Baltimore: Penguin Books, 1956. An excellent, detailed, authoritative history of the arts in traditional China: sculpture and painting by Sickman, architecture by Soper; with 190 pages of black and white plates and a comprehensive bibliography arranged by topics.

1395
Willetts, William. *Chinese Art.* 2 vols. New York: George Braziller, 1958; paperbound ed., Harmondsworth, England: Penguin Books, 1958. A comprehensive, detailed, authoritative history of all forms including architecture, w.in numerous illustrations; tends to emphasize sociological and technical aspects more than aesthetic.

1396
Munsterberg, Hugo. *A Short History of Chinese Art.* New York: Philosophical Library, 1949. A brief but authoritative introduction, arranged by periods; with 50 plates.

1397
Carter, Dagny. *Four Thousand Years of China's Art.* New York: Ronald Press, 1948. A standard, authoritative textbook survey, with profuse illustrations; arranged by periods.

1398
Sullivan, Michael. *An Introduction to Chinese Art.* Berkeley: University of California Press, 1961. A profusely illustrated general survey of China's fine and decorative arts, period by period; an excellent introduction for the general reader.

1399
Ashton, Leigh and Basil Gray. *Chinese Art.* London: Faber and Faber, 1935. A standard, authoritative history of all art forms, with very brief introductory essays, period by period, and numerous photographic illustrations.

1400
Bachhofer, Ludwig. *A Short History of Chinese Art.* New York: Pantheon, 1946. An authoritative, brief history of traditional Chinese bronzes, sculpture, and painting, with special emphasis on the analysis of forms or shapes; with 129 illustrations.

1401
Paul-David, Madeleine. *Arts et styles de la Chine.* Paris: Larousse, 1951. An excellent introductory history of Chinese arts of all forms, with too few illustrations.

1402
Grousset, René. *Chinese Art and Culture* trans, by H. Chevalier. New York: Orion Press, 1959; paperbound

reprint, New York: Grove Press, 1961. A long interpretive history of the arts in a broad cultural context by a French authority, with 82 illustrations.

1403

Bushell, Stephen W. *Chinese Art*. Rev. ed. 2 vols. London: Victoria and Albert Museum, 1909; repeatedly reissued. A comprehensive, detailed history, arranged by art forms, with more than 200 illustrations; of outdated scholarship, but still useful.

1404

Hajek, Lubor. *Chinese Art*. London: Spring Books, 1958. A profusely and beautifully illustrated general history of all art forms, based on holdings in Czechoslovakia.

1405

Fitzgerald, C. P. *China: A Short Cultural History*. 3d ed. New York: Praeger, 1950. Incorporates good chapters on the historical development of the arts and architecture.

1406

Balazs, E. and others. *Aspects de la Chine*. 2 vols. Paris: Presses Universitaires de France, 1959. Part 5 (vol. 2, pp. 319-437) is devoted to excellent brief historical and interpretive essays on all forms of Chinese art, mostly by M. Paul-David and V. Elisséeff.

1407

Burling, Judith and A. H. Burling. *Chinese Art*. New York: Studio Publications, 1953. A non-technical history, arranged by art forms; with numerous illustrations. A good popular introduction to Chinese arts and their study.

1408

Soper, Alexander C. *Literary Evidence for Early Buddhist Art in China*. Ascona, Switzerland: 1959. (Artibus Asiae Supplementum XIX) A major contribution to the history of Chinese art, with detailed descriptions of iconography, inscriptions, and literary references; concerns the era of North-South division.

1409

Davidson, J. LeRoy. *The Lotus Sutra in Chinese Art*. New Haven: Yale University Press, 1954. An interpretive history of Buddhist art in China up to the year 1000, with 40 black and white illustrations.

1410

The Arts of the Ming Dynasty. New York: Collings, 1958. Essays on the history and characteristics of paintings, ceramics, lacquer wares, metal work, etc., in the Ming era by Basil Gray and others, with 104 black and white plates; representing an exhibition held in London in 1957 by the Oriental Ceramic Society and the Arts Council of Great Britain.

1411

Fenollosa, Ernest Francisco. *Epochs of Chinese and Japanese Art*. Rev. ed. 2 vols. New York: Stokes, 1921. A classical study by a pioneer, introducing a long-dominant practice of interpreting Chinese art from a Japanese point of view; still of some use, but almost entirely superseded. Has abundant illustrations.

1412

Lin Yutang. *My Country and My People*. Rev. ed. New York: John Day, 1935. Chap. 8, "Artistic Life," offers an enthusiastic, interpretive introduction to Chinese calligraphy, painting, and architecture for the general reader.

* * *

1413

Hansford, S. Howard. *A Glossary of Chinese Art and Archaeology*. London: The China Society, 1954. A useful handbook explaining Chinese terms used in the study of art and archaeology, grouped by topics; with some illustrative charts of forms of bronze vessels, etc.

* * *

1414

Sullivan, Michael. *Chinese Art in the Twentieth Century*. Berkeley: University of California Press, 1959. A brief,

well illustrated summary of developments into the 1950's with reference both to traditional and to Western art forms.

1415

Chao Chung. *The Communist Program for Literature and Art in China*. Kowloon: Union Research Institute, 1955. A brief critical study of the subjection of art and artists to government direction during the early years of the People's Republic.

1416

Herstand, A. L. "Art and the Artist in Communist China," *College Art Journal*, XIX (1959–60), 23-29. On the subjugation of art to politics in the People's Republic; with some illustrations.

* * *

1417

Chinese Art. Hollywood: Dr. Block Color Productions, 1958. (Series 24). A set of 257 excellent color slides illustrating the history of all forms of traditional Chinese art from earliest times.

Ancient bronzes

1418

Karlgren, Bernhard. *A Catalogue of the Chinese Bronzes in the Alfred F. Pillsbury Collection*. Minneapolis: University of Minnesota Press, 1952. On one of the world's great collections of Shang and Chou bronzes, now in the Minneapolis Institute of Fine Arts; a detailed, authoritative description of the 106 pieces, with 114 plates and a long introduction on the chronology of ancient Chinese bronze developments.

1419

Freer Gallery of Art. *A Descriptive and Illustrative Catalogue of Chinese Bronzes Acquired During the Administration of John Ellerton Lodge*. Washington: Smithsonian Institute, 1946. On one of the great American collections of Shang and Chou bronze vessels; introductory essays by J. E. Lodge, A. G. Wenley, and J. A. Pope, with 50 plates and translations of all inscriptions.

1420

Loehr, Max. "The Bronze Styles of the Anyang Period (1300–1028 B.C.)," *Archives of the Chinese Art Society of America*, VII (1953), 42-53. An authoritative reappraisal, with illustrations.

1421

White, William C. *Bronze Culture of Ancient China*. Toronto: University of Toronto Press, 1956. A detailed study of numerous bronze objects from the Yellow River valley, of Shang and early Chou times (1400–771 B.C.); with maps, charts, and 100 plates.

1422

Kelley, C. F. and Ch'en Meng-chia. *Chinese Bronzes from the Buckingham Collection*. Chicago: Art Institute of Chicago, 1946. On another noted collection of Shang and Chou vessels, with 84 plates and translations of all inscriptions.

1423

Kidder, J. Edward. *Early Chinese Bronzes in the City Art Museum of St. Louis*. St. Louis: City Art Museum, 1956. A catalogue of vessels, weapons, mirrors, etc. from Shang to Han times, but especially of the Shang and early Chou periods; with 34 plates.

1424

Loehr, Max. *Chinese Bronze Age Weapons*. Ann Arbor: University of Michigan Press, 1956. A detailed, technical study of more than 100 axes, spearheads, dagger axes, knives, daggers, and swords of Shang and early Chou times; with authoritative comment on the difficulties of relating early Chinese culture to outside cultures through stylistic and technological analysis.

1425

Watson, William. *Archaeology in China*. London: Parrish, 1960. Excellent black and white plates of ceramic and bronze pieces from the prehistoric, Shang, Chou, and Han periods excavated in the 1950's, with a very brief introductory survey.

1426

Yetts, W. Perceval. *The George Eumorfopoulos Collection: Catalogue of the Chinese and Corean Bronzes, Sculpture, Jades; Jewellery and Miscellaneous Objects.* 3 vols. London: Benn, 1929–33. On one of the world's great collections, now in the British Museum.

1427

Karlgren, Bernhard. "Some Weapons and Tools of the Yin Dynasty," *Bulletin of the Museum of Far Eastern Antiquities,* Stockholm, XVII (1945), 101-144. Highly technical study of some Shang dynasty styles and techniques, suggesting that they contributed to the nomadic art styles of Central Asia.

1428

Karlgren, Bernhard. "Yin and Chou in Chinese Bronzes," *Bulletin of the Museum of Far Eastern Antiquities,* Stockholm, VIII (1936), 9-154. A standard, but highly technical, analysis of Shang and Chou bronze vessels, with numerous illustrations. Cf. the author's subsequent article, "New Studies on Chinese Bronzes," *op. cit.,* IX (1937), 1-118. Both articles emphasize dating problems.

1429

Li Chi. *The Beginnings of Chinese Civilization.* Seattle: University of Washington Press, 1957. Has much data on bronze technology in Shang times.

1430

Cheng Te-k'un. *Archaeology in China.* Vol. 2: *Shang China.* Cambridge: Heffer, 1960. Includes information and plates on Shang bronzes.

Ceramics

1431

Honey, William. *The Ceramic Art of China and Other Countries of the Far East.* London: Faber and Faber, 1945. A standard, detailed history, emphasizing China; with 192 black and white plates and 2 color inserts.

1432

Hobson, R. L. *Chinese Art.* 2d rev. ed. London: Benn, 1952. A very brief introduction, with 100 color plates, mostly of ceramics.

1433

Jenyns, Soame. *Ming Pottery and Porcelain.* London: Faber and Faber, 1953. A comprehensive, authoritative history of ceramic arts in Ming China, with 120 plates.

1434

Jenyns, Soame. *Later Chinese Porcelain: The Ch'ing Dynasty, 1644–1912.* 2d ed. London: Faber and Faber, 1959. A history of pottery production at the imperial kilns of Ching-te-chen in Kiangsi province from the 17th into the 20th century, with 120 black and white plates.

1435

Gray, Basil. *Early Chinese Pottery and Porcelain.* New York: Pitman, 1952 (?). A brief, authoritative history of Chinese ceramics from antiquity through the Yüan dynasty, with 96 black and white plates.

1436

Phillips, John Goldsmith. *China-Trade Porcelain.* Cambridge: Harvard University Press, 1956. A study of porcelain tablewares made in China for the European and American markets in the 18th and early 19th centuries, and of the porcelain trade; with 109 plates. Based on the collection of Helena Woolworth McCann.

1437

Hobson, R. L. *Handbook of the Pottery and Porcelain of the Far East.* 2d ed. London: British Museum, 1937. An authoritative history of Chinese and Japanese ceramics, with more than 200 illustrations from the British Museum collections.

1438

Hobson, R. L. and A. L. Hetherington. *The Art of the Chinese Potter.* New York: Knopf, 1923. A thick volume of 152 black and white and color plates of notable ceramic productions in historical sequence, with brief comments on each; also with a brief introduction on the characteristics of China's ceramic art.

1439

Pope, John Alexander. *Chinese Porcelains from the Ardebil Shrine.* Washington: Freer Gallery of Art, 1956. A history of Ming porcelains emphasizing stylistic changes, based on a magnificent, little-known Iranian collection of more than 800 pieces; with 142 black and white plates.

1440

Sayer, Geoffrey R. (trans.) *Ching-Tê-Chên T'ao-Lu, or The Potteries of China.* London: Routledge and Kegan Paul, 1951. A fully annotated translation of an early 19th century Chinese treatise on the history and techniques of the imperial kilns at Ching-te-chen in Kiangsi province.

1441

Mahler, Jane Gaston. *The Westerners Among the Figurines of the T'ang Dynasty in China.* Rome: Instituto Italiano per il Medio ed Estremo Oriente, 1959. An illustrated study of T'ang ceramic figurines representing non-mongoloids.

1442

Honey, W. B. *Guide to the Later Chinese Porcelain.* London: Victoria and Albert Museum, 1927. An analysis of the styles and decorations of porcelains produced at the imperial kilns of Ching-te-chen in Kiangsi province from the 1680's into the 1850's, with 120 black and white illustrations.

1443

Hobson, R. L. *The George Eumorfopoulos Collection: Catalogue of the Chinese, Corean and Persian Pottery and Porcelain.* 6 vols. London: Benn, 1925–28. On one of the world's great collections, now in the British Museum; overwhelmingly devoted to China.

1444

Hobson, R. L. *The Wares of the Ming Dynasty.* London: Benn, 1923. A standard, voluminous history of Ming porcelain production, with profuse black and white illustrations.

1445

Hetherington, Arthur L. *Chinese Ceramic Glazes.* 2nd rev. ed. South Pasadena: P. D. and Ione Perkins, 1948. On the chemistry and technology of glazes.

1446

Osgood, Cornelius. *Blue-and-White Chinese Porcelain,* New York: Ronald Press, 1956. An analysis of the forms of blue and white porcelains of the Ming and Ch'ing periods, with detailed descriptions of 92 major form classes and their sub-classes, and with 64 black and white plates.

* * *

1447

Rudolph, Richard C. and Wen Yu. *Han Tomb Art of West China.* Berkeley: University of California Press, 1951. Reproductions of 100 tomb reliefs of the 1st and 2d centuries, with an introduction and descriptions of the plates.

1448

White, William C. *Tomb Tile Pictures of Ancient China.* Toronto: University of Toronto Press, 1939. A study of pictures inscribed on ceramic tiles of about the 3d century B.C., from tombs of Honan province; with more than 100 plates of ink-rubbings.

1449

Watson, William. *Archaeology in China.* London: Parrish, 1960. Excellent black and white plates of ceramic and bronze pieces from the prehistoric, Shang, Chou, and Han periods excavated in the 1950's, with a very brief introductory survey.

1450

Wu, G. D. *Prehistoric Pottery in China.* London: Kegan Paul, 1938. A classification of pre-Shang pottery remains, with detailed technical descriptions.

1451

Cheng Te-k'un. *Archaeology in China*. Vol. 1: *Prehistoric China*. Cambridge: Heffer, 1959. An up to date synthesis of information about pre-Shang China, with much data on pottery and 45 plates.

1452

Cheng Te-k'un. *Archaeology in China*. Vol. 2: *Shang China*. Cambridge: Heffer, 1960. Includes information and plates on Shang ceramics.

Sculpture, including jade and ivory carving

1453

Munsterberg, Hugo. *The Art of the Chinese Sculptor*. Rutland, Vt.: C. E. Tuttle, 1960. A brief introduction to the history of Chinese sculpture, with 12 beautiful color plates.

1454

Priest, Alan. *Chinese Sculptures in the Metropolitan Museum of Art*. New York: Metropolitan Museum of Art, 1944. A brief, authoritative history of Chinese sculpture, with 132 black and white plates.

1455

Sickman, Laurence and Alexander Soper. *The Art and Architecture of China*. Baltimore: Penguin Books, 1956. Chaps. 2, 5, 8-10, 12 and 14, by Sickman, provide a detailed general survey of Chinese sculpture from earliest times through the 14th century; with many plates.

1456

Siren, Osvald. *Chinese Sculpture from the Fifth to the Fourteenth Centuries*. 4 vols. London: Benn, 1925. A comprehensive, standard study of more than 900 specimens of stone, bronze, lacquer, and wood sculpture, with more than 600 plates.

1457

Yetts, W. Perceval. *The George Eumorfopoulos Collection: Catalogue of the Chinese and Corean Bronzes, Sculpture, Jades; Jewellery and Miscellaneous Objects*. 3 vols. London: Benn, 1929-33. On one of the world's great collections, now in the British Museum.

1458

Soper, Alexander C. "Northern Liang and Northern Wei in Kansu," *Artibus Asiae*, XXI (1958), 131-164. An illustrated study of some Buddhist cave sculptures of far western China, dating from the 5th century.

1459

Ecke, G. and P. Demiéville. *The Twin Pagodas of Zayton*. Cambridge: Harvard University Press, 1935. An illustrated study of Sung dynasty Buddhist iconography on two famous pagodas at Ch'üan-chou in Fukien province.

* * *

1460

Hansford, S. Howard. *Chinese Jade Carving*. London: Lund Humphries, 1950. An authoritative study of China's sources of jade and of the history and techniques of jade carving, with 32 plates.

1461

Nott, Stanley Charles. *Chinese Jade Throughout the Ages*. New York: Scribner, 1937. A comprehensive, detailed history of Chinese jade carving, with numerous illustrations, many in color.

1462

Laufer, Berthold. *Jade: A Study in Chinese Archaeology and Religion*. Chicago: 1912. (Field Museum of Natural History Publication 154) A classical, voluminous study of the uses and symbolism of jade carvings, with more than 200 illustrations.

1463

Cheng Te-k'un. *Archaeology in China*. Vol. 2: *Shang China*. Cambridge: Heffer, 1960. Includes information and plates on jade carving in Shang times.

* * *

1464

Eastham, Barry C. *Chinese Art Ivory*. Tientsin: J. E. Paradissis, 1940. A brief general history and appreciation of ivory carving, with 32 plates.

Painting and calligraphy: general

1465

Cahill, James. *Chinese Painting*. Cleveland: World Publishing Co., 1960. Probably the best available introduction to the history of Chinese painting, in a fresh interpretive approach; with 110 beautiful color plates.

1466

Siren, Osvald. *Chinese Painting: Leading Masters and Principles*. 7 vols. New York: Ronald Press, 1956-58. A monumental, authoritative history in a not overly technical style; with biographical data about more than 1400 painters, including notations of where their works can be located. Vol. I: the pre-Sung era. II: Sung. III: 388 plates to accompany vols. 1 and 2. IV: Yüan and early Ming periods. V: later Ming and Ch'ing periods. VI: 464 plates to accompany vols. 4 and 5. VII: annotated lists of painters to accompany vols. 4 and 5. This compendium largely supersedes Siren's earlier standard works, *A History of Early Chinese Painting* (2 vols. London: The Medici Society, 1933) and *A History of Later Chinese Painting* (2 vols. London: The Medici Society, 1938).

1467

Sickman, Laurence and Alexander Soper. *The Art and Architecture of China*. Baltimore: Penguin Books, 1956. Chaps. 3, 6-7, 11, 13, and 15-30, by Sickman, provide a detailed general survey of Chinese painting from earliest times through the 18th century; with many plates.

1468

Cohn, William. *Chinese Painting*. 2nd rev .ed. London: Phaidon, 1951. A brief but authoritative history, with more than 200 black and white illustrations.

1469

Waley, Arthur. *An Introduction to the Study of Chinese Painting*. New York: Grove Press, 1958. A long history of Chinese painting, with 49 black and white plates; originally published in 1923, but still authoritative.

1470

Swann, Peter C. *Chinese Painting*. New York: Universe Books, 1958. A brief interpretive history for the general reader, with many color plates of somewhat uneven quality.

1471

Sze Mai-mai. *The Tao of Painting*. 2 vols. New York: Bollingen Foundation, 1956; abbreviated single-volume paperbound ed., New York: Modern Library, 1959, under the title *The Way of Chinese Painting*. Part 1 on the spirit and styles of traditional Chinese painting; part 2 a complete translation (selections only in the 1959 ed.) of *Chieh-tzu yüan hua-chuan*, a 17th century Chinese handbook on the techniques of painting various objects, with profuse illustrative drawings from the original Chinese publication.

1472

Rowley, George. *Principles of Chinese Painting*. 2nd ed. Princeton: Princeton University Press, 1959. An authoritative discussion of the subject matter and styles of traditional painting, with 47 photographic illustrations.

1473

Gulik, R. H. van. *Chinese Pictorial Art as Viewed by the Connoisseur*. London: Luzac, 1959. A new approach to the appreciation of Chinese painting through the study of the art of mounting scrolls and other aspects of traditional connoisseurship in China and Japan; with 160 plates.

1474

Lee, Sherman E. and Wen Fong. *Streams and Mountains Without End*. Ascona, Switzerland: Artibus Asiae, 1955. (Artibus Asiae Supplementum XIV). A study of a

12th century landscape scroll in the Cleveland Museum of Art, with explanations of the seals and poetry colophons inscribed and with 25 illustrative plates.

1475

Jenyns, Soame. *A Background to Chinese Painting.* London: Sidgwick and Jackson, 1935. An authoritative general introduction to the major styles, the subject matter, the techniques, and the cultural context of traditional Chinese painting, with 40 illustrations.

1476

Binyon, Laurence. *Painting in the Far East.* 3d ed. rev. London: Edward Arnold, 1923; paperbound reprint, New York: Dover, 1959. An authoritative, interpretive history of Chinese and Japanese painting.

1477

Chiang Yee. *The Chinese Eye.* 2nd ed. London: Methuen, 1936. A popular introduction to the "style" of Chinese painting, with comments on its relations with philosophy and literature, its subject matter, and its techniques.

1478

Chang Shu-chi. *Painting in the Chinese Manner,* trans. by Helen F. Chang. New York: Viking Press, 1960. A discussion of traditional painting techniques by a modern Chinese painter, with many illustrations from his own work.

1479

Rowland, Benjamin. *Art in East and West.* Cambridge: Harvard University Press, 1954. Essays touching on the major characteristics of Chinese painting in contrast with those of the West; authoritative.

1480

Vanderstappen, Harrie. "Painters at the Early Ming Court (1368–1435) and the Problem of a Ming Painting Academy," *Monumenta Serica,* XV (1956), 259-302; XVI (1957), 315-346. A detailed compendium of information about officially-sponsored painters, with much biographical data; concludes there was no formally-organized Painting Academy *(Hua-yüan)* in Ming times.

1481

March, Benjamin. *Some Technical Terms of Chinese Painting.* Baltimore: Waverly Press, 1935. A technical handbook explaining Chinese terms relating to painting.

*   *   *

1482

Gray, Basil. *Buddhist Cave Paintings at Tun-huang.* Chicago: University of Chicago Press, 1959. A brief description by an authority of T'ang and pre-T'ang murals in famous Central Asian caves, with 70 plates.

1483

Vincent, Irene. *The Sacred Oasis.* Chicago: University of Chicago Press, 1953. An illustrated description of the magnificent mural art of the caves at Tun-huang in far western China, famous storehouses of data on the introduction of Buddhist art into China; for the general reader.

1484

Warner, Langdon. *Buddhist Wall Painting.* Cambridge: Harvard University Press, 1938. An illustrated study of 9th century Buddhist murals in the Wan Fo hsia caves in Central Asia.

1485

Mizuno Seiichi. "Archaeological Survey of the Yün-kang Grottoes," *Archives of the Chinese Art Society of America,* IV (1950), 39-60. On pre-T'ang Buddhist art in a famous group of North China caves.

*   *   *

1486

Chiang Yee. *Chinese Calligraphy.* 2nd ed. Cambridge: Harvard University Press, 1954. A standard, authoritative introduction to the aesthetics, the styles, and the techniques of calligraphy and its importance in China's art tradition.

1487

Driscoll, Lucy and Toda Kenji. *Chinese Calligraphy.* Chicago: University of Chicago Press, 1935. A standard introduction to the theory and aesthetics of brushwork, with numerous illustrations from rubbings.

Painting and calligraphy: theory and criticism

1488

Acker, William R. B. (trans.) *Some T'ang and Pre-T'ang Texts on Chinese Painting.* Leiden: E. J. Brill, 1954. A voluminous, technical compendium of early Chinese writings in the realm of art criticism, especially representing the canonical judgments of Hsieh Ho (5th century), which have been the bases of all subsequent art theory in China; with reproductions of the original Chinese texts.

1489

Soper, Alexander C. (trans.) *Kuo Jo-hsü's Experiences in Painting.* Washington: American Council of Learned Societies, 1951. An 11th century Chinese treatise on art history and art theory, abundantly annotated; somewhat technical.

1490

Sakanishi Shio (trans.). *The Spirit of the Brush.* London: John Murray, 1939. (Wisdom of the East Series) Ten brief essays on art theory, especially as related to landscape painting, attributed to great painters from the 4th to 10th centuries, including Ku K'ai-chih (344-406) and Hsieh Ho (late 5th century); with interpretive introductions of each.

1491

Sakanishi Shio (trans.). *An Essay on Landscape Painting by Kuo Hsi.* London: John Murray, 1935. (Wisdom of the East Series) A brief but important and influential explanation of art theory by an 11th century painter-official.

1492

Siren, Osvald. *The Chinese On the Art of Painting.* Peiping: H. Vetch, 1936. A history of Chinese art theory and criticism, arranged by historical periods and incorporating selected Chinese passages in translation; by an authority, but not his best work.

1493

Cahill, James F. "Confucian Elements in the Theory of Painting," in *The Confucian Persuasion* (A. F. Wright, ed; Stanford: Stanford University Press, 1960), pp. 115-140. Urges reconsideration of the common thesis that Chinese painting has been chiefly influenced by Taoism and Buddhism.

1494

Frankel, Hans H. "Poetry and Painting: Chinese and Western Views of Their Convertibility," *Comparative Literature,* IX (1957), 289-307. On the gradual rise of painting as a distinguished art rather than a craft in medieval times, and on the concepts that painting is visual poetry and poetry is aural painting.

1495

Levenson, Joseph R. "The Amateur Ideal in Ming and Early Ch'ing Society: Evidence from Painting," in *Chinese Thought and Institutions* (J. K. Fairbank, ed.; Chicago: University of Chicago Press, 1957), pp. 320-341. On the ideal of the non-specialist gentleman-painter; an important contribution to the understanding of traditional aesthetic values.

1496

Binyon, Laurence. *The Flight of the Dragon.* London: John Murray, 1911; paperbound reprint, New York: Grove Press, 1960. (Wisdom of the East Series) A standard brief interpretation of Chinese and Japanese art and art theory, especially in regard to painting.

1497

Chang, H. C. "Inscriptions, Stylistic Analysis, and Traditional Judgment in Yüan, Ming and Ch'ing Painting," *Asia Major,* VII (1959), 207-227. On some of the characteristics of traditional art criticism; principally disagrees with some of Osvald Siren's stylistic analyses.

Architecture and gardens

1498

Sickman, Laurence and Alexander Soper. *The Art and Architecture of China.* Baltimore: Penguin Books, 1956. Part 2, by Soper, provides an authoritative, detailed survey of Chinese architecture from earliest times through the 19th century; with many illustrations.

1499

Siren, Osvald. *The Imperial Palaces of Peking.* 3 vols. Paris: G. Van Oest, 1926. A magnificent collection of 274 photographic plates representing traditional China's greatest architectural masterpieces, with a brief historical introduction and several architectural drawings.

1500

Siren, Osvald. *Walls and Gates of Peking.* London: John Lane, 1924. A voluminous description of some of traditional China's architectural marvels, with many architectural drawings and 109 photographic plates.

1501

Siren, Osvald. *Gardens of China.* New York: Ronald Press, 1949. An authoritative study of the aesthetics, the components, and the architecture of traditional Chinese gardens, with detailed descriptions of the imperial parks and gardens in Peking and some other noted gardens, with 208 plates.

1502

Malone, Carroll. *History of the Peking Summer Palaces under the Ch'ing Dynasty.* Urbana: University of Illinois, 1934. An illustrated study of Chinese architecture in late traditional times, with special reference to the activities of European architects and decorators in China in the 18th century.

1503

Inn, Henry. *Chinese Houses and Gardens.* Honolulu: Fong Inn's Ltd., 1940. Includes essays on various aspects of house and garden architecture by Ch'en Shou-yi, Chan Wing-tsit, and others, as well as numerous photographic and drawn illustrations.

1504

Kates, George N. *Chinese Household Furniture.* New York: Harper, 1948. On the varieties and uses of household furniture, with 112 plates amply annotated.

1505

Fugl-Meyer, H. *Chinese Bridges.* Shanghai: Kelly and Walsh, 1937. A detailed, illustrated explanation of Chinese bridge-building techniques, cautiously estimating there may be 2.5 million bridges of all sorts in China.

1506

Schafer, Edward H. *Tu Wan's Stone Catalogue of Cloudy Forest.* Berkeley: University of California Press, 1961. An annotated synopsis of the 12th century work on stones for garden use, with addenda on the symbolic significance of stones, etc.

Designs and symbolism

1507

Cammann, Schuyler. "Types of Symbols in Chinese Art," in *Studies in Chinese Thought* (A. F. Wright, ed.; Chicago: University of Chicago Press, 1953), pp. 195-231. On the original meanings of certain graphic symbols: the ancient "T'ao-t'ieh" monster mask, cosmic symbols, imperial symbols, Buddhist and Taoist symbols, nature symbols, etc.

1508

Williams, Charles A. S. *Outlines of Chinese Symbolism and Art Motives.* Rev. ed. Shanghai: Kelly and Walsh, 1932. Reprinted New York: Julian Press, 1960, under the title *Encyclopedia of Chinese Symbolism and Art Motives.* A monumental catalogue of symbols and their explanations, arranged alphabetically; with numerous illustrations.

1509

Nott, Stanley Charles. *Chinese Culture in the Arts.* New York: Chinese Culture Study Group of America, 1946. On the meanings of emblems and symbols in Chinese art, with numerous photographic and drawn illustrations.

1510

Salmony, Alfred. *Antler and Tongue.* Ascona, Switzerland: Artibus Asiae, 1954. (Artibus Asiae Supplementum XIII) A detailed study of the symbolism of stag antlers and long tongues in Chinese art of Shang and Chou times, with comparative reference to other cultures and numerous illustrations.

1511

Dye, Daniel Sheets. *A Grammar of Chinese Lattice.* 2 vols. Cambridge: Harvard University Press, 1937. (Harvard-Yenching Institute Monograph Series, 5-6) A voluminous sourcebook on the designs traditionally used in Chinese windows and grilles, with profuse illustrations and a brief introduction.

1512

Sowerby, Arthur de Carle. *Nature in Chinese Art.* New York: John Day, 1940. An analysis of the representation of flora and fauna in all forms of Chinese art, with numerous illustrations.

1513

Bulling, A. *The Meaning of China's Most Ancient Art.* Leiden: E. J. Brill, 1952. An analysis of the designs and symbolism of pottery from the Shang, Chou, and Han periods.

1514

Cammann, Schuyler. *Chinese Mandarin Squares.* Philadelphia: 1953. (*University Museum Bulletin,* vol 17, no. 3). An illustrated catalog of badges of rank worn by Ming and Ch'ing officials, from the collection of J. S. Letcher; with a long introduction.

1515

Waterbury, Florance. *Early Chinese Symbols and Literature: Vestiges and Speculations.* New York: Weyhe, 1942. An analysis of the meanings of animal and bird motifs on Shang bronze vessels; with 77 plates.

1516

Cheng Te-k'un. "*Yin-yang Wu-hsing* and Han Art," "*Harvard Journal of Asiatic Studies,* XX (1957), 162-186. On manifestations of cosmological theories in Han art motifs; with illustrations.

1517

Cammann, Schuyler. "Some Strange Ming Beasts," *Oriental Art,* II (1956), 3-11. On some dragon designs used in Ming dynasty art.

LITERATURE

Literature has been one of the greatest glories of Chinese civilization; perhaps no people have been more prolific producers or assiduous preservers of artistic writing. Literature has been written in two basic styles: (1) literary or classical Chinese, a rather artificial style that has never had a close resemblance to spoken Chinese and is very difficult to master; and (2) colloquial Chinese, which in traditional times was looked down upon as a style not proper for written expression. The total corpus of Chinese literature includes every major genre except the epic. In literary style — in addition to philosophical and other, even more non-artistic writings — it includes historical writings, poetry in myriad forms, essays, and short stories. Colloquial literature, stemming orginally from the activities of professional story-tellers, began to appear in substantial amounts only after the 13th century and was long restricted chiefly to prose fiction, in both short and long forms. Traditional Chinese drama, as well as much prose fiction, is a mixture of literary and colloquial styles. In the 20th century the impact of the west on China has introduced many new themes into Chinese literature, and the colloquial style of writing has become increasingly dominant. Of all Chinese forms of literature, poetry has probably been most esteemed by the Chinese themselves and by foreign students of China.

General Works

1518

Hightower, James R. *Topics in Chinese Literature*. Rev. ed. Cambridge: Harvard University Press, 1953. (Harvard-Yenching Institute Studies, III)Somewhat technical, but still the best general introduction to the study of Chinese literature; contains essays on the nature and history of the various periods and genres of literary development and extended, analytical bibliographies.

1519

Ch'en Shou-Yi. *Chinese Literature: A Historical Introduction*. New York: Ronald Press, 1961. A voluminous, chronological narrative of literary developments throughout history, with anecdotal sketches of China's literary masters and sample translations of their masterpieces.

1520

Davidson, Martha. *A List of Published Translations from Chinese into English, French and German: Literature, Exclusive of Poetry*. Washington: American Council of Learned Societies, 1952. The most comprehensive bibliography of its kind; an invaluable reference tool.

1521

Hightower, James R. "Chinese Literature in the Context of World Literature," *Comparative Literature*, V (1953), 117-124. Brief evaluative comments on characterstics of the major Chinese literary genres and on the importance of Chinese literature for the study of world literature in general.

1522

Wang Chi-chen. "Traditional Literature: Nature and Limitations," in *China* (H. F. MacNair, ed.; Berkeley: University of California Press, 1946), pp. 386-396. A good general survey of the historical evolution of Chinese literary forms from earliest times into the 20th century.

1523

Ceadel, Eric B. (ed.) *Literatures of the East, an Appreciation*. London: John Murray, 1953. (Wisdom of the East Series) Chap. 6, by A. R. Davis, is a brief historical survey of the development of Chinese literature from earliest times into the 20th century.

1524

Lin Yutang. *My Country and My People*. Rev. ed. New York: John Day, 1935. Chap. 7, "Literary Life," offers an enthusiastic, interpretive introduction to the role of literature in traditional Chinese life, the various genres and masterpieces of traditional literature, and the literary changes that have come about in the 20th century; for the general reader.

1525

Balazs, E. and others. *Aspects de la Chine*. Vol. 2. Paris: Presses Universitaires de France, 1959. Pp. 211-316: essays on all aspects of traditional Chinese literature by M.-R. Guignard, Wu Chi-yu, M. and O. Kaltenmark, Y. Hervout, R. Ruhlmann, Li Tche-houa, and P. Demiéville; in popular style, but authoritative.

1526

Feng Yuan-chun. *A Short History of Classical Chinese Literature*. Peking: Foreign Languages Press, 1958. A very brief summary, arranged in large chronological epochs, of China's classical literary history up to 1919; strongly reflecting a Marxist-Maoist interpretation of Chinese history in general.

The Chinese classics

What the Chinese call *ching* or "classics" are diverse writings that are among the oldest known literary remains of China. Confucians have particularly esteemed them, have used them as the basic texts of all education, and have claimed that they were in part written or edited by Confucius himself. The usual list of classics includes five categories: (1) *I-ching* ("Classic of Changes"), which seems to have originated as a handbook for diviners and came to be used as a reference in astrological, numerological, and other forms of prophesying; (2) *Shih-ching* ("Classic of Odes"), a compilation of more than 300 ancient folk songs, religious odes, and court ceremonial hymns, many dating from the early Chou period and some perhaps from earlier times; (3) *Shu-ching* ("Classic of Documents"), a collection of speeches and other documents attributed to the kings and ministers of highest antiquity down through the first 300 years of the Chou dynasty; (4) *Ch'un-ch'iu* ("Spring and Autumn Annals"), a cryptic chronicle of events from 721 to 481 B.C., particularly emphasizing the history of Confucius' native state, Lu; and (5) *Li* ("rituals"). The last category actually includes three works: (a) *I-li*, a systematic description of ritual practices and rules of conduct applicable in selected situations; (b) *Li-chi*, a heterogeneous collection of treatises on mourning, marriage, banquets, sacrifices, etc.; and (c) *Chou-li*, a late and unreliable reconstruction of the Chou governmental system. Four other works, known as "the Four Books," are often included in lists of the classics: (1) *Lun-yü* (the "Analects" of Confucius), (2) *Meng-tzu* (the book of Mencius), (3) *Ta-hsüeh* (the "Great Learning"), and (4) *Chung-yung* (the "Doctrine of the Mean"). The latter two are both chapters of the *Li-chi* singled out for special esteem. Problems relating to the authorship and authenticity of the various classics have provoked great and continuing controversies among Chinese and foreign scholars.

1527

Hightower, James R. *Topics in Chinese Literature*. Rev. ed. Cambridge: Harvard University Press, 1953. Chap. 1 includes general descriptions of the various classics, with bibliographic references.

1528

Galt, Howard S. *A History of Chinese Educational Institutions*. Vol. 1. London: Probsthain, 1951. Pp. 2-32 provide an excellent general description of the classical works, noting problems concerning their authorship and authenticity; derived from good modern scholarship.

1529

Tjan Tjoe Som. *Po Hu T'ung: The Comprehensive Discussion in the White Tiger Hall*. 2 vols. Leiden: E. J.

Brill, 1949–52. Translation of a report of a court-sponsored conference on the classics in A.D. 79, with a long technical introduction; a major contribution toward understanding traditional Chinese classical scholarship.

* * *
1530
Legge, James (trans.). *The Chinese Classics.* Vols. 1-2. 2d ed. rev. Oxford: Clarendon Press, 1893–95. Vols. 3-5 in 6 parts. London: 1865–72. (Being reprinted in 5 volumes by Hong Kong University Press, 1961.) Standard, annotated translations of the *Analects* of Confucius, the *Great Learning,* the *Doctrine of the Mean* (vol. 1), the *Mencius* (vol. 2), the *Classic of Documents* (vol. 3 in 2 parts), the *Classic of Odes* (vol 4 in 2 parts), and the *Spring and Autumn Annals* with its most influential commentary, *Tso-chuan* (vol. 4 in 2 parts); with reproductions of the Chinese texts. In some instances the Legge translations have been superseded, but they remain basic referencs for scholarly purposes.

1531
Müller, Max (ed.). *Sacred Books of the East.* 50 vols. Oxford: Clarendon Press, 1879–1910. Includes authoritative translations by James Legge of the *Shu-ching* and *Shih-ching* (vol. 1: 1879), the *I-ching* (16: 1882), and the *Li-chi* (27-28: 1885).

* * *
1532
Wilhelm, Hellmut. *Change: Eight Lectures on the I Ching,* trans. by Cary F. Baynes. New York: Pantheon Books: 1960. (Bollingen Series, LXII) A brief, readable introduction to the "Classic of Changes."

1533
Wilhelm, Richard (trans.). *The I Ching or Book of Changes,* rendered into English by Cary F. Baynes. 2 vols. New York: Pantheon, 1950. The standard translation, with detailed explications of the cryptic text; with an introductory appreciation by C. G. Jung.

1534
Waley, Arthur. "The Book of Changes," *Bulletin of the Museum of Far Eastern Antiquities,* Stockholm, V (1933), 121-142. A theoretical analysis of the meanings of the *I-ching* omens and the techniques of manipulating them; somewhat technical.

1535
Harlez, C. de (trans.). *Le livre des mutations.* Paris: Denoël, 1959. A standard French translation of *I-ching* made in 1888, newly annotated by Raymond de Becker, principally to call attention to differences of interpretation between Harlez and Richard Wilhelm; with an introduction discussing the importance and use of the text in the Chinese tradition.

* * *
1536
Waley, Arthur (trans.). *The Book of Songs.* 2d ed. reprinted. New York: Grove Press, 1960; paperbound reprint by the same publisher, 1960. A standard, complete translation of the *Shih-ching;* poems grouped according to subject matter.

1537
Karlgren, Bernhard (trans.). *The Book of Odes.* Stockholm: Museum of Far Eastern Antiquities, 1950. A complete, authoritative, literal translation of the *Shih-ching,* complete with the Chinese text; reprinted from *Bulletin of the Museum of Far Eastern Antiquities,* XVI and XVII.

1538
Pound, Ezra (trans.). *The Confucian Odes: The Classic Anthology Defined by Confucius.* Cambridge: Harvard University Press, 1954; paperbound reprint New York: New Directions, 1959. A very free, highly readable translation of the *Shih-ching* by a brilliant modern poet-translator; useful for consultation, but not to be relied on for scholarly purposes.

* * *
1539
Karlgren, Bernhard (trans.). "The Book of Documents," *Bulletin of the Museum of Far Eastern Antiquities,* Stockholm, XXII (1950), 1-81. A complete, authoritative translation of the *Shu-ching,* in very literal and precise terms.

* * *
1540
Couvreur, S. (trans.) *Tch'ouen ts'iou et Tso tchouan.* 3 vols. Ho Kien Fou: Mission Catholique, 1914; reprinted Paris: Cathasia, 1951. Complete, authoritative French translation of *Ch'un-ch'iu* and its commentary *Tso-chuan.*

* * *
1541
Steele, John (trans.). *The I-li or Book of Etiquette and Ceremonial.* 2 vols. London: Probsthain, 1917. A standard, complete translation.

1542
Couvreur, S. (trans.) *I Li: Ceremonial.* 2d ed. Sien Hsien: Mission Catholique, 1928. A standard French translation, with reproduction of the Chinese text.

1543
Biot, Édouard (trans.). *Le Tcheou-li ou Rites des Tcheou.* 3 vols. Paris: Imprimerie Nationale, 1851. The only complete translation in a Western language of the *Chou-li,* which purports to describe and establish regulations for the ancient Chou government but now is generally believed to be a utopian reconstruction attributable to a very late Chou or perhaps even later period.

* * *
1544
Waley, Arthur (trans.). *The Analects of Confucius.* New York: Macmillan, 1938; reprinted 1956. The most often recommended modern translation, with critical textual and historical annotations.

1545
Soothill, W. E. (trans.) *The Analects of Confucius.* London: Oxford University Press, 1937. (The World's Classics series) A standard, authoritative translation with very limited annotations.

1546
Ware, James R. (trans.) *The Sayings of Mencius.* New York: Mentor Books, 1960. A complete, reliable translation, but without annotations.

1547
Lin Yutang. *The Wisdom of China and India.* New York: Modern Library, 1942. Includes original, reliable translations of the *Analects* of Confucius (pp. 811-842; incomplete), the *Mencius* (743-784; incomplete), and the *Chung-yung* (843-866; complete).

1548
Hughes, E. R. *The Great Learning and the Mean-in-Action.* New York: Dutton, 1943. Standard, original translations of *Ta-hsüeh* and *Chung-yung,* with detailed studies of their meaning and significance.

Poetry

Poetry is probably the oldest extant form of literary expression in China, and the Chinese have undoubtedly published a greater volume of poetry than any other people. Most of their poetic forms originated as song-words, so that metrical rhythm is the dominant poetic element, and rhyme is generally present. But their repertoire ranges from starkly simple forms into elaborately complex forms and through almost all the moods and themes known in the West. Western readers are usually struck by the terse impressionism of much Chinese poetry, by the abundance of similes and metaphors and often undecipherable allusions, and by the relative unimportance of romantic love, religious passion, and martial exploits as poetic themes. The poetry of every historic period has its special characteristics, but the T'ang dynasty (618–907) is considered to have been the period of greatest poetic creativity. Among the most renowned Chinese poets are Ch'ü Yüan (4th century B.C.?), a semi-mythical creator of a tradition of long, ornate, turbulent, highly emotional poems; T'ao Ch'ien (365–427), a master of short descriptive poems, especially about nature; Wang Wei (699–750), especially noted for his impressionistic poems about nature; Li Po (699–762), one of the most spontaneous lyricists of world literature; Tu Fu (712–770), a poignant commentator on life's sadness; Po Chü-i (772–846), an almost reportorial observer of society; and Su Tung-p'o (1037–1101), one of the most brilliant all-around litterateurs of traditional China. However, since in traditional times every educated Chinese was a practising and publishing poet, a complete list of even great Chinese poets would have to be a very long one.

Reference aids and general studies

1549

Hightower, James R. *Topics in Chinese Literature*. Rev. ed. Cambridge: Harvard University Press, 1953. Chaps. 4, 7-10, 13-14 discuss the various poetic genres in their historical sequence, with bibliographic references.

1550

Davidson, Martha. *A List of Published Translations from Chinese into English, French and German: Poetry*. Washington: American Council of Learned Societies, 1957. The most comprehensive bibliography of its kind; an invaluable reference tool.

1551

Waley, Arthur (trans.). *The Temple and Other Poems*. New York: Alfred A. Knopf, 1923. Includes a long, authoritative history of Chinese poetic genres up to T'ang times in the introduction and an appendix on the forms of Chinese poetry.

1552

Waley, Arthur. "The Limitations of Chinese Literature," in his *170 Chinese Poems* (London: Constable, 1918; repeatedly reissued), pp. 3-18. A useful general discussion, by an eminent modern translator, of the history and techniques of traditional Chinese poetry.

1553

Bishop, John L. "Prosodic Elements in T'ang Poetry," in *Indiana University Conference on Oriental-Western Literary Relations* (Horst Frenz and G. L. Anderson, ed.; Chapel Hill: University of North Carolina Press, 1955), pp. 49-63. On how traditional Chinese poetry achieves its effects: the technical devices.

1554

Bynner, Witter and Kiang Kang-hu (trans.). *The Jade Mountain*. New York: Alfred A. Knopf, 1929; repeatedly reissued. Includes an authoritative introductory explanation by Kiang Kang-hu of traditional Chinese poetic techniques.

1555

Frankel, Hans H. "Poetry and Painting: Chinese and Western Views of Their Convertibility," *Comparative Literature*, IX (1957), 289-307. On the close interrelation between poetry and painting in the Chinese literati tradition.

1556

Frodsham, J. D. "The Origins of Chinese Nature Poetry," *Asia Major*, VIII, part 1 (1960), 68-103. The development of "landscape poetry" in the post-Han era; its relations to Taoist and Buddhist thought.

1557

Baxter, Glen W. "Metrical Origins of the *Tz'u*," *Harvard Journal of Asiatic Studies*, XVI (1953), 108-145. On a song form used by poets of the T'ang and Sung periods; technical.

1558

Teele, Roy E. *Through a Glass Darkly*. Ann Arbor: 1949. A detailed analysis of the changing styles and techniques that have characterized translators of Chinese poetry into English.

1559

Margoulies, George. *Histoire de la littérature chinoise: poesie*. Paris: Payot, 1948. A general chronological account of the evolution of the various traditional genres of Chinese poetry, with examples of masterpieces in each.

General anthologies

1560

Payne, Robert (ed.). *The White Pony*. New York: John Day, 1947; paperback reprint New York: Mentor Books, 1960. The most representative English-language anthology of Chinese poetry from earliest times into the 20th century, in translations of somewhat variable quality; with biographical introduction to each major poet.

1561

Waley, Arthur (trans.). *Translations from the Chinese*. New York: Alfred A. Knopf, 1941. More than 200 poems ranging from earliest times to the 17th century, including more than 100 by the 9th century poet-official Po Chü-i, rendered freely into poetic English by the most distinguished and deft modern translator from the Chinese; mostly reprinted from Waley's *170 Chinese Poems* (London: Constable, 1918; repeatedly reissued).

1562

Ch'u Ta-kao (trans.). *Chinese Lyrics*. Cambridge: Cambridge University Press, 1937. An anthology of poems mostly by Sung poets (Li Yü, Fan Chung-yen, Su Tung-p'o, Chu Tun-ju, et al.), in expert translations.

1563

French, Joseph L. (ed.) *Lotus and Chrysanthemum*. New York: Liveright, 1928. A large symposium of standard translations of Chinese and Japanese poetry, arranged by poets.

1564

Hart, Henry H. (trans.) *Poems of the Hundred Names*. Stanford: Stanford University Press, 1954. (Originally published in 1933 by the University of California Press under the title *The Hundred Names*.) Selections of representative Chinese poems, arranged in groups by dynasties; with a brief introduction on the characteristics, techniques, and history of poetry in China.

1565

Bynner, Witter and Kiang Kang-hu (trans.). *The Jade Mountain*. New York: Alfred A. Knopf, 1929; repeatedly reissued. A complete translation, in poetic but not versified English, of a standard anthology of 311 poems of the T'ang dynasty (*T'ang-shih san-pai shou*), with Li Po, Tu Fu, Wang Wei, and Po Chü-i strongly represented.

1566

Ayscough, Florence and Amy Lowell (trans.). *Fir-flower Tablets*. Boston: Houghton Mifflin, 1921. A substantial selection of Chinese poetry, mostly by Li Po, Tu Fu, and other T'ang poets; with a long introduction on the history and characteristics of Chinese poetry and the personalities of some major poets.

1567

Jenyns, Soame (trans.). *Selections from the Three Hundred Poems of the T'ang Dynasty*. London: John Murray, 1940. (Wisdom of the East Series) A selection of poems by Tu Fu, Li Po, Wang Wei, Po Chü-i, Meng Hao-jan and others from the Chinese anthology *T'ang-shih san-pai shou*, arranged according to topics.

1568

Jenyns, Soame (trans.). *A Further Selection from the Three Hundred Poems of the T'ang Dynasty*. London: John Murray, 1944. (Wisdom of the East Series) Addenda to Jenyns' earlier selection; also from *T'ang-shih san-pai shou*.

1569

Waley, Arthur (trans.). *The Temple and Other Poems*. New York: Alfred A. Knopf, 1923. A selection of long poems dating from Han to Sung times.

1570

Candlin, Clara M. (trans.) *The Herald Wind*. London: Murray, 1933. (Wisdom of the East Series) Selections from Sung poets, including Ou-yang Hsiu, Ssu-ma Kuang, Wang An-shih, Su Tung-p'o, and Lu Yu.

1571

Cranmer-Byng, L. (trans.) *A Feast of Lanterns*. London: John Murray, 1916; repeatedly reissued. (Wisdom of the East Series) A brief selection of poems, mostly from the T'ang and Sung periods, representing Li Po, Tu Fu, Wang Wei, Po Chü-i, Su Tung-p'o, Lu Yu, etc.

1572

Cranmer-Byng, L. (trans.) *A Lute of Jade*. London: John Murray, 1909; repeatedly reissued. (Wisdom of the East Series) Poems from antiquity into Sung times, but mostly by T'ang poets; with an introduction on the history and characteristics of Chinese poetry and biographical notes on all poets represented.

1573

Lin Yutang. *The Wisdom of China and India*. New York: Modern Library, 1942. Pp. 867-934: selected poems in translations by different hands, representing the ancient *Shih-ching*, Ch'ü Yüan, and Li Po, and including a famous "drum song" (monologue recitation with drum accompaniment), "The Tale of Meng Chiang," about a tragic bride of the Ch'in dynasty whose husband was drafted to help build the Great Wall.

1574

Fletcher, W. J. B. (trans.) *Gems of Chinese Verse*. Shanghai: Commercial Press, 1932. Nearly 200 poems of the T'ang dynasty, mostly by Li Po, Tu Fu, and Wang Wei, with reproductions of the Chinese originals; one of the more respected efforts — now increasingly rare — to render Chinese poetry into rhyming English verse.

1575

Giles, Herbert A. (trans.) *Gems of Chinese Literature: Verse*. 2d ed. Shanghai: Kelly and Walsh, 1923. Selections from all historic periods, rendered in rhyming English; representing Ch'ü Yüan, T'ao Ch'ien, Li Po, Tu Fu, Po Chü-i, Su Tung-p'o, and others.

1576

Robinson, Richard (trans.). *Chinese Buddhist Verse*. London: John Murray, 1954. (Wisdom of the East Series) A selection of Buddhist hymns, with an introduction on the history, style, and techniques of this little-known aspect of the Chinese poetic tradition.

1577

Rexroth, Kenneth (trans.). *One Hundred Poems from the Chinese*. New York: New Directions, 1955. English poems based on the Chinese of Tu Fu, Su Tung-p'o, Lu Yu, etc.; cannot always be relied on to retain the original meaning.

1578

Margoulies, George. *Anthologie raisonée de la littérature chinoise*. Paris: Payot, 1948. A collection of both prose and poetry of traditional times, arranged under topical headings such as war, death, separation, etc.

Particular poets and works (in chronological order)

1579

Waley, Arthur (trans.). *The Book of Songs*. 2d ed. reprinted. New York: Grove Press, 1960; paperbound reprint by the same publisher, 1960. A standard, complete translation of the ancient, classical poetry compilation called *Shih-ching*; poems grouped according to subject matter.

1580

Waddell, Helen (trans.). *Lyrics from the Chinese*. Boston: Houghton Mifflin, 1913. A selection of 36 poems from the *Shih-ching*, in notably poetic English renderings.

1581

Karlgren, Bernhard (trans.). *The Book of Odes*. Stockholm: Museum of Far Eastern Antiquities, 1950. A complete, authoritative, literal translation of the *Shih-ching*, complete with the Chinese text; reprinted from *Bulletin of the Museum of Far Eastern Antiquities*, XVI and XVII.

1582

Legge, James (trans.). *The Chinese Classics*. Vol. 4 in 2 parts. London: Henry Frowde, 1871. (Being reprinted by Hong Kong University Press, 1961.) An authoritative, annotated translation of *Shih-ching*, the ancient "Classic of Poetry"; remains a standard reference for scholarly purposes.

* * *

1583

Hawkes, David (trans.). *Ch'u Tz'u: The Songs of the South, An Ancient Chinese Anthology*. New York: Oxford University Press, 1959. A complete translation of an influential anthology of the 4th and 3rd centuries B.C., including the famous *Li Sao* ("On Encountering Sorrow") by Ch'ü Yüan.

1584

Waley, Arthur. *The Nine Songs: A Study of Shamanism in Ancient China*. London: Allen and Unwin, 1955. Authoritative, thoroughly annotated translations of nine poems from the pre-Han collection *Ch'u-tz'u*, with an introduction and commentaries about the South China shamanistic tradition from which they emerged.

1585

Hightower, James R. "Ch'ü Yüan Studies," in *Silver Jubilee Volume of the Zinbun-Kagaku-Kenkyusyo*, Kyoto University (Kyoto: 1954), pp. 192-223. An evaluation of modern scholarship concerning China's earliest identifiable poet and the anthology associated with his name, the *Ch'u Tz'u*.

* * *

1586

Hughes, Ernest R. *Two Chinese Poets: Vignettes of Han Life and Thought*. Princeton: Princeton University Press, 1960. Translations of Pan Ku's "Fu on the Western Capital" and "Fu on the Eastern Capital" and Chang Heng's two *fu* prose-poems of the same titles, with extensive critiques.

* * *

1587

Roy, David T. "The Theme of the Neglected Wife in the Poetry of Ts'ao Chih," *Journal of Asian Studies*, XIX (1959–60), 25-31. On the artistry of an influential 3d century poet, particularly noting his fusion of literary and folk traditions.

* * *

1588

Hughes, E. R. *The Art of Letters*. New York: Pantheon, 1951. (Bollingen Series, XXIX) A highly theoretical study of early Chinese poetics and aesthetics as reflected in the *Wen-fu* of Lu Chi (261-303), incorporating an annotated translation.

1589

Fang, Achilles (trans.). "Rhymeprose on Literature: The *Wen-fu* of Lu Chi (A.D. 261-303)," *Harvard Journal of Asiatic Studies,* XIV (1951), 527-566. A classical treatise on poetics in technical translations.

* * *

1590

Gulik, R. H. Van. *Hsi K'ang and his Poetical Essay on the Lute.* Tokyo: Sophia University, 1941. Includes an annotated translation of a 3rd century prose-poem *(fu)* on the history and theory of instrumental music.

* * *

1591

Acker, William (trans.). *T'ao the Hermit: Sixty Poems by T'ao Ch'ien.* London: Thames and Hudson, 1952. On one of China's greatest "nature-poets" (4th-5th centuries), with a long introduction on his life and poetic art.

1592

Chang, Lily Pao-hu and Marjorie Sinclair (trans.). *The Poems of T'ao Ch'ien.* Honolulu: University of Hawaii Press, 1953. Translations of all the known poems of the 4th-5th century nature poet.

1593

Hightower, James R. "The *Fu* of T'ao Ch'ien," *Harvard Journal of Asiatic Studies,* XVII (1954), 169-230. A critical study of three long prose-poems by the 4th-5th century nature poet, with complete, annotated translations.

* * *

1594

Mather, Richard. "The Landscape Buddhism of the Fifth-century Poet Hsieh Ling-yün," *Journal of Asian Studies,* XVIII (1958-59), 67-79. On an early "landscape poet" who was also an ardent Buddhist, with translations of some of his poems.

* * *

1595

Wu Chi-yu. "A Study of Han-shan," *T'oung Pao,* XLV (1957), 392-450. A technical study on the life of a 7th century Buddhist poet, with translations of some of his poems.

* * *

1596

Chang Yin-nan and Lewis C. Walmsley (trans.). *Poems by Wang Wei.* Rutland, Vt.: C. E. Tuttle, 1958. Free translations of 167 poems by a great T'ang dynasty nature poet, with an introduction on the nature of Chinese poetry.

* * *

1597

Waley, Arthur. *The Poetry and Career of Li Po.* New York: Macmillan, 1950. On a famous Taoist-inspired poet of the 8th century, a self-identified "immortal banished from Heaven" who has come to be the special darling of Western connoisseurs of Chinese literature; including translations of many poems.

1598

Obata Shigeyoshi (trans.). *The Works of Li Po the Chinese Poet.* New York: Dutton, 1922. A standard reference on Li Po, including translations of 124 of his poems and brief biographical information.

* * *

1599

Hung, William. *Tu Fu, China's Greatest Poet.* 2 vols. Cambridge: Harvard University Press, 1952. A detailed biography of the sober, troubled poet-bureaucrat of the 8th century whom the Chinese have considered their outstanding poetic genius, incorporating many translations; vol. 2 consists entirely of notes.

* * *

1600

Von Zach, Erwin (trans.). *Han Yü's poetische Werke,* ed. by J. R. Hightower. Cambridge: Harvard University Press, 1952. (Harvard-Yenching Institute Studies, VII)

The poetry of a great 9th century scholar, best known as a prose stylist and anti-Buddhist propagandist; the only complete translation.

* * *

1601

Waley, Arthur. *The Life and Times of Po Chü-i.* New York: Macmillan, 1949. A detailed, authoritative biography of a great 9th century poet-official, incorporating translations of about 100 of his poems.

* * *

1602

Liu Yih-ling and Shahid Suhrawardy (trans.). *Poems of Lee Hou-chu.* Bombay: Orient Longmans, 1948. Literal and sometimes awkward translations of 39 wistful poems (mostly of the song-word variety called *tz'u*) by Li Hou-chu (or Li Yü, 937-978), the last king of Southern T'ang who was deposed by the founder of the Sung dynasty, whose poems in exile are masterpieces of nostalgic melancholy; with a brief biographical introduction.

* * *

1603

Lin Yutang. *The Gay Genius.* New York: John Day, 1947. A somewhat romanticized account of the life and times of the great 11th century poet-official Su Tung-p'o, incorporating translations of many of his poems.

1604

Clark, Cyril D. le Gros (trans.). *Selections from the Works of Su Tung-p'o.* London: Jonathan Cape, 1931. Includes some prose-poems *(fu);* with brief introductory sections on Su's life and times.

1605

Clark, Cyril D. le Gros (trans.). *The Prose-Poetry of Su Tung-p'o.* London: Kegan Paul, 1935. A selection of prose-poems *(fu).*

* * *

1606

Candlin, Clara M. (trans.) *The Rapier of Lu.* London: John Murray, 1946. (Wisdom of the East Series) A brief selection of the poems of Lu Yu (1125-1210), the best known poet of the Southern Sung period; with a biographical introduction.

* * *

1607

Waley, Arthur. *Yuan Mei: Eighteenth Century Chinese Poet.* New York: Macmillan, 1956; paperbound reprint New York: Grove Press, 1958. On Yüan Mei's life and times, incorporating translations of many of his poems.

Classical prose

Chinese writings in classical prose styles — a great bulk of which is contributed by scholarly works, letters, and official documents — include notable masterpieces in the forms of historiography, literary criticism, essays, and fiction. There is a particularly strong tradition of historiography, stemming from the ancient *Shu-ching* ("Classic of Documents") and including a long series of voluminous dynastic histories produced largely by official historiographic commissions, not one of which has been wholly translated into any Western language. The greatest masterpiece in this form is *Shih-chi* ("Memoirs of a Historian") by Ssu-ma Ch'ien (145-90 B.C.), a comprehensive history of the Chinese world up to the author's time. Offering topical treatises, comparative charts, and numerous biographical sketches as well as a narrative of major events, it established the pattern for much subsequent history writing. Both histories and early philosophical writings contributed to an anecdotal tradition that blossomed in the T'ang period (618–907) with the production of numerous short imaginative tales and culminated in the elegant short-story collection called *Liao-chai chih-i,* by P'u Sung-ling (1640–1715), which is widely considered a model of classical prose style. The most admired prose stylist of all is Han Yü (768–824), a literary reformer who championed a vigorous, straightforward, unornamented style and wrote it superbly. Despite his influence, much classical prose has a semi-poetic rhythmic quality, and it is always characteristically terse, erudite, and full of stylistic graces that defy translation.

Prose writing: general

1608

Hightower, James R. *Topics in Chinese Literature.* Rev. ed. Cambridge: Harvard University Press, 1953. Chaps. 2-3, 5-6, 11-12 discuss the historical development of prose forms and styles, with bibliographic references.

1609

Lin Yutang (trans.). *The Importance of Understanding.* Cleveland: World Publishing Co., 1960. More than 100 selections from Chinese literature of all periods, but mostly essays and anecdotes in classical style, grouped according to subject matter.

1610

Shih, Vincent Y. C. (trans.) *The Literary Mind and the Carving of Dragons.* New York: Columbia University Press, 1959. An annotated translation, with a long introduction, of Liu Hsieh's *Wen-hsin tiao-lung,* a classic of literary theory and criticism written in the 6th century; very difficult reading, but an indispensable source for the study of Chinese aesthetics.

1611

Edwards, E. D. *Chinese Prose Literature of the T'ang Period (A.D. 618–906).* 2 vols. London: Probsthain, 1937-38. A critical summary of *T'ang-tai ts'ung-shu,* an anthology of T'ang belles-lettres representing various literary genres including fiction; with specimen translations.

1612

Hightower, James R. "Some Characteristics of Parallel Prose," in *Studia Serica Bernhard Karlgren Dedicata* (Copenhagen: Ejnar Munksgaard, 1959), pp. 60-91. Analysis of various parallelisms and allusions common in the elaborate, metrical prose called parallel prose; with English renderings of two famous pieces by K'ung Chih-kuei (447-501) and Hsü Ling (507-583).

1613

Hightower, James R. "The *Wen Hsüan* and Genre Theory," *Harvard Journal of Asiatic Studies,* XX (1957), 512-533. On a 6th century categorization of literary forms; technical, with annotated translations.

1614

Yoshikawa Kojiro. "The *Shih-shuo hsin-yü* and Six Dynasties Prose Style," trans. by Glen W. Baxter. *Harvard Journal of Asiatic Studies,* XVIII (1955), 124-141. On a 5th century collection of anecdotes as a forerunner of the luxuriant "parallel prose" style that characterized much medieval writing; technical.

1615

Williamson, Henry R. *Wang An-shih, Chinese Statesman and Educationalist of the Sung Dynasty.* Vol. 2. Lon-

don: Arthur Probsthain, 1937. Includes translations of many essays by a major prose stylist of the 11th century, best known as a controversial political reformer.

1616

Teng Ssu-yü and Knight Biggerstaff. *An Annotated Bibliography of Selected Chinese Reference Works.* Rev. ed. Cambridge: Harvard University Press, 1950. (Harvard-Yenching Institute Studies, II) A descriptive study of several hundred standard bibliographies, encyclopedias, dictionaries, geographical works, biographical works, etc., in the Chinese language; an indispensable reference tool for serious students of traditional China, and useful as a survey of some important aspects of traditional Chinese scholarship.

1617

Franke, Herbert (trans.). *Beiträge zur Kulturgeschichtechinas unter der Mongolenherrschaft: Das Shan-kü sinhua des Yang Yü.* Wiesbaden: Franz Steiner, 1956. Anecdotes and essays from *Shan-chü hsin-hua,* a 14th century scholar's notebook of miscellany; a type of classical literature (*pi-chi*) that is rare in translation.

1618

Margoulies, George. *Histoire de la littérature chinoise: prose.* Paris: Payot, 1949. A general history, in a chronological approach, of artistic prose writings in the classical style, with important evaluations of the successive schools of stylists.

1619

Margoulies, George. *Anthologie raisonée de la littérature chinoise.* Paris: Payot, 1948. A collection of both prose and poetry of traditional times, arranged under topical headings such as war, death, separation, etc.

1620

Tsien Tsuen-hsuin. "A History of Bibliographic Classification in China," *Library Quarterly,* XXII (1952), 307-324. An authoritative survey of one important aspect of traditional Chinese scholarship.

Historiography

1620-a

Beasley, W. G. and E. G. Pulleyblank (ed.). *Historians of China and Japan.* London: Oxford University Press, 1961. A collection of essays on the general character of Chinese historiography and on particular historians and historical works by P. van der Loon, A. F. P. Hulsewé, L. S. Yang, W. Franke, E. Balazs, D. Twitchett, H. Franke, P. Demiéville, et al.

1621

Watson, Burton. *Ssu-ma Ch'ien, Grand Historian of China.* New York: Columbia University Press, 1958. A thorough scholarly study of the life and historiographic work of Ssu-ma Ch'ien.

1622

Gardner, Charles S. *Chinese Traditional Historiography.* Cambridge: Harvard University Press, 1938. A standard analytical study of the Chinese tradition of history writing, in a topical approach (motivation, textual and historical criticism, synthesis, style, etc.); authoritative and technical.

1623

Dawson, Raymond. "The Writing of History in China," *History Today,* II (1952), 281-286. A general survey of the evolution of historiographic techniques and ideals, from Ssu-ma Ch'ien to the 20th century Marxists.

1624

Bielenstein, Hans. "The Restoration of the Han dynasty, with Prolegomena on the Historiography of the Hou Han Shu," *Bulletin of the Museum of Far Eastern Antiquities,* Stockholm, XXVI (1954), 1-209. Pp. 20-81 provide a thorough and detailed analysis of the purpose, the objectivity, and the techique of the *History of the Later Han;* a most important contribution to the study of historiographic aspects of the dynastic histories in general.

1625

Sargent, Clyde B. "Subsidized History: Pan Ku and the Historical Records of the Former Han Dynasty," *The Far Eastern Quarterly,* III (1943–44), 119-143. On the organization, sources, authorship, and especially the historiographic techniques of the *Han-shu,* concluding that Pan Ku was subject to significant political control as regards his interpretations. Cf. Homer H. Dubs, "The Reliability of Chinese Histories," *op. cit.,* VI (1946–47), 23-43, largely a critique of Sargent's views.

1626

Wang Gung-wu. "The *Chiu Wu-tai shih* and History-writing during the Five Dynasties," *Asia Major,* VI (1957–58), 1-22. On the techniques and products of official historians in the 5 Dynasties era.

1627

Han Yu-shan. *Elements of Chinese Historiography.* Hollywood: W. M. Hawley, 1955. A technical handbook for students explaining traditional categories of historical writings, terms commonly used in histories, the lives and significance of many noted historians, etc.; offers some data about the role of the historian and the characteristics of history-writing in China, but is somewhat traditionalistic and uncritical.

1628

Hummel, Arthur W. (trans.) *The Autobiography of a Chinese Historian.* Leiden: E. J. Brill, 1931. A general discussion of China's historiographic development by Ku Chieh-kang, an outstanding 20th century scholar: Ku's preface to *Ku-shih pien,* a series of critical studies of ancient history.

1629

Wright, Arthur F. "Sui Yang-ti: Personality and Stereotype," in *The Confucian Persuasion* (A. F. Wright, ed.; Stanford, Stanford University Press, 1960), pp. 47-76. A valuable contribution to the understanding of traditional historiographic biases: a case study of the last Sui emperor, a classic type of "bad last emperors."

1630

Parsons, James B. "Attitudes toward the Late Ming Rebellions," *Oriens Extremus,* VI (1959–60), 177-209. An analysis of historiographic interpretations of, and biases toward, some 17th century rebels, ranging from traditional Confucian historians to modern communist historians.

1631

Wright, Arthur F. "Biography and Hagiography: Hui-chiao's *Lives of Eminent Monks,*" in *Silver Jubilee Volume of the Zinbun-Kagaku-Kenkyusyo,* Kyoto University (Kyoto: 1954), pp. 383-432. A critical study of the historiographic techniques and hagiographic attitudes displayed in a famous 6th century compendium of biographies of Buddhist monks, with comments about other early biographical compendiums.

*   *   *

1632

Frankel, Hans H. *Catalogue of Translations from the Chinese Dynastic Histories for the Period 220-960.* Berkeley: University of California Press, 1957. A useful reference tool for the study of traditional Chinese historiographic techniques.

1633

Watson, Burton (trans.). *Records of the Grand Historian of China.* 2 vols. New York: Columbia University Press, 1961. An extensive selection from Ssu-ma Ch'ien's *Shih-chi,* in authoritative translations. Vol. 1 offers annals and biographies relating to the rise and early reigns of the Han dynasty; vol. 2 relates to the age of Emperor Wu (140–87 B.C.) and includes some topical treatises.

1634

Dubs, Homer H. (trans.) *The History of the Former Han Dynasty.* 3 vols. of a projected 5. Baltimore: Waverly Press, 1938–55. An annotated translation of the annals sections of Pan Ku's *Han-shu,* with much data in prolegomena and appendices that bear on the author's historiographic techniques.

1635

Chavannes, Édouard (trans.). *Les mémoires historiques de Se-ma Ts'ien.* 5 vols. in 6. Paris: Ernest Leroux, 1895-1905. A monumental annotated translation of the annals sections, the chronological tables, the topical treatises, and some of the sections on great families from Ssu-ma Ch'ien's *Shih-chi,* with a valuable introductory study of the authors, the sources, the methodology, and the history of the text.

1636

Legge, James (trans.). *The Chinese Classics.* Vol. 3 in 2 parts. London: Henry Frowde and Trübner and Co., 1865. (Being reprinted by Hong Kong University Press, 1961) The *Shu-ching,* a classical collection of speeches and other historical documents attributed to highest antiquity; the prolegomena include a translation of *Chu-shu chi-nien* ("The Bamboo Annals"), a very cryptic chronicle of events from highest antiquity down into the 4th century B.C., of very questionable authenticity. Both texts are traditionally considered forerunners of the great historiographic tradition. Cf. the more literal rendering of the *Shu-ching* by Bernhard Karlgren in *Bulletin of the Museum of Far Eastern Antiquities,* Stockholm, XXII (1950), 1-81.

1637

Legge, James (trans.). *The Chinese Classics.* Vol. 5 in 2 parts. London: Henry Frowde, 1872. (Being reprinted by Hong Kong University Press, 1961). The *Ch'un-ch'iu* ("Spring and Autumn Annals") and its principal commentary *Tso-chuan,* classical chronicles of events from 721 to 481 B.C., in a complete, authoritative translation. The *Tso-chuan* is considered one of China's greatest masterpieces of historical narrative.

1638

Fang, Achilles (trans.). *The Chronicle of the Three Kingdoms* (220-265). Cambridge: Harvard University Press, 1952. Authoritative translation of chaps. 68-78 of Ssu-Ma Kuang's comprehensive narrative history of pre-Sung China, *Tzu-chih t'ung-chien.*

1639

Swann, Nancy Lee. *Food and Money in Ancient China.* Princeton: Princeton University Press, 1950. Incorporates annotated translations of treatises on economic history from Pan Ku's *Han-shu* and Ssu-ma Ch'ien's *Shih-chi.*

1640

Blue, Rhea C. "The Argumentation of the *Shih-huo chih* Chapters of the Han, Wei, and Sui Dynasty Histories," *Harvard Journal of Asiatic Studies,* XI (1948), 1-118. Detailed, annotated translations of the evaluating and summing-up portions of China's earliest historiographic treatises on economics.

1641

Chinese Dynastic Histories Translations. Berkeley: University of California Press, 1952–. A series of pamphlet-size translations of chapters and sections from dynastic histories of post-Han times up into T'ang times, under the general editorship of Hans H. Frankel; includes biographies of notable individuals and treatises on foreign peoples, etc. Excellent source materials for the study of Chinese historiography, and well annotated.

1642

Bodde, Derk (trans.). *Statesman, Patriot, and General in Ancient China.* New Haven: American Oriental Society, 1940. Three biographies from Ssu-ma Ch'ien's *Shih-chi:* Lü Pu-wei, Ching K'o, and Meng T'ien, all of the Ch'in period.

1643

Schafer, Edward H. (trans.) "The History of the Empire of Southern Han," in *Silver Jubilee Volume of the Zinbun-Kagaku-Kenkyusyo,* Kyoto University (Kyoto: 1954), pp. 339-369. Ou-yang Hsiu's account of one of the 10th century "southern Kingdoms" in the *Wu-tai shih,* in a technical, awkwardly literal translation.

1644

De Francis, John (trans.). "Biography of the Marquis of Huai-yin," *Harvard Journal of Asiatic Studies*, X (1947), 179-215. A somewhat irreverent biography from Ssu-ma Ch'ien's *Shih-Chi;* annotated.

1645

Giles, Lionel (trans.). *A Gallery of Chinese Immortals*. London: John Murray, 1948. (Wisdom of the East Series) Translations or adaptations of early biographical notices, principally from two early biographical compendiums about Taoist marvel-workers: *Lieh-hsien chuan* (3d century) and *Shen-hsien chuan* by Ko Hung (4th century).

1646

Solomon, Bernard S. (trans.) *The Veritable Record of the T'ang Emperor Shun-tsung (February 28, 805–August 31, 805): Han Yü's Shun-tsung shih-lu*. Cambridge: Harvard University Press, 1955. Complete, annotated translation of the only extant T'ang reign-history. On textual problems, cf. E. G. Pulleyblank, "The *Shun-tsung Shih-lu*," *Bulletin of the School of Oriental and African Studies*, London University, XIX (1957), 336-44.

Classical prose fiction

1647

Lu Hsün. *A Brief History of Chinese Fiction*. Peking: Foreign Languages Press, 1959. A standard modern Chinese work, first presented as a series of lectures in 1920-24; deals with both classical and colloquial fiction.

1648

Giles, Herbert A. (trans.) *Gems of Chinese Literature: Prose*. 2d ed. Shanghai: Kelly and Walsh, 1923. Selections from every historic period, mostly in classical style and mostly of anecdotal or fictional genres.

1649

Wang Chi-chen (trans.). *Traditional Chinese Tales*. New York: Columbia University Press, 1944. Includes 15 short stories of the classical-language type, mostly from the T'ang dynasty.

1650

Lin Yutang (trans.). *Famous Chinese Short Stories*. New York: John Day, 1952; paperbound reprint New York: Pocket Library, 1954. Adaptations of twenty tales, mostly of the T'ang and Sung periods.

1651

Giles, Herbert A. (trans.) *Strange Tales from a Chinese Studio*. 4th ed. rev. Shanghai: Kelly and Walsh, 1926. The most extensive selection (164 stories) from *Liao-chai Chih-i*. Cf. an investigation of the life of the author to determine the cause of his critical and satirical tone: Jaroslav Prusek's "Liao-chai chi-i by P'u Sung-ling: An inquiry into the Circumstances under which the Collection Arose," in *Studia Serica Bernhard Karlgren Dedicata* (Copenhagen: Ejnar Munksgaard, 1959), pp. 128-146.

1652

Quong, Rose (trans.). *Chinese Ghost and Love Stories*. New York: Pantheon, 1946. Selections from *Liao-chai chih-i*.

1653

Lin Yutang. *The Wisdom of China and India*. New York: Modern Library, 1942. Pp. 939-963 offer 9 short stories in classical style from ancient and medieval sources; pp. 1054-1067 offer 18 famous anecdotes in classical literature, mostly from ancient philosophical writings.

1654

Kao, George (ed.). *Chinese Wit and Humor*. New York: Coward-McCann, 1946. Includes many humorous anecdotes from ancient philosophical and historical writings, in classical style.

1655

Edwards, E. D. (ed.) *The Dragon Book*. London: William Hodge, 1938. Pp. 163-277; translations of an-ecdotes and very short tales, mostly from classical-language sources.

1656

Bodde, Derk. "Some Chinese Tales of the Supernatural: Kan Pao and his *Sou-shen chi*," *Harvard Journal of Asiatic Studies*, VI (1942), 338-344. Translations of 8 ghost stories from a 4th century collection, with introductory data about the work and its author as well as the ghost-story genre in Chinese fiction.

1657

Hightower, James R. (trans.) *Han Shih Wai Chuan: Han Ying's Illustrations of the Didactic Application of the Classic of Songs*. Cambridge: Harvard University Press, 1952. (Harvard-Yenching Institute Monograph Series, XI) Annotated translation of a Han dynasty compendium of earlier literature with moralistic implications, chiefly representing the ancient anecdotal tradition.

1658

Waley, Arthur. *The Real Tripitaka and Other Pieces*. London: Allen and Unwin, 1952. Pp. 171-213 offer 7 anecdotes or short tales from the T'ang period and one long tale of the 18th century, all translated from classical-style Chinese.

1659

Birch, Cyril (trans.). *Stories from a Ming Collection*. London: The Bodley Head, 1958. Includes one classical-language tale, "The Story of Wu Pao-an," by Niu Su of the T'ang dynasty.

Drama

Chinese theatrical productions are characteristically semi-operatic, in that there is alternation between spoken dialogue (in relatively colloquial language) and lyrics sung to orchestral accompaniment (in relatively classical language). Themes are commonly drawn from history and are heavily moralistic, and action is not very dramatic except in military dramas, which stress acrobatics. Characters tend to be stereotypes, readily identifiable to the audience by their costumes and facial makeup. In form, the drama apparently developed out of narrative song recitations. The fully-developed drama has evolved through three dominant forms: (1) *tsa-chü*, regularized operatic performances in four acts that developed in North China during the 13th century; (2) *nan-hsi*, multi-act productions with different musical styles that developed concurrently in South China and became the most vigorous form in the 15th century; and (3) *ching-hsi*, the still dominant, rather heterogeneous form that developed around Peking in the latter half of the 19th century. The introduction of Western dramatic forms in the 20th century has not lessened the popularity of these traditional dramas.

1660

Hightower, James R. *Topics in Chinese Literature*. Rev ed. Cambridge: Harvard University Press, 1953. Chap. 15 discusses the history and nature of traditional Chinese drama, with bibliographic references.

1661

Scott, A. C. *The Classical Theatre of China*. London: Allen and Unwin, 1957. A detailed description of the history, staging, music, plays, and playhouses of traditional opera-drama, with special emphasis on the training, roles, and techniques of the actors; a "practical handbook" by an authority.

1662

Delza, Sophia. "The Classic Chinese Theater," *Journal of Aesthetics and Art Criticism,* XV (1956), 181-197. A good interpretive introduction to traditional opera-drama, emphasizing the theatrical atmosphere and techniques.

1663

Hsiung Shih-i. "Drama," in *China* (H. F. MacNair, ed.; Berkeley: University of California Press, 1946), pp. 372-385. An excellent brief survey of the history of traditional Chinese opera-dramas.

1664

Zucker, A. E. *The Chinese Theater.* London: Jarrolds, 1925. A general description of theater arts in China, with a fairly detailed history of the opera-drama form from the Yüan dynasty into the 20th century.

1665

Crump, James I. "The Elements of Yüan Opera," *Journal of Asian Studies,* XVII (1957–58), 417-434. Discussion of the main characteristics of classical *tsa-chü* drama.

1666

Liu, James. *Elizabethan and Yuan.* London: The China Society, 1955. A brief essay comparing the dramatic conventions of England's Elizabethan drama with those of China's *tsa-chü* of the Yüan era.

1667

Scott, A. C. *"Ch'ou chiao erh:* The Comic Roles of the Chinese Classical Theatre," in *Akten des vierundzwansigsten Internationalen Orientalisten-Kongresses München, 1957* (Herbert Franke, ed.; Wiesbaden: Franz Steiner, 1959).

1668

Yao Hsin-nung. "The Theme and Structure of the Yüan Drama," *T'ien Hsia Monthly,* I (1935), 388-403. A general description of the classical *tsa-chü* opera.

1669

Yao Hsin-nung. "The Rise and Fall of the K'un Ch'ü (Quinsan Drama)," *T'ien Hsia Monthly,* II (1936), 63-84. The nature and history of a lyrical dramatic form that dominated the Chinese stage in the latter half of the Ming dynasty.

1670

Liu Wu-chi. "The Original Orphan of China," *Comparative Literature,* V (1953), 193-212. A study of a Yüan dynasty operatic drama *(Chao-shih ku-erh)* that was adapted to the European stage and became a smash hit in the 18th century, as "The Chinese Orphan."

1671

Kalvodova-Sis-Vanis. *Chinese Theatre.* London: Spring Books, 1957. An essay on the staging, acting, and "atmosphere" of traditional Chinese opera-dramas; a romanticized "appreciation," but with 44 beautiful color plates.

1672

Bowers, Faubion. *Theatre in the East.* New York: Nelson, 1956; paperbound reprint New York: Grove Press, 1960. Pp. 272-302: a brief survey of the place of theatrical arts in Chinese life, the characteristics of both traditional and modern dramas, and the styles and techniques of acting.

*   *   *

1673

Wimsatt, Genevieve. *Chinese Shadow Shows.* Cambridge: Harvard University Press, 1936. An unscholarly introduction to a minor but highly popular Chinese theatrical art, with photographic illustrations of shadow-puppet stages, scenes, and techniques; with an English rendering of one representative libretto.

1674

March, Benjamin. *Chinese Shadow-figure Plays and their Making.* Detroit: Puppetry Imprints, 1938. An abundantly illustrated introduction, in popular style; with English renderings of three representative librettos.

*   *   *

1675

Hsiung, S. I. (trans.) *The Romance of the Western Chamber.* New York: Liveright, 1936. One of the great classics of 13th century drama, *Hsi-hsiang chi,* a *tsa-chü* based on a famous T'ang dynasty short story about the love of a young examination candidate for Ts'ui Ying-ying, one of traditional China's most popular heroines.

1676

Arlington, L. C. and Harold Acton. *Famous Chinese Plays.* Peiping: Henri Vetch, 1937. Free translations of traditional Chinese operatic dramas, including 31 of the *ching-hsi* form and 2 of the earlier *k'un-ch'ü* form, a peculiarly melodic form of *nan-hsi* in which the flute is the major accompaniment.

1677

Hart, Henry H. *West Chamber.* Stanford: Stanford University Press, 1936. Another translation of *Hsi-hsiang chi.*

1678

Hsiung, S. I. (trans.) *Lady Precious Stream.* New York: Liveright, 1935. A Ch'ing dynasty *ching-hsi* drama.

1679

Irwin, Will and Sidney Howard. *Lute Song.* Chicago: Dramatic Publishing Co., 1954. A popular American adaptation of one of the most famous *nan-hsi* opera-dramas of Ming times, *P'i-pa chi.*

*   *   *

1680

The Ruse of the Empty City: A Peking Opera Recorded in China. Folkways Records album FW 8882. New York: 1960. A famous *ching-hsi* drama about military stratagems of Chu-ko Liang in the Three Kingdoms era, completely recorded on one long-play record; with an English translation of the libretto.

Colloquial prose fiction

Fiction in colloquial language became a vigorous force in Chinese literature after the 14th century though studiously ignored by most Chinese of the ruling class, who read it in private and sometimes wrote it but considered it vulgar and immoral. It is characteristically longer, more rambling and unstructured, and more broad-ranging in sentiments and situations than classical-style fiction. Colloquial fiction is also commonly of unidentifiable authorship. Long tales or novels include works in several genres. Of historical novels, the earliest and most esteemed is *San-kuo yen-i* (14th century?), a romanticized chronicle about the 3rd-century 3 Kingdoms era. Among picaresque or adventure novels, *Shui-hu chuan* (15th century?) is the acknowledged masterpiece; a loose, anecdotal tale of the exploits of a 12th-century bandit gang, it is probably the story best loved by the Chinese people. Novels of the supernatural notably include *Hsi-yu chi* (16th century), an allegorical account of a pilgrimage to India made by the 7th-century Buddhist monk Hsüan-tsang. *Ju-lin wai-shih* (18th century), a semi-comical attack on corrupt and stupid officials, is the most famous satirical novel. Two outstanding novels of domestic life and romance are *Chin P'ing Mei* (16th century), a rather pornographic tale of bourgeois life, and *Hung-lou meng* (18th century), a panoramic and highly stylized account of the rise and decay of a great family that is generally recognized by 20th-century Chinese as their greatest fictional masterpiece. Three 17th-century works collectively called *San-yen* are the best known compendiums of colloquial short stories. Such short stories, like many novels, betray origins in long-perpetuated oral tradition.

Critical studies

1681

Hightower, James R. *Topics in Chinese Literature.* Rev. ed. Cambridge: Harvard University Press, 1953. Chap. 16 discusses the history, general nature, and masterpieces of traditional colloquial-language short stories and novels, with bibliographic references.

1682

Feuerwerker, Yi-tse Mei. "The Chinese Novel," in *Approaches to the Oriental Classics* (W. T. de Bary, ed.; New York: Columbia University Press, 1959), pp. 171-185. On the major characteristics of traditional Chinese novels, from the point of view of their use by Western readers.

1683

Bishop, John L. "Some Limitations of Chinese Fiction," *Far Eastern Quarterly,* XV (1955–56), 239-247. On some characteristics of traditional colloquial fiction that disappoint Western readers—uniformity of style, shallow characterization, etc.; with comments on the early development of the story-telling craft.

1684

Ruhlmann, Robert. "Traditional Heroes in Chinese Popular Fiction," in *The Confucian Persuasion* (A. F. Wright, ed.; Stanford: Stanford University Press, 1960), pp. 141-176. An informative essay on the different value systems of classical and popular literature, with analyses of the treatments of the princes, scholars, and swordsmen who are the principal heroes of popular fiction.

1685

Lu Hsün. *A Brief History of Chinese Fiction.* Peking: Foreign Languages Press, 1959. A standard modern Chinese work, first presented as a series of lectures in 1920–24; detailed summaries and evaluations of the great colloquial novels.

1686

Irwin, Richard G. *The Evolution of a Chinese Novel: Shui-hu-chuan.* Cambridge: Harvard University Press, 1953. (Harvard-Yenching Institute Studies, X) A detailed, authoritative textual history of China's earliest novel in colloquial language, with a long summary of its fullest form.

1687

Prusek, Jaroslav. "Researches into the Beginnings of the Chinese Popular Novel," *Archiv Orientalni,* XI (1939), 91-132. A detailed, authoritative study of the Sung dynasty literary forms and practices from which the colloquial-language novels later emerged; should be used in conjunction with the author's "Popular Novels in the Collection of Ch'ien Tseng," *op. cit.,* X (1938), 281-294, and "The Narrators of Buddhist Scriptures and Religious Tales in the Sung Period," *op cit.,* X (1938), 375-389.

1688

Birch, Cyril. "Feng Meng-Lung and the *Ku Chin Hsiao Shuo,*" *Bulletin of the School of Oriental and African Studies,* London University, XVIII (1956), 64-83. A technical study of the nature of the editor's contribution to a 17th century anthology of story-tellers' tales.

1689

Birch, Cyril. "Some Formal Characteristics of the *Hua-pen* Story," *Bulletin of the School of Oriental and African Studies,* London University, XVII 1955), 346-364. On early written versions of tales told by story-tellers in the Sung, Yüan, and Ming dynasties, with special reference to a 17th century anthology called *Ku-chin hsiao-shuo.*

1690

Ou Itai. *Essai critique et bibliographique sur le roman chinois.* Paris: Les Editions Vega, 1933. A standard reference on the history of traditional China's colloquial-language novels.

1691

Ho Shih-chun. *Jou Lin Wai Che, le Roman des Lettrés.* Paris: L. Rodstein, 1933. A critical analysis of *Ju-lin wai-shih,* including studies of its authorship and its ideas, a resumé of the story, analyses of its chief characters, and translations of representative sections.

1692

Schurmann, H. F. "On Social Themes in Sung Tales," *Harvard Journal of Asiatic Studies,* XX (1957), 239-261. An analysis of several short stories from a socio-historical point of view.

Novels

1693

Kao, George (ed.). *Chinese Wit and Humor.* New York: Coward-McCann, 1946. Includes long excerpts from *Shui-hu chuan, Hsi-yu chi, Chin P'ing Mei, Hung-lou meng, Ju-lin wai-shih,* and other traditional fiction in colloquial style.

1694

Brewitt-Taylor, C. H. (trans.) *Romance of the Three Kingdoms.* 2 vols. Rutland, Vt.: C. E. Tuttle Co., 1959. A Ming dynasty romanticized retelling of the troubled history of 3d century China, following the fall of the Han dynasty; the classic model of all traditional historical fiction.

1695

Buck, Pearl S. (trans.) *All Men Are Brothers.* 2 vols. New York: Grove Press, 1957. China's greatest traditional adventure novel, *Shui-hu chuan,* in a complete translation of the 70-chapter version; the Chinese counterpart of the Robin Hood tradition, glorifying the struggles of honest and brave men against a corrupt and oppressive government.

1696

Jackson, J. H. (trans.) *Water Margin.* 2 vols. Shanghai: Commercial Press, 1937. A somewhat abridged translation of *Shui-hu chuan.*

1697

Waley, Arthur (trans.). *Monkey.* New York: John Day, 1943; paperbound reprint New York: Grove Press, 1958. An abridged translation of *Hsi-yu chi,* a highly allegorical retelling of the adventures of a famous 7th century Buddhist pilgrim to India, Hsüan-tsang, by Wu Ch'eng-en (ca. 1505–80); sometimes called the Chinese "Pilgrim's Progress," but very lively and comic. A substantial excerpt from Waley's translation is reprinted in *Masterpieces of the Orient* (G. L. Anderson, ed.; New York: Norton, 1961), pp. 235-254.

1698

Yang Hsien-yi and Gladys Yang (trans.). *The Scholars.* Peking: Foreign Languages Press, 1957. The only extensive English translation from *Ju-lin wai-shih,* a rambling Ch'ing dynasty satire on the corruption and incompetence of traditional scholar-officials.

1699

Chin P'ing Mei. 2 vols. New York: Putnam, 1940. Single-volume edition by same publisher, 1947; paperbound reprint New York: Capricorn Books, 1960. A somewhat abridged English translation of a classic 16th century novel about a prosperous pharmacist and his six concurrent wives, with a moral lesson but many rather pornographic passages; translator not indicated, but apparently Bernard Miall from the German version of Franz Kuhn.

1700

Egerton, Clement (trans.). *The Golden Lotus.* 4 vols. New York: Grove Press, 1954. A complete translation of *Chin P'ing Mei,* shifting from English into Latin for the more pornographic passages.

1701

Kuhn, Franz (trans.). *Flower Shadows Behind the Curtain: Ko Lien Hua Ying,* rendered into English by Vladimir Kean. London: The Bodley Head, 1959. A sequel, written in the Ch'ing dynasty, to the great Ming novel *Chin P'ing Mei,* with most of the original characters reincarnated and up to their old amorous tricks; the English rendering is somewhat abridged from Kuhn's complete German translation.

1702

Wang Chi-chen (trans.). *Dream of the Red Chamber.* New York: Twayne, 1958; abridged paperbound reprint New York: Doubleday, 1958. An authoritative rendering of *Hung-lou meng,* the 18th century novel of domestic life and romance by Tsao Hsüeh-chin that has come to be revered as the greatest of all Chinese novels.

1703

Kuhn, Franz (trans.). *Dream of the Red Chamber,* trans. from the German version by Florence and Isabel McHugh. New York: Pantheon, 1958. Another rendering of *Hung-lou meng,* done second-hand from a standard and popular German translation.

1704

Shadick, Harold (trans.). *The Travels of Lao Ts'an.* Ithaca: Cornell University Press, 1952. A late 19th century satirical novel by Liu E; with a useful introduction. A substantial excerpt from Shadick's translation is reprinted in *Masterpieces of the Orient* (G. L. Anderson, ed.; New York: Norton, 1961), pp. 254-288.

Short stories

1705

Birch, Cyril (trans.). *Stories from a Ming Collection.* London: The Bodley Head, 1958. Six colloquial stories from the 17th century anthology *Ku-chin hsiao-shuo.*

1706

Wang Chi-chen (trans.). *Traditional Chinese Tales.* New York: Columbia University Press, 1944. Includes 5 short stories of the colloquial-language type, from the *San-yen* collections.

1707

Acton, Harold and Lee Yi-hsieh (trans.). *Four Cautionary Tales.* New York: A. A. Wyn, 1948. Short stories selected from the *San-yen* collections.

1708

Howell, E. B. (trans.) *The Restitution of the Bride and Other Stories.* New York: Brentano, 1926. Six short stories from the 17th century anthology *Chin-ku ch'i-kuan.*

1709

Howell, E. B. (trans.) *The Inconstancy of Madame Chuang and Other Stories.* London: T. W. Laurie, 1924. Five short stories selected from an important 17th century anthology, *Chin-ku ch'i-kuan.*

1710

Lin Yutang. *Widow, Nun and Courtesan.* New York: John Day, 1950. Includes free adaptations of "Miss Tu," from the *San-yen* collections, and "A Nun of Taishan," by Liu E, a late Ch'ing author, intended as a sequel to his satirical novel *Lao-ts'an yu-chi.*

*   *   *

1711

Black, Shirley M. (trans.) *Chapters from a Floating Life.* London: Oxford University Press, 1960. The memoirs of a minor litterateur dogged by tragedy, Shen Fu (1763–?), chiefly concerned with his love for his wife: "a literary masterpiece; poetic, romantic, nostalgic and filled with emotion, it recreates a life essentially tragic, which yet held innumerable moments of an almost magical happiness and beauty." Cf. an abridged translation in Lin Yutang's *The Wisdom of China and India* (New York: Modern Library, 1942), pp. 964-1052.

1712

Eberhard, Wolfram. *Chinese Fairy Tales and Folk Tales.* London: Kegan Paul, 1937. A voluminous compendium of traditional tales, mostly recorded directly from informants; folklore rather than created literature.

Modern literary movements

Perhaps no aspect of Chinese life has had a more turbulent history in the 20th century than literature. Literary theories, forms, and techniques have been very notably changed under the impact of Western examples. A dynamic literary renaissance began in the second decade of the century under the principal leadership of Hu Shih and with close ties to the May 4th movement (1919) of socio-political agitation. Its basic stimulus was the rapidly accepted conviction that literature should be written in the living language of the people and that the artificialities of the classical style should be abolished. The literary revolution or "New Tide" (also called "New Culture Movement" and "New Thought Movement") through the 1920's and 1930's spawned literary journals, contending schools of literary criticism, and mutually antagonistic organizations of writers in large numbers and in bewildering succession. Political and social issues gradually became dominant in the attitudes of such groups as the Creation Society, the Crescent Moon Society, and the League of Left-Wing Writers, so that during the 1930's the traditional didactic character of Chinese literature became ever more reapparent. This tendency was accelerated by the upsurging nationalism of the Sino-Japanese War period and, later, by the increasing appeal of the communist movement among intellectuals. After communism won control of the mainland in 1949, literature became totally subordinated to ideological control by the state, and "socialist realism" became the uniform literary style. In general, the 20th century modernization of literature has been most effective in the novel, short story, and essay forms. A new, Western-style, spoken drama began to thrive but could not quickly overtake the traditional operatic drama in artistry and popularity, and new poetic forms failed to be taken seriously in competition with the old classical forms. The single most influential Chinese writer of the 20th century was Lu Hsün (or Lusin, pseud. of Chou Shu-jen, 1881–1936), a leader in the leftist movement and a skillful satirist. Leading writers of the communist era include Mao Tun, Ting Ling, Lao She, and Chao Shu-li.

Histories and critical studies

1713

Hsia, C. T. *A History of Modern Chinese Fiction, 1917–1957.* New Haven: Yale University Press, 1961. A voluminous, detailed, critical study, full of biographical information about major writers, evaluations of literary movements, critical reviews of literary works, and analyses of governmental control of literature under the communists; in readable narrative style. Includes a brief appendix on literary developments in Taiwan during the 1950's by Hsia Tsi-an.

1714

Hightower, James R. *Topics in Chinese Literature.* Rev. ed. Cambridge: Harvard University Press, 1953. Chap. 17 discusses 20th century literature, with bibliographic references.

1715

Li Tien-yi. "Continuity and Change in Modern Chinese Literature," *Annals of the American Academy of Political and Social Science,* 321 (January 1959), 90-99. An excellent general survey of 20th century literary developments in China.

1716

Huang Sung-k'ang. *Lu Hsün and the New Culture Movement of Modern China.* Amsterdam: Djambatan, 1957. A scholarly, authoritative analysis of literary currents in republican China up to 1936, especially focusing on the role of Lu Hsün and including a critical study of his literary work.

1717

Hughes, E. R. *The Invasion of China by the Western World.* New York: Macmillan, 1938. Chap. 6, "The New Literature," provides an authoritative introductory survey of the literary renaissance of the 20th century.

1718

Hu Shih. *The Chinese Renaissance.* Chicago: University of Chicago Press, 1934. An early evaluation of the New Culture Movement by one of its prime movers; a good introduction to Chinese intellectual history of the 20th century.

1719

Liu Chun-jo. "The Heroes and Heroines of Modern Chinese Fiction: From Ah Q to Wu Tzu-hsü," *Journal of Asian Studies,* XVI (1956–57), 201-211. A critical analysis of some creations of Lu Hsün, Lao She, Mao Tun, Feng Chih, and others.

1720

Mei Yi-tsi. "Tradition and Experiment in Modern Chinese Literature," in *Indiana University Conference on Oriental-Western Literary Relations* (Horst Frenz and G. L. Anderson, ed.; Chapel Hill: University of North Carolina Press, 1955), pp. 107-121. An interpretive evaluation of 20th century trends in Chinese literature.

1721

Scott, A. C. *Mei Lan-fang, Leader of the Pear Garden.* Hong Kong: Hong Kong University Press, 1959. A biography of China's most admired 20th century actor, especially noted for his female roles in traditional operatic dramas.

1722

Schyns, Joseph and others. *1500 Modern Chinese Novels and Plays.* Peiping: Catholic University Press, 1948. A voluminous compendium on 20th century literature, including a historical survey by Su Hsüeh-lin, brief biographical notices of 200 authors, reviews of 1013 works of fiction (novels and volumes of short stories), reviews of more than 200 plays, etc.; much useful data, though marred by moralistic judgments and proscriptions.

1723

Liu Chun-jo. "People, Places, and Time in Five Modern Chinese Novels," in *Asia and the Humanities* (Horst Frenz, ed.; Bloomington, Ind.; Indiana University Comparative Literature Committee, 1959), pp. 15-25. An analysis of the varieties of realism demonstrated by five 20th century novelists, including Lu Hsün, Mao Tun, and Lao She.

1724

Fang, Achilles. "From Imagism to Whitmanism in Recent Chinese Poetry: A Search for Poetics that Failed," in *Indiana University Conference on Oriental-Western Literary Relations* (Horst Frenz and G. L. Anderson, ed.; Chapel Hill: University of North Carolina Press, 1955), pp. 177-189. On modern Chinese difficulties in finding an acceptable replacement for the traditional forms of poetry, especially noting the work of Hu Shih and Kuo Mo-jo.

1725

Chen, David Y. "The Trilogy of Ts'ao Yü and Western Drama," in *Asia and the Humanities* (Horst Frenz, ed.; Bloomington, Ind.; Indiana University Comparative Literature Committee, 1959), pp. 26-37. On the evolution of Western-influenced "spoken drama" in 20th century China, and one of its most noted practitioners.

1726

Houn, Franklin W. "The Stage as a Medium of Propaganda in Communist China," *Public Opinion Quarterly,* XXIII (1959–60), 223-235. An authoritative study of the devices by which the Peking regime has utilized all theatrical activities for political purposes.

1727

Teng, S. Y. "Chinese Historiography in the Last Fifty Years," *Far Eastern Quarterly,* VIII (1948–49), 131-156. General survey of the major trends and new developments in 20th century historical scholarship, noting the outstanding authorities in each field.

1728

McAleavy, Henry. "Tseng P'u and the Nieh Hai Hua," in *St. Antony's Papers,* VII (London: Chatto and Windus, 1960), 88-137. An introduction to and summary of an early 20th century novel about Sino-Western relations, with a biographical study of a remarkable Chinese woman on whose life it was based.

* * *

1729

Chen, Theodore H. E. *Thought Reform of the Chinese Intellectuals.* Hong Kong: Hong Kong University Press, 1960. A detailed, authoritative history of anti-intellectual programs pursued by the Chinese communists during the 1950's; includes case studies of many litterateurs caught in "rectification" campaigns.

1730

Birch, Cyril. "Fiction of the Yenan Period," *China Quarterly,* no. 4 (October-December 1960), 1-11. An evaluative survey of communist-inspired novels and short stories published between 1935 and 1949, with comments on the communist attitude toward literature as an instrument of political policy.

1731

Chen, S. H. "Multiplicity in Uniformity: Poetry and the Great Leap Forward," *China Quarterly,* no. 3 (July-September 1960), 1-15. On the fostering of spontaneous folk poetry by the Peking government and its quantitative measurement as an indicator of cultural progress.

1732

Chao Chung. *The Communist Program for Literature and Art in China.* Kowloon: Union Research Institute, 1955. A brief critical study of Chinese communist policies and organizations concerning literature and of literary productions under government sponsorship in the early communist period.

1733

Mao Tse-tung. *Selected Works.* Vol. IV. London: Lawrence and Wishart, 1956. Pp. 63-93, "Talks at the Yenan

Forum on Art and Literature" (1942), set forth the official Chinese Communist Party views concerning "socialist realism" in literature.

1734

Mills, Harriet C. "Lu Hsün and the Communist Party," *China Quarterly,* no. 4 (October-December 1960), 17-27. On the actual political sympathies of the great 20th century writer, honored posthumously as a great cultural hero by the Chinese communist government.

1735

Feuerwerker, Albert. "China's History in Marxian Dress," *American Historical Review,* LXVI (1960-61), 323-353. On the reinterpretation of China's past under communist influence, and some controversies involved in it.

1736

Feuerwerker, Albert. "From 'Feudalism' to 'Capitalism' in Recent Historical Writing from Mainland China," *Journal of Asian Studies,* XVIII (1958–59), 107-115. A critical discussion of some communist reinterpretations of traditional economic history.

1737

Fairbank, John K. and Mary C. Wright (ed.). "Documentary Collections on Modern Chinese History," *Journal of Asian Studies,* XVII (1957–58), 55-111. Critical evaluations of some monumental historiographic compilations in mainland China on 19th century events: the Opium War, Taiping rebellion, Nien rebellion, Moslem uprisings, Sino-French war of 1882-85, Sino-Japanese war of 1894–95, 1898 reform movement, and Boxer rebellion.

1738

Grieder, Jerome B. "The Communist Critique of *Hung lou meng,*" *Papers on China,* X (Cambridge: Harvard University Committee on Regional Studies, 1956; privately distributed), 142-168. A seminar paper on the political aspects of literary criticism in communist China, as reflected in the modern revaluation of *Dream of the Red Chamber.*

1739

Goldman, Merle. "Hu Feng's Conflict with the Communist Literary Authorities," *Papers on China,* XI (Cambridge: Harvard University Center for East Asian Studies, 1957; privately distributed), 149-191. A seminar paper on state control of literature in communist China, focusing on the ideological rehabilitation of an influential literary critic in 1955.

1740

Yang I-fan. *The Case of Hu Feng.* Kowloon: Union Research Institute, 1956. A case study of ideological attack on a dissenting literary critic, in the context of the history of literary-political controversies under the communists.

1741

Ting Yi. *A Short History of Modern Chinese Literature.* Peking: Foreign Languages Press, 1959. An officially-sponsored Chinese communist interpretation of literary history from the May 4th Movement of 1919 to the communist conquest of the mainland in 1949.

1742

Moy, Clarence. "Communist China's Use of the Yang-ko," *Papers on China,* VI (Cambridge: Harvard University Committee on International and Regional Studies, 1952; privately distributed), 112-148. A seminar paper on a form of "peasant opera" developed under the communists: its history, content, and propaganda use.

1743

Johnson, Chalmers A. *Communist Policies Toward the Intellectual Class.* Kowloon: Union Research Institute, 1959. A critical analysis of thought-control in mainland China during the 1950's, with special reference to philosophical and literary spheres; with background on the general intellectual and literary history of the 20th century.

Translations

1744

Milton, D. L. and W. Clifford (ed.). *A Treasury of Modern Asian Stories.* New York: Mentor Books, 1961. Pp. 166-213: representative short stories and anecdotes by 20th century Chinese writers, including Lao She, Mao Tun, Lu Hsün, et al.; with brief biographical notes.

1745

Wang Chi-chen (trans.). *Contemporary Chinese Stories.* New York: Columbia University Press, 1944. Twenty-one short stories published between 1918 and 1937, representing Lu Hsün, Lao She, Mao Tun, Chang T'ien-yi and others.

1746

Wang Chi-chen (ed.). *Stories of China at War.* New York: Columbia University Press, 1947. An anthology of 16 short stories of the period 1937–42, by Lao She, Mao Tun, Kuo Mo-jo, and others; by various translators.

1747

Payne, Robert (ed). *Contemporary Chinese Poetry.* London: Routledge, 1947. Translations of more than 100 poems of the Literary Renaissance era, by Wen I-to, Ai Ching, Tien Chien and others; with a useful introductory essay on the poets and poetry of the 20th century, and with brief biographical sketches of the 9 poets represented.

1748

Kao, George (ed). *Chinese Wit and Humor.* New York: Coward-McCann, 1946. Includes representative selections from such 20th century writers as Lao She, Lin Yutang, Lu Hsün, et al.

1749

Snow, Edgar (ed). *Living China.* New York: Reynal and Hitchcock, 1937. Short stories by 15 writers of the 1930's, including Lu Hsün, with useful biographical data on each derived from personal interviews.

1750

Payne, Robert (ed.). *The White Pony.* New York: John Day, 1947; paperbound reprint New York: Mentor Books, 1960. Pp. 381-414 provide a brief introduction to and selective translations from 20th century poets.

1751

Wang Chi-chen (trans.). *Ah Q and Others.* New York: Columbia University Press, 1941. Authoritative translations of 11 short stories by the 20th century master satirist Lu Hsün, with a brief introductory appreciation.

1752

Kyn Yn-yu (trans.). *The Tragedy of Ah Qui and Other Modern Chinese Stories.* New York: Dial Press, 1931. An anthology of 3 short stories by Lu Hsün, together with 6 by other 20th century authors.

1753

Lu Hsün. *Selected Works.* 3 vols. of a projected 4. Peking: Foreign Languages Press, 1956–59. The most complete anthology in English of the writings (fiction, criticism, and other sorts) of the great 20th century social critic who has been adopted by the Chinese communists as nearly a patron saint of literature; renderings by various translators.

1754

Lau Shaw (Lao She; pseud. of Shu Ch'ing-ch'un). *Rickshaw Boy,* trans. by Evan King. New York: Reynal and Hitchcock, 1945. A novel of social protest about the lives of the poor in Peking in the 1930's.

1755

Lau Shaw (Lao She; pseud. of Shu Ch'ing-ch'un). *The Yellow Storm,* trans. by Ida Pruitt. New York: Harcourt, Brace, 1951. A social-protest novel about life in Peking during the early years of the Sino-Japanese war.

1756

Lin Yutang. *Widow, Nun and Courtesan.* New York: John Day, 1950. Includes the long tale "Widow Chuan," by the modern humorist Wang Hsiang-ch'en.

Representative fiction of the communist era
(all published by the Foreign Languages Press, Peking)

1757

Chinese Literature, 1951–. A literary quarterly (issued monthly since 1959) in English, including translations of current short stories and novelettes, literary criticism, articles on literary history, and classics of traditional literature.

1758

Ho Ching-chih and Ting Yi. *The White-haired Girl,* trans. by Yang Hsien-yi and Gladys Yang. The most phenomenal success among the new communist-inspired operatic dramas, in a style called *yang-ko* incorporating peasant songs and dances; about a servant girl who was raped, and whose father was murdered, by an evil landlord and the eventual triumph of justice upon "liberation" of the area by the Red Army.

1759

Chao Shu-li. *Changes in Li Village,* trans. by Gladys Yang. 1953.

1760

Chao Shu-li. *Rhymes of Li Yu-ts'ai and Other Stories.* 1950.

1761

Che'n Ch'i-t'ung. *The Long March.* 1956.

1762

Chou Li-po. *The Hurricane,* trans. by Hsü Meng-hsiung. 1955.

1763

Hu K'o. *Steeled in Battles,* trans by Tang Sheng. 1955.

1764

Hsü Kuang-yao. *The Plains are Ablaze,* trans by Sidney Shapiro. 1955.

1765

Lao She. *Dragon Beard Ditch,* trans by Liao Hung-ying. 1956.

1766

Liu Ch'ing. *Wall of Bronze,* trans by Sidney Shapiro. 1954.

1767

Liu Pai-yü. *Flames Ahead.* 1954.

1768

Liu Pai-yü. *Six A. M. and Other Stories.* 1953.

1769

Mao Tun (pseud. of Shen Yen-ping). *Midnight,* trans. by Hsü Meng-hsiung. 1957.

1770

Ting Ling. *The Sun Shines Over the Sangkan River,* trans. by Yang Hsien-yi and Gladys Yang. 1954.

1771

Yang Shuo. *A Thousand Miles of Lovely Land,* trans. by Yüan Ko-chia. 1957.

MUSIC

Music is one of the least studied aspects of traditional Chinese culture, although the Chinese have been a very musical people who even recite all forms of literature in a sing-song chant. Their singing is normally solo rather than choral except in folk singing and is done either in a "thin," nonresonant voice resembling the speaking voice or in a rather strained falsetto. Instrumental music is normally played solo or in small chamber-music accompaniment groups rather than in large orchestras, on various string, wind, and percussion instruments, none of which has great volume or sustaining power. Among the most familiar instruments are a 7-stringed zither called the *ch'in,* a 2-stringed fiddle called the *hu-ch'in,* and a flute called the *ti-tzu.* Much instrumental music and many instruments are used only to accompany singing. In general, all Chinese music is melodic rather than harmonic and uses a 5-tone scale rather than the West's 7-tone scale. In comparison with the West, China's musical repertoire seems quite small, comprising many variations on relatively few themes; and compositions seem meandering and structureless. Under the influence of the West, new instruments and styles have been introduced in modern times, but traditional music still predominates — and by far.

1772

Picken, Laurence. "The Music of Far Eastern Asia, 1. China," in *Ancient and Oriental Music* (Egon Wellesz, ed.; London: Oxford University Press, 1957; "New Oxford History of Music," vol. 1), pp. 83-134. An excellent general introduction to music history, music theory, instruments and techniques, notation, etc.; with illustrations and selected transcriptions.

1773

Crossley-Holland, P. C. "Chinese Music," in *Grove's Dictionary of Music and Muscians,* vol. 2 (5th ed., E. Blom, ed.; London: Macmillan, 1954), pp. 219-248. A general introductory survey, with a comprehensive bibliography.

1774

Reinhard, Kurt. *Chinesische Musik.* Eisenach und Kassel: Erich Röth, 1956. A detailed study of the history, theory, and practice of Chinese music; with photographic and other illustrations, and with many transcriptions.

1775

Sachs, Curt. *The Rise of Music in the Ancient World, East and West.* New York: Norton, 1943. Section 3, principally on China and Japan, provides an authoritative introduction for the student of comparative musicology.

1776

Chao Yuen Ren. "Music," in *Symposium on Chinese Culture* (Sophia H. Zen, ed.; Shanghai: Institute of Pacific Relations, 1931), pp. 82-96. An excellent general survey of traditional Chinese musicology.

1777

Chao Mei-pa. *The Yellow Bell.* Baldwin, Md.: Barberry Hill, 1934. A brief explanation of the theory and practice of music in China by a noted performer, with illustrations and transcriptions.

1778

Gulik, R. H. Van. *The Lore of the Chinese Lute.* Tokyo: Sophia University, 1940. A detailed history of the classical seven-stringed *ch'in,* with special reference to its cultural significance and with comments on the instrument itself and the technique of playing it.

1779

Soulie, C. G. *Theatre et musique modernes en Chine.* Paris: P. Geunther, 1926. Includes a general history of music and a description of musicianship in China; with illustrations and many transcriptions for piano of traditional Chinese melodies.

1780

Fernald, Helen E. "Ancient Chinese Musical Instruments," in *A Harp with a Thousand Strings* (Hsiao Ch'ien, ed.; London: Pilot Press, 1944), pp. 395-440. A general history of traditional music, musicians, and instruments, with many illustrations.

1781

Gulik, R. H. Van. *Hsi K'ang and his Poetical Essay on the Lute.* Tokyo: Sophia University, 1941. Includes an annotated translation of a 3d century prose-poem *(fu)* on the history and theory of the instrument called *ch'in.*

1782

Kishibe Shigeo. "The Origin of the P'i-pa," *Transactions of the Asiatic Society of Japan,* 2d series, XIX (1940), 259-301. A detailed investigation of the history of the *p'i-pa* lute in China, tracing it back to Iran; with photographic illustrations.

* * *

1783

Chinese Classical Music. Lyrichord record LL 27 (n.d.). Eight pieces played on traditional instruments by Wei Chung Loh, demonstrating the fiddle, flutes, the *p'i-pa* lute, etc.; on a single long-play record.

1784

Chinese Classic Music. Folkways Records FP 12 (1951). Five instrumental pieces on one long-play record, demonstrating fiddles, flutes, gongs, bells, cymbals, etc.

1785

Folk Songs and Dances of China. Folkways Records album FP 802 (1954). Eight songs and dance-songs from scattered parts of China on a single long-play record, with a spoken introduction by Julian Schuman.

POLITICAL PATTERNS

The Chinese have not indulged very notably in systematic theorizing about politics, but their practical accomplishments in statecraft have been among the chief reasons for China's long history of national cohesion. The structure of government has changed repeatedly, passing through an ancient phase of feudal decentralization, through a long imperial epoch of bureaucratic centralization, finally in the 20th century into a pattern of one-party dictatorship — and, recurringly, through transitional periods of regional warlordism. But, in the long view, Chinese government has been remarkably stable, resilient, and responsive to the needs of changing times. It has been characterized by elaborate administrative organizations and procedures, sophisticated personnel practices, a strong military tradition, and the implicit assumption that China must dominate all neighboring peoples. Another of its notable characteristics throughout history has been a conception that the state has unlimited responsibility for and almost unchallengeable authority over all aspects of Chinese life. It has been thought that rulers rule by "the mandate of Heaven," which can be withdrawn if a ruler does not respect Heaven's wish that the people be contented. Therefore, the Chinese state, though tending always to be totalitarian, has also been paternalistic. From the dawn of history until 1912 it was monarchical in form, with a semi-theocratic aspect; and even in the 20th century there has been a persistent inclination toward a traditional type of charismatic one-man rule.

GENERAL WORKS

1786

Linebarger, Paul M. A., Djang Chu, and Ardath W. Burks.

Far Eastern Governments and Politics: China and Japan. 2d ed. Princeton: Van Nostrand, 1956. Includes an over-all, authoritative description and interpretive analysis of the evolution of Chinese government from earliest times into the 1950's; an excellent introductory reference.

1787

Ch'ien Tuan-sheng. *The Government and Politics of China.* Cambridge: Harvard University Press, 1950. The only general history of Chinese government from antiquity into the 20th century in the English language; emphasizes the modern period, but provides analyses of the traditional patterns from antiquity.

TRADITIONAL GOVERNMENT

At the dawn of history Chinese government seems to have been a relatively simple monarchy. The Chou conquerors (1122 B.C.?) parceled out land feudal-fashion to regional lords. The hereditary aristocrats of the feudal states gradually usurped power from the Chou central government, and after the 6th century B.C. there was increasingly devastating inter-state competition. In the 3rd century B.C. the state of Ch'in imposed its control over all China, undermined the old aristocratic class, and created a unitary empire administered at all levels by appointees of the central government. This general form of government persisted until 1912, despite changing dynasties. To some extent from the 2nd century B.C. on, and especially after the 7th century, it was staffed chiefly by a non-hereditary civil service of Confucian scholar-officials recruited in highly competitive written examinations. Their management of the state was occasionally disrupted by palace women and eunuchs and by officers of a somewhat professional and hereditary military corps, but it was never seriously challenged. State support of Confucianism as the official orthodoxy assured a moralistic and paternalistic style of government. The state therefore assumed responsibility for the total well-being of Chinese as individuals and as a society, and it developed an elaborate array of governmental agencies, as well as sophisticated bureaucratic procedures, for fulfilling this responsibility. At the same time, it expected tribute-giving submission on the part of all surrounding peoples. In the 19th century the traditional state apparatus and policies proved inadequate in the face of problems created by the impact of the modern West, and the so-called Confucian state system, which symbolized and dominated China's whole traditional way of life, was rather easily swept away by revolutionary tides early in the 20th century.

The traditional state system and ideology in general

1788

Fairbank, John King. *The United States and China.* Rev. ed. Cambridge: Harvard University Press, 1958. Chaps. 3-6 provide general interpretive analyses of various aspects of China's political tradition, especially the elite role of the scholar-bureaucrat, the ideological foundations, and the historic patterns of alien conquest and rule.

1789

Linebarger, Paul M. A., Djang Chu, and Ardath W. Burks. *Far Eastern Governments and Politics:* China and Japan. 2d ed. Princeton: Van Nostrand, 1956. Chaps. 1-4 describe traditional governmental patterns in China, with special emphasis on the Ch'ing dynasty.

1790

Ch'ien Tuan-sheng. *The Government and Politics of China.* Cambridge: Harvard University Press, 1950. Pp. 3-60 survey the nature and history of traditional Chinese government.

1791

Wittfogel, Karl A. *Oriental Despotism: A Comparative Study of Total Power.* New Haven: Yale University Press, 1957. A voluminous, controversial interpretation of "hydraulic societies," notably including that of traditional China. Suggests that the need for control of water resources brought about a concentration of all power in a centralized, bureaucratic state apparatus to which all societal groups were totally subordinate — a theory that is widely influential among social scientists but not generally accepted by China specialists. For a critical review, see N. S. Eisenstadt in *Journal of Asian Studies,* XVII (1957–58), 435-446.

1792

Hughes, E. R. *The Invasion of China by the Western World.* New York: Macmillan, 1938. Chap. 3: a historical survey of the impact of Western political thought on traditional institutions in the 19th century and China's difficulties in adopting Western governmental institutions in the 20th century.

1793

Latourette, K. S. *The Chinese, Their History and Culture.* 3d ed. rev. New York: Macmillan, 1946. Chap. 14 provides a general survey of traditional governmental principles and practices, particularly referring to the Manchu era; a useful introduction, but somewhat out of date.

1794

Yang Lien-sheng. "Schedules of Work and Rest in Imperial China," in his book *Studies in Chinese Institutional History* (Cambridge: Harvard University Press, 1961), pp. 18-42; previously published in *Harvard Journal of Asiatic Studies,* XVIII (1955), 301-325. Includes interesting data about the daily routine of officialdom from dynasty to dynasty in traditional China.

* * *

1795

Lin Mousheng. *Men and Ideas.* New York: John Day, 1942. Subtitled "An Informal History of Chinese Political Thought," though more a general survey of Chinese intellectual history interpreted with an emphasis on political theory; for the general reader, but reliable.

1796

Duyvendak, J. J. L. (trans.) *The Book of Lord Shang, a Classic of the Chinese School of Law.* London: Probsthain, 1928. An introduction to the Legalist school of thought in ancient China, which advocated rule by rigid laws and contributed many concepts to the state system of imperial China.

1797

Liang Ch'i-ch'ao. *History of Chinese Political Thought During the Early Tsin Period,* trans. by L. T. Chen. New York: Harcourt, Brace, 1930. A general evaluation of the political aspects and implications of the various schools of ancient Chinese philosophy prior to the 3d century B.C. Ch'in dynasty, by a noted 20th century scholar-philosopher.

1798

De Bary, William Theodore. "Chinese Despotism and the Confucian Ideal: A Seventeenth-Century View," in *Chinese Thought and Institutions* (J. K. Fairbank, ed.;

Chicago: University of Chicago Press, 1957), pp. 163-203. An analytical summary of a socio-political critique by an eminent Neo-Confucian scholar: Huang Tsunghsi's *Ming-i Tai-fang Lu.*

1799

Levenson, Joseph R. "*T'ien-hsia* and *Kuo* and the Transvaluation of Values," *Far Eastern Quarterly,* XI (1951–52), 447-451. On the difficult transition from a universalist empire to a modern nation-state in modern Chinese political thinking.

1800

Hsü, Leonard Shihlien. *The Political Philosophy of Confucianism.* London: Routledge, 1932. A rather traditionalistic analysis of the ideological foundations of the "Confucian state" system; more relevant to classical ideas in the abstract than to the actual workings of the state in imperial times.

General studies, by periods

1801

Cheng Te-k'un. *Archaeology in China.* Vol. 2: *Shang China.* Cambridge: Heffer, 1960. The most up-to-date compendium of what is known of China at the dawn of history, including data on the Shang governmental system.

* * *

1802

Bodde, Derk. "Feudalism in China," in *Feudalism in History* (R. Coulborn, ed.; Princeton: Princeton University Press, 1956), pp. 49-92. Includes a brief introduction to the early Chou governmental system.

1803

Creel, H. G. *The Birth of China.* Reprint ed. New York: Ungar, 1954. Chap. 9 describes the ancient Shang state, and part III describes the inauguration and early character of Chou feudalism.

1804

Walker, Richard Louis. *The Multi-state System of Ancient China.* Hamden, Conn.: Shoe String Press, 1953. Analyzes inter-state relations of the Ch'un-ch'iu period; a good introduction to Chou government.

1805

Bodde, Derk. "Authority and Law in Ancient China," in Supplement 17 to the *Journal of the American Oriental Society:* "Authority and Law in the Ancient Orient" (1954), pp. 46-55. On Chinese ideas about kingship and the "mandate of heaven" in Chou times.

1806

Kaizuka Shigeki. *Confucius,* trans. by G. Bownas. New York: Macmillan, 1956. Includes data on the political structure of late Chou China.

1807

Bodde, Derk, *China's First Unifier: A Study of the Ch'in Dynasty as Seen in the Life of Li Ssu, 280?–208 B.C.* Leiden: E. J. Brill, 1938. Includes the best discussion in English of the highly centralized Ch'in governmental system, which inaugurated China's imperial tradition.

* * *

1808

Wang Yü-ch'üan. "An Outline of the Central Government of the Former Han Dynasty," *Harvard Journal of Asiatic Studies,* XII (1949), 134-187. A standard reference on the organization, functions, and ideological basis of early Han government.

1809

Yang Lien-sheng. "Great Families of Eastern Han," in *Chinese Social History* (E-tu Zen Sun and John de Francis, ed.; Washington: American Council of Learned Societies, 1956), pp. 103-134. Includes an analysis of the political deterioration of the Later Han dynasty.

* * *

1810

Rotours, Robert des (trans.). *Traité des fonctionnaires et traité de l'armé.* 2 vols. Leiden: E. J. Brill, 1947–

48. An authoritative, highly technical, thoroughly annotated translation of treatises from the *Hsin T'ang-shu* on the civil government and military establishment of T'ang times; one of the monuments of modern Sinological scholarship.

1811

Rideout, John K. "The Rise of the Eunuchs During the T'ang Dynasty," *Asia Major,* I (1949–50), 53-72; III (1952), 42-58. On the recruitment, training, functions, and influence of palace eunuchs.

* * *

1812

Kracke, Edward A., Jr. *Civil Service in Early Sung China, 960–1067.* Cambridge: Harvard University Press, 1953. Includes the only substantial description in English of the Sung dynasty governmental organization.

* * *

1813

Wittfogel, Karl A. and Feng Chia-sheng. *History of Chinese Society: Liao (907–1125).* Philadelphia: American Philosophical Society, 1949. (Transactions of the American Philosophical Society, new series, XXXVI) Includes a detailed analysis of governmental organization and functions under the Liao dynasty of the Ch'itan invaders.

* * *

1814

Ratchnevsky, Paul. *Un code des Yuan.* Paris: Ernest Leroux, 1937. A fully annotated, technical translation of parts of the Yüan dynasty law code, from the *Yüan-shih;* an indispensable guide to Yüan governmental institutions.

1815

Olbricht, Peter. *Das Postwesen in China under der Mongolenherrschaft im 13. und 14. Jahrhundert.* Wiesbaden: Otto Harrassowitz, 1954. A technical study of the administration of postal relays and transport systems in Yüan China.

* * *

1816

Hucker, Charles O. *The Traditional Chinese State in Ming Times (1368–1644).* Tucson: University of Arizona Press, 1961. A general interpretive description of the organization, personnel, societal relations, functions, and ideology of the Ming state system.

1817

Hucker, Charles O. "Governmental Organization of the Ming Dynasty," *Harvard Journal of Asiatic Studies,* XXI (1958), 1-66. A technical description of the agencies of the Ming government and of their major functions.

1818

Crawford, Robert B., Harry M. Lamley, and Albert B. Mann. "Fang Hsiao-ju in the Light of Early Ming Society," *Monumenta Serica,* XV (1956), 303-327. Includes comment on the despotic character of government under the early Ming emperors.

1819

Grimm, Tilemann. "Das Neiko der Ming-zeit, von den Anfängen bis 1506," *Oriens Extremus,* I (1954), 139-177. On the early history and organization of the Ming dynasty Grand Secretariat.

* * *

1820

Hsieh Pao-chao. *The Government of China (1644–1911).* Baltimore: The Johns Hopkins Press, 1925. A standard interpretive discussion of the organization and functions of the Ch'ing government.

1821

Hsiao Kung-ch'uan. *Rural China: Imperial Control in the Nineteenth Century.* Seattle: University of Washington Press, 1960. A voluminous, authoritative, thoroughly documented analysis of the Ch'ing government's sponsorship and utilization of "self-government" organizations in villages and towns as instruments of political and ideological control, and of the deterioration of the imperial government's efficiency in local government in

the 19th century; a very important contribution to the understanding of the traditional Confucian governmental system.

1822

Fairbank, John K. and Teng Ssu-yü. *Ch'ing Administration: Three Studies.* Cambridge: Harvard University Press, 1960. (Harvard-Yenching Institute Studies, XIX) Three technical studies originally published in the *Harvard Journal of Asiatic Studies,* IV, V, and VI: "On the Transmission of Ch'ing Documents," "On the Types and Uses of Ch'ing Documents," and "On the Ch'ing Tributary System."

1823

Ho, Alfred K. L. "The Grand Council in the Ch'ing Dynasty," *Far Eastern Quarterly,* XI (1951–52), 167-182. On the establishment of the *Chün-chi-ch'u,* the highest ranking advisory body in the Ch'ing government, in 1729; its organization, procedures, and personnel.

1824

Hu Ch'ang-tu. "The Yellow River Administration in the Ch'ing Dynasty," *Far Eastern Quarterly,* XIV (1954–55), 505-513. How bureaucratization and corruption led to the stagnation of an important state water-control enterprise in the 19th century.

1825

Cameron, Meribeth E. *The Reform Movement in China, 1898–1912.* Stanford: Stanford University Press, 1931. (Stanford University Publications, University Series: History, Economics, and Political Science, vol. III, no. 1) An authoritative scholarly study of efforts to modernize the Ch'ing governmental system during the last decade of the dynasty, with particular emphasis on constitution-making efforts.

1826

Mayers, William Frederick. *The Chinese Government.* 3d ed. rev. by G. M. H. Playfair. Shanghai: Kelly and Walsh, 1897. A technical manual of Chinese governmental titles in the Ch'ing dynasty.

1827

Brunnert, H. S. and V. V. Hagelstrom. *Present Day Political Organization of China,* rev. by N. Th. Kolessoff, trans. by A. Beltchenko and E. E. Moran. Shanghai: Kelly and Walsh, 1912. A standard manual of Ch'ing governmental agencies, including the innovations of the dynasty's last years.

1828

Hoang, Pierre. *Mélanges sur l'administration.* Shanghai: Mission Catholique, 1902. (Variétés Sinologiques, 21) A monumental sourcebook of miscellaneous data concerning administrative practices of the Ch'ing dynasty.

1829

Hsiao Kung-ch'uan. "Rural Control in Nineteenth Century China," *Far Eastern Quarterly,* XII (1952–53), 173-181. A brief study of local "self-government" as an instrument of political and imperial control in Ch'ing times; the subject is dealt with more fully in Hsiao's book, *Rural China.*

Bureaucracy and civil service examinations

1830

Kracke, Edward A., Jr. *Civil Service in Early Sung China, 960–1067.* Cambridge: Harvard University Press, 1953. An authoritative study of the Sung dynasty's elaborate techniques of personnel administration, with special reference to a system of "controlled sponsorship" or "guaranteed recommendations" for selecting men for high office.

1831

Chang Chung-li. *The Chinese Gentry: Studies on Their Role in Nineteenth-century Chinese Society.* Seattle: University of Washington Press, 1955. A detailed scholarly analysis of the bureaucratic elite in Ch'ing times: social origins, privileges, numbers, etc.; includes an authoritative description of the civil service examination system.

1832

Michael, Franz. "State and Society in Nineteenth-century China," *World Politics,* VII (1955), 419-433. A brief interpretation of the socio-political role of scholar-officials of the Ch'ing period.

1833

Teng Ssu-yü. "Chinese Influence on the Western Examination System," *Harvard Journal of Asiatic Studies,* VII (1943), 267-312. On European admirers of China's civil service system from the 16th century on, and their influence on the introduction of written examinations and especially civil service examinations in Western life. Cf. Teng's shorter article, "China's Examination System and the West," in *China* (H. F. MacNair, ed.; Berkeley: University of California Press, 1946), pp. 441-451.

1834

Liu, James T. C. "Some Classifications of Bureaucrats in Chinese Historiography," in *Confucianism in Action* (D. S. Nivison and A. F. Wright, ed.; Stanford: Stanford University Press, 1959), pp. 165-181. On traditional typologies of officials according to their political behavior, with examples mainly from the Sung period. Cf. Liu's article "Eleventh-century Chinese Bureaucrats: Some Historical Classifications and Behavioral Types," in *Administrative Science Quarterly,* IV (1959), 207-226.

1835

Yang, C. K. "Some Characteristics of Chinese Bureaucratic Behavior," in *Confucianism in Action* (D. S. Nivison and A. F. Wright, ed.; Stanford: Stanford University Press, 1959), pp. 134-164. On some traditional Chinese deviations from "rational" bureaucratic structures: the preference for generalists rather than specialists, the prestige of moral norms as against formal rules, and the conflict of informal relationships with the ideal of impersonality.

1836

Kracke, E. A., Jr. "Region, Family, and Individual in the Chinese Examination System," in *Chinese Thought and Institutions* (J. K. Fairbank, ed.; Chicago: University of Chicago Press, 1957), pp. 251-268. On the ideal and the reality of free opportunity in the civil service examinations, with special reference to the Sung, Ming, and Ch'ing periods.

1837

Houn, Franklin W. "The Civil Service Recruitment System of the Han Dynasty," *Tsing Hua Journal of Chinese Studies,* I (1956), 138-164. Analysis and evaluation of many types of personnel recruitment used in both Former and Later Han governments, including examinations.

1838

Rotours, Robert des. *Le traité des examens.* Paris: Ernest Leroux, 1932. An authoritative study of the T'ang system of recruiting personnel for bureaucratic office through competitive examinations, based on translations from the *Hsin T'ang-shu.*

1839

Grimm, Tilemann. *Erziehung und Politik im konfuzianischen China der Ming-zeit (1368-1644).* Wiesbaden: Otto Harrassowitz, 1960. (Mitteilungen der Gesellschaft für Natur- und Völkerkunde Ostasiens, XXXV B) On education and its utilization for civil service recruitment in Ming times; chap. 2 deals with the development of state schools and civil service examinations from T'ang up to Ming times.

1840

Zi, Étienne. *Pratique des examens littéraires en Chine.* Shanghai: Mission Catholique, 1894. (Variétés Sinologiques, 5) A detailed description of the civil service examination system of the Ch'ing period.

1841

Creel, Herrlee G. "The Meaning of *Hsing Ming,*" in *Studia Serica Bernhard Karlgren Dedicata* (Copenhagen: Ejnar Munksgaard, 1959), pp. 199-211. On a doctrine of personnel control and testing that was current in late Chou, Ch'in, and early Han times; cf. Creel's article "On the Origins of the Chinese Examination System," in *Akten des vierundzwansigsten Internationalen Orientalisten-Kongresses München, 1957* (Herbert Franke, ed.; Wiesbaden: Franz Steiner, 1959).

1842

Weber, Max. *The Religion of China,* trans. by Hans. H. Gerth. Glencoe, Ill.: Free Press, 1951. A classic sociological analysis of the traditional Chinese bureaucracy; of theoretical value, but not to be relied on for descriptive detail. Cf. Helen Constas, "Max Weber's Two Conceptions of Bureaucracy," *American Journal of Sociology,* LXIII (1957-58), 400-409, distinguishing between legal-rational bureaucracy and charismatic bureaucracy, and classing the Chinese form among the latter. For an excellent general summation of Weber's influential views on China see Reinhard Bendix, *Max Weber: An Intellectual Portrait* (Garden City, N. Y.: Doubleday, 1960), pp. 117-157.

1843

Liu, James T. C. "An Early Sung Reformer: Fan Chung-yen," in *Chinese Thought and Institutions* (J. K. Fairbank, ed.; Chicago: University of Chicago Press, 1957), pp. 104-131. Includes an analysis of the traditional civil service in terms of "idealistic bureaucrats" and "career-minded bureaucrats," with special reference to the 11th century.

1844

Nivison, David S. "Ho-shen and His Accusers: Ideology and Political Behavior in the Eighteenth Century," in *Confucianism in Action* (D. S. Nivison and A. F. Wright, ed.; Stanford: Stanford University Press, 1959), pp. 209-243. An analysis of the attitudes involved in ruler-minister relations in the late, highly authoritarian form of the traditional imperial system.

1845

Levenson, Joseph R. "The Suggestiveness of Vestiges: Confucianism and Monarchy at the Last," in *Confucianism in Action* (D. S. Nivison and A. F. Wright, ed.; Stanford: Stanford University Press, 1959), pp. 244-267. A highly interpretive analysis of the persistent conflict between traditional bureaucrats and monarchs, focused on the nostalgic attempt of the early republican president Yüan Shih-k'ai to keep alive a monarchical mystique.

1846

Marsh, Robert M. "Bureaucratic Constraints on Nepotism in the Ch'ing Period," *Journal of Asian Studies,* XIX (1959-60), 117-133. A statistical study, suggesting that seniority qualifications were used to equalize opportunities for promotion between scions of official families and of commoner families.

1847

Hulsewé, A. F. P. "The Shuo-wen Dictionary as a Source for Ancient Chinese Law," in *Studia Serica Bernhard Karlgren Dedicata* (Copenhagen: Ejnar Munksgaard, 1959), pp. 239-258. On the recruitment of personnel for local government clerical positions in Han times; technical.

1848

Parsons, James B. *A Preliminary Analysis of the Ming Dynasty Bureaucracy.* Kyoto: Kansai Asiatic Society, 1959. (Occasional Papers of the Kansai Asiatic Society, VII) A statistical analysis of the tenure in office, the geographical origins, the kinship relations, etc., of a selected group of office holders.

1849

Sprenkel, O. B. van der. "High Officials of the Ming," *Bulletin of the School of Oriental and African Studies,* London University, XIV (1952), 87-114. A statistical study of career patterns among high-ranking civil officials of the Ming period; based on chronological tables in the *Ming-shih.*

1850

Liu, James T. C. *Reform in Sung China: Wang An-shih (1021-1086) and his new Policies.* Cambridge: Harvard

University Press, 1959. (Harvard East Asian Studies, 3) Especially valuable for its interpretive analyses of political theories and bureaucratic behavior in the 11th century.

1851

Herson, Lawrence J. R. "China's Imperial Bureaucracy: Its Direction and Control," *Public Administration Review,* XVII (1957), 44-53. Traditional governmental techniques for maintaining control and direction of the civil service bureaucracy; a generalized, ahistorical treatment based on secondary sources.

1852

Eisenstadt, S. N. "Political Struggle in Bureaucratic Societies," *World Politics,* IX (1956–57), 15-23. The sociological aspects of bureaucratic systems; especially concerned with problems of bureaucratic legitimation, bureaucratic autonomy, and political struggle. Relates to ancient Egypt, Byzantium, China, Ottoman Turkey, and Europe in the age of absolutism.

Patterns of foreign relations

1853

Linebarger, Paul M. A., Djang Chu, and Ardath W. Burks. *Far Eastern Governments and Politics: China and Japan.* 2d ed. Princeton: Van Nostrand, 1956. Chap. 4, "Old China's Colonial Empire and the Chinese Family of Nations," provides an authoritative survey of traditional patterns of China's international relations.

1854

Fairbank, John King. *Trade and Diplomacy on the China Coast.* Vol. 1. Cambridge: Harvard University Press, 1953. Pp. 3-53 summarize traditional Chinese views and practices regarding relations with foreigners, with particular reference to the tributary system under the early Ch'ing dynasty.

1855

Levi, Werner. *Modern China's Foreign Policy.* Minneapolis: University of Minnesota Press, 1953. Chaps. 1-2 provide an interpretive description of China's traditional tributary system of relations with neighboring peoples and an analysis of the difficulties this created for early Sino-Western contacts.

1856

Nelson, M. Frederick. *Korea and the Old Orders in Eastern Asia.* Baton Rouge: Louisiana State University Press, 1945. Chap. 1, "Confucian Familism and the Inequality of Nations," gives an excellent brief summary of the theory and practice of international relations in traditional China.

1857

Hsü, Immanuel C. Y. *China's Entrance into the Family of Nations: The Diplomatic Phase, 1858–1880.* Cambridge: Harvard University Press, 1960. (Harvard East Asian Studies, 5) The prologue contains a brief, generalized summary of traditional Chinese attitudes toward foreigners and international-relations practices.

1858

Wang Yi-t'ung. *Official Relations between China and Japan, 1368–1549.* Cambridge: Harvard University Press, 1953. (Harvard-Yenching Institute Series, IX) A technical, authoritative study of the Ming government's attempts to impose tributary status on Japan so as to halt coastal raiding by Japanese pirate fleets.

1859

Fairbank, John K. and Teng Ssu-yü. "On the Ch'ing Tributary System," in their book *Ch'ing Administration: Three Studies* (Cambridge: Harvard University Press, 1960), pp. 107-210. An authoritative, technical study of the official relations between the Manchus and neighboring, tribute-giving states; reprinted from *Harvard Journal of Asiatic Studies,* VI (1941), 135-246.

1860

Lin, T. C. "Manchurian Trade and Tribute in the Ming Dynasty," *Nankai Social and Economic Quarterly,* IX (1936), 855-892. An analysis of Chinese theories and

practices used in dominating the proto-Manchu peoples of Manchuria in the 15th and 16th centuries.

1861

Hall, John. "Notes on the Early Ch'ing Copper Trade with Japan," *Harvard Journal of Asiatic Studies,* XIV (1949), 444-461. On junk trade between China and Japan in the 17th and 18th centuries, with reference to the traditional patterns of China's foreign relations.

1862

Pritchard, Earl H. "The Kotow in the Macartney Embassy to China in 1793," *Far Eastern Quarterly,* II (1942–43), 163-203. Includes general information about the *k'ou-t'ou* prostration as an element in traditional China's domination of foreigners.

1863

Wright, Mary C. "The Adaptibility of Ch'ing Diplomacy—The Case of Korea," *Journal of Asian Studies,* XVII (1957–58), 363-381. A sympathetic analysis of China's difficulties in adapting its traditional system of tributary relations with neighboring peoples to 19th century realities.

1864

Petech, Luciano. *China and Tibet in the Early Eighteenth Century.* Leiden: E. J. Brill, 1950. An authoritative study of the establishment of a Chinese protectorate over Tibet between 1705 and 1751, based on both Chinese and Tibetan sources.

1865

Cammann, Schuyler. "The Panchen Lama's Visit to China in 1780: an Episode in Anglo-Tibetan Relations," *Far Eastern Quarterly,* IX (1949–50), 3-19. A case study in traditional tributary relations.

1866

Cammann, Schuyler. "Presentation of Dragon Robes by the Ming and Ch'ing Court for Diplomatic Purposes," *Sinologica,* III (1951–53), 193-202. On one aspect of traditional China's treatment of tributary princes.

1867

Farquhar, David M. "Oirat-Chinese Tribute Relations, 1408–1446," in *Studia Altaica: Festschrift für Nikolaus Poppe* (Wiesbaden: Otto Harrassowitz, 1957), pp. 60-68. On 43 tributary missions sent to the Ming court by the western Mongols, with detailed information about the gifts exchanged.

1868

Serruys, Henry. *Sino-Jurced Relations during the Yung-lo Period (1403–1424).* Wiesbaden: Otto Harrassowitz, 1955. On Ming Chinese techniques in dealing with the proto-Manchu peoples of the far northeast.

1869

Wild, Norman. "Materials for the Study of the Ssu I Kuan," *Bulletin of the School of Oriental and African Studies,* London University, XI (1943–46), 617-640. On the history and functions of the Ming government's College of Translators, which handled communications to and from tributary states; cf. Paul Pelliot, "Le Sseu-yi-kouan et le Houei-t'ong-kouan," *T'oung Pao,* XXXVIII (1948), 207-290, for a technical study of the same subject.

1870

Fairbank, John K. "Synarchy under the Treaties," in *Chinese Thought and Institutions* (J. K. Fairbank, ed.; Chicago: University of Chicago Press, 1957), pp. 204-231. On foreign participation in Chinese government under the "Treaty Port System" of the 19th century, with reference to the traditional (and perhaps persisting) Chinese practice of incorporating outsiders into the universal state structure.

1871

Serruys, Henry. "The Mongols of Kansu during the Ming," *Mélanges Chinois et Bouddhiques,* X (1955), 215-346. Includes data on Mongol relations with the Ming government.

Law

1872

Hulsewé, A. F. P. *Remnants of Han Law.* Vol. 1. Leiden: E. J. Brill, 1955. A detailed study of the punitive laws and judicial administration of the Han era, with annotated translations from the *Han-shu.*

1873

Escarra, Jean. *Le droit chinois.* Peking: Henri Vetch, 1936. An interpretive study of the historical development and 20th century status of legal theory, legislative institutions and practices, law codes, judicial organizations and procedures, etc.; the most comprehensive work of its kind. Uses an analytical rather than a chronological organization, but has historical resumés under each topic.

1874

Gulik, R. H. van (trans.). *T'ang-yin-pi-shih: Parallel Cases from Under the Pear-tree.* Leiden: E. J. Brill, 1956. A 13th century casebook for magistrates, with anecdotes about famous ancient and medieval judges.

1875

Hsü, Francis L. K. "Some Problems of Chinese Law in Operation Today," *Far Eastern Quarterly,* III (1943–44), 211-221. Some case studies illustrating the difficulties of imposing modern Chinese law upon a rural population whose mores contradict it.

1876

Gilpatrick, Meredith. "The Status of Law and Lawmaking Procedure under the Kuomintang, 1925–46," *Far Eastern Quarterly,* X (1950–51), 38-55. An analysis of difficulties encountered by the nationalist government in modernizing its law codes, with special reference to traditional legal practices and ideas.

1877

Pelliot, Paul. "Notes de bibliographie chinoise: le droit chinois," *Bulletin de l'Éole Francaise d'Extrème-Orient,* IX (1909), 123-152. A survey of the history of Chinese law codes; technical.

1878

Alabaster, Ernest. *Notes and Commentaries on Chinese Criminal Law.* London: Luzac, 1899. Voluminous data about legal and judicial processes in the Ch'ing period.

1879

Needham, Joseph. *Science and Civilisation in China.* Vol. 2. Cambridge: Cambridge University Press, 1956. Pp. 518-583, "Human Law and the Laws of Nature in China and the West," provide a detailed, heavily interpretive survey of traditional Chinese attitudes toward law and the natural order; previously published in *Journal of the History of Ideas,* XII (1951), 3-30, 194-230.

1880

Staunton, George T. (trans.) *Ta Tsing Leu Lee.* London: T. Cadell and W. Davies, 1810. Partial translation of the Ch'ing dynasty law code, *Ta Ch'ing lü-li.*

1881

Bünger, Karl. *Quellen zur Rechtsgeschichte der T'ang-zeit.* Peking: 1946. (Monumenta Serica Monograph IX) A classical study of the T'ang law code, which was the basis for all subsequent codifications in China and served also as a model for East Asia as a whole.

1882

Balazs, Étienne. *Le traité juridique du "Souei-Chou."* Leiden: E. J. Brill, 1954. Translation of the section on law in the *Sui-shu,* with introductory data and appendices; a basic work on the development of legal thought and judicial institutions between the Han and T'ang periods.

1883

Riasanovsky, V. A. "Mongol Law and Chinese Law in the Yuan Dynasty," *Chinese Social and Political Science Review,* XX (1936–37), 266-289. A study revealing continuity of the principles of the T'ang law code even through the period of Mongol domination in China; especially notes the influence of the T'ang code on the *Yüan Tien-chang,* the Yüan dynasty code.

1884

Riasanovsky, V. A. "The Influence of Chinese Law upon Mongolian Law," *Chinese Social and Political Science Review,* XV (1931), 402-421. A study of the history and characteristics of traditional Chinese criminal law, with an analysis of its influence on Chingis Khan's *Yasa* and subsequent Mongol codes.

1885

Twitchett, Denis C. "The Fragment of the T'ang Ordinances of the Department of Waterways Discovered at Tun-huang," *Asia Major,* VI (1957–58), 23-79. A valuable, technical study of codified administrative law in T'ang times, with an annotated translation of an important 8th century document.

1886

Boulais, Guy. *Manuel du code chinois.* 2 vols. Shanghai: Mission Catholique, 1923–24. (Variétés Sinologiques, 55) Complete, annotated translation of the Ch'ing law code.

1887

Ratchnevsky, Paul. *Un code des Yuan.* Paris: Ernest Leroux, 1937. A fully annotated, technical translation of parts of the Yüan dynasty law code, from the *Yüan-shih.*

1888

Gernet, Jacques. "La vente en Chine d'après les contrats de Touen-houang (IXe-Xe siècles)," *T'oung Pao,* XLV (1957), 295-391. Provides important data on the legal aspects of contractual relations in T'ang and Sung times; technical.

1889

Franke, Wolfgang. "Ein Document Prozess gegen Yü Ch'ien im Jahr 1457," *Studia Serica,* VI (1947), 193-208. On legal proceedings against a powerful Ming minister, put to death for treason.

Censors

1890

Walker, Richard L. "The Control System of the Chinese Government," *Far Eastern Quarterly,* VII (1947–48), 2-21. A superficial survey of the history of traditional China's censorial institutions.

1891

Hucker, Charles O. "Confucianism and the Chinese Censorial System," in *Confucianism in Action* (D. S. Nivison and A. F. Wright, ed.; Stanford: Stanford University Press, 1959), pp. 182-208. On the ideological bases and implications of censorial activities in Ming times.

1892

Hucker, Charles O. "The Traditional Chinese Censorate and the New Peking Regime," *American Political Science Review,* XLV (1951), 1041-1057. On the organization and functions of the Censorate in Ming times and on modern vestiges of the traditional censorial system.

1893

Sah Mong-wu. "The Impact of Hanfeism on the Earlier Han Censorial System," *Chinese Culture,* I (1957), 75-111. A theoretical analysis of the function of censors in Han times and its relation to Legalistic principles of government.

1894

Hucker, Charles O. "The Yüan Contribution to Censorial History," *Bulletin of the Institute of History and Philology, Academia Sinica,* extra vol. no. 4 (1960), 219-227. On the institutional aspects of China's traditional surveillance and remonstrance apparatus at a time of increasing authoritarianism.

1895

Wist, Hans, *Das chinesische Zensorat.* Hamburg: 1932. A brief survey of the over-all history of China's traditional Censorate.

1896

Li Hsiung-fei. *Les censeurs sous la dynastie Mandchoue (1616–1911) en Chine.* Paris: Imprimeries Les Presses Modernes, 1936. A detailed, technical study of the personnel and activities of the Censorate in Ch'ing times.

1897

Seuberlich, Wolfgang. "Kaisertrue oder auflehnung? Eine Episode aus der Ming-zeit," *Zeitschrift der Deutschen Morgenländischen Gesellschaft,* CII (1952), 304-314. On a censorial official who in 1517 won a battle of wills with the emperor Wu-tsung, with comments on the nature of imperial despotism in Ming times.

The military tradition

1898

Fried, Morton H. "Military Status in Chinese Society," *American Journal of Sociology,* LVII (1951–52), 347-357. A sociological analysis of military prestige in the Chinese tradition, suggesting that military status has recurringly been higher than is commonly thought; with an appendix of unfavorable comment by Lee Shu-ching and rejoinder by Fried.

1899

Giles, Lionel (trans.). *Sun Tzu on the Art of War.* London: Luzac, 1910. Complete, annotated translation of a strikingly sophisticated treatise on tactics, strategy, logistics, espionage, etc., of the 6th century B.C., recognized as one of the world's great classics on military theory; reprinted without annotations and the Chinese text under the title *The Art of War* (Harrisburg, Pa.: Military Service Publishing Co., 1944).

1900

Powell, Ralph. *The Rise of Chinese Military Power, 1895–1912.* Princeton: Princeton University Press, 1955. Chap. 1 surveys the military tradition of China, with special emphasis on the Ch'ing dynasty.

1901

Rotours, Robert des (trans.). *Traité des fonctionnaires et traité de l'armée.* 2 vols. Leiden: E. J. Brill, 1947-48. Includes an authoritative, technical, annotated translation of the treatise from the *Hsin T'ang-shu* on the military establishment of T'ang times.

1902

Goodrich, L. C. and Feng Chia-sheng. "The Early Development of Firearms in China," *Isis,* XXXVI (1945-46), 114-123, 250-251. On the use of gunpowder for firearms by the Sung Chinese against Mongol invaders in the 13th century.

1903

Wang Ling. "On the Invention and Use of Gunpowder and Firearms in China," *Isis,* XXXVII (1947), 160-178. Data on Sung military technology, supplementary to "The Early Development of Firearms in China" by Goodrich and Feng.

1904

Lo Jung-pang. "The Emergence of China as a Sea Power during the late Sung and Early Yüan Periods," *Far Eastern Quarterly,* XIV (1954–55), 489-503. On 13th century developments in naval techniques and technology. Cf. Lo's "The Decline of the Early Ming Navy," *Oriens Extremus,* V (1958), 149-158.

1905

Zi, Étienne. *Pratique des examens militaires en Chine.* Shanghai: Mission Catholique, 1896. (Variétés Sinologiques, 9) A detailed description of the military counterpart of the civil service examination system in the Ch'ing period.

1906

Balazs, Étienne. *Le traité économique de "Souei-Chou."* Leiden: E. J. Brill, 1953. Pp. 241-75 on military organization and conditions of military service among the North China states in the 6th century.

1907

Martin, Henry Desmond. *The Rise of Chingis Khan and his Conquest of North China.* Baltimore: Johns Hopkins Press, 1950. Contains important data on the state of military science in the Chinese world of the 13th century.

1908

Wu Wei-p'ing. "The Rise of the Anhwei Army," *Papers on China,* XIV (Cambridge: Harvard University East Asian Research Center, 1960; privately distributed), 30-49. A seminar paper on the early history (1860–64) of an important anti-Taiping army organized by Tseng Kuo-fan and Li Hung-chang.

1909

Pelliot, Paul. "La date de l'apparition en Chine des canons *Fo-lang-ki,*" *T'oung Pao,* XXXVIII (1948), 199-207. On China's adoption of Portuguese-style guns in the 16th century.

1910

Laufer, Berthold. *Chinese Clay Figures.* Part 1. *Prolegomena on the History of Defensive Armor.* Chicago: 1914. (Field Museum of Natural History Publication 177) A voluminous, technical study of the history of Chinese armor from the earliest times through the T'ang period, with numerous illustrations including those of many clay figurines on which the study is partly based.

1911

Werner, E. T. C. *Chinese Weapons.* Shanghai: Royal Asiatic Society, North China Branch, 1932. An illustrated history and description of traditional Chinese weapons, armor, etc., including early firearms; outdated in scholarship, but not wholly superseded.

1912

Fang Chaoying. "A Technique for Estimating the Numerical Strength of the Early Manchu Military Forces," *Harvard Journal of Asiatic Studies,* XIII (1950), 192-215. A useful description and statistical analysis of the early Ch'ing military organization.

Education

1913

Galt, Howard S. *A History of Chinese Educational Institutions.* Vol. 1 (all published). London: Probsthain, 1951. A detailed compilation of information about the development of educational ideas and institutions from highest antiquity to the end of the 5 Dynasties era in A.D. 960, arranged chronologically by dynasties; critical and annotated, but not always based on the best sources.

1914

Kuo Ping-wen. *The Chinese System of Public Education.* New York: Columbia University Teachers College, 1915. A history of Chinese educational organization and practices from earliest times, with emphasis on the development of a new system in the 19th and early 20th centuries under Western influence; somewhat uncritical and conventional as regards the historical treatment.

1915

Hughes, E. R. *The Invasion of China by the Western World.* New York: Macmillan, 1938. Chap. 4: a historical study of the collapse of the traditional educational system in the 19th and early 20th centuries and the gradual introduction of Western-style educational ideas and practices in the republican era.

1916

Grimm, Tilemann. *Erziehung und Politik im konfuzianischen China der Ming-zeit (1368–1644).* Wiesbaden: Otto Harrassowitz, 1960. (Mitteilungen der Gesellschaft für Natur- und Völkerkunde Ostasiens, XXXV B) Includes much data on the history of Chinese education from the 7th to the 17th centuries, and especially during the Ming period.

1917

Galt, Howard S. "Kuo Tzu Chien: Its Historical Development and Present Condition," *Chinese Social and Political Review,* XXIII (1939–40), 441-462. On China's traditional "national university," with special reference to the Ch'ing dynasty system.

1918

Grimm, Tilemann. "War das China der Ming-Zeit totalitär?" *Nachrichten der Gesellschaft für Natur- und Völkerkunde Ostasiens,* No. 79-80 (1956), 30-36. A brief but informative essay on state control, and the content, of education in Ming times, as related to the problem of totalitarianism.

MODERN GOVERNMENT

The republican government at Peking that nomially governed China from 1912 to 1927 was a facade maintained by shifting cliques of regional warlords and provided no national leadership. Its successor, the republican government dominated by Chiang Kai-shek and the Kuomintang (Nationalist Party), with Sun Yat-sen's *San-min chu-i* ("Three Principles of the People") as its platform of political organization and action, is a representative government in form but a one-party dictatorship in practice. Its major organs are a Legislative Yüan, an Executive Yüan, a Judicial Yüan, a Control Yüan (an audit and surveillance agency), and an Examination Yüan (for certifying candidates for governmental offices). Its support has come largely from military and business groups, and its policies have generally been conservative and favorable to middle-class capitalistic interests. Restricted to Taiwan (Formosa) since 1949, it still represents the Chinese people as a whole in the United Nations. The Chinese People's Republic that has controlled the mainland since 1949 practices communist-style "democratic centralism" and is even more notably a one-party dictatorship. Its basic governing body is an elective National People's Congress. Its chief original support was among intellectuals and the peasantry, and its policies are those of Marxism-Leninism, as interpreted by Mao Tse-tung, the dominant figure in the Chinese Communist Party. It has emphasized the development of pervasive political and ideological controls over the Chinese population and rapid economic growth, in both agriculture and industry. Whereas the nationalist government during the 1950's consistently aligned itself with the United States in international affairs, the Chinese People's Republic consistently aligned itself with the Soviet Union.

General works

1919

Linebarger, Paul M. A., Djang Chu, and Ardath W. Burks. *Far Eastern Governments and Politics: China and Japan.* 2d ed. Princeton: Van Nostrand, 1956. Authoritative summaries: the warlord-dominated Peking republic (chap. 6), the nationalist republic in mainland China (7) and on Taiwan (8), and the Chinese communist government (9). Appendices includes the nationalist constitution of 1947 and the communist constitution of 1954.

1920

Fried, Morton H. "Military Status in Chinese Society," *American Journal of Sociology,* LVII (1951–52), 347-357. A sociological analysis of military prestige in both traditional and modern China, suggesting that military status has recurringly been higher than is commonly thought; with an appendix of unfavorable comment by Lee Shu-ching and a rejoinder by Fried.

Early republican government

1921

Houn, Franklin W. *Central Government of China, 1912–1928.* Madison: University of Wisconsin Press, 1957. A detailed, scholarly analysis of the organization and operations of the Peking government from Yüan Shih-k'ai's time until the Kuomintang's conquest of North China; a valuable study of the little-known warlord period of republican development.

1922

Powell, Ralph. *The Rise of Chinese Military Power, 1895–1912.* Princeton: Princeton University Press, 1955. A detailed analysis of the military reforms undertaken and accomplished in the last years of the Manchu empire, especially by such leaders as Chang Chih-tung and Yüan Shih-k'ai, which set the stage for warlordism in the early republican years.

1923

Cheng Sih-gung. *Modern China: A Political Study.* Oxford: Clarendon Press, 1919. A detailed study of governmental organization, procedures, and problems at the beginning of the republican era.

Nationalist government

1924

Ch'ien Tuan-sheng. *The Government and Politics of China.* Cambridge: Harvard University Press, 1950. A detailed study of the organization, functioning, and policies of the nationalist government in a partly historical, partly topical approach; critical of the Kuomintang's shortcomings. Appendices include the text of the 1947 constitution.

1925

China Yearbook, 1959–60. Taipei: China Publishing Co., 1960. An almanac-like compendium of historical and statistical data about life in nationalist China, with much descriptive and documentary material about governmental organization and procedures. Published annually, but originally issued irregularly under the title *China Handbook,* beginning with a 1937–43 edition (New York: Macmillan).

1926

Tsao, W. Y. *The Constitutional Structure of Modern China.* Melbourne: Melbourne University Press, 1947. A comprehensive analysis of the nationalist government as provided for in the permanent constitution of 1947, with an introductory survey of the constitution-making process from 1929 to 1946; appendices include the text of the 1947 constitution.

1927

Linebarger, Paul M. A. *The China of Chiang Kai-shek: A Political Study.* Boston: World Peace Foundation, 1941. A detailed, authoritative description of the governmental institutions, ideology, and procedures of the nationalist government during the 1930's with discussions of the roles of the Kuomintang, the Chinese Communist Party, and Japanese puppet governments.

1928

North, Robert C. *Kuomintang and Chinese Communist Elites.* Stanford: Stanford University Press, 1952. (Hoover Institute Studies, series B, no. 8) A sociological, statistical analysis of the social backgrounds, education, and careers of the leaders of both the Kuomintang and the Chinese Communist Party throughout history; with brief histories of changing currents evidenced in the leadership of the two parties from their origins.

1929

Linebarger, Paul M. A. *The Political Doctrines of Sun Yat-sen*. Baltimore: Johns Hopkins Press, 1937. A thorough explication of the *San-min chu-i*, "The Three Principles of the People," which became the ideological platform of the Kuomintang.

1930

Sun Yat-sen. *San Min Chu I: The Three Principles of the People*, trans. by F. W. Price, ed. by L. T. Chen. Shanghai: Commercial Press, 1929. The standard English translation of Sun Yat-sen's lectures setting forth the basic Kuomintang doctrines; the canonical statement of principles of the revolutionary party.

1931

Pan Wei-tung. *The Chinese Constitution*. Washington: Catholic University of America Press, 1945. A detailed history of constitutions and constitution-making from the last years of the Ch'ing empire through the early provisional constitutions of the nationalist government under Chiang Kai-shek.

1932

Riasanovski, V. A. *Chinese Civil Law*. Tientsin: 1938. An authoritative study of civil law under the nationalist government.

1933

Chang Chao-yuan (trans.). *The Criminal Code of the Republic of China*. Shanghai: Kelly and Walsh, 1935. The official code of the nationalist government, adopted in 1928; with supplementary laws concerning the military forces, etc.

1934

Linebarger, Paul M. A. *Government in Republican China*. New York: McGraw-Hill, 1938. A brief survey of governmental organization and processes in the early years of Chiang Kai-shek's supremacy.

*   *   *

1935

Liu, F. F. *A Military History of Modern China, 1924–1949*. Princeton: Princeton University Press, 1956. A detailed analysis of the military establishment developed by Chiang Kai-shek and its political influence.

1936

MacFarquhar, Roderick L. "The Whampoa Military Academy," *Papers on China*, IX (Cambridge: Harvard University Committee on Regional Studies, 1955; privately distributed), 146-172. A seminar paper on the organization, operation, and influence of "the Kuomintang West Pont" in the 1920's.

1937

Carlson, Evans F. *The Chinese Army*. New York: Institute of Pacific Relations, 1940. A historical analysis of China's total war effort during the early years of the Sino-Japanese war, with special emphasis on the organization, leadership, and tactics of both Kuomintang-controlled forces and communist forces (the 8th Route Army); by a U. S. Marine officer who had first-hand experience of the military activity in China.

*   *   *

1938

Pott, Francis L. H. "Modern Education," in *China* (H. F. MacNair, ed.; Berkeley: University of California Press, 1946), pp. 427-440. A very general survey of progress in modernizing China's educational system up to the Sino-Japanese war.

1939

Purcell, V. W. W. S. *Problems of Chinese Education*. London: Kegan Paul, 1936. On the modernization of education under the nationalist government; authoritative.

1940

Buck, Pearl S. *Tell the People*. New York: John Day, 1945. On a mass education movement of the 1920's and 1930's, founded by James Yen, aiming at teaching a minimum vocabulary of written characters to every Chinese.

1941

Ch'en Li-fu. *Four Years of Chinese Education (1937–1941)*. Chungking: China Information Committee, 1941. A brief report on the educational setbacks in China during the Sino-Japanese war.

Communist government

1942

Kahin, George M. (ed.) *Major Governments of Asia*. Ithaca: Cornell University Press, 1958. Pp. 52-120: an excellent, readable survey of political history, political behavior, and domestic and foreign policies in China under communism, by Harold C. Hinton.

1943

Hu Chang-tu and others. *China: Its People, Its Society, Its Culture*. New Haven: HRAF Press, 1960. Includes extensive descriptions of governmental organization and functioning in mainland China, especially in chap 9: "Dynamics of Political Behavior," and 10: "Theory and structure of Government."

1944

Thomas, S. B. *Government and Administration in Communist China*. Rev. ed. New York: Institute of Pacific Relations, 1955. The most comprehensive survey in English of the organization and operation of the Peking government, with various useful documentary appendices including the 1954 constitution.

1945

Barnett, A. Doak. *Communist China and Asia*. New York: Council on Foreign Relations, 1960; paperbound reprint, New York: Random House, 1961. An interpretive, detailed analysis of state power in communist China, with particular emphasis on foreign relations.

1946

North, Robert C. *Kuomintang and Chinese Communist Elites*. Stanford: Stanford University Press, 1952. (Hoover Institute Studies, series B, no. 8. A sociological, statistical analysis of the social backgrounds, education, and careers of the leaders of both the Kuomintang and the Chinese Communist Party throughout history; with brief histories of changing currents evidenced in the leaderships of the two parties from their origins.

1947

Djang Chu. "Leadership in Communist China," *Current History*, XXXII (1957), 13-18. A brief survey of the evolution of governmental organizations, techniques, and especially leadership throughout the history of the Chinese communist movement.

1948

Gluckstein, Ygael. *Mao's China*. London: Allen and Unwin, 1957. Pp. 317-380: a highly unsympathetic evaluation of political organization and leadership in communist China.

1949

Houn, Franklin W. "The Eighth Central Committee of the Chinese Communist Party: A Study of an Elite," *American Political Science Review*, LI (1957), 392-404. A sociological analysis of the 97-member board of party leaders chosen in 1956, emphasizing their middle-class origins, their extensive (and in many cases foreign) education, and their representation of the hinterland rather than the coastal areas; with comparative comments regarding Kuomintang leadership.

1950

Compton, Boyd (trans.). *Mao's China: Party Reform Documents, 1942–44*. Seattle: University of Washington Press, 1952. A collection of documents that became an extra-constitutional basis for party organization, party policies, and party discipline, principally including writings of Mao Tse-tung and Liu Shao-ch'i; with an introduction on the history of the Chinese Communist Party.

1951

Steiner, H. Arthur. "Chinese Communist Urban Policy," *American Political Science Review*, XLIV (1950), 47-

63. On the problems that confronted the Chinese communists when they gained control of cities in the late 1940's and on the governmental policies and administrative techniques they developed to deal with urban populations.

1952

Liu Shao-ch'i. *On the Party.* Peking: Foreign Languages Press, 1952. A canonical discussion of the organization, policies, and functions of the Chinese Communist Party; an appendix provides the party constitution adopted in 1945.

* * *

1953

Steiner, H. Arthur. "Constitutionalism in Communist China," *American Political Science Review,* XLIX (1955), 1-21. An analysis of the constitution of 1954, its effects on the organizational structure of the communist regime, its nature as an instrument of socioeconomic revolution, and the processes by which it was drafted and adopted; authoritative and enlightening.

1954

Houn, Franklin W. "Communist China's New Constitution," *Western Political Quarterly,* VIII (1955), 199-233. A detailed, authoritative study of communist China's governmental structure as provided for in the constitution of 1954.

1955

Chang Yu-Nan. "Chinese Communist State System under the Constitution of 1954," *Journal of Politics,* XVIII (1956), 520-546. A general analysis, emphasizing the influence of communist ideology.

* * *

1956

Pool, Ithiel de Sola and others. *Satellite Generals: A Study of Military Elites in the Soviet Sphere.* Stanford: Stanford University Press, 1955. (Hoover Institute Studies, series B, no. 5) Pp. 123-146 analyze the organization of the communist Chinese military forces, the personalities of their outstanding generals, and the social composition of the military elite.

1957

Nanes, Allan. "The Armies of Red China," *Current History,* XXXIX (1960), 338-342. A brief survey of the size, leadership, capabilities, and nuclear-war potential of communist China's armed forces.

1958

Powell, Ralph L. "Everyone a Soldier: The Chinese Communist Militia," *Foreign Affairs,* XXXIX (1960-61), 101-111. A general, authoritative survey of 1958-59 reorganizations of irregular military forces in mainland China, for economic as well as military purposes; with comments on communist China's military power in general.

1959

Ting Li. *Militia of Communist China.* Kowloon: Union Research Institute, 1954. On the civilian soldiery of mainland China and its activities in economic production and in anti-subversive work; with a rather pronounced antagonism to the communist regime.

1960

Rigg, Robert B. *Red China's Fighting Hordes.* Harrisburg, Pa.: Military Service Publishing Co., 1952. A detailed description of the organization, leadership, equipment, morale, and tactics of the Chinese communist Red Army during the middle 1940's, by a U. S. Army officer personally acquainted with the situation. Includes much useful data but is in a bitterly antagonistic, often contemptuous tone.

1961

Rigg, Robert B. "Red Army in Retreat," *Current History,* XXXII (1957), 1-6. A brief evaluation of the organization and strength of communist China's military forces; untechnical.

1962

Katzenbach, E. L., Jr. and Gene Z. Hanrahan. "Revolutionary Strategy of Mao Tse-tung," *Political Science Quarterly,* LXX (1955), 321-340. An analysis of the military theories of the Chinese communist leader as they have developed from the establishment of the Red Army in the early 1930's.

* * *

1963

Hu Chang-tu and others. *China: Its People, Its Society, Its Culture.* New Haven: HRAF Press, 1960. Chap. 20 provides a general, up to date description of education under Chinese communism.

1964

Yen, Maria (pseud.). *The Umbrella Garden.* New York: Macmillan, 1954. A first-hand account, by a not overly embittered refugee, of the communist impact on academic life at National Peking University in 1949-50.

1965

Hunter, Edward. *Brain-washing in Red China.* New York: Vanguard Press, 1953. Interviews with Chinese refugees about ideological remolding in the early years of communist control on the mainland, with special reference to schools and colleges.

1966

Chao Chung and Yang I-fan. *Students in Mainland China.* Kowloon: Union Research Institute, 1958. A survey of education at all levels under the Chinese communists, emphasizing non-academic and especially political aspects of student life.

1967

Chung Shih. *Higher Education in Communist China.* 3d ed. Kowloon: Union Research Institute, 1958. A general survey of the organization, administration, and policies of higher education in the 1950's.

1968

Chi Tung-wei. *Education for the Proletariat in Communist China.* Kowloon: Union Research Institute, 1954. A brief critical study of mass education techniques and developments.

SOCIAL PATTERNS

Social cohesion has been one of the most remarkable characteristics of the Chinese people and has given their communities a distinctive quality, whether in or outside China. Traditional society was an authoritarian pyramid-like hierarchy encompassed within and subordinate to the state structure; the nation was spoken of as an enlarged family, the emperor as father and mother of the people, and governmental officials in lower echelons as "father-mother officials." The individual was subordinate to the family, the family to the community, and the community to the society at large (that is, the state). Distinctions between social superiors and inferiors were clearly drawn, and social relationships were burdened with prescribed formalities that gave traditional Chinese life an unusually ritualized style.

Class stratification has not been rigid. Officialdom has always been the most prestigeful group; and since in traditional times officials were largely recruited on the basis of personal merit demonstrated in competitive examinations the ideal persisted that any person of good moral character and respectable origins could rise dramatically in the social scale. The peasantry was considered second in prestige. Artisans and merchants were discriminated against in some ways, and entertainers, soldiers, and vagrants were considered unrespectable. The degree of social mobility that existed in traditional times is a matter of scholarly dispute, but it is clear that China has not had a closed society.

The Chinese have been abnormally group-oriented and have responded principally to family and other locally-focused obligations. The social unit was the nuclear family, not the individual. The family was patriarchal, parilineal, patrilocal, and patronymic, bound together as an indefinitely-perpetuated corporation by ancestor worship. Women were subordinate in all things to men, and polygamy was an approved means of assuring male heirs. Marriages were arranged by the families rather than by the individuals concerned, and often through semi-professional go-betweens. The large extended family, incorporating in one residential compound all the descendants of an aged patriarch, was the ideal to which all persons of means aspired. The immediate kin-group, whether a nuclear or an extended family, in turn belonged to a regional clan comprising all people bearing the same surname. This had a somewhat informal organization, sometimes collectively held property, and offered various charitable, educational, and religious services to its members. Clan elders usually joined in a community council that had semi-official status, functions, and powers. At the village level, such community councils were the only governmental agencies with which many individuals ever had contact. In addition to the family and clan, Chinese society has included many other non-governmental or semi-governmental organizations to which individuals owed loyalty and support and from which they derived services and a sense of security. There were benevolent societies, scholarly groups, religious organizations, craft and mercantile guilds, and secret societies of both religious and political bents. The Chinese habitually thought to provide for their social needs and to attain their social wants through such groups rather than by individual action; and every Chinese consequently "belonged" in some sense.

The peasant village has always been the dominant form of community in China. At the same time, however, the Chinese have had the most striking urban tradition of Asia. From the 8th century China has had metropolitan concentrations of a million or more population, so that the earliest European visitors were most impressed by the sophisticated city life that was evident everywhere. Until modern times, Chinese cities were principally administrative centers and were walled. However great the population concentration, they retain a distinctively rural atmosphere.

Under the impact of the modern West, and especially under communist control since 1949, China's traditional patterns of social organization have been breaking down. Women have been emancipated at least in law, the domination of family elders has been weakened, and with industrialization the process of urbanization has been greatly accelerated. Nationalism has become the basis for new patterns of social cohesion, in which family loyalties and local patriotism are de-emphasized.

GENERAL WORKS

1969

Fairbank, John King. *The United States and China.* Rev. ed. Cambridge: Harvard University Press, 1958. Chap. 3 provides a general, interpretive analysis of traditional Chinese society, emphasizing the elite role of the scholar-gentry class.

1970

Sun, E-tu Zen and John de Francis (trans.). *Chinese Social History.* Washington: American Council of Learned Societies, 1956. Translations of 25 articles by modern Chinese scholars, chiefly dating from the 1930's, relating to socioeconomic aspects of Chinese life from earliest antiquity into the 19th century; an invaluable reference.

1971

Latourette, K. S. *The Chinese, Their History and Culture.* 3d ed. rev. New York: Macmillan, 1946. Chap. 17 provides a reliable general description of traditional Chinese social organization and attitudes: the family, relations between the sexes, secret societies and other organizations, social stratification, recreations and entertainments, etc.; a useful introduction, but somewhat out of date.

1972

Yüan Tung-Li. *Economic and Social Development of Modern China: A Bibliographical Guide.* New Haven: Human Relations Area Files, 1956. Part 2, "Social Development," is a long, unannotated list of 20th century books in Western languages on social life and customs, social institutions, social work, social pathology, labor problems, immigration and emigration, and ethnology, with an author index; an indispensable reference.

1973

Yang Lien-sheng. *Studies in Chinese Institutional History.* Cambridge: Harvard University Press, 1961. (Harvard-Yenching Institute Studies, XX) Includes three studies relevant to general social history: "Schedules of Work and Rest in Imperial China," "Hostages in Chinese History," and "Notes on the Economic History of the Chin Dynasty," reprinted from the *Harvard Journal of Asiatic Studies,* XVIII (1955), 301-325; XV (1952), 507-521; and IX (1945–47), 107-185.

1974

Kirby, E. Stuart. *Introduction to the Economic History of China.* London: Allen and Unwin, 1954. A theoretical evaluation of the kinds of studies that are being made, and that could be made, on the social as well as economic development of China throughout history, period by period; with special reference to Marxist reinterpretations of China's past and to modern Japanese scholarship. Highly technical.

1975

Wiens, Herold J. *China's March Toward the Tropics.* Hamden, Conn.: Shoe String Press, 1954. A history of Chinese expansion southward out of the Yellow River Valley and of China's historic relations with the aboriginal inhabitants of South and Southwest China.

1976

Li Chi. *The Formation of the Chinese People.* Cambridge: Harvard University Press, 1928. An anthropological-historical study of the evolution in China of a conscious "we-group" and its migrations leading toward its dominance of the whole of China Proper, at the expense of southern aboriginal groups and despite the invasions of northern nomads.

1977

Eberhard, Wolfram. "The Formation of Chinese Civilization According to Socio-Anthropological Analysis," *Sociologus*, VII (1957), 97-112. Discussion of possible new approaches to an explanation of how, in Shang or pre-Shang times, a high-civilization "Chinese" group emerged among non-Chinese "local cultures." This interpretation of China's social origins is developed most fully in Eberhard's *Lokalkulturen im alten China* (2 vols.; Leiden: E. J. Brill, 1942).

1978

Miyakawa Hisayuki. "The Confucianization of South China," in *The Confucian Persuasion* (A. F. Wright, ed.; Stanford: Stanford University Press, 1960), pp. 21-46. On the gradual expansion of dominant North Chinese culture patterns into the south coastal regions and Taiwan, from the 3d century B.C. into the 19th century.

1979

Bielenstein, Hans. "The Chinese Colonization of Fukien until the End of T'ang," in *Studia Serica Bernhard Karlgren Dedicata* (Copenhagen: Ejnar Munksgaard, 1959), pp. 98-122. On the chronology and patterns of Chinese migration into the mountainous southeast coastal region, with details on the history of each settlement in an appendix.

1980

Balazs, Stefan. "Beitrage zur Wirtschaftsgeschichte der T'angzeit," *Mitteilung des Seminars für Orientalische Sprachen*, XXXIV (1931), 1-92; XXXV (1932), 1-73. A classical, indispensable study of population problems, migrations, land distribution, etc., in T'ang times.

1981

Eberhard, Wolfram. "Notes on the Population of the Tunhuang Area," *Sinologica*, IV (1954–56), 69-90. Sociological analyses of fragmentary data about inhabitants of Northwest China from 102 B.C. to A.D. 995, with suggestions about life expectancy, age of soldiers, age at marriage, recruitment and geographical origin of soldiers, etc. For related data, see two subsequent articles by Eberhard: "The Origin of the Commoners in Ancient Tun-huang," *op cit.*, 141-155; and "The Leading Families of Ancient Tun-huang," *op. cit.*, 209-232.

1982

Sun, E-tu Zen and John de Francis. *Bibliography on Chinese Social History.* New Haven: Far Eastern Publications, Yale University, 1952. An annotated list of 176 modern scholarly articles in Chinese about socioeconomic aspects of Chinese history from antiquity; a valuable reference for those who can use the language.

1983

Granet, Marcel. *Chinese Civilization.* London: Kegan Paul, 1930; paperbound reprint New York: Meridian Books, 1958. A highly theoretical reconstruction of social institutions in ancient Chou dynasty times, but not generally considered authoritative.

BASIC SOCIAL ATTITUDES

1984

Hsü, Francis L. K. *American and Chinese: Two Ways of Life.* New York: Henry Schuman, 1953. An ambitious theoretical attempt to generalize about the traditional social psychology or national character of the Chinese in contrast to Americans, emphasizing the differences that spring from Chinese polytheism and American monotheism; a highly readable and fascinating analysis that is unavoidably susceptible to criticism in detail.

1985

Lin Yutang. *My Country and My People.* Rev. ed. New York: John Day, 1935. A sweeping, interpretive, considerably idealized introduction to traditional Chinese values or attitudes toward life, by China's most effective modern publicist.

1986

Hu Chang-tu and others. *China: Its People, Its Society, Its Culture.* New Haven: HRAF Press, 1960. Chaps. 23-24 survey traditional Chinese social values and attitudes and their changes under the communist regime in the 1950's.

1987

Hu Hsien-chin. "The Chinese Concepts of Face," in *Personal Character and Cultural Milieu* (D. G. Haring, ed.; 3d rev. ed.; Syracuse: Syracuse University Press, 1956), pp. 447-467; reprinted from *American Anthropologist*, XLVI (1944), 45-64. A detailed, authoritative description of face-saving, face-losing, etc., in Chinese social relations. The volume *Personal Character and Cultural Milieu* has an excellent, long bibliography of articles and books, many of which pertain to Chinese personality and national character.

1988

Yang Lien-sheng. "The Concept of *Pao* as a Basis for Social Relations in China," in *Chinese Thought and Institutions* (J. K. Fairbank, ed.; Chicago: University of Chicago Press, 1957), pp. 291-309. On the pervasiveness of "reciprocity" as an ideal in Chinese life and thought.

1989

Abegg, Lily. *The Mind of East Asia.* London: Thames and Hudson, 1952. An interpretive analysis of national character in Japan and China, based on long familiarity with the people rather than on controlled research, by a well-informed journalist; frequently offers stimulating insights and contrasts with the West.

1990

Wei, Francis C. M. *The Spirit of Chinese Culture.* New York: Scribner, 1947. An attempt to explain the Chinese national character to Americans, with special reference to the religio-philosophical tradition and the problems of instituting Christianity successfully among the Chinese.

1991

Chiang Yee. *A Chinese Childhood.* New York: John Day, 1952. The autobiography of a popular interpreter of Chinese art; an excellent introduction to social customs and everyday life in 20th century China, with many illustrations.

1992

Hsü, Francis L. K. *Religion, Science and Human Crises.* London: Routledge and Kegan Paul, 1952. A detailed anthropological study of the reaction to a cholera epidemic among the Chinese of a Yunnan town, throwing much light on Chinese national character and socioreligious ideas.

1993

Balazs, Étienne. "Les aspects significatifs de la société chinoise," *Asiatische Studien*, VI (1952) 77-87. A brief survey of anti-specialization and other social values and characteristics of traditional China.

1994

Lin Yutang (trans.). *The Importance of Understanding.* Cleveland: World Publishing Co., 1960. More than 100 selections from Chinese literature of all periods, reflecting traditional Chinese outlooks on life; a fascinating sourcebook for the study of China's traditional values, but all representing the literature classes more than the folk.

1995

Smith, Arthur H. *Chinese Characteristics.* 2d. ed. New York: Revell, 1894. A classic reference on traditional Chinese attitudes and values, but with a strong missionary bias.

1996

Hosie, Dorothea. *Two Gentlemen of China.* 5th ed. London: Seeley, Service, 1929. A first-hand, intimate description of the home lives of two upper-class families at the end of the Manchu era, with much data on customs and attitudes; from a distinctively feminine point of view.

1997

Headland, Isaac Taylor. *Home Life in China.* New York: Macmillan, 1914. A standard description of everyday life in traditional China, arranged analytically by topics.

1998

Levenson, Joseph R. "The Amateur Ideal in Ming and Early Ch'ing Society: Evidence from Painting," in *Chinese Thought and Institutions* (J. K. Fairbank, ed.; Chicago: University of Chicago Press, 1957), pp. 320-341. On the social values of China's traditional elite.

1999

Stratton, G. M. and F. M. Henry. "Emotion in Chinese, Japanese, and Whites; Racial and National Difference and Likeness in Physiological Reactions to an Emotional Stimulus," *American Journal of Psychology,* LVI (1943), 161-180. Technical and inconclusive, but suggesting that Chinese and Japanese react about equally to stimuli, but both more strongly than Caucasoids.

2000

Lin Yutang. *The Wisdom of China and India.* New York: Modern Library, 1942. Pp. 1091-1101 offer 100 traditional Chinese proverbs, reflecting basic social values.

2001

Abel, Theodora M. and F. L. K. Hsü. "Some Aspects of Personality of Chinese as Revealed by the Rorschach Test," *Journal of Projective Techniques,* XIII (1949), 285-301.

2002

Hsiao, H. H. "Mentality of the Chinese and Japanese," *Journal of Applied Psychology,* XIII (1929), 9-31.

2003

Lin Tsung-Yi. "A study of the Incidence of Mental Disorder in Chinese and other Cultures," *Psychiatry,* XVI (1953), 313-336.

2004

Granet, Marcel. *Festivals and Songs of Ancient China.* New York: Dutton, 1932. A highly theoretical reconstruction of social customs in very ancient China on the basis of literary remains in the *Shih-ching* ("Classic of Odes").

SOCIAL STRUCTURE AND MOBILITY

2005

Ch'ü T'ung-tsu. "Chinese Class Structure and its Ideology," in *Chinese Thought and Institutions* (J. K. Fairbank, ed.; Chicago: University of Chicago Press, 1957), pp. 235-250. A general, authoritative description of the persisting patterns of social stratification in traditional China.

2006

Levy, Marion J., Jr. "Contrasting Factors in the Modernization of China and Japan," *Economic Development and Cultural Change,* II (1953), 161-197; reprinted in Simon Kuznets and others, *Economic Growth: Brazil, India, Japan* (Durham, N. C.: Duke University Press, 1955), pp. 496-536. A sociological analysis, suggesting that the difficulty of change in China and the ease of change in Japan have stemmed basically from the social structures of each country rather than from the nature of outside forces upon them; includes a useful general interpretation of traditional Chinese social patterns and ideals.

2007

Fei Hsiao-t'ung. "Peasantry and Gentry: An Interpretation of Chinese Social Structure and Its Changes," *American Journal of Sociology,* LII (1946-47), 1-17; reprinted in *Class, Status, and Power: A Reader in Social Stratification* (R. Bendix and S. M. Lipset, ed.; Glencoe, Ill.: Free Press, 1953), pp. 631-650. An authoritative general interpretation of China's traditional social structure, explaining why the old rural elite has proved incapable of leadership in the modernization of China.

2008

Hu Chang-tu and others. *China: Its People, Its Society, Its Culture.* New Haven: HRAF Press, 1960. Chap. 7, "Social Organization," provides a reliable, up-to-date survey of traditional patterns and changes brought about by the communist government.

2009

Eberhard, Wolfram. *A History of China.* Rev. ed. Berkeley: University of California Press, 1960. A highly interpretive and provocative presentation of Chinese history from a sociological point of view: as a one-sided class struggle in which an agrarian-minded gentry class, by keeping control of the imperial government, consistently repressed bourgeois middle classes and prevented commercial and industrial revolutions of the kind that transformed modern Europe. The same analysis appears in Eberhard's book *Conquerors and Rulers: Social Forces in Medieval China* (Leiden: E. J. Brill, 1952). It is harshly criticized in E. G. Pulleyblank, "Gentry Society: Some Remarks on Recent Work by W. Eberhard," *Bulletin of the School of Oriental and African Studies,* London University, XV (1953), 588-597.

2010

Chang Chung-li. *The Chinese Gentry: Studies on Their Role in Nineteenth-century Chinese Society.* Seattle: University of Washington Press, 1955. An analysis of the social composition, social functions, size, and governmental relations of China's traditional elite; equates "gentry" with "degree-holders," and suggests that the gentry should not be considered primarily a landowning class.

2011

Wittfogel, Karl A. "Chinese Society: A Historical Survey," *Journal of Asian Studies,* XVI (1956-57), 343-364. A highly theoretical and controversial interpretation of traditional China as a "hydraulic society" or an "Oriental despotism," suggesting that the need for control of water resources brought about a concentration of all power in a centralized, bureaucratic state apparatus to which all societal groups were totally subordinate, and tracing the relationship between traditional despotism and modern communist government. This interpretation is more broadly developed in Wittfogel's voluminous *Oriental Despotism: A Comparative Study of Total Power* (New Haven: Yale University Press, 1957). For a critical review, see S. N. Eisenstadt in *Journal of Asian Studies,* XVII (1957-58), 435-446.

2012

Hsiao Kung-chuan. *Rural China: Imperial Control in the Nineteenth Century.* Seattle: University of Washington Press, 1960. A voluminous, authoritative, thoroughly documented analysis of the Ch'ing government's sponsorship and utilization of "self-government" organizations in villages and towns as instruments of political and ideological control; an important contribution to the understanding of peasant-gentry-government relations in traditional times.

2013

Fei Hsiao-t'ung. *China's Gentry: Essays in Rural-Urban Relations.* Rev. and ed. by Margaret Park Redfield. Chicago: University of Chicago Press, 1953. On the social role of the scholar-gentry in imperial and modern China, the power structure in rural communities, and the relations between villages and towns; with life histories of six varied families collected by Chow Yung-teh.

2014

Weber, Max. *The Religion of China,* trans. by Hans H. Gerth. Glencoe, Ill.: Free Press, 1951. A classic sociological analysis of traditional Chinese civilization as an integrated whole; of theoretical value, but not to be relied on for descriptive detail. For an excellent summation of Weber's influential views on China see Reinhard Bendix, *Max Weber: An Intellectual Portrait* (Garden City, N. Y.: Doubleday, 1960), pp. 117-157.

2015

Kracke, Edward A., Jr. "Sung Society: Change Within Tradition," *Far Eastern Quarterly*, XIV (1954–55), 479-488. An important refutation of the common belief that traditional Chinese social organization did not permit significant change from within; based on the social changes that accompanied urbanization in Sung times.

2016

Wang, Y. C. "Western Impact and Social Mobility in China," *American Sociological Review*, XXV (1960), 843-855. On the decrease in social mobility that resulted when the civil service examinations were abolished and expensive education abroad became the principal avenue to success; with statistical tables.

2017

Kracke, E. A., Jr. "Region, Family, and Individual in the Chinese Examination System," in *Chinese Thought and Institutions* (J. K. Fairbank, ed.; Chicago: University of Chicago Press, 1957), pp. 251-268. On the ideal of free opportunity in the civil service examinations and the actual degrees of social mobility reflected in statistical data concerning examination graduates of the Sung, Ming, and Ch'ing periods.

2018

Ho Ping-ti. "Aspects of Social Mobility in China, 1368–1911," *Comparative Studies in Society and History*, I (1958–59), 330-359. An interpretive study of both upward and downward mobility in Ming and Ch'ing times, based chiefly on data concerning civil service examination graduates; with informative preliminary remarks about the changing character of China's class structure throughout history. Concludes that "probably more careers ran 'from rags to riches' in Ming and Ch'ing China than in modern Western societies." Cf. a debate between Ho and V. K. Dibble on the meaning and uses of Ho's statistics in *op. cit.*, III (1960–61), 315-327.

2019

Hsü, Francis L. K. "Social Mobility in China," *American Sociological Review*, XIV (1949), 764-771. A technical study, suggesting that a high rate of social mobility obtained in China over the last millenium.

2020

Wang, Y. Chu. "The Intelligentsia in Changing China," *Foreign Affairs*, XXXVI (1957–58), 315-329. On the disappearance of the old Confucian elite in republican times and the rise of a new, urban intelligentsia which did not take its place in the social structure; one aspect of the deterioration of the old regime that helped prepare China for communist conquest.

2021

Ho Ping-ti. "The Salt Merchants of Yang-chou: a Study of Commercial Capitalism in Eighteenth-century China," *Harvard Journal of Asiatic Studies*, XVII (1954), 130-168. A detailed analysis of the private accumulation and dissipation of wealth in the Yangtze valley and its relation to social mobility.

2022

Balazs, E. "The Birth of Capitalism in China," *Journal of the Economic and Social History of the Orient*, III (1960), 196-216. An authoritative, interpretive study of traditional Chinese society to explain why competitive free-enterprise capitalism did not develop indigenously.

2023

Bodde, Derk. "Feudalism in China," in *Feudalism in History* (R. Coulborn, ed.; Princeton: Princeton University Press, 1956), pp. 49-92. On the Chou feudal structure of society and the reemergence of "feudalistic phenomena" during the era of North-South division.

2024

Hucker, Charles O. *The Traditional Chinese State in Ming Times (1368–1644)*. Tucson: University of Arizona Press, 1961. Includes a general interpretive description of the nature of Chinese society and of state-society relations, with critical reference to the theories of Wittfogel and Eberhard.

2025

Feuerwerker, Albert. "From 'Feudalism' to 'Capitalism' in Recent Historical Writing from Mainland China," *Journal of Asian Studies*, XVIII (1958–59), 107-115. A critical discussion of communist studies suggesting that the Ming dynasty was a period of "incipient capitalism" and thus an important turning point in China's social history.

2026

Wittfogel, Karl A. and Feng Chia-sheng. *History of Chinese Society: Liao (907–1125)*. Philadelphia: American Philosophical Society, 1949. (Transactions of the American Philosophical Society, new series, XXXVI) A monumental compendium of data on the organization of Chinese society under a conquering "barbarian" dynasty, with introductory comments of value about the impact of non-Chinese groups on the over-all development of Chinese social organization; refutes the traditional assumption that Chinese society has always absorbed invaders.

2027

Wilbur, C. Martin. *Slavery in China During the Former Han Dynasty, 206 B.C.-A.D. 25*. Chicago: Field Museum of Natural History, 1943. A standard source on socioeconomic conditions in Former Han China.

2028

Jacobs, Norman. *The Origin of Modern Capitalism and Eastern Asia*. Hong Kong: Hong Kong University Press, 1958. A sociological study of why industrial capitalism has developed in modern Japan but not in China, including a highly theoretical interpretation of China as a rigid two-class society.

2029

Pulleyblank, E. G. "The Origins and Nature of Chattel Slavery in China," *Journal of the Economic and Social History of the Orient*, I (1957–58), 185-220. An essay surveying the history and conditions of slavery from earliest times to the T'ang dynasty, emphasizing social rather than economic aspects but suggesting that China never was a "slave society."

2030

Wang Yi-t'ung. "Slaves and Other Comparable Social Groups During the Northern Dynasties (386-618)," *Harvard Journal of Asiatic Studies*, XVI (1953), 293-364. A detailed study of the sources, status, and functions of private and public slaves, as well as comparable groups such as tomb-tenders, government grazers, musicians, private soldiery, etc., in medieval times.

2031

Levy, Marion J., Jr. and Shih Kuo-Heng. *The Rise of the Modern Chinese Business Class*. New York: Institute of Pacific Relations, 1949. Two brief but authoritative studies of the social backgrounds, attitudes, and problems of merchants and industrial promoters and executives in the 20th century.

2032

Eberhard, Wolfram. *Das Toba-reich nordchinas: eine soziologische Untersuchung*. Leiden: E. J. Brill, 1949. A technical study of the social organization of the T'o-pa invaders in the 5th and 6th centuries, who influenced the Chinese social structure of Sui and T'ang times.

FAMILY AND CLAN

2033

Yang, C. K. *The Chinese Family in the Communist Revolution*. Cambridge, Mass.: The Technology Press, 1959. A detailed, authoritative study of the traditional family structure, the effects on it of gradual modernization in nationalist times, and especially the nature and effects of the communist assaults on it during the 1950's.

2034

Levy, Marion J., Jr. *The Family Revolution in Modern China*. Cambridge: Harvard University Press, 1949. A sociological analysis of traditional family structure in China and its changing character in a time of increasing industrialization and urbanization.

2035

Hsü, Francis L. K. "The Family in China," in *The Family: Its Function and Destiny* (R. N. Anshen, ed.; New York, Harper, 1949), pp. 73-92. An authoritative general interpretation of the traditional family system and its changing character in the 20th century.

2036

Lee Shu-ching. "China's Traditional Family, its Characteristics and Distintegration," *America Sociological Review,* XVIII (1953), 272-280. A general interpretive description of the large family system of traditional China and 20th century trends toward a nuclear family system, with comments on possible consequences of communist domination.

2037

Ch'en, Theodore Hsi-en and Wen-hui Chung Chen. "Changing Attitudes Toward Parents in Communist China," *Sociology and Social Research,* XLIII (1959), 175-182. A survey of the Chinese communist assault on filial piety in the early 1950's and its reversal of policy in the late 1950's to reinculcate respect for parents in the young.

2038

Hu Chang-tu and others. *China: Its People, Its Society, Its Culture.* New Haven: HRAF Press, 1960. Chap. 8, "Family," provides a reliable, up-to-date survey of traditional patterns and changes brought about by the communist government.

2039

Liu, Hui-chen Wang. *The Traditional Chinese Clan Rules.* Locust Valley, N.Y.: J. J. Augustin, 1959. (Monographs of the Association for Asian Studies, VII) An analysis of the content of clan rules found in a selection of 151 published clan genealogies; a valuable contribution to the study of the traditional family and clan system.

2040

Hu Hsien-chin. *The Common Descent Group in China and its Functions.* New York: The Viking Fund, 1948. (Viking Fund Publications in Anthropology, 10) A detailed, authoritative analysis of the clan system, emphasizing its religious, judicial, and economic aspects; the appendices include lengthy translations from various clan regulations and other documents illustrating the history and nature of the clan system.

2041

Yang, Martin C. *A Chinese Village.* New York: Columbia University Press, 1945. Chaps. 5-11 provide an excellent introduction to the traditional family system from an anthropological point of view, based on the author's recollections of his own native village in Shantung province.

2042

Tao, L. K. "Some Chinese Characteristics in the Light of the Chinese Family," in *Essays Presented to C. G. Seligman* (E. E. Evans-Pritchard and others, ed.; London: Kegan Paul, 1934), pp. 335-344. A brief introductory description of family organization and relations, with reference to the Chinese national character.

2043

Lang, Olga. *Chinese Family and Society.* New Haven: Yale University Press, 1946. One of the most comprehensive analytical descriptions of the traditional Chinese family system and the family's relations with society at large; based on field research from 1935 to 1937.

2044

Liu, Hui-chen Wang. "An Analysis of Chinese Clan Rules: Confucian Theories in Action," in *Confucianism in Action* (D. S. Nivison and A. F. Wright, ed; Stanford: Stanford University Press, 1959), pp. 63-96. On the Confucian-dominated value system of various sets of by-laws governing traditional clan organization.

2045

Feng Han-yi. *The Chinese Kinship System.* Cambridge: Harvard University Press, 1948; reprinted from *Harvard Journal of Asiatic Studies,* II (1937), 141-275. A de-

tailed, technical history of kinship structure and terminology.

2046

Twitchett, Denis. "The Fan Clan's Charitable Estate, 1050-1760," in *Confucianism in Action* (D. S. Nivison and A. F. Wright, ed.; Stanford: Stanford University Press, 1959), pp. 97-133. A case study of the history of a famous clan's management of its jointly held clan property; an important contribution to the understanding of traditional socioeconomic patterns.

2047

Freedman, Maurice. *Lineage Organization in Southeastern China.* London: Athlone Press, 1958. (London School of Economics Monographs on Social Anthropology, 18) On family and clan systems of Fukien and Kwangtung provinces; based on Western and Chinese writings.

2048

Levi, Werner, "The Family in Modern Chinese Law," *Far Eastern Quarterly,* IV (1944-45), 263-273. An examination of the implications for family organization and customs of the civil law code adopted by the nationalist government in 1929.

2049

Hsü, Francis L. K. "Observations on Cross-Cousin Marriage in China," *American Anthropologist,* XLVII (1945), 83-103. An anthropological field report on some Chinese ideas concerning the effects of cross-cousin marriages on family harmony, etc.

2050

Lin Yueh-hwa. *The Golden Wing.* London: Kegan Paul, 1947. An anthropologist's recreation of the social life and social evolution of a merchant family in an urban area of Fukien province during three generations from the 19th century into the 1940's; written in the form of a novel, but an authoritative generalization.

2051

Twitchett, Denis C. "Documents on Clan Administration: I," *Asia Major,* VIII (1960), 1-35. An annotated translation of 11th century rules for administration of the jointly-held lands of the famous Fan family, with addena about organization and management of the clan estates in Sung times.

2052

Lee, Rose Hum. "Research on the Chinese Family," *American Journal of Sociology,* LIV (1949), 497-504. A review of available research reports with suggestions about areas of needed work.

2053

McAleavy, Henry. "Certain Aspects of Chinese Customary Law in the Light of Japanese Scholarship," *Bulletin of the School of Oriental and African Studies,* London University, XVII (1955), 535-547. A review of recent Japanese findings about traditional legal relations with Chinese families, especially noting that women's rights have traditionally been stronger than is ordinarily thought.

*   *   *

2054

Hsieh Ping-ying. *Autobiography of a Chinese Girl,* trans. by Tsui Chi. London: Allen and Unwin, 1948. The story of a very liberal-minded girl's struggles to free herself from the repression of a traditional-minded family; principally relating to the 1920's.

2055

Pruitt, Ida. *A Daughter of Han.* New Haven: Yale University Press, 1945. The autobiography of a Chinese woman of poor parentage, Mrs. Ning, who worked as a servant for officials, military officers, and foreigners from Ch'ing times into the nationalist era; throws much light on the attitudes and changing status of Chinese women.

2056

Lewis, Ida Belle. *The Education of Girls in China.* New York: Columbia University Teachers College, 1919. A useful reference on the traditional upbringing of girls in China and the effects of early 20th century modernization in education on their social status and values.

2057

Cusak, Dymphna. *Chinese Women Speak*. London: Angus and Robertson, 1959. A sympathetic report of 18 months spent in communist China, with character sketches of numerous women encountered; not scholarly, and not entirely objective, but showing many aspects of what modernization and communization have done to Chinese women's lives and attitudes.

2058

Ayscough, Florence. *Chinese Women Yesterday and Today*. Boston: Houghton Mifflin, 1937. An unscholarly, unsystematic "appreciation" of Chinese women, with observations on their traditional status and its 20th century improvement; including biographical sketches of many famous ladies of the past and of the republican era and many very awkward renderings of poems by and about women.

NON-KIN SOCIAL GROUPS

2059

Topley, Marjorie. "The Emergence and Social Function of Chinese Religious Associations in Singapore," *Comparative Studies in Society and History*, III (1960–61), 289-314. On spirit cults, secret societies, charitable and ideological groups, etc.; useful on Chinese "togetherness" in general.

2060

Glick, Carl and Hong Sheng-hua. *Swords of Silence*. New York: Whittlesey House, 1947. A popular history of Chinese societies, with descriptions of their organization and activities in modern times; not authoritative, but a useful introduction.

2061

Ward, John S. M. and W. G. Stirling. *The Hung Society, or the Society of Heaven and Earth*. 3 vols. London: Baskerville Press, 1925–26. A monumental, classic study of the organization and activities of one of China's largest and most influential secret societies.

2062

Comber, Leon. *Chinese Secret Societies in Malaya: a Survey of the Triad Society from 1800 to 1900*. Locust Valley, N. Y.: J. J. Augustin, 1959. (Monographs of the Association for Asian Studies, 6) Serves as a useful introduction to the traditional organization and activities of secret societies; by a long-time Malayan police officer.

2063

Faure, Benoit. *Les sociétés secrets en Chine*. Paris: Courtrai, 1933. A brief but good survey of the history and nature of secret societies.

*   *   *

2064

Burgess, John S. *The Guilds of Peking*. New York: Columbia University Press, 1928. A detailed sociological analysis of the number, organization, membership, religious life, and economic functions of all types of guilds operating in Peking in the 1920's.

2065

Kato Shigeshi. "On the Hang or the Associations of Merchants in China," *Memoirs of the Research Department of The Toyo Bunko*, VIII (1936), 45-83. A general history of mercantile guilds, with special reference to their development in T'ang and Sung times.

2066

Wales, Nym (pseud. of Helen Foster Snow). *The Chinese Labor Movement*. New York: John Day, 1945. A detailed survey of the history of organized labor in China in the 20th century, including data on labor legislation and welfare work.

2067

Eichhorn, Werner. "Zur Vorgeschichte der chinesischen Arbeiterbewegung," *Saeculum*, XII (1961), 30-60. On the labor movement of early republican days, and especially its role in the May 4th movement of 1919.

RURAL COMMUNITIES

2068

Fried, Morton H. "Community Studies in China," *Far Eastern Quarterly*, XIV (1954–55), 11-36. A critical evaluation of traditional and modern studies of selected Chinese communities: their methodology, distribution, etc.; a useful introduction to this type of literature on China, but in technical terms.

2069

Yang, Martin C. *A Chinese Village*. New York: Columbia University Press, 1945. An anthropological analysis of family, interfamily, and intervillage relations in the North China village in which the author grew up: Taitou in Shantung province.

2070

Yang, C. K. *A Chinese Village in Early Communist Transition*. Cambridge, Mass.: The Technology Press, 1959. A comprehensive analytical description of the life of a suburban village outside Peking, emphasizing the effects of communist domination prior to the appearance of communal organization.

2071

Fei Hsiao-t'ung. *Peasant Life in China*. London: Kegan Paul, 1943. A thorough, general study of the social and economic life of a rural village; based on field research in 1939–40 at Kaihsienkung, in the Yangtze delta area west of Shanghai. An extensive summary of Fei's book is given in E. R. Service, *A Profile of Primitive Culture* (New York: Harper, 1958), chap. 19.

2072

Hsü, Francis L. K. *Under the Ancestors' Shadow*. New York: Columbia University Press, 1948. An anthropological field report on family, religion, and personality among rural Chinese of a Yunnan town; research conducted in 1941–43.

2073

Crook, David and Isabel Crook. *Revolution in a Chinese Village: Ten Mile Inn*. London: Routledge and Kegan Paul, 1959. A socioeconomic study of how communism affected a small agricultural village, based on field research during 1947–48 in Shansi province; generally sympathetic in its appraisal of communist influence.

2074

Gamble, Sidney D. *Ting Hsien, a North China Rural Community*. New York: Institute of Pacific Relations, 1954. An intensive, compendious description of the administrative, social, economic, and religious life of a rural county south of Peking, based on field residence from 1926 to 1937; with more than 100 tables.

2075

Fried, Morton H. *Fabric of Chinese Society*. New York: Praeger, 1953. An analytical study of how economic, social, political, and religious elements interact in the social life of a county seat near Nanking; based on field research in 1947–48.

2076

Ch'en Ta. *Emigrant Communities In South China*. New York: Institute of Pacific Relations, 1940. A sociologist's comprehensive report on socioeconomic conditions and social change in several selected villages in Kwangtung and Fukien provinces during the middle 1930's, with special reference to the causes and effects of overseas migration to Southeast Asia. Cf. Francis L. K. Hsü, "Influence of South-seas Emigration on Certain Chinese Provinces," *Far Eastern Quarterly*, V (1945–46), 47-59, for some contradictory views.

2077

Ward, Barbara E. "A Hong Kong Fishing Village," *Journal of Oriental Studies*, I (1954), 195-214. A social and economic analysis of a settlement of landless boat-dwellers, representative of a large floating population in South China; with data on their everyday lives and attitudes derived from field residence and research.

2078

Kulp, Daniel H. *Country Life in South China; the Sociology of Familism*. New York: Teachers College, Columbia University, 1925. A detailed analysis of social structure and relations in a rural village of Kwangtung province, emphasizing the importance of the family as the primary social unit; with many illustrations, charts, and maps and an introductory statement of 71 "significant facts" about Chinese society gleaned from the study.

2079

Leong, Y. K. and L. K. Tao. *Village and Town Life in China.* London: Allen and Unwin, 1915. A standard reference, describing social and religious life of both villages and towns under the empire.

2080

Gamble, Sidney D. "Hsin Chuang: A Study of Chinese Village Finance," *Harvard Journal of Asiatic Studies,* VIII (1944–45), 1-33. A case study of revenue-gathering and expenditures for local needs in a peasant village, 1907–31; with statistical tables.

2081

Smith, Arthur H. *Village Life in China.* New York: Revell, 1899. A classic study of traditional family and village life in China in a generalized approach but based on the author's long missionary experience in Shantung province; covers a wide range of customs and attitudes, but descriptive rather than analytical.

URBAN COMMUNITIES

2082

Murphey, Rhoads, "The City as the Center of Change: Western Europe and China," *Annals of the Association of American Geographers,* XLIV (1954), 349-362. Includes a general sociological analysis of urbanization in traditional China, suggesting reasons why Chinese cities, as administrative centers, were not European-style centers of social change.

2083

Trewartha, Glenn T. "Chinese Cities: Numbers and Distribution," *Annals of the Association of American Geographers,* XLI (1951), 331-347. A survey of studies and estimates of urban distribution from the 1920's to 1949, with numerous statistical charts and maps; suggests that modern China contains more than 200 cities of more than 50,000 population. Cf. Trewartha's article "Chinese Cities: Origins and Functions," *op. cit.,* XLII (1952), 69-93.

2084

Orleans, Leo A. "The Recent Growth of China's Urban Population," *Geographical Review,* XLIX (1959), 43-57. An interpretive statistical study of migration to the cities in communist China between 1949 and 1959, suggesting an annual urban increase of 4 million and noting socioeconomic problems associated with such growth.

2085

Murphey, Rhoads. *Shanghai, Key to Modern China.* Cambridge: Harvard University Press, 1953. A general geographic study of modern Shanghai: its site and advantages, its history as a treaty port, its functions as a distributor, producer, and consumer of goods, etc.; with speculative comments about its future under communism.

2086

Gamble, Sidney D. and J. S. Burgess. *Peking, A Social Survey.* New York: Doran, 1921. A voluminous, heavily statistical and descriptive survey of life in Peking in about 1917; probably the only standard social survey of any major Chinese city.

2087

Arlington, L. C. and William Lewisohn. *In Search of Old Peking.* Peking: Henri Vetch, 1935. A comprehensive tourist guide to Peking of the 1930's with much data on its customs and history.

2088

Keyes, Fenton. "Urbanism and Population Distribution in China," *American Journal of Sociology,* LVI (1950–51), 519-527. A review of demographic studies concerning the urban percentage of China's population, with specu-

lation about the effects of communization and industrialization.

2089

Johnstone, William C., Jr. *The Shanghai Problem.* Stanford: Stanford University Press, 1937. On the history and administration of the focal point of the "treaty port system" that characterized Chinese-Western relations in the 19th and early 20th centuries.

2090

Jones, F. C. *Shanghai and Tientsin.* London: Oxford University Press, 1940. On the political and economic conditions of two of China's great treaty-port cities before and after Japanese occupation in the 1930's.

2091

Gernet, Jacques. *La vie quotidienne en Chine a la veille de l'invasion Mongole (1250–1276).* Paris: Hachette, 1959. A panoramic description of city life in the magnificent Southern Sung capital, Hangchow; a valuable, authoritative contribution to Chinese social history.

2092

Balazs, Étienne. "Les villes chinoises: histoire des institutions administratives et judiciares," *Société Jean Bodin Recuels,* VI (1954), 225-240.

2093

Balazs, Étienne. "Marco Polo dans la capitale de la Chine," in *Oriente Poliana* (Rome: Instituto Italiano per il Medio ed Estremo Oriente, 1957), pp. 133-154. On city life in China in the 13th century, with special reference to the splendid metropolis of medieval Southeast China, Hang-chou.

2094

Leong, Y. K. and L. K. Tao. *Village and Town Life in China.* London: Allen and Unwin, 1915. A standard reference, describing social and religious life of both villages and towns under the empire.

2095

Bredon, Juliet. *Peking.* 2d ed. Shanghai: Kelly and Walsh, 1922. An extensive tourist guide.

OVERSEAS COMMUNITIES

2096

Purcell, Victor. *The Chinese in Southeast Asia.* New York: Oxford University Press, 1951. A voluminous compendium of historical data concerning Chinese migration and settlement to the south, arranged according to the various countries of Southeast Asia.

2097

Skinner, George W. *Chinese Society in Thailand: An Analytical History.* Ithaca: Cornell University Press, 1957. A detailed history of the emigrant Chinese community in Thailand from a sociological point of view, with a general survey of its condition and problems since World War II; the most comprehensive analysis available of any single group of overseas Chinese.

2098

Skinner, George W. *Leadership and Power in the Chinese Community of Thailand.* Ithaca: Cornell University Press, 1958. (Monographs of the Association for Asian Studies, III) On the backgrounds, activities, and influence of the elite group of the Chinese community in Thailand, with special reference to the 1950's.

2099

Purcell, Victor. *The Chinese in Modern Malaya.* Singapore: Donald Moore, 1956. A brief history of the Chinese emigrant community in Malaya from earliest times, with special emphasis on its problems in anticipation of Malayan independence.

2100

Purcell, Victor. *The Chinese in Malaya.* London: Oxford University Press, 1948. A detailed history and social analysis of the overseas Chinese community in Malaya; should be used to supplement Purcell's later work, *The Chinese in Modern Malaya.*

2101

Freedman, Maurice. "Colonial Law and Chinese Society," *Journal of the Royal Anthropological Institute of Great Britain and Ireland*, LXXX (1950), 97-126. On conflicts between "government law" and the customs of overseas Chinese in Singapore, regarding marriage, divorce, adoption, property rights, etc.

2102

Freedman, Maurice. "Immigrants and Associations: Chinese in Nineteenth-century Singapore," *Comparative Studies in Society and History*, III (1960-61), 25-48. How overseas Chinese organized their community in Singapore through secret societies and voluntary organizations.

2103

Williams, Lea E. *Overseas Chinese Nationalism: The Genesis of the Pan-Chinese Movement in Indonesia, 1900-1916*. Glencoe, Ill.: Free Press, 1960. A sociological-historical study of how the Chinese of Java first organized themselves to achieve political influence.

2104

Appleton, Sheldon. "Overseas Chinese and Economic Nationalization in the Philippines," *Journal of Asian Studies*, XIX, (1959-60), 151-161. On Chinese dominance of retail trade in the Philippines and Filipino legislation to curb it. Cf. Appleton's article "Communism and the Chinese in the Philippines," *Pacific Affairs*, XXXII (1959), 376-391, for an appraisal of the political loyalties of the Philippines Chinese.

2105

T'ien Ju-K'ang. *The Chinese of Sarawak*. London: London School of Economics and Political Science, 1953. (Department of Anthropology Monographs on Social Anthropology, No. 12) A technical anthropological report on the origins, associations, clans, occupations, etc., of an overseas Chinese community.

2106

Willmott, Donald E. *The Chinese of Semarang*. Ithaca: Cornell University Press, 1960. A field study emphasizing socio-cultural changes observed in 1955.

2107

Chung Wen-hui. *Changing Social-Cultural Patterns of the Chinese Community in Los Angeles*. Los Angeles: University of Southern California, 1952.

MINORITY COMMUNITIES

2108

Hu Chang-tu and others. *China: Its People, Its Society, Its Culture*. New Haven: HRAF Press, 1960. Chap. 4, "Ethnic Minorities," gives a reliable survey of the various minority groups in China's population and of modern governmental policies toward them.

2109

Wiens, Herold J. *China's March Toward the Tropics*. Hamden, Conn.: Shoe String Press, 1954. A history of China's historic relations with the aboriginal inhabitants of South and Southwest China, with information about their 20th century conditions.

2110

Rock, Joseph F. *The Ancient Na-Khi Kingdom of Southwest China*. 2 vols. Cambridge: Harvard University Press, 1947. Technical studies of an aboriginal tribe of the Chinese-Tibetan border regions known to the Chinese as the Mo-so; more geographical and historical than anthropological.

2111

Hsieh Ting-yu. "Origin and Migrations of the Hakkas," *Chinese Social and Political Science Review*, XIII (1929), 202-227. A general survey of the history and modern status of an important minority group of South China, especially tracing their four great migration waves, from pre-Han into Sung times.

2112

Graham, David Crockett. *The Customs and Religion of the Ch'iang*. Washington: Smithsonian Institution, 1958. On an important aboriginal people of western Szechwan province, historically a buffer group between the Chinese and the Tibetans.

2113

Feng Han-yi and J. K. Shryock. "The Historical Origins of the Lolo," *Harvard Journal of Asiatic Studies*, III (1938), 103-127. A survey of the history and culture of an important southwestern aboriginal group, with translations of early Chinese descriptions; inconclusively reviews theories about Lolo origins and ethnic affiliations.

2114

Lin Yüeh-hwa. "The Miao-Man Peoples of Kweichow," *Harvard Journal of Asiatic Studies*, V (1940-41), 261-345. An annotated translation of a 19th century Chinese account of the history and customs of various southwestern aboriginal tribes; with addenda about their customs from other sources.

2115

Fitzgerald, Charles Patrick. *The Tower of Five Glories*. London: Cresset, 1941. An ethnological study of the Min Chia people, one of the notable aboriginal groups of Yunnan province; with special emphasis on their religions.

2116

Chen Han-seng. *Frontier Land Systems in Southernmost China*. New York: Institute of Pacific Relations, 1949. A detailed study of two little-known minority groups of southwestern China: the Pai Yi of Yunnan province and the Kamba of Sikang province.

2117

Ekvall, Robert B. *Cultural Relations on the Kansu-Tibetan Border*. Chicago: University of Chicago Press, 1939. (University of Chicago Publications in Anthropology: Occasional Papers, 1) A brief analytical study of the social and economic relations between four ethnic groups in southwestern China and Tibet: the Han Chinese, the Moslems, the nomadic Tibetans, and the sedentary Tibetans.

2118

Rock, J. F. "Contributions to the Shamanism of the Tibetan-Chinese Borderland," *Anthropos*, LIV (1959), 796-818. A technical study of religious practices among an important group of the Mo-so aborigines of Yunnan province, with photographic illustrations.

2119

Lin Yüeh-hwa. "Kinship System of the Lolo," *Harvard Journal of Asiatic Studies*, IX (1945-47), 81-100. On one of the important groups of southwestern aborigines.

2120

Schram, Louis M. J. *The Monguors of the Kansu-Tibetan Border*. 3 vols. Philadelphia: American Philosophical Society, 1954-61. (Transactions of the American Philosophical Society, vol. XLIV, part 1; XLVII, part 1; and LI, part 3) A monumental study of the social organization, religion, and history of an important minority people, of mixed Mongol-Turkish background, on China's far western frontier.

2121

Broomhall, Marshall. *Islam in China: A Neglected Problem*. London: Morgan and Scott, 1910. The only substantial study yet available on the history and modern status of China's Moslem population.

ECONOMIC PATTERNS

Throughout history agriculture has been the backbone of China's economic life. The principal crops have been millet and wheat in the arid north and rice in the well-irrigated south. Such crops have been produced typically on very small, garden-like plots of land through the intensive application of human labor, so that Chinese farmers have attained remarkably high yields per acre but remarkably low yields per man hour. Farming has traditionally included the production of tea, silk, and cotton and animal husbandry on a small scale (notably pigs and chickens). Money, transportation, and communications were developed to relatively high levels in traditional times, but mercantile and industrial activities suffered from social discrimination and from monopolization and repression on the part of the government. Nevertheless, from very early times regional and international trade contributed significantly to China's wealth, and craft-scale production of iron, textile, and many other goods flourished. Until perhaps the 18th century China was unquestionably one of the world's most prosperous nations.

Historically, China's economic development has passed through several phases. Prior to the 3d century B.C. the feudal-like political structure of China was complemented by a feudal-like economy, in which peasants were serfs bound to the land of their lords and commerce and industry began to flourish under aristocratic patronage. The succeeding imperial age, lasting to the beginning of the 20th century, was characterized by governmental fostering of agriculture to the detriment of independent commerce and industry and by the free purchase and sale of land. Recurringly, the economy suffered from inequitable distribution of wealth (that is, of land, which was the only approved form of investment) between peasant landholders and absentee landlords, although the lack of any system of primogeniture or entailment prevented the appearance of a hereditary landlord class. Recurringly, too, the economy suffered from excessive governmental demands to support wars, luxurious life at court, or official corruption; and from the ravages of floods, droughts, and insect infestations. For two thousand years economic factors of these sorts contributed to the rise and fall of dynasty after dynasty and kept the population fairly stable between 60 and 100 millions.

The impact of the modern West, coupled with a dramatic population growth during the 17th and 18th centuries, provoked severe economic dislocations that played a major part in China's 19th century decline. When the republican era began in 1912 China found itself overpopulated, underdeveloped, and burdened with a semi-colonial type of economic dependence on the outside world. Efforts of the nationalist government at economic development during the 1930's and 1940's were frustrated by a lack of skilled technicians and managers, by an inclination to benefit landlord-entrepreneur groups rather than the peasantry, by monetary instability and lack of capital, by official corruption

— and, most importantly, by the Japanese invasion of China. Since 1949 the Chinese communist government has been guiding economic development more efficiently, if more ruthlessly. Its principal technique has been to increase agricultural production while restraining consumption, so that an agricultural surplus can be used as investment capital for the rapid industrialization that is considered China's only hope for improving its standard of living. In this process, agriculture has been increasingly collectivized and communalized, and all other economic activities have been increasingly socialized. A high rate of population growth (now nearing 700 millions), a lack of adequate plans and statistics, overly coercive pressures on the people, and the insistent intrusion of political dogma into all economic considerations have hampered the effort; but it appears that China may be approaching a level of economic strength and stability that it has not enjoyed for more than a century.

GENERAL: PRE-1949

2122

Yuan Tung-li. *Economic and Social Development of Modern China: A Bibliographical Guide.* New Haven: Human Relations Area Files, 1956. Part 1, "Economic Development," is a long, unannotated list of 20th century books in Western languages on statistics, economic history, resources, agriculture, industry, commerce, transportation, communication, money and banking, public finance, international trade, regional surveys, etc., with an author index; an indispensable reference.

2123

Fairbank, John K., Alexander Eckstein, and L. S. Yang. "Economic Change in Early Modern China: An Analytic Framework," *Economic Development and Cultural Change,* IX (1960–61), 1-26. A brief, authoritative analysis of traditional patterns of economic organization in 19th century China, emphasizing factors that retarded economic growth in the Western pattern.

2124

Fairbank, John King. *The United States and China.* Rev. ed. Cambridge: Harvard University Press, 1958. Chap. 3 includes an authoritative, interpretive analysis of the major patterns of China's traditional economic organization.

2125

Latourette, K. S. *The Chinese, Their History and Culture.* 3d ed. rev. New York: Macmillan, 1946. Chap. 15 provides a reliable general description of the main patterns of traditional Chinese economic life: agriculture, industry, commerce, money and banking, transportation, etc.; a useful introduction, but somewhat out of date.

2126

Tawney, Richard Henry. *Land and Labor in China.* New York: Harcourt, Brace, 1932. A classical, authoritative evaluation of China's general economic situation in the earliest years under the nationalist government.

2127

Kirby, E. Stuart. *Introduction to the Economic History of China.* London: Allen and Unwin, 1954. A theoretical evaluation of the kinds of studies that are being made, and that could be made, on the socioeconomic development of China throughout history, period by period; with special reference to Marxist reinterpretations of China's past and to modern Japanese scholarship. Highly technical.

2128
Allen, G. C. and Audrey G. Donnithorne. *Western Enterprise in Far Eastern Economic Development: China and Japan*. London: Allen and Unwin, 1954. An analysis of the activities of Western merchants, engineers, and financiers in China from the Opium War to the 1950's, with an evaluation of their influence on China's general economic development.

2129
Sun, E-tu Zen and John de Francis (trans.). *Chinese Social History*. Washington: American Council of Learned Societies, 1956. Translations of 25 articles by modern Chinese scholars, chiefly dating from the 1930's, relating to socioeconomic aspects of Chinese life from earliest antiquity into the 19th century; an invaluable reference.

2130
Jacobs, Norman. *The Origin of Modern Capitalism and Eastern Asia*. Hong Kong: Hong Kong University Press, 1958. A theoretical, sociological study of why industrial capitalism has developed in modern Japan but not in China.

2131
Balazs, E. "The Birth of Capitalism in China," *Journal of the Economic and Social History of the Orient*, III (1960), 196-216. An authoritative, interpretive study of China's socioeconomic tradition to explain why competitive free-enterprise capitalism did not develop indigenously.

2132
Chi Ch'ao-ting. *Key Economic Areas in Chinese History*. London: Allen and Unwin, 1936. An influential economic interpretation of the development of China throughout history, based principally on a study of public works for water control from dynasty to dynasty.

2133
Yang Lien-sheng. *Studies in Chinese Institutional History*. Cambridge: Harvard University Press, 1961. (Harvard-Yenching Institute Studies, XX) Includes 3 studies relevant to general economic history: "Economic Justification for Spending—An Uncommon Idea in Traditional China," "Numbers and Units in Chinese Economic History," and "Buddhist Monasteries and Four Money-raising Institutions in Chinese History," all previously published as articles in the *Harvard Journal of Asiatic Studies*, respectively: XX (1957), 36-52; XII (1949), 216-225; XIII (1950), 174-191.

2134
Lee, Mabel Ping-hua. *The Economic History of China*. New York: Columbia University Press, 1921. A standard reference on land distribution and land tax problems and practices throughout history, but somewhat uncritical.

2135
Weber, Max. *The Religion of China*, trans. by Hans H. Gerth. Glencoe, Ill.: Free Press, 1951. A classical sociological attempt to determine why capitalism did not develop in traditional China, ranging over the whole of Chinese society and civilization; of theoretical value, but not to be relied on for descriptive detail. For an excellent summation of Weber's influential views on China see Reinhard Bendix, *Max Weber: An Intellectual Portrait* (Garden City, N.Y.: Doubleday, 1960), pp. 117-157.

2136
Wang Yü-ch'üan. "The Rise of Land Tax and the Fall of Dynasties in Chinese History," *Pacific Affairs*, IX (1936), 201-220. A brief but influential essay suggesting an economic interpretation of China's traditional dynastic cycle.

2137
Yao Shan-yu. "The Geographical Distribution of Floods and Droughts in Chinese History, 206 B.C.-A.D. 1911," *Far Eastern Quarterly*, II (1942-43), 357-378. A statistical study, by province and by dynasty; quantitative data only.

2138
Sun, E-tu Zen and John de Francis. *Bibliography on Chinese Social History*. New Haven: Far Eastern Publicatons, Yale University, 1952. An annotated list of 176 modern scholarly articles in Chinese about socioeconomic aspects of Chinese history from antiquity; a valuable reference for those who can use the language.

2139
Chen Huan-chang. *The Economic Principles of Confucius and His School*. 2 vols. New York: Columbia University Press, 1911. On the economic implications of early Chinese philosophy of all schools, empasizing reasons for the relatively stationary nature of Chinese economic life in traditional times; somewhat uncritical and outdated, but still of some use.

2140
Maverick, Lewis (ed.). *Economic Dialogues in Ancient China: Selections from the Kuan-Tzu*, trans. by T'an Po-fu and Wen Kung-wen. Carbondale, Ill.: 1954. Early Chinese economic theories, probably of the 3d century B.C. though attributed by tradition to a statesman of the 7th century B.C., Kuan Chung; with a useful introduction about early economic history and thought in China.

2141
Bodde, Derk. "Henry A. Wallace and the Ever-Normal Granary," *Far Eastern Quarterly*, V (1945-46), 411-426. On the influence of traditional Chinese economic theories and practices on an American social reformer in the 1920's and 1930's.

* * *

2142
Swann, Nancy Lee. *Food and Money in Ancient China*. Princeton: Princeton University Press, 1950. A monumental, technical study of China's economic life from earliest times into the Han dynasty, incorporating annotated translations from Pan Ku's *Han-shu* and Ssu-ma Ch'ien's *Shih-chi* treatises on economics; an indispensable reference.

2143
Wilbur, C. Martin. *Slavery in China During the Former Han Dynasty, 206 B.C.-A.D. 25*. Chicago: Field Museum of Natural History, 1943. A standard source on socioeconomic conditions in Former Han China.

2144
Gale, Esson M. (trans.) *Discourses on Salt and Iron: A Debate on State Control of Commerce and Industry in Ancient China*. Leiden: E. J. Brill, 1931. On emergent welfare-state ideas in Han times; translation of chaps. 1-19 of Huan K'uan's *Yen-t'ieh lun*, reporting a court debate in 81 B.C. Chaps. 20-28 are translated in *Journal of the North China Branch of the Royal Asiatic Society*, LXV (1934), 73-110.

2145
Blue, Rhea C. "The Argumentation of the *Shih-huo chih* Chapters of the Han, Wei, and Sui Dynasty Histories," *Harvard Journal of Asiatic Studies*, XI (1948), 1-118. A valuable contribution on the development of welfare-state concepts and other concepts regarding state controls of economic life in pre-T'ang China.

2146
Gernet, Jacques. *Les aspects économiques du Bouddhisme dans la Société chinoise du Ve au Xe siècle*. Saigon: École Francaise d'Extreme-Orient, 1956. Includes indispensable information about economic history in general during China's medieval age. Cf. extensive comments by A. F. Wright in *Journal of Asian Studies*, XVI (1956-57), 408-414, and by D. C. Twitchett in *Bulletin of the School of Oriental and African Studies*, London University, XIX (1957), 526-549.

2147
Balazs, Étienne. *Le traité économique du "Souei-Chou."* Leiden: E. J. Brill, 1953. Translation, with copious introduction and appendices, of the section on economic

history in the *Sui-shu;* a basic work on the development of economic conditions and institutions between the Han and T'ang periods.

2148

Twitchett, Denis. "Monastic Estates in T'ang China," *Asia Major,* V (1955–56), 123-146. A detailed, technical study of the extent and economic influence of land-ownership by Buddhist establishments and of government efforts to regulate and control it.

2149

Twitchett, Denis. "The Salt Commissioners after An Lu-shan's Rebellion," *Asia Major,* IV (1954–55), 60-89. A technical study of the history, personnel, and techniques of a government salt monopoly that was relied upon to shore up the T'ang dynasty's sagging economic strength in its final century.

2150

Gernet, Jacques. "La vente en Chine d'après les contrats de Touen-houang (IXe-Xe siècles)," *T'oung Pao,* XLV (1957), 295-391. On sale contracts, prices, seller-buyer relations, etc., of the T'ang and Sung periods, based on contemporary contracts; technical.

2151

Hsiao Kung-chuan. *Rural China: Imperial Control in the Nineteenth Century.* Seattle: University of Washington Press, 1960. Includes important, detailed data on tax collection, famine control, and other aspects of economic life in rural China during the Ch'ing period.

2152

Gamble, Sidney D. "Daily Wages of Unskilled Chinese Laborers," *Far Eastern Quarterly,* III (1943–44), 41-73. A statistical study of wage rates in 19th century China, principally based on the records of a fuel store near Peking, covering the years from 1807 to 1902.

2153

Paauw, Douglas S. "The Koumintang and Economic Stagnation, 1928–1937," *Journal of Asian Studies,* XVI (1956–57), 213-220. Criticizes the nationalist government's failures to promote economic development.

2154

Freyn, Herbert. *Free China's New Deal.* New York: Macmillan, 1943. A general survey of the total economy of nationalist China in 1940–41, during wartime; with a sympathetic evaluation of the government's developmental plans and programs.

2155

Lieu, D. K. *China's Economic Stabilization and Reconstruction.* New Brunswick: Rutgers University Press, 1948. A general survey of Nationalist China's plans and projects for economic development after World War II.

2156

Sun Yat-sen. *International Development of China.* London: Hutchinson, 1928 (?). Dr. Sun's rather visionary program for industrial development in China through Western investment: a plan to "make capitalism create socialism in China."

GENERAL: COMMUNIST CHINA

2157

United Nations Economic Commission for Asia and the Far East. *Economic Survey of Asia and the Far East.* 1947–. An annual publication including statistical and interpretive reports on current economic conditions in both mainland China and Taiwan.

2158

Far Eastern Economic Review. Hong Kong: 1946–. Published weekly; includes interpretive articles and statistical reports on current economic conditions in mainland China.

2159

China Reconstructs. Peking: Foreign Languages Press, 1952–. The Peking government's official propaganda journal on economic development; published monthly and handsomely illustrated.

*   *   *

2160

Li Choh-ming. *Economic Development of Communist China.* Berkeley: University of California Press, 1959. A general, objective survey, principally emphasizing industrial growth; based almost entirely on communist China's own statistical reports.

2161

Hughes, T. J. and D. E. T. Luard. *The Economic Development of Communist China, 1949–1958.* London: Oxford University Press, 1959. A readable, objective general survey of accomplishments and future prospects in both agriculture and industry.

2162

Hu Chang-tu and others. *China: Its People, Its Society, Its Culture.* New Haven: HRAF Press, 1960. Chaps. 13-18 provide up-to-date descriptions of over-all economic life under the Chinese communists, with some historical background.

2163

Gluckstein, Ygael. *Mao's China.* London: Allen and Unwin, 1957. An unsympathetic technical study of economic development in communist China, emphasizing state regimentation of all economic activity.

2164

Wu Yuan-li. *An Economic Survey of Communist China.* New York: Bookman Associates, 1956. On China's success in rapid industrialization through harsh over-regimentation of labor.

2165

Rostow, W. W. and others. *The Prospects for Communist China.* New York: Wiley, 1954. An excellent, dispassionate analysis of the early economic development of communist China and of its economic potential.

2166

Moorsten, Richard. "Economic Prospects for Communist China," *World Politics,* XI (1958–59), 192-220. A general evaluation by an economist of China's economic growth during its first 5-year plan, in contrast with contemporary growth in India, growth in Japan during the 1930's, and especially growth in the Soviet Union during its early industrialization following 1928.

2167

Hollister, William W. *China's Gross National Product and Social Accounts, 1950–1957.* Glencoe, Ill.: Free Press, 1958. An authoritative analysis of China's national income under communism.

2168

Yin, Helen and Yin Yi-chang. *Economic Statistics of Mainland China (1949–1957).* Cambridge: Harvard University Press, 1960. A compilation of statistical tables based on official Peking reports, reflecting all facets of economic life.

2169

Wu Yuan-li (ed.). *Realities of Communist China.* Milwaukee: Marquette University, 1960. (Marquette University Studies in Business and Economics) Five essays, principally on economic development.

2170

Malenbaum, Wilfred. "India and China: Development Contrasts," *Journal of Political Economy,* LXIV (1956), 1-24. A comparison of economic development and planning during the early years of the Peking regime and the Republic of India, emphasizing the democratic, privately-oriented aspects of Indian economics and the totalitarian, publicly-oriented aspects of the Chinese economy.

2171

Hsia, Ronald. *Economic Planning in Communist China.* New York: Institute of Pacific Relations, 1955. A technical study of communist China's first 5-year plan for economic development, with introductory data on earlier stages in Chinese communist economic planning.

2172

Adler, Solomon. *The Chinese Economy.* New York: Monthly Review Press, 1957. A sympathetic and admiring survey of China's over-all economic development under communism during the 1950's.

2173

Iyer, Raghavan. "Economic Planning in India and China," *St. Antony's Papers,* II (London: Chatto and Windus, 1957), 34-74. An Indian economist's comparative analysis of China's first two 5-year plans.

2174

Chin, Calvin S. K. *A Study of Chinese Dependence Upon the Soviet Union for Economic Development as a Factor in Communist China's Foreign Policy.* Kowloon: Union Research Institute, 1959. A critical analysis of communist China's economic support from the U.S.S.R.

2175

Chen Chu-yuan. *Income and Standard of Living in Mainland China.* 2 vols. Kowloon: Union Research Institute, 1957. A critical technical study.

2176

Clubb, O. E. *Chinese Communist Development Programs in Manchuria.* New York: Institute of Pacific Relations, 1954. On the reinvigoration of industry and agriculture in Manchuria from 1950 through 1952; with a supplement on the Inner Mongolian Autonomous Region.

GENERAL: MODERN TAIWAN

2177

China Yearbook, 1959-60. Taipei: China Publishing Co., 1960. An almanac-like compendium of historical and statistical data about life in nationalist China, especially valuable as a reference on economic activities. Published annually, but originally issued irregularly under the title *China Handbook,* beginning with a 1937-43 edition (New York: Macmillan).

2178

General Report of the Joint Commission on Rural Reconstruction. Taipei: 1950-. Annual evaluations for the general reader of agricultural development in Taiwan.

2179

United Nations Economic Commission for Asia and the Far East. *Economic Survey of Asia and the Far East.* 1947-. A annual publication, including statistical and interpretive reports on current economic conditions in both mainland China and Taiwan.

2180

Industry of Free China. Taipei: 1954-. A monthly journal in English, with articles, current statistics, etc., about general economic development in Taiwan.

* * *

2181

Joint Commission on Rural Reconstruction. *A Decade of Rural Progress, 1948-1958.* Taipei: Republic of China, 1958. A popular, illustrated summation of agricultural development in Taiwan under Kuomintang control.

2182

Economic Progress of Free China, 1951-1958. Taipei: International Cooperation Administration Mutual Security Mission to China, 1958. A survey of various programs for socioeconomic development in Taiwan and their achievements, with statistical charts and illustrations; for the general reader.

2183

Klein, Sidney. *The Pattern of Land Tenure Reform in East Asia after World War II.* New York: Bookman Associates, 1958. Pp. 52-82: on the land redistribution program in Taiwan during the 1950's.

2184

Ginsburg, Norton S. *Economic Resources and Development of Formosa.* New York: Institute of Pacific Relations, 1953. A general survey of the economic base of the nationalist government in the 1950's, with comments on Taiwan's economic potential.

2185

Raper, Arthur F. and others. *Urban and Industrial Taiwan— Crowded and Resourceful.* Taipei: Foreign Operations Administration Mutual Security Mission to China and National Taiwan University, 1954. A comprehensive, analytical survey of social and economic conditions in Taiwan and a delineation of developmental needs, with statistical tables and illustrations; of use to both the general reader and the specialist.

POPULATION

2186

Ho Ping-ti. *Studies on the Population of China, 1368-1953.* Cambridge: Harvard University Press, 1959. A thorough, authoritative analysis of the techniques and findings of Chinese census registrations in modern centuries.

2187

Taeuber, Irene B. "China's Population: Riddle of the Past, Enigma of the Future," *Antioch Review,* XVII (1957), 7-18. A general evaluation of the census registration of 1953 against the background of China's population growth during recent centuries; authoritative but untechnical.

2188

Borrie, W. D. "The 'Population Explosion' and the Far East," *Pacific Affairs,* XXXIII (1960), 181-190. A brief review of recent literature on population in China and the rest of the Far East, with general comments about the size and growth rate of China's population in the 1950's.

2189

United Nations. *The Population of Asia and the Far East, 1950-1980: Future Estimates by Sex and Age, Report IV.* New York: United Nations, 1959. Part 3, on China, cautiously suggests for 1983 a possible range between 800 millions and 1.28 billions; highly technical.

2190

Chandrasekhar, S. *China's Population.* Hong Kong: Hong Kong University Press, 1959. A brief report on the techniques and findings of the mainland registration of 1953, by a leading Indian demographer who has visited China and consulted with Chinese demographers.

2191

Ch'en Ta. *Population in Modern China.* Chicago: University of Chicago Press, 1946. An authoritative study of the development of modern demographic methods under the nationalist government, with statistics and descriptions concerning the demographic aspects of limited groups of Chinese in the early 1940's.

2192

Thompson, Warren S. *Population and Progress in the Far East.* Chicago: University of Chicago Press, 1959. A speculative essay on population growth and economic development in South and East Asia in general, including a general evaluation of present and potential population pressures in China; by a distinguished demographer.

2193

Krader, Lawrence and John Aird. "Sources of Demographic Data on Mainland China," *American Sociological Review,* XXIV (1959), 623-630. An evaluation of communist China's census procedures and results, and of their reliability.

2194

Bielenstein, Hans. "The Census of China during the Period 2-742 A.D.," *Bulletin of the Museum of Far Eastern Antiquities, Stockholm,* XIX (1947), 125-163. An analysis of China's earliest registrations of population, touching on their reliability, their evidence on the size of families, their tracing of population migrations, etc.

2195

Lao Kan. "Population and Geography in the Two Han Dynasties," in *Chinese Social History* (E-tu Zen Sun and John de Francis, ed.; Washington: American Council of Learned Societies, 1956), pp. 83-102. On fluctuation in population and in population distribution, with special reference to Chinese settlement south of the Yangtze River.

2196

Sprenkel, O. B. van der. "Population Statistics of Ming China," *Bulletin of the School of Oriental and African Studies,* London University, XV (1953), 289-326. A detailed, technical study of Ming census registration procedures and findings; with many statistical charts.

2197

Taeuber, Irene B. and Nai-chi Wang. "Population Reports in the Ch'ing Dynasty," *Journal of Asian Studies,* XIX (1959–60), 403-417. A critical evaluation of registration techniques and population counts of the 18th and 19th centuries.

AGRICULTURE

2198

Shen, T. H. *Agricultural Resources of China.* Ithaca: Cornell University Press, 1951. A modern, authoritative survey of China's agricultural economy, especially of the late 1940's; emphasizes the various kinds of food crops and livestock, transportation and consumption of foodstuffs, international trade in agricultural products, etc.

2199

Buck, John Lossing. *Land Utilization in China.* 3 vols. Nanking: University of Nanking, 1937. Reprint ed. of vol. 1 New York: Council on Economic and Cultural Affairs, 1956. The most comprehensive descriptive study ever made on China's modern agricultural economy, based on a survey of 16,786 farms in 22 provinces from 1929 to 1933. Vol. 1 is a general report, filled with statistical tables, maps, and photographic illustrations; vol. 2 is a detailed land-utilization atlas; vol. 3 is devoted entirely to detailed statistical tables. The survey suggests that tenancy has not been as serious a problem as often thought.

2200

Buck, John Lossing. *Chinese Farm Economy.* Nanking: University of Nanking, 1930. A voluminous statistical study of farm management and various socioeconomic aspects of farm life in 2,866 farms of North China, the Yangtze delta region, and the southeast coastal provinces of Chekiang and Fukien, based on field surveys made between 1921 and 1925. A valuable sourcebook on the state of the agricultural economy, with many tables, maps, and photographic illustrations.

2201

Mallory, Walter H. *China: Land of Famine.* New York: American Geographical Society, 1926. An authoritative evaluation of the causes and possible cures of recurrent famines in China, considering natural, economic, social, and political factors.

2202

Fei Hsiao-t'ung and Chang Chih-i. *Earthbound China.* Chicago: University of Chicago Press, 1945. A sociological analysis of the total economic life of three communities in Yunnan province, representing rural agriculture, rural industry, and rural commerce.

2203

Wickizer, V. D. and M. K. Bennett. *The Rice Economy of Monsoon Asia.* Stanford: Food Research Institute, 1941. (Grain Economics Series, 3) A standard reference on the production and consumption of rice in India, Southeast Asia, China, Korea, and Japan, with special attention given to the international rice trade.

2204

Ho Ping-ti. "Early-ripening Rice in Chinese History," *Economic History Review,* IX (1956–57), 200-218. On the introduction of new rice varieties from Southeast Asia in the 11th century and its revolutionary economic consequences: double-cropping, terracing, steady population growth, etc.

2205

Ho Ping-ti. "The Introduction of American Food Plants into China," *American Anthropologist,* LVII (1955), 191-201. On the basis of Chinese references, suggests that peanuts, sweet potatoes, and maize were introduced to China in the midde or earlier years of the 16th century.

2206

Jones, Fred O. "Tukiangyien: China's Ancient Irrigation System," *Geographical Review,* XLIV (1954), 543-559. An illustrated description of a famous Chinese water-control system in the Chengtu plain of Szechwan province, designed during the 3d century B.C. and maintained continuously ever since.

2207

Schurmann, H. F. "Traditional Property Concepts in China," *Far Eastern Quarterly,* XV (1955–56), 507-516. A brief survey of some traditional ideas and practices concerning landownership, with special reference to the Sung and Yüan periods; contrasts Chinese concepts with the concept of alienability that developed in Europe.

2208

King, F. H. *Farmers of Forty Centuries.* London: Jonathan Cape, 1911. Reprint ed. Emmaus, Pa.; Organic Gardening Press, 1948. An early classical description of agricultural life and products in China, Korea, and Japan.

2209

Laufer, Berthold. *Sino-Iranica.* Chicago: 1919. (Field Museum of Natural History Publications, 201) A classical study of the interchange of agricultural plants, textiles, and other products between China and Iran in early times.

2210

Chen Han-seng. *Landlord and Peasant in China.* New York: International Publishers, 1936. A denunciatory analysis of landlord abuses in Kwangtung province; suggests that a violent peasant revolution is the only hope for improvement in the agrarian situation.

* * *

2211

Hudson, G. F., A. V. Sherman, and A. Zauberman. *The Chinese Communes: a Documentary Review and Analysis of the "Great Leap Forward."* London: Soviet Survey, 1959. Three well-documented essays giving an early appraisal of the rise and meaning of communal developments in agriculture during 1958–59.

2212

Donnithorne, Audrey. "Background to the People's Communes: Changes in China's Economic Organization in 1958," *Pacific Affairs,* XXXII (1959), 339-353. A critical, authoritative analysis of rearrangements in the management of commercial and agricultural life during 1958, noting the Peking government's emphasis on decentralizing economic control.

2213

Chao Kuo-chun. *Agrarian Policies of Mainland China.* Cambridge: Harvard University Press, 1957. A detailed history of pre-commune agricultural developments under the Chinese communists, with translations of numerous relevant documents.

2214

Klein, Sidney. *The Pattern of Land Tenure Reform in East Asia after World War II.* New York: Bookman Associates, 1958. Includes surveys of land redistribution programs in Taiwan (pp. 52-82) and mainland China (pp. 134-188) during the 1950's.

2215

Crook, David and Isabel Crook. *Revolution in a Chinese Village: Ten Mile Inn.* London: Routledge and Kegan Paul, 1959. A generally sympathetic analysis of early communist land reform movements, based on field research during 1947-48 in a village of Shansi province.

2216

Henze, Paul B. "Agricultural Collectivization in Communist China," *Royal Central Asian Journal,* XLI

(1954), 238-248. On early trends toward collectivization under the Chinese communists, in comparison and contrast with the experience of the Soviet Union; emphasizes the subservice of economics to politics.

2217

Thomas, S. B. "Communist China's Agrarian Policy, 1954–1956," *Pacific Affairs*, XXIX (1956), 141-160. On the collectivization of agriculture under the first 5-year plan, in pre-commune times.

2218

Luard, D. E. T. "The Chinese Co-operative Farm," *St. Antony's Papers*, VII (London: Chatto and Windus, 1960), pp. 37-50. On the progress of collectivization prior to the appearance of communes in 1958.

INDUSTRY

2219

Feuerwerker, Albert. *China's Early Industrialization.* Cambridge: Harvard University Press, 1958. A valuable contribution on the nature of the old economic order and 19th century difficulties in transforming it along the lines of Western industrial enterprise, with special reference to the China Merchants' Steam Navigation Company and other officially-sponsored enterprises managed by Shen Hsuan-huai (1844–1916).

2220

Cheng Yu-kwei. *Foreign Trade and Industrial Development of China.* Washington: University Press of Washington, 1956. A technical study of commercial and industrial development from 1840 to 1948, emphasizing developments under the nationalist government in the 1930's; with many statistical charts.

2221

Fei Hsiao-t'ung and Chang Chih-i. *Earthbound China.* Chicago: University of Chicago Press, 1945. Includes much data on rural industry.

2222

Shih Kuo-heng. *China Enters the Machine Age,* trans. and ed. by Fei Hsiao-t'ung and Francis L. K. Hsü. Cambridge: Harvard University Press, 1944. A sociological study of the sources, attitudes, living and working conditions, and wages of industrial laborers in war industries in Yunnan province.

2223

Wang, Y. C. "Free Enterprise in China: The Case of a Cigarette Concern, 1905–1953," *Pacific Historical Review*, XXIX (1960), 395-414. On the Kwangtung Nanyang Tobacco Company of Hong Kong; a useful contribution to the study of industrial development and management in the republican period.

2224

Carlson, Ellsworth C. *The Kaiping Mines (1877-1912).* Cambridge: Harvard University Press, 1957. A study of the development and management of a coal-mining enterprise in Shantung Province under official sponsorship, with general reference to China's difficulties in industrial development under the imperial regime.

2225

Lieu, D. K. *The Silk Industry of China.* Shanghai: Kelly and Walsh, 1941. A descriptive and statistical study of silk-raising in Wuhsin district of Chekiang province, the silk-reeling industry of Shanghai, and the silk-weaving industry of Shanghai, noting developments under Japanese occupation.

2226

Ukers, William H. *All About Tea.* 2 vols. New York: The Tea and Coffee Trade Journal Co., 1935. A monumental reference work including detailed descriptions of the history and production of tea in China and the development of the world tea trade.

2227

Liu Kwang-ching. "Steamship Enterprise in Nineteenth-century China," *Journal of Asian Studies*, XVIII (1958–

59), 435-455. A brief analysis of the founding and management of the government-sponsored China Merchants' Steam Navigation Company.

2228

Schafer, Edward H. "The Pearl Fisheries of Ho-p'u," *Journal of the American Oriental Society*, LXXII (1952), 155-168. Miscellaneous, technical notes about the history of the pearl gathering industry of Kwangtung province from the 2d century B.C. into the 12th century A.D.

* * *

2229

Orleans, Leo A. *Professional Manpower and Education in Communist China.* Washington: National Science Foundation, 1961. A detailed, authoritative analysis of technological training and technically-trained manpower resources of mainland China, in relation to its industrial potential.

2230

Cheng Chu-yuan. *Anshan Steel Factory in Communist China.* Kowloon: Union Research Institute, 1955. A critical technical study of the use and development of mainland China's greatest industrial establishment under communism.

TRADE AND COMMERCE

2231

Kato Shigeshi. "On the Hang or the Associations of Merchants in China," *Memoirs of the Research Department of The Toyo Bunko*, VIII (1936), 45-83. A general history of mercantile guilds, with special reference to the development in T'ang and Sung times; a valuable source on medieval mercantile practices in general.

2232

Chang T'ien-tse. *Sino-Portuguese Trade from 1514 to 1644.* Leiden: E. J. Brill, 1934. The standard reference for the first modern European trading contacts with China; with an introductory survey of pre-Ming history of mercantile relations between China and the Mediterranean world. Cf. the detailed critique by Paul Pelliot in *T'oung Pao*, XXXI (1935), 58-94.

2233

Hall, John. "Notes on the Early Ch'ing Copper Trade with Japan," *Harvard Journal of Asiatic Studies*, XIV (1949), 444-461. On the background, conditions, and extent of China's import of copper from Japan in the 17th and 18th centuries.

2234

Chang Teh-ch'ang. "Maritime Trade at Canton during the Ming Dynasty," *Chinese Social and Political Science Review*, XVII (1933-34), 264-282. Should be used to supplement Chang T'ien-tse's *Sino-Portuguese Trade from 1514 to 1644.*

2235

Boxer, C. R. "The Manila Galleon: 1565–1815," *History Today*, VIII (1958), 538-547. A brief summary of Spain's early system of exchanging Mexican silver for Chinese silk through Manila, for the general reader. For further detail, see W. L. Schurz's *The Manila Galleon* (New York: Dutton, 1939; paperbound reprint by same publisher, 1959).

2236

Hirth, Friedrich and W. W. Rockhill (trans.). *Chau Ju-kua.* St. Petersburg: Imperial Academy of Sciences, 1911. A 13th century description of the outside world and of the various spices and other produce that China obtained from abroad; with an introduction on the historical development of East-West sea trade and its status in Sung times.

2237

Kuwabara Jitsuzo. "On P'u Shou-keng," *Memoirs of the Research Department of The Toyo Bunko*, II (1928), 1-79; VII (1935), 1-104. A compendium of miscellany on Arab trade with China in T'ang and Sung times, focused on a long-resident Arab family that gained official control of foreign trade at Canton and, later, at

Ch'üan-chou in Fukien and prospered by serving the Mongols.

2238

Hourani, George Fadlo. *Arab Seafaring in the Indian Ocean in Ancient and Early Medieval Times.* Princeton: Princeton University Press, 1951. Pp. 61-79 on Persian and Arab trading relations with T'ang China.

2239

Chao Ch'üan-ch'eng. "A Ship's Voyage from Luzon to China in the Eighteenth Century," in *Chinese Social History* (E-tu Zen Sun and John de Francis, ed.; Washington: American Council of Learned Societies, 1956), pp. 353-360. On Chinese official treatment of a shipwrecked Filipino crew at Amoy in 1747–50, with comments on the nature of China's traditional South Seas trade.

*   *   *

2240

Cheng Yu-kwei. *Foreign Trade and Industrial Development of China.* Washington: University Press of Washington, 1956. A technical study of commercial and industrial development from 1840 to 1948, emphasizing developments under the nationalist government in the 1930's; with many statistical charts.

2241

Ho Ping-ti. "The Salt Merchants of Yang-chou: a Study of Commercial Capitalism in Eighteenth-century China," *Harvard Journal of Asiatic Studies,* XVII (1954), 130-168. A detailed analysis of private exploitation of a public monopoly; a valuable contribution to the understanding of China's traditional economic system.

2242

Sheldon, Charles D. "Some Economic Reasons for the Marked Contrast in Japanese and Chinese Modernization," *Kyoto University Economic Review,* XXIII (1953–54), 30-60. A case study of traditional practices in shipping and trading by water.

2243

Fei Hsiao-t'ung and Chang Chih-i. *Earthbound China.* Chicago: University of Chicago Press, 1945. Includes much data on rural commerce.

2244

Wiens, Herold J. "Riverine and Coastal Junks in China's Commerce," *Economic Geography,* XXXI (1955), 248-264. On the history and modern importance of transport in wooden ships, with maps and statistical tables.

2245

Tsang Chih. *China's Postwar Markets.* New York: Macmillan, 1945. A statistical analysis of China's international trade during the 1930's and of its potential as both a producer and consumer of international trade goods after World War II.

2246

Morse, Hosea Ballou. *The Trade and Administration of China.* 3d rev. ed. London: Longmans, Green, 1920. A standard descriptive and statistical account of the fiscal administration, domestic trade, and foreign trade of China during the late 19th and early 20th centuries.

2247

Morse, Hosea Ballou. *The Chronicles of the East India Company Trading to China, 1635–1834.* 5 vols. Oxford: Clarendon Press, 1926–29. The voluminous standard reference on the famous "John Company's" relations with China; based entirely on official company records, many of which are quoted extensively.

2248

Pritchard, Earl H. "Private Trade between England and China in the Eighteenth Century (1680–1833)," *Journal of the Economic and Social History of the Orient,* I (1957–58), 108-137, 221-256. On the conditions and amounts of private trade permitted to use the East India Company's ships, with many statistical tables.

2249

Dulles, Foster Rhea. *The Old China Trade.* Boston: Houghton Mifflin, 1930. The mercantile details of Sino-American relations up to 1844, in popular presentation.

2250

Wickizer, V. D. and M. K. Bennett. *The Rice Economy of Monsoon Asia.* Stanford: Food Research Institute, 1941. (Grain Economics Series, 3). On the production and consumption of rice in Asia and the international rice trade.

2251

Ukers, William H. *All About Tea.* 2 vols. New York: The Tea and Coffee Trade Journal Co., 1935. A monumental reference work including detailed descriptions of the history and production of tea in China and the development of the world tea trade.

*   *   *

2252

Remer, C. F. (ed.) *Three Essays on the International Economics of Communist China.* Ann Arbor: University of Michigan Press, 1959. Includes "International Economics and the Rise of Chinese Communism" by Remer, a good introduction to the 20th century economic history of China; "The First Five-Year Plan and Its International Aspects" by F. H. Mah; and "The International Trade of Communist China" by R. F. Dernberger.

2253

Hsin Ying. *The Foreign Trade of Communist China.* Kowloon: Union Research Institute, 1958. A general study of the patterns and extent of China's trade, both with the Soviet bloc countries and others.

2254

Cheng Cho-yuan. *The China Mainland Market under Communist Control.* Kowloon: Union Research Institute, 1956. On import-export trade, with special reference to trading relations with the Soviet Union.

2255

Mikesell, R. F. and D. Wells. "State Trading in the Sino-Soviet Bloc," *Law and Contemporary Problems,* XXIV (1959), 435-453.

TRANSPORTATION

2256

Murphey, Rhoads. "China's Transport Problem and Communist Planning; Example of the Burma Road," *Economic Geography,* XXXII (1956), 17-28. A general study of the techniques and difficulties of transportation in China throughout history, with special reference to the operation of the Burma Road during World War II and brief comments about communist planning as regards transport problems.

2257

Sun, E-tu Zen. "The Pattern of Railway Development in China," *Far Eastern Quarterly,* XIV (1954–55), 179-199. A brief history of railway-building in China from the 1880's into the 1950's, emphasizing financing and administering problems.

2258

Hinton, Harold C. *The Grain Tribute System of China (1845–1911).* Cambridge: Harvard University Press, 1956. On the gradual decline of the Grand Canal transport system in the last Ch'ing decades and the reappearance of sea transport of tax revenues.

2259

Wiens, Herold J. "Riverine and Coastal Junks in China's Commerce," *Economic Geography,* XXXI (1955), 248-264. On the history and modern importance of transport in wooden ships in China.

2260

Chao Yung Seen. *Railways in Communist China.* Kowloon: Union Research Institute, 1955. On railway construction and administration.

2261

Lo Jung-pang. "The Controversy over Grain Conveyance During the Reign of Qubilai Qaqan, 1260–94," *Far Eastern Quarterly*, XIII (1953-54), 263-285. On the extension of the Grand Canal to its final length (Hangchou to Peking) and the development of both canal and coastal fleets to haul Yangtze valley grain to North China.

2262

Sun, E-tu Zen. *Chinese Railways and British Interests, 1898–1911.* New York: King's Crown Press, 1954. On one aspect of exploitation by capital investment on the part of the foreign powers during the last days of the Ch'ing dynasty.

2263

Gandar, D. *Le canal impérial.* Shanghai: Mission Catholique, 1903. (Variétés Sinologiques, 4) The most detailed study of the Grand Canal, emphasizing its operation in Ch'ing times.

MONEY AND FINANCE

2264

Yang Lien-sheng. *Money and Credit in China: a Short History.* Cambridge: Harvard University Press, 1952. The most scholarly and up to date history of money and banking in traditional China.

2265

Tullock, Gordon. "Paper Money — a Cycle in Cathay," *Economic Historical Review*, IX (1956–57), 393-407. A general survey of the history of paper money in China from T'ang to Ming times.

2266

Gamble, Sidney D. "A Chinese Mutual Savings Society," *Far Eastern Quarterly*, IV (1944–45), 41-52. A statistical case study of how the modern Chinese have gone about meeting their small loan needs.

2267

Morse, Hosea Ballou. *The Trade and Administration of China.* 3d rev. ed. London: Longmans, Green, 1920. Chap. 5 surveys the history of money in China from earliest times into the 20th century.

2268

Franke, Herbert A. *Geld und Wirtschaft in China unter der Mongolenherrschaft: Beiträge zur Wirtschaftsgeschichte der Yüan-zeit.* Leipzig: Otto Harrassowitz, 1949. A detailed analysis of the Yüan dynasty monetary system, especially emphasizing the Mongols' inflationary experiments with paper money; with many statistical tables.

2269

Vissering, Willem. *On Chinese Currency: Coin and Paper Money.* Leiden: E. J. Brill, 1877. A standard, detailed history of Chinese money from earliest times through the Sung dynasty; partly superseded, but still useful. Reproduces and translates many Chinese references.

* * *

2270

Kato Shigeru. "A Study of the Suan-fu, the Poll Tax of the Han Dynasty," *Memoirs of the Research Department of the Toyo Bunko*, I (1926), 51-68. Includes useful data on the Han fiscal system in general.

2271

Twitchett, Denis. "Lands Under State Cultivation under the T'ang," *Journal of the Economic and Social History of the Orient*, II (1959), 162-203. A technical historical study of the role of state-owned lands in T'ang fiscal operations.

2272

Ch'en, Kenneth K. S. "The Economic Background of the Hui-ch'ang Suppression of Buddhism," *Harvard Journal of Asiatic Studies*, XIX (1956), 67-105. An analysis of how tax-exempt church estates disrupted the T'ang revenue system, with a general survey of the T'ang economic structure.

2273

Balazs, Stefan. "Beitrage zur Wirtschaftsgeschichte der T'ang-zeit," *Mitteilung des Seminars für Orientalische Sprachen*, XXXIV (1931), 1-92; XXXV (1932), 1-73. A classical, indispensable study of fiscal administration in T'ang times.

2274

Schurmann, H. F. (trans.) *Economic Structure of the Yüan Dynasty.* Cambridge: Harvard University Press, 1956. (Harvard-Yenching Institute Studies, XVI) *Yüan-shih* treatises on economic and fiscal policies of the Mongol government in 13th-14th century China, with useful introductions to all sections.

2275

Liang Fang-chung. *The Single-whip Method of Taxation in China*, trans. by Wang Yü-ch'üan. Cambridge: Harvard University Press, 1956. A general study of the Ming fiscal system, emphasizing a tax reform instituted in the 16th century.

2276

Franke, Wolfgang. "Zur Grundsteuer in China während der Ming-Dynastie (1368–1644)," *Zeitschrift für vergleichende Rechtswissenschaft*, LVI (1953), 93-103. A general history of the land tax system throughout the Ming period.

2277

Friese, Heinz. *Das Dienstleistungs-System der Ming-zeit.* Wiesbaden: Otto Harrassowitz, 1959. (Mitteilungen der Gesellschaft für Natur- und Völkerkunde Ostasiens, XXXV A) An authoritative, technical analysis of the Ming dynasty's corvée system, with details of types of labor assignments, of classifications of citizens from whom labor was required, of organization and direction of the labor forces, of abuses and reforms in the system, etc.

2278

Chen Shao-kwan. *The System of Taxation in China in the Tsing Dynasty, 1644–1911.* New York: Columbia University, 1914. (Studies in History, Economics, and Public Law, Vol. LIX, No. 2) An early technical study, not wholly superseded.

2279

Beal, Edwin George, Jr. *The Origin of Likin, 1853–1864.* Cambridge: Harvard University Press, 1958. On the background and early development of a system of domestic customs duties by the Ch'ing government, with translations of relevant Chinese texts; technical.

* * *

2280

Chang Chia-ao. *The Inflationary Spiral: the Experience in China, 1939–1950.* Cambridge, Mass.: The Technology Press, 1958. A voluminous study of nationalist China's monetary and fiscal difficulties during and after World War II.

2281

Paauw, Douglas S. "Chinese National Expenditures During the Nanking Period," *Far Eastern Quarterly*, XII (1952–53), 3-26. A general evaluation of the fiscal operations of the nationalist government.

2282

Cheng Chü-yüan. *Monetary Affairs of Communist China.* Kowloon: Union Research Institute, 1954. A comprehensive analysis of all aspects of fiscal and banking activities, noting strict adherence to Leninist doctrines.

2283

Hsia, Ronald. *Price Control in Communist China.* New York: Institute of Pacific Relations, 1953. An analytical review of the Peking government's early efforts to rectify the extreme inflation of the late nationalist years.

2284

Hsiao Chi-jung. *Revenue and Disbursement of Communist China.* Kowloon: Union Research Institute, 1954. A critical technical study of early fiscal administration under communism.

2285

Hsin Ying. *The Price Problems of Communist China.* Kowloon: Union Research Institute, 1954. On early price-stabilization programs of the Peking regime, with data on money, revenues, etc.

INDEX